ON THIS DAY IN CHRISTIAN HISTORY

365 AMAZING AND INSPIRING STORIES
ABOUT SAINTS, MARTYRS, AND HEROES

ROBERT J. MORGAN

THOMAS NELSON
Since 1798

NASHVILLE DALLAS MEXICO CITY RIO DE JANEIRO

Previously published as *On This Day*

Published in Nashville, Tennessee, by Thomas Nelson. Thomas Nelson is a registered trademark of Thomas Nelson, Inc.

Thomas Nelson, Inc., titles may be purchased in bulk for educational, business, fund-raising, or sales promotional use. For information, please e-mail SpecialMarkets@ThomasNelson.com.

ISBN 978-0-7852-3189-9

Library of Congress Cataloging-in-Publication Data

Morgan, Robert J., 1952–
On This Day / Robert J. Morgan.
p. cm.
ISBN 0-7852-1162-4
1. Christian saints—Meditations. 2. Christian martyrs—Meditations. 3. Devotional calendars.
BR1710.M67 1997
270'.092'2—dc21
[B] 97–8956
CIP

Printed in the United States of America
13 14 QG 14 13 12 11

Preface

The October 22, 1996, headlines of the *Times* of London cried: "Lost Forever: A Nation's Heritage Looted by Its Own People." Afghanistan's National Museum in Kabul is rubble, said the newspaper. It once held one of the earth's greatest multicultural antique collections: Persian, Indian, Chinese, Central Asian, and beyond. But Mujahidin rebels blasted into vaults and shattered display cases, looted the relics, and sold them here and there around the world for quick cash. Rockets slammed into the museum's roof, burying ancient bronzes under tons of debris. Pottery from prehistory was thrown into bags like cheap china. The Bagram collection, one of the greatest archaeological finds of the twentieth century, disappeared. Nearly forty thousand coins, some of the world's oldest, vanished. The museum, once a repository for Afghan history, became a military post, and the storied past has now been ruined by the unbridled present. A nation has lost its history. With no history, there is no heritage. And with no heritage from the past, there is no legacy for the future.

The same could happen to the church of Jesus Christ. Contemporary Christianity is interested in recent trends, current challenges, and modern methods. So am I. But nothing braces me to face these days like visiting the cloud of witnesses that comprise church history.

Aleksandr Solzhenitsyn observed, "If we don't know our own history, we will simply have to endure all the same mistakes, sacrifices, and absurdities all over again."

"How shall we labor with any effect to build up the church" asks Philip Schaff, "if we have no thorough knowledge of her history? History is, and must ever continue to be, next to God's word, the richest foundation of wisdom, and the surest guide to all successful practical activity."

This is one of the reasons I'm providing this armchair tour of the chronicles of Christianity in a devotional format—to inspire, amuse, challenge, and deepen the soul with two thouand years of anecdotes from an alphabet of characters from Ambrose to Zinzendorf. Each story is told on the date it occurred.

Christian history provides humanity's most riveting storehouse of adventures. Its menagerie of characters, both saintly and eccentric, is the most colorful host of men and women ever assembled on one stage. Some of them make us shudder with horror, others make us laugh, and many sober us and call us to greater dedication to our mission and Master. In preaching to my young congregation in Nashville, I use many kinds of illustrations, but there's seldom such a hush as when I launch into a story about a stalwart, struggling hero or villain from the tapestry of history. The Christian past is the highest drama.

Each day of every century since the resurrection of Jesus Christ, God's people have been about his business, building his kingdom, using their gifts, shedding their blood. A million stories have been acted out. Most are known only to heaven. Some have come down to us, and a few are presented here for your consideration. Secondary sources are not always accurate, and whenever possible, I have tracked down details and verified facts. Any inadvertent inaccuracies made known to me will be corrected in future editions. My deepest thanks go to Steve Camp, who suggested this project, and to Dr. Paul Harrison, church historian, and Charles Sherrill of the Tennessee State Library, who reviewed each of these installments, providing excellent input. Kevin Harper helped with research. I'm grateful for the encouragement and excellence that Phil Stoner and Teri Mitchell of Thomas Nelson brought to this project. My wife, Katrina, researched and reviewed this book, made excellent suggestions about it, and cared for its author. My brother-in-law and sister, Steve and Ann Campbell, shouldered heavy family burdens during my final phase of writing.

Finally, I'm particularly grateful for the assistance and affection of my colleagues at the Donelson Fellowship in Nashville who are making history in their own corner of the Lord's church. They sustain me more than they know, and to them this book is affectionately dedicated—

Mark McPeak

Mike Hollifield

Jeff Nichols

Jerry Carraway

Sherry Anderson

Bob Hill

On This Day in Christian History...

JANUARY

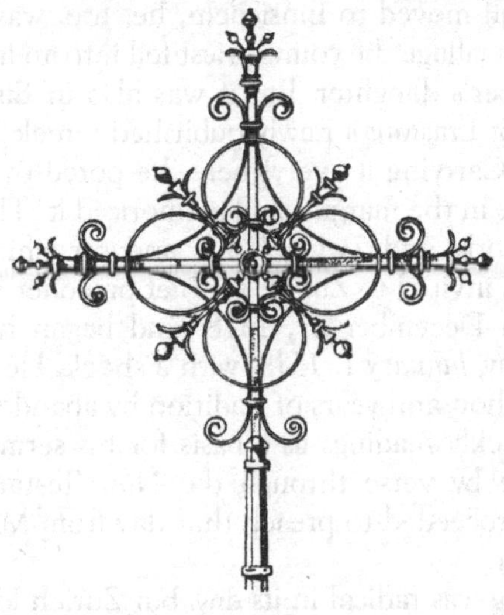

January 1

Verse by Verse

When preached simply and purely, verse by verse and book by book, the Bible can change lives and transform history. Just ask Zwingli.

Ulrich Zwingli was born on *January 1, 1484*, in a Swiss shepherd's cottage in the Alps. His parents instilled in him a love for God. The young man proved a brilliant student, and following a brief stint as a schoolteacher, he entered the priesthood. For ten years he labored in the village of Glarus, and there he began corresponding with the famous Greek scholar Erasmus.

The Swiss church was bubbling with corruption during this time. In 1516, when Zwingli moved to Einsiedeln, he, too, was struggling hard with sin. In his new village the young priest fell into an intimate relationship with the barber's daughter. But it was also in Einsiedeln that he borrowed a copy of Erasmus's newly published Greek New Testament. Zwingli copied it. Carrying it everywhere, he pored over it continually and scribbled notes in the margins and memorized it. The pure scripture began doing its work, and Zwingli's life and preaching took on new vigor. Soon he was invited to Zurich as chief preacher in the cathedral.

He arrived on December 27, 1518, and began his duties on his thirty-sixth birthday, *January 1, 1519*, with a shock. He announced that he would break a thousand years of tradition by abandoning the church liturgy and the weekly readings as a basis for his sermons. Instead, he would teach verse by verse through the New Testament, beginning immediately. He proceeded to preach that day from Matthew 1 on the genealogy of Christ.

Such preaching was radical in its day, but Zurich loved it. Zwingli's concern for the city's youth, his courage during the plague, and his cheerful temper dispelled initial doubts about his Reformation ideas. Later when opposition arose, Zurich's City Council and six hundred other interested citizens gathered to evaluate his actions. The assembly (the First Zurich Disputation, 1523) affirmed Zwingli and encouraged his work. Lives were changed; history was made. The Swiss Reformation had begun.

Jesus Christ came from the family of King David and also from the family of Abraham . . . The Lord's promise came true, just as the prophet had said, "A virgin will have a baby boy, and he will be called Immanuel," which means "God is with us." (Matthew 1:1, 22–23)

Famous or Faithful?

"Not many of you came from important families," Paul told the Corinthians. Not many, perhaps, but some—like the one born three centuries after Christ in a wealthy Christian home in Caesarea of Cappadocia (Turkey). His parents named him *Basil*, meaning "Kingly." They sent him to the finest schools in Constantinople and Athens, and Basil graduated with honors. He thought highly of himself and returned home dreaming of becoming great in public life. But his sister, who led him to faith in Christ, counseled humility. "It's better to be faithful before God," she insisted, "than famous before men."

Basil craved a quiet life of study, prayer, and writing. He settled along the bank of the Iris River on the family estate, preaching to and helping the poor. But his stature was already so great that Emperor Julian the Apostate, though a fierce opponent of Christianity, tried to recruit him as advisor. Basil declined.

But he couldn't refuse the appeal of his own bishop, Eusebius, who warned that the church faced both imperial attacks from without and dangerous heresy from within. Basil left his quiet retreat to spend the rest of his life in public ministry. He championed orthodoxy, preaching and writing brilliant messages on the nature of Jesus Christ and the composition of the Trinity.

In 370, Basil succeeded Eusebius and proved himself a gifted bishop who organized the ministries of the church. Using his own fortune, Basil founded a hospital, perhaps the first in Christian history, for the care of lepers. He was a kind man, often personally treating the diseased. Basil's complex of churches, schools, hospitals, hostels, monasteries, and almshouses outside Caesarea became a town within itself called Basiliad. His rules for monks and monasteries are used to this day in the Greek church.

Worn out before his fiftieth year, Basil died on January 1, 379. News spread like wildfire the next day, and he was mourned deeply. He is remembered every *January 2*, which is designated in Western tradition as the Feast Day of St. Basil the Great.

Everyone should be humble toward everyone else. The Scriptures say, "God opposes proud people, but he helps everyone who is humble." Be humble in the presence of God's mighty power, and he will honor you when the time comes. (1 Peter 5:5–6)

January 3 Send Me to the Rough

David Brainard was a frail young man, tubercular, sickly, and easily depressed. He longed to reach out to the Indians of Colonial America, but his first venture to a tribe in Massachusetts was fraught with danger. Unknown to him, his every move was monitored by warriors intent on killing him. But as they raised their bows, they saw a rattlesnake slithering alongside him, lifting its head, flicking its tongue, preparing to strike Brainard. Suddenly the snake uncoiled and glided away. The Indians attributed Brainard's safety to the "Great Spirit."

But the incident didn't lead to sustained evangelistic fruitfulness, and Brainard's missionary work in 1743 saw little success. His despondency increased during Christmas. He wrote, "I was very fatigued with my journey, wherein I underwent great hardships; much exposed and very wet by falling into the river." The next year was no better; he grew even more depressed.

On *January 3, 1745*, Brainard set aside the entire day for fasting and prayer, pleading for an outpouring of spiritual power. He claimed the promise found in John 7: "Have faith in me, and you will have life-giving waters flowing from deep inside you."

Then he preached repeatedly from John 7, and the unfolding year proved the most fruitful of his ministry. His interpreter, an alcoholic named Tattamy, was converted. An immediate change seemed to transform Tattamy's life and his translating of Brainard's sermons. Scores of Indians were saved and baptized.

Brainard grew weaker, and in 1747, he died at age twenty-nine in the home of Jonathan Edwards. But his story moved his generation—Henry Martyn, William Carey, Adoniram Judson—toward missions. His diary became one of the most powerful Christian books in early American history, containing such entries as this one: "Here am I, send me; send me to the ends of the earth; send me to the rough, the savage pagans of the wilderness; send me from all that is called comfort on earth; send me even to death itself, if it be but in Thy service and to promote Thy kingdom."

On the last and most important day of the festival, Jesus stood up and shouted, "If you are thirsty, come to me and drink! Have faith in me, and you will have life-giving water flowing from deep inside you, just as the Scriptures say." Jesus was talking about the Holy Spirit. (John 7:37–39)

The Tongue Screw

Travel brochures of the Netherlands tell of windmills, dikes, and boys with their silver skates. But the years 1531 to 1578 were not so peaceful there. Hundreds of Protestants were slaughtered, including a young man named Hans.

Hans Bret supported his widowed mother by working in a bakery in Antwerp. The two belonged to a Protestant group there, and in his spare time Hans studied the Bible and taught new converts in the church, preparing them for baptism. One evening a knock sounded on the bakery door. Hans opened it to find a delegation of officers. The house was surrounded and Hans was arrested. For the next several months, authorities alternately questioned and tortured him. From his dark isolation hole, Hans managed to smuggle letters to his mother.

> From him alone we expect our strength to withstand these cruel wolves, so that they have no power over our souls. They are really more cruel than wolves—they are not satisfied with our bodies, tearing at them; but they seek to devour and kill our souls.

Hans's treatment worsened, and when intense torture failed to break his spirit, he was sentenced to the stake. Early on Saturday, *January 4, 1577*, the executioner came to Hans's cell and ordered him to stick out his tongue. Over it he clamped an iron tongue screw, twisting it tightly with a vise grip. Then he seared the end of Hans's tongue with a red-hot iron so that the tongue would swell and couldn't slip out of the clamp. The officials didn't want Hans preaching at his execution. The young man was taken by wagon to the marketplace, secured to a post with winding chains, and burned alive.

In the crowd, another Hans watched in horror—Hans de Ries, Bret's pastor and friend. After the ashes cooled, he sifted through them and retrieved a keepsake—the tongue screw that had fallen from Bret's consumed body. Shortly after, Hans de Ries married Hans Bret's mother, and the tongue screw became a symbol of faithfulness, passed from generation to generation.

> Each generation will announce
> to the next
> your wonderful
> and powerful deeds.
> I will keep thinking about
> your marvelous glory
> and your mighty miracles.
> Everyone will talk about
> your fearsome deeds,
> and I will tell all nations
> how great you are. (Psalm 145:4–6)

January 5

Pillar Piety

As the church grew institutionally during its first centuries, those flooding through its doors were not always of high caliber. In reaction, a number of Christians withdrew to a life of poverty, chastity, and separation. Monastic forms developed, and sometimes rivalry arose among monks concerning self-denial. Simeon seems to have won the contest.

He was born about 390 to a shepherd's family in Cilicia. He kept flocks as a boy, but at age thirteen he was moved by listening to the Beatitudes. He left home to join a cloister but was soon dismissed because of his acts of self-torture. Simeon moved to the Syrian desert and lived with an iron chain on his feet before having himself buried up to the neck for several months.

When crowds flocked to view his acts of perceived holiness, Simeon determined to escape the distractions by living atop a pillar. His first column was six feet high, but soon he built higher ones until his permanent abode towered sixty feet above ground.

The tiny perch wouldn't allow for comfort, but a railing and a rope kept Simeon from falling while asleep. Disciples took his food and removed his waste by ladder. The rope eventually became embedded in his flesh, rotted, and teemed with worms. When worms fell from his sores, Simeon would pick them up and replace them, saying, "Eat what God has given you."

Simeon lived atop his pole for thirty years, exposed to blistering heat, driving rain, and chilling frost. But if his motive was crowd avoidance, he failed. Huge numbers came to gawk at him, and Simeon preached to them daily, stressing the importance of prayer, selflessness, and justice. He settled disputes between neighbors and persuaded lenders to reduce their interest.

He was likened to a candle on a candlestick.

He died at age sixty-nine, but his example created a fashion of pillar hermits lasting over a thousand years. His name has been remembered throughout church history on *January 5*—in western tradition, the Feast Day of St. Simeon Stylites.

You would have to leave this world to get away from everyone who is immoral or greedy or who cheats or worships idols. (1 Corinthians 5:10)

Charles Spurgeon - London pastor 1854
Huge numbers came to hear him preach.

No Small Churches

January 6

Discouragement is the occupational hazard of ministry, and many of God's workers are disheartened by small crowds and meager results. Charles Spurgeon could teach them a lesson.

It isn't that Spurgeon ever struggled with small crowds. Almost from the beginning, multitudes flocked to his feet. When he assumed his London pastorate in 1854, the church had 232 members. Soon so many were crowding his auditoriums that he sometimes asked his members to stay away the next Sunday to accommodate newcomers. He seldom preached to fewer than six thousand, and on one occasion his audience numbered almost twenty-four thousand—all this before the day of microphones. During his lifetime, Spurgeon preached to approximately ten million people.

He also became history's most widely read preacher. Today there is more material written by Spurgeon than by any other Christian author of any generation. The collection of his Sunday sermons stands as the largest set of books by a single author in the history of the church. He is called the *Prince of Preachers*.

But ironically Spurgeon himself is a testimony to the power of a *small* church. On Sunday, *January 6, 1850*, a blizzard hit England, and fifteen-year-old Charles was unable to reach the church he usually attended. He turned down Artillery Street and ducked into a Primitive Methodist church, finding only a few people standing around the stove. Not even the preacher arrived.

A thin-looking man stood and read Isaiah 45:22: "Look unto me, and be ye saved, all the ends of the earth" (KJV). The speaker, groping for something to say, kept repeating his text. Finally, he spied young Charles in the back. Pointing his bony finger at the boy, he cried, "Look, young man! Look! Look to Christ!"

The young man did look, and Spurgeon later said, "As the snow fell on my road home from the little house of prayer, I thought every snowflake talked with me and told of the pardon I had found." Arriving home, his mother saw his expression and exclaimed, "Something wonderful has happened to you." It had, proving that smaller ponds often yield the biggest fish.

Does anyone remember how glorious this temple used to be? Now it looks like nothing. But cheer up! Because I, the LORD All-Powerful, will be here to help you with the work, just as I promised . . . My Spirit is right here with you. (Haggai 2:3–5)

January 7

. . . Whose Will Be Done

Faithfulness eclipses fame as the mark of greatness. Not everyone is named Augustine, Luther, or Graham. The names of some are obscured by time, but they have done the Father's will. Take John Hooper, for example—born in Sommersetshire, England, in 1495. While studying at Oxford, he discovered the book of Romans, which "seriously affected the salvation of my soul," he wrote, "and my everlasting welfare. Therefore with an earnest study, I employed myself therein both night and day." Hooper found the death of Christ sufficient for salvation without additional work or merit. He confessed, "I had blasphemed God by wicked worship and an almost idolatrous heart until I became rightly acquainted with the Lord."

His Reformation beliefs put him at risk, and he escaped to the coast on a borrowed horse, then to France and later to Zurich, where he studied Greek, theology, and the writings of Zwingli. Returning to England during King Edward's reign, he preached to packed houses and before the king himself. When Queen Mary ascended the throne and unleashed a storm against Protestants. Hooper was thrown into Fleet prison, where his clammy bed of rotten straw lay beside the city sewer. Hooper described conditions in a letter on *January 7, 1554*: "On the one side is the stink and filth of the house, and on the other side the town ditch, so that the stench hath infected me with sundry diseases—during which time I have been sick; and the doors, bars, and chains being closed, and made fast upon me, I have mourned and cried for help . . . neither is there suffered any to come at me whereby I might have relief. But I commit my cause to God, whose will be done, whether it be by life or death."

While being burned at the stake, his voice joined those of the assembled crowd praying, "Our Father which art in heaven, Hallowed be thy name . . ." (KJV).

> Here is a true message:
> "If we died with Christ,
> we will live with him.
> If we don't give up,
> we will rule with him.
> If we deny
> that we know him,
> he will deny
> that he knows us.
> If we are not faithful,
> he will still be faithful.
> Christ cannot deny
> who he is." (2 Timothy 2:11–13)

Tough as Nails

January 8

Women are tough as nails when it comes to working for Christ, as George Fox realized when he began the Quaker movement in the 1600s. From the beginning, he welcomed women preachers. His first convert was a well-to-do, middle-aged mother named Elizabeth Hooton from Nottingham, England. She soon became the Quakers' first woman preacher. Her new beliefs landed her in jail, and she was sent to a grim succession of English prisons before being released at age sixty. She booked passage to Boston, but when authorities there wouldn't admit her, she sailed to Virginia and started for New England by foot.

She was stepping from pan to fire.

Governor John Endicott demanded the reason for her coming to America. She answered, "To do the will of Him that sent me." She found herself behind bars again, and over the next several years she was in and out of Boston, and in and out of jail. Even worse, her grandmotherly age didn't keep her from the whipping post. At Cambridge, she was given ten stripes with a three-stringed whip, knotted at the ends. At Watertown, she was whipped again. At Dedham, she again felt the lash.

She remained undaunted, and when nearly seventy, she said, "The love I bear to the souls of men makes me willing to undergo whatsoever can be inflicted to me." At length she returned to England and wrote King Charles II, saying: "Oh that thou would give up thy kingdom to ye Lord, God of heaven and earth, whose it is, and thy strength and power to Jesus Christ, who is King of kings, and then thou wilt be more honorable than ever thou wast."

The message was not well received, and in 1671 she boarded ship for the West Indies to do missionary work and to escape further abuse. The ship reached the islands the first week of 1672, but Elizabeth Hooton, the Quakers' first convert and first woman preacher, had fallen ill. She died on *January* 8 and was buried in the Jamaican sands like a soldier falling in the line of duty.

Three times the Romans beat me with a big stick, and once my enemies stoned me. I have been shipwrecked three times, and I even had to spend a night and a day in the sea. During my many travels, I have been in danger from rivers, robbers, my own people, and foreigners. My life has been in danger in cities, in deserts, at sea, and with people who only pretended to be the Lord's followers. (2 Corinthians 11:24–26)

Sheffey 1820 Virginia preacher. Powerful in prayer.

January 9 The Peculiar Preacher

The Lord gives each of us a unique personality, and his choicest servants have sometimes been, well, peculiar. "Uncle" Bob Sheffey was among them.

Sheffey was born on Independence Day, 1820. When his mother died, an aunt in Abingdon, Virginia, took him in. There, over Greenway's Store, he was converted on *January 9, 1839*. He was nineteen. Feeling the call to preach, he dropped out of college and started through the Virginia hills as a Methodist circuit rider preaching the gospel.

He did it oddly. For example, one day he was called to a cabin on Wolfe Creek. He had previously tried to win this family to Christ, but without success. As he rode up this time, things were different. A member had been bitten by a rattlesnake. There seemed little hope. Entering the house, Sheffey sank to his knees and prayed, "O Lord, we do thank thee for rattlesnakes. If it had not been for a rattlesnake they would not have called on You. Send a rattlesnake to bite Bill, one to bite John, and send a great big one to bite the old man!"

He is well remembered for prayers like that. An acquaintance said, "Brother Sheffey was the most powerful man in prayer I ever heard, but he couldn't preach a lick." Once, encountering moonshiners in the mountains, he dismounted, knelt, and offered a long prayer for God to "smash the still into smithereens." He rose, smoothed his trousers, and continued his journey. A heavy tree fell on the still, wrecking it. The owner rebuilt it, and Sheffey prayed again. This time a flash flood did the job.

His prayers were honest, down-to-earth, and plainspoken—even routine prayers like grace at meals. Once, being entertained in a neighborhood home, he was asked to offer thanks. Sheffey, who loved chicken and dumplings, said, "Lord, we thank Thee for this good woman; we thank Thee for this good dinner—but it would have been better if the chicken had dumplings in it. Amen."

Robert Sheffey's unorthodox prayers and sermons ushered many mountaineers into the kingdom and earned him the title the *Peculiar Preacher*.

Each of you has been blessed with one of God's many wonderful gifts to be used in the service of others. So use your gift well. If you have the gift of speaking, preach God's message. If you have the gift of helping others, do it with the strength that God supplies. (1 Peter 4:10–11)

Closed Doors

When God closes a door, someone said, he always opens a window. In George Whitefield's case, many doors closed, but God opened up the world.

Whitefield became a Christian while attending Oxford in 1735. He soon began preaching, finding huge crowds whenever he mounted a pulpit. On Wednesday, *January 10, 1739*, having preached the previous night, he rose to leave for Oxford to be ordained to the Anglican ministry. His diary reads: "Slept about three hours, rose at five, set out at ten, and reached Oxford by five in the evening. As I entered the city, I called to mind the mercies I had received since I left it. They are more than I am able to express. Oh that my heart may be melted by the sense of them."

He expected church doors to open following his ordination, but the reverse occurred. Many ministers envied his success. Some didn't trust his association with Methodists, Moravians, and other nonconformists. And Whitefield alienated others by sometimes speaking too critically.

A Welsh evangelist, Howell Harris, was creating a storm by preaching in the fields, and Whitefield wondered if he, too, should take to the open air. Outside Bristol among coal miners, Whitefield preached out-of-doors for the first time on February 17. About two hundred heard him. Soon ten thousand were showing up, and that launched a lifetime of preaching from tombstones, tree stumps, and makeshift platforms.

Whitefield's sermons were electric. His vivid imagination, prodigious memory, powerful voice, and ardent sincerity mesmerized listeners. He could be heard a mile away, and his voice was so rich that British actor David Garrick said, "I would give 100 guineas if I could say 'O' like Mr. Whitefield."

Later that year Whitefield, then twenty-five, toured the American colonies, sparking the Great Awakening and bringing multitudes to Christ. His final sermon in Boston drew the largest crowd that had ever gathered in America—twenty-three thousand people, more than Boston's entire population. He has been called the greatest evangelist in history, save for Paul.

The LORD said:
"... I chose you to speak for me
to the nations."
I replied, "I'm not a good speaker, LORD, and I'm too young."
"Don't say you're too young," the LORD answered. "If I tell you to go and speak to someone, then go! ..." (Jeremiah 1:4–7)

Scandal of the Century

American Christianity suffered from clergy scandals long before the televangelist disgraces of the 1980s. The most popular pastor of his time, Henry Ward Beecher, created "the scandal of the century" in 1870, and to this day no one knows the full story.

Beecher, pastor of Brooklyn's Plymouth Church, was a witty, dynamic, larger-than-life political activist, promoting heartfelt causes such as racial equality and woman suffrage. Though theologically liberal, he became the best-known preacher in America.

But his speaking engagements and church duties kept him away from home, and he grew distant from his wife, Eunice. Beecher was an imposing man with broad shoulders, flowing hair, and grayish-blue eyes full of expression. He exuded vitality and charm, especially with women. Rumors began surfacing about his involvements, and when Elizabeth Tilton came into his life, the rumors rose to the surface like gaseous bubbles.

"Libby's" husband, journalist Theodore Tilton, traveled widely, and she was lonely. She approached Beecher for counseling and soon became his closest confidante. In 1870, Libby confessed that she and Beecher had become intimate. Beecher denied all but kissing Libby and giving her emotional support, and the situation simmered for years.

It burst on the public on *January 11, 1875*, when Tilton sued Beecher for alienating his wife's affections. The trial dragged on, becoming the talk of the nation. In the end the jury was deadlocked. While Beecher's supporters gave him the benefit of the doubt, the *New York Times* spoke for most when it editorialized on July 3, 1875: "Sensible men throughout the country will in their hearts be compelled to acknowledge that Mr. Beecher's management of his private affairs has been entirely unworthy of his name, position, and sacred calling."

Beecher himself admitted as much to attorneys who once apologized for disturbing him on a Sunday. "We have it on good authority," he said, "that it is lawful to pull an ass out of the pit on the Sabbath. Well, there never was a bigger ass or a deeper pit."

Anyone who desires to be a church official wants to be something worthwhile. That's why officials must have a good reputation and be faithful in marriage. They must be self-controlled, sensible, well-behaved, friendly to strangers, and able to teach. (1 Timothy 3:1–2)

The Hampton Court Conference

How odd that the most famous Bible in history should bear the name of a hard-drinking, foulmouthed, ego-driven homosexual who rejected all demands for reform within the church.

James IV of Scotland, son of imprisoned Mary, Queen of Scots, was raised in drafty Scottish castles by self-serving lords. He grew up religious and was well trained in theology. He went to church every day. But he was rude, rough, loud, conceited, and bisexually immoral. He was also shrewd. At age thirty-seven he managed to succeed his cousin, Elizabeth I, as England's monarch.

As he traveled from Scotland to London, he met a group of Puritans bearing a Millenary Petition signed by approximately one thousand pastors. It demanded renewal within the church. The Puritans, stirred by the Geneva translation of the Bible and by Foxe's popular *Book of Martyrs*, wanted to purify the church.

The established clergy opposed Puritan demands, and the new king realized his kingdom was torn. He convened a conference for church leaders at his Hampton Court estate on *January 12, 1604*, and the Puritans vigorously presented their concerns. James rejected their requests, sometimes thundering against them, white with rage. At the conclusion of the conference, he flung his arm toward the Puritans, shouting, "I shall make them conform or I will harry them out of this land, or do worse."

Many of the dispirited Puritans, abandoning hope for the Anglican Church, began worshiping in small groups as they felt the Bible taught them. They were tagged Separatists, but from these persecuted cells came the Baptists in 1611, the Pilgrims who fled to America in 1620, and other dissenting groups.

But on one issue at Hampton Court the king and Puritans had agreed. When Puritan John Rainolds requested a new translation of the Bible, James promptly approved it, saying, "I have never yet seen a Bible well translated. But I think the Geneva is the worst." Seven years later the authorized version was unveiled, ironically making vice-prone King James one of the best recognized names in English church history.

The LORD controls rulers,
just as he determines
the course of rivers.
We may think we are doing
the right thing,
but the LORD always knows
what is in our hearts. (Proverbs 21:1–2)

Finding Her Place

Sometimes it takes a while for young people to find themselves. Amy Carmichael grew up in Belfast, enjoying a carefree life until her father died and left the family debt ridden. The ensuing pressure helped direct her attention to spiritual things, and in 1886 she gave her life to Christ. She struggled vocationally till the words *Go ye* so impressed her that on *January 13, 1892*, she yielded to overseas service. She sailed to Japan.

But she didn't seem to fit there, and Amy struggled to find her place. She left for Shanghai then, to the dismay of family and friends, abruptly sailed for Ceylon. Returning to England, she decided on India. But for several years, she couldn't find her niche there, and she was often criticized by fellow missionaries.

But she gradually noticed that children were drawn to her, so much so that Indian parents feared Amy was "bewitching" their youngsters. One day, she met a girl who had escaped from the Hindu temple with stories of horror. The Hindus were secretly using children as temple prostitutes. Evidently, parents sold baby girls to the temple, and when the children were eight or nine, they "married" the idol and were pressed into harlotry.

Most people disbelieved such stories, and for several years Amy worked as a detective, assembling evidence to prove the atrocities real. She rescued several more children, and by 1904, was responsible for seventeen youngsters. Amy was occasionally hauled into court for kidnapping, and death threats were common.

But children multiplied on her doorstep, and by 1945, thousands had been placed in Amy's Dohnavur Fellowship, a series of homes for outcast children. Many youngsters grew up becoming Christian husbands, wives, and leaders.

During these years, Amy Carmichael also made time for another ministry—writing. By the time of her death at Dohnavur in 1951, at age eighty-three, she had written thirty-five books on her work in India and on the victorious Christian life. She had found her place and filled it well.

The ones who pleased the Lord will ask, "When did we give you something to eat or drink? When did we . . . give you clothes to wear or visit you while you were sick or in jail?" The king will answer, "Whenever you did it for any of my people, no matter how unimportant they seemed, you did it for me." (Matthew 25:37–40)

My Head to My Feet January 14

Walter Lewis Wilson, medical doctor and Christian, agonized over his fruitless efforts at witnessing. One day in 1913, a French missionary visiting in the Wilson home asked the doctor, "Who is the Holy Spirit to you?"

Wilson replied, "One of the Persons of the Godhead . . . Teacher, Guide, Third Person of the Trinity." The friend challenged Wilson: "You haven't answered my question." To this Wilson replied sadly: "He is nothing to me. I have no contact with Him and could get along quite well without Him."

The next year, on *January 14, 1914*, Wilson heard a sermon by James M. Gray, Reformed Episcopal clergyman and later president of Moody Bible Institute. Speaking from Romans 12:1, Gray leaned over the pulpit and said, "Have you noticed that this verse does not tell us to whom we should give our bodies? It is not the Lord Jesus. He has His own body. It is not the Father. He remains on His throne. Another has come to earth without a body. God gives you the indescribable honor of presenting your bodies to the Holy Spirit, to be His dwelling place on earth."

Wilson returned home and fell on the carpet. There in the quiet of that late hour, he said, "My Lord, I have treated You like a servant. When I wanted You I called for You. Now I give You this body from my head to my feet. I give you my hands, my limbs, my eyes and lips, my brain. You may send this body to Africa, or lay it on a bed with cancer. It is your body from this moment on."

The next morning, two ladies came to Wilson's office selling advertising. He promptly led both to Christ, and that was the beginning of a life of evangelistic fruitfulness. Wilson later founded Central Bible Church in Kansas City, Flagstaff Indian Mission, and Calvary Bible College; he also wrote the best-selling *Romance of a Doctor's Visits*. "With regard to my own experience with the Holy Spirit, the transformation in my life on January 14, 1914, was much greater than the change that took place when I was saved December 21, 1896."

Dear friends, God is good. So I beg you to offer your bodies to him as a living sacrifice, pure and pleasing. That's the most sensible way to serve God. Don't be like the people of this world, but let God change the way you think. Then you will know how to do everything that is good and pleasing to him. (Romans 12:1–2)

God's Handwriting

Missionaries Dick and Margaret Hillis found themselves caught in China during the Japanese invasion. The couple lived with their two children in the inland town of Shenkiu. The village was tense with fear, for every day brought terrifying reports of the Japanese advance. At the worst possible time, Dick developed appendicitis, and he knew his life depended on making the long journey by rickshaw to the hospital. On *January 15, 1941*, with deep foreboding, Margaret watched him leave.

Soon the Chinese colonel came with news. The enemy was near and townspeople must evacuate. Margaret shivered, knowing that one-year-old Johnny and two-month-old Margaret Anne would never survive as refugees. So she stayed put. Early next morning she tore the page from the wall calendar and read the new day's scripture. It was Psalm 56:3: "What time I am afraid, I will trust in thee" (KJV).

The town emptied during the day, and next morning Margaret arose, feeling abandoned. The new verse on the calendar was Psalm 9:10: "Thou, LORD, hast not forsaken them that seek thee" (KJV).

The next morning she arose to distant sounds of gunfire and worried about food for her children. The calendar verse was Genesis 50:21: "I will nourish you, and your little ones" (KJV). An old woman suddenly popped in with a pail of steaming goat's milk, and another straggler arrived with a basket of eggs.

Through the day, sounds of warfare grew louder, and during the night Margaret prayed for deliverance. The next morning she tore the page from the calendar to read Psalm 56:9: "When I cry unto thee, then shall mine enemies turn back" (KJV). The battle was looming closer, and Margaret didn't go to bed that night. Invasion seemed imminent. But the next morning, all was quiet. Suddenly villagers began returning to their homes, and the colonel knocked on her door. For some reason, he told her, the Japanese had withdrawn their troops. No one could understand it, but the danger had passed. They were safe.

Margaret glanced at her wall calendar and felt she had been reading the handwriting of God.

When I pray, LORD God,
my enemies will retreat,
because I know for certain
that you are with me.
I praise your promises!
I trust you and am not afraid.
No one can harm me. (Psalm 56:9–11)

"Young Man . . ."

On a cold Sunday in 1873, a dignified woman and her portly companion trudged across Clark Street Bridge in Chicago. College administrator Emma Dryer and evangelist D. L. Moody were discussing a Christian school for Chicago. Dryer insisted that such a school be coeducational, but Moody disagreed.

Miss Dryer decided to raise the money herself, and in 1882, her institute opened with fifty students. Moody, watching from afar, was impressed and agreed to lend his support if Chicagoans could raise $250,000: "I will tell you what I have on my heart. I would like to see $250,000 raised at once; $250,000 for Chicago is not anything. Take $50,000 and put up a building that will house 75 or 100 people, where they can eat and sleep. Take $200,000 and invest it at 5 percent, and that gives you $10,000 a year to run this work. Then take men that have the gifts and train them for this work of reaching the people." Men and, he finally agreed, women.

It happened, and Emma Dryer, who had kept the vision before Moody for years and provided educational and organizational expertise to the school's beginnings, resigned to make room for his leadership. Land and buildings were acquired, and on *January 16, 1890*, Moody Bible Institute was dedicated.

Two years later, William Evans became MBI's first graduate. Evans, a New York journalist, had first heard Moody in New York City. Preaching from Luke 5, Moody had challenged young people to give themselves for Christian service. Suddenly the evangelist had looked down at young Evans and said, "Young man, I mean you."

Afterward Moody found Evans and continued, "Young man, somehow or other God told me He meant you. Have you never been called to give your life to the service of Jesus Christ?" When Evans mentioned his comfortable salary, Moody retorted, "Pack up your trunk and go to my school in Chicago. Never mind about money."

Evans went. And he became the first of thousands who, for over a century, have spanned the globe for Christ from the Moody Bible Institute of Chicago.

Timothy, my child, Christ Jesus is kind, and you must let him make you strong. You have often heard me teach. Now I want you to tell these same things to followers who can be trusted to tell others. (2 Timothy 2:1–2)

January 17

Death by Baptism

As Ulrich Zwingli preached in Zurich, he sought to bring reformation to Switzerland within the context of the established state church. In Zurich and throughout Europe there was little difference between state and church. All babies baptized were thereby considered members of the church and citizens of the city. But Conrad Grebel and Felix Manz, impatient with Zwingli's reforms, began holding Bible classes in private homes, and their investigation of Scripture raised questions about state-sponsored sprinkling of infants.

When Grebel's wife gave birth to a son, the stage was set for conflict. On *January 17, 1525*, the Zurich City Council arranged a public debate on the issue. Zwingli insisted that all children be baptized by their eighth day, while Grebel and Manz argued that baptism symbolized a believer's commitment to Christ. They lost.

Four days later under cloak of darkness, a dozen men trudged through falling snow to Manz's house. After kneeling in prayer, one of them, George Blaurock, asked Grebel to baptize him in the apostolic fashion—upon his confession of personal faith in Christ. Grebel did so; then Blaurock, a former priest, baptized the others.

Zwingli was incensed, and these radical reformers were soon driven from Zurich. They established a congregation in the nearby village of Zollikon, the first "free" church of modern times. But they weren't free from Zwingli, who hounded them, or from Zurich's arm of persecution.

Grebel, his health failing in prison, died of the plague. Blaurock was burned at the stake. And Zurich officials decided that if Manz wanted baptism so badly, they would give it to him. Taking him from Wellenberg prison, they bound his arms and legs. As they rowed down the middle of Zurich's Limmat River, his mother shouted over the splashing oars for him to remain true to Christ. After he sang "Into thy hands, O Lord, I commend my spirit," he was rolled overboard, and the cold waters of Lake Zurich closed over his head.

As they were going along the road, they came to a place where there was some water. The official said, "Look! Here is some water. Why can't I be baptized?" He ordered the chariot to stop. Then they both went down into the water, and Philip baptized him. (Acts 8:36–38)

Perfidious Prelates

Jesus surely chose his disciples knowing that sooner or later most of us would identify with impetuous, impulsive Peter.

James Mitchell was a Peter: part preacher/part assassin—and perhaps with good reason for being both. He was a Covenanter, one of the Scottish Presbyterians who vowed to resist English efforts to impose Anglo-Catholic forms on their churches. Their resistance drew fire from the monarchy and from the church itself, the chief tormentor being the prelate, Archbishop James Sharp, who caught and killed Presbyterians like dogs.

Something had to be done, Mitchell reasoned. On July 11, 1668, as the archbishop sat in his horse-drawn coach, Mitchell pointed a pistol at him and fired through the open door. He missed, hitting another bishop in the hand. Eventually Mitchell was captured, imprisoned, and tortured with the boot, a tight box fitted around the leg, into which staves were slowly driven, shattering the leg an inch at a time. Mitchell and his crushed limb were then thrown into a series of squalid prisons where he subsisted on snow water sprinkled with oatmeal.

On *January 18, 1678*, the preacher and would-be assassin was taken to the center of Edinburgh for execution. Loud drumming drowned out his last words, but he had hidden away two copies of his message, and from the scaffold he flung them to the crowd. The next day these words were plastered across Scotland:

> I acknowledge my private and particular sins have been such as deserved a worse death; but I hope in the merits of Jesus Christ to be free from the eternal punishment due me for sin. I am brought here that I might be a witness for his despised truths and interests in this land, where I am called to seal the same with my blood: and I wish heartily that my poor life may put an end to the persecution of the true members of Christ in this place, so much actuated by these perfidious prelates . . .

The perfidious prelates, however, found more blood to drink in the years to come.

Simon Peter had brought along a sword. He now pulled it out and struck at the servant of the high priest. The servant's name was Malchus, and Peter cut off his right ear. Jesus told Peter, "Put your sword away. I must drink from the cup that the Father has given me." (John 18:10–11)

Charles I

The mixing of politics and spirituality can be explosive for a head of state or the head of a church—and especially when both heads occupy one set of shoulders.

The English Reformation occurred when King Henry VIII declared himself head of the Anglican church, replacing the pope. But it didn't satisfy those desiring genuine renewal. The Puritans didn't feel Henry went far enough in purifying the church from the "rags of popery" and returning it to the Scriptures.

Henry's daughter, Queen Elizabeth I, opposed the Puritans. Her successor, King James I, threatened at the Hampton Court Conference to "harry them out of the kingdom." But it was James's son, Charles I, who lost his head over them.

Charles was born in 1600, and assumed the throne twenty-five years later. He was deeply religious and morally unsullied, a perfect family man. He was an obstinate monarch, however, and committed to the divine right of kings. He took a Catholic wife and appointed a Catholic-leaning archbishop of Canterbury. He oppressed the Puritans, and thousands of them fled to America; the rest stayed and simmered.

Charles ruled long without a Parliament, but when he tried to force changes in the Scottish church, his northern kingdom revolted. Needing money and arms, Charles at last summoned Parliament. But it proved even more opposed to Charles than the Scots, and when Charles attempted to arrest its leaders, civil war erupted. Oliver Cromwell's Puritan forces, aided by the Scots, defeated the king's supporters in 1645.

On *January 19, 1649*, King Charles was placed on trial. The judges sat on a raised dais at one end of Westminster Hall, soldiers stood at the other end, and Charles sat alone in the center. The drama gripped the nation, and in the end the king, condemned, went to the scaffold calmly. His head was severed with one swing of the ax while a groan rose from the horrified crowd. If he could have governed his kingdom as he had cared for his family, they said, he would have been among England's greatest monarchs.

He didn't, and the head of the head of the Anglican church was lost.

We humans make plans,
but the LORD
has the final word.
We may think we know
what is right,
but the LORD is the judge
of our motives. (Proverbs 16:1–2)

Still Going

The church of Jesus Christ is indestructible. Even the weakest Christians are precious in God's sight, and death itself has no power over his people.

Decius didn't understand that. When Decius Trajan became ruler of Rome in 249, the empire was weakening. Barbarians were threatening northern borders, and morale was low. Decius, a soldier rigid and determined, blamed Christians for the weakness and unwieldiness of his empire.

The emperor had a strategy. He thought if he removed the leaders of the church the entire fabric would dissolve. If you cut off the head, he said, the body will soon die. So in December 249, arrest warrants went out across the empire for prominent Christians, igniting the first empire-wide attack on the church. On *January 20, 250*, Fabian, nineteenth bishop of Rome (or pope), was arrested, tried, and became the first to die.

Decius reportedly said, "I would far rather receive news of a rival to the throne than of another bishop of Rome."

Few records remain of Fabian's life and ministry. We know he improved the organization of the Roman church both above and below ground. He divided the city into seven congregations with a deacon in charge of each section, and he directed work on the catacombs. In those catacombs his broken body was later buried.

But the church wasn't buried. Brave Christians in Rome wrote from prison to Bishop Cyprian of Carthage: "What more glorious and blessed lot can fall to man by the grace of God, than to confess God the Lord amidst tortures and in the face of death itself; to confess Christ the Son of God with lacerated body and with a spirit departing, yet free; and to become fellow-sufferers with Christ? Though we have not yet shed our blood, we are ready to do so."

Decius died the next year, but the church he persecuted is still going strong.

Jesus told him: Simon, son of Jonah, you are blessed! You didn't discover this on your own. It was shown to you by my Father in heaven. So I will call you Peter, which means "a rock." On this rock I will build my church, and death itself will not have any power over it. (Matthew 16:17–18)

January 21 The Pint-Size Pope

Would you stand barefoot in the snow for three days to receive forgiveness of sin?

One man did. In the eleventh century the church fell into widespread corruption, and a dwarf-size reformer named Hildebrand became Pope Gregory VII. Gregory immediately instituted change, insisting that he—not secular kings—had the prerogative of appointing church leaders in the various nations of Europe.

Germany's emperor Henry IV resisted and tried to replace Gregory. The pope excommunicated Henry, dispatching an edict that the emperor's subjects should no longer obey him. Henry flew into a rage, storming around for months as his subjects rebelled. He finally realized the only way to save his crown was by seeking Gregory's forgiveness.

The winter of 1077 was among the coldest in memory. Even so, a few days before Christmas Henry left Germany with his wife and infant son, crossing the Alps as a penitent seeking absolution. The queen and child were lifted and lowered across the icy slopes in rough sledges of oxhide. Horses were killed for warmth and food. The little entourage arrived at the palace housing the pope in Canossa, Italy, on *January 21, 1077*, when the cold was severest. For three days Henry stood in the snow, a penitent with bare head and feet, in a coarse woolen shirt, shivering, and knocking for entrance. "The stern old pope, as hard as a rock and as cold as the snow, refused till he was satisfied that the cup of humiliation was drained to the dregs."* Henry was finally allowed into the presence of the pint-size pope, throwing himself at his feet and bursting into tears, saying, "Spare me, holy father, spare me!"

Gregory forgave him.

We don't have to stand barefoot in the cold, for Christ hung on Calvary that our sins, though scarlet, should be as white as snow.

I, the LORD, invite you
to come and talk it over.
Your sins are scarlet red,
but they will be whiter
than snow or wool. (Isaiah 1:18)

---

*Philip Schaff, *History of the Christian Church, Volume 5: The Middle Ages* (Grand Rapids: Eerdman's Publishing Company, 1907), p. 55.

The Pope's Hope

The little man before whom Henry IV had stood half-frozen, Gregory VII, didn't become pope in the usual manner. He had not been elected behind closed doors by cardinals but proclaimed pope by the people.

His name was actually Hildebrand. His insight and integrity had made him advisor to five popes, and he preferred working behind the scenes to foster reform. That reputation earned him the respect of the people.

During the funeral of Pope Alexander II in 1073, the crowds began shouting "Hildebrand shall be pope!" When Hildebrand tried to ascend the pulpit to quiet the people, Cardinal Candidus stopped him. "Men and brethren," shouted the cardinal. "We cannot find for the papacy a better man or even one his equal. Let us elect him." The cardinals and clergy, using the ancient formula, all exclaimed, "St. Peter elects Gregory (Hildebrand) pope."

Gregory VII tried to bring integrity and revival to the church, but many church leaders opposed him. One who didn't was his friend Hugo, a monk in Cluny. On *January 22, 1075*, the pope wrote to his friend about his burdens:

> The Eastern Church fallen from the faith, and attacked by infidels from without. In the West, South, or North, scarcely any bishops who have obtained their office regularly, or whose life and conduct correspond to their calling, and who are actuated by the love of Christ instead of worldly ambition. Nowhere princes who prefer God's honor to their own, and justice to gain. The Romans among whom I live are worse than heathens. And when I look to myself, I feel oppressed by such a burden of sin that no other hope of salvation is left me but in the mercy of Christ alone.

Hildebrand did his best to free the church from corruption and from political control by secular princes. But frostbitten Henry IV eventually regained strength enough for revenge. He marched to Rome, reduced it nearly to ruins, and drove Gregory into exile. The pope died in Salerno, heartbroken, in 1085.

No hope nourished him but the mercy of Christ alone.

Only God can save me,
and I calmly wait for him.
I feel like a shaky fence
or a sagging wall . . .
You want to bring me down
from my place of honor . . .
Only God gives inward peace,
and I depend on him.
. . . God is our place of safety. (Psalm 62:1, 3–5, 8)

God's Image in Ebony

"Work hard at whatever you do," as it is written in Ecclesiastes 9:10.

Perhaps no one worked harder than Amanda Smith, who learned this trait from her father. Amanda was born into slavery in Maryland on *January 23, 1837*. Her father, Samuel Berry, worked tirelessly to free his children. He made brooms by day, walked miles to work in the fields until one or two o'clock in the morning. He slept for an hour or two; then he was up again. Thus he eventually purchased freedom for every member of his family.

Amanda grew up committed to Christ. Her mother and grandmother were full of faith, and the Methodist revivals sweeping the area profoundly affected her. She labored in the kitchen, earning a reputation for Maryland biscuits and fried chicken. She also became known as the area's best scrubwoman. When her sister Frances accidentally destroyed her freedom papers, Amanda worked hard to repurchase them. She often stood at her washtub for twelve hours, then worked for hours at her ironing board. Overcome by fatigue, she would lean her head on the window ledge and sleep a few moments till the need passed.

She somehow found time for witnessing, and her power as an evangelist gained notice. She began accepting invitations and was soon in demand as a Methodist holiness evangelist. She evangelized all across the South, including such places as Knoxville and as far west as Austin. She traveled alone by train and with simplicity, her belongings rolled in a carpetbag. Her fame leaped the Atlantic, and she was called to England for meetings, then to India, then to Africa. She organized women's bands, young people's groups, temperance societies, children's meetings. She adopted homeless youngsters and started an orphanage near Chicago.

She was called God's image carved in ebony.

Though never ordained, she brought many to Christ through her preaching. She said, "The thought of ordination never entered my mind, for I had received my ordination from him who said, 'Ye have not chosen Me, but I have chosen you, and ordained you, that you might go and bring forth fruit.'"

Do your work willingly, as though you were serving the Lord himself, not just your earthly master. In fact, the Lord Christ is the one you are really serving, and you know that he will reward you. (Colossians 3:23–24)

Finished

My God, why . . . ? is not an unknown prayer among Christians—Why did she contract cancer? Why was I fired? Why does God seem to forget us? Yet Jesus, having uttered "My God, why . . . ?" on the cross, then whispered, "It is finished," signaling not only the end of his suffering, but the completion of his work.

Irene Ferrel graduated from the Bible Institute of Los Angeles with a burden for overseas missions. She found her place in the Congo (Zaire), where for ten years she taught school, shared Christ, and worked in a dispensary in the Kwilu bush.

In 1964, Communist rebels mounted guerrilla raids to overthrow the government. Missionaries in the Kwilu Province were threatened. Irene and her coworker, Ruth Hege, decided to evacuate from their station. A helicopter was ordered, and on *January 24, 1964*, the two prepared to leave.

They packed essential belongings then gathered their Congolese workers for a final time of worship, Irene playing the organ. The final songs died down, the last prayers were offered, and the women began anticipating the chopper's arrival. When it didn't come, they decided to retire and rise early to await it the next day.

Shortly after midnight, young, intoxicated rebels attacked. The youngsters, some barely teenagers, were smoking hemp, smashing windows, and screaming for blood. Storming the house, they dragged the women from their beds and danced around them in wild circles in the moonlight. One youth shot an arrow into Irene's neck. With her last ounce of strength she pulled it out, whispering, "I am finished," and died.

Ruth Hege, also struck by arrows, pretended to be dead, not even moving when one of the rebels jerked out a handful of her hair. Only after the attackers finally ran into the forest could Ruth crawl to safety.

Many other Christians perished during the 1960s Congolese turmoil, including both Protestant and Catholic missionaries. It was a killing time. Why was the helicopter late? Why do God's servants sometimes perish? We'll understand someday.

Till then we trust, knowing his kindness never fails.

> I tell myself, "I am finished!
> I can't count on the LORD
> to do anything for me."
> Just thinking of my troubles
> and my lonely wandering
> makes me miserable.
> That's all I ever think about,
> and I am depressed.
> Then I remember something
> that fills me with hope.
> The LORD's kindness never fails. (Lamentations 3:18–22)

January 25 "This Superstition . . ."

Emperor Nerva, dying suddenly on *January 25*, 98, was succeeded by his adopted son, Trajan. The young man was a soldier, a general with rigid posture, vigorous energy, and conservative ideas. He proved a tireless and able administrator, lowering taxes, publishing a budget, and cutting the cost of government. His building projects benefited the empire, and, in contrast to fellow emperors, he remained faithful to his wife.

Trajan sent his advisor Pliny the Younger to Bithynia when troubling reports arose in 110 about corruption there. Arriving at the Black Sea, Pliny encountered Christians, and he didn't know what to do with them. His famous letter to Trajan—the earliest extant Roman document regarding Christianity (which Pliny called a *superstition*)—described a worship service and asked for advice:

> Their guilt or error amounted to this: on an appointed day they meet before daybreak, recite a hymn antiphonally to Christ, as to a god, and bind themselves by an oath to abstain from theft, robbery, adultery and breach of faith. After the conclusion of this ceremony it was their custom to depart and meet again to take food; but it was ordinary and harmless food. I applied torture to two maidservants who were called deaconesses. But I found nothing but a depraved and extravagant superstition. The matter seemed to justify my consulting you, especially on account of the number of those imperiled; many of all ages and classes and of both sexes are being put in peril by accusation. This superstition has spread not only in the cities, but in the villages and rural districts as well.

Trajan wrote back, and his answer established Roman policy for years. It was a "Don't ask, don't tell" policy. Christians, he said, were not to be tracked down like animals, but if any were found in the normal course of affairs, they were to be punished. If they recanted, they were to be pardoned.

Though moderate, Trajan became the first to persecute Christians as distinct from the Jews, and among those who perished under his reign was Ignatius, bishop of Antioch.

"I praise and honor
God Most High . . .
When God does something,
we cannot change it
or even ask why." (Daniel 4:34–35)

The Reaper

Cyrus McCormick's father dreamed of inventing a machine to harvest crops. He tinkered for years, but it was Cyrus who became famous for inventing the reaper. Cyrus went to Chicago at age thirty-eight with sixty dollars in his pocket to open his factory. Two years later he was a millionaire.

He met a young lady from New York, Nettie Fowler. Nettie was striking, tall, graceful, with shining brown eyes. The radiance on her face, Cyrus learned, came from her relationship with Christ. They fell in love and married on *January 26, 1859.* Nettie was twenty-six years younger than Cyrus, and the couple enjoyed twenty-six years together. Cyrus's death in 1884 left Nettie wealthy beyond belief. What did she do with her money?

She established McCormick Theological Seminary in Chicago for young Presbyterian ministers. She enabled John R. Mott of the Student Volunteer Movement to go to the ends of the earth to organize student missions. She helped form the World Student Christian Federation. She contributed to the evangelic campaigns of D. L. Moody. She supported Wilfred Grenfell, missionary to Labrador, and George Livingstone Robinson, archaeologist to Petra (Jordan). She funded Tusculum College in Tennessee and gave generously to educational efforts in Appalachia.

She absorbed herself in Asian missions, and her house off Michigan Avenue in Chicago became a Christian halfway house between the Orient and the West, a center of international Christianity. It was always full of missionaries and overseas Christians.

She improved the water supply in one country, provided a hospital in another, and a Christian college in another. She built a women's clinic in Persia and a seminary in Korea. She sent agricultural machines to India.

She did it all in the name of Christ. But she never thought of herself as a great giver. Others, she felt, did more. She could give money, but "the greatest gift of all comes from the self-sacrifice and devotion of missionaries," she said.

You can tell where people's hearts are by looking at their check stubs.

Don't store up treasures on earth! Moths and rust can destroy them, and thieves can break in and steal them. Instead, store up your treasures in heaven, where moths and rust cannot destroy them, and thieves cannot break in and steal them. Your heart will always be where your treasure is. (Matthew 6:19–21)

Hush, My Soul

Life spans were shorter in earlier days, and the Lord's workers were not unaffected. Medical science was young, hospitals were scarce, disease was rampant, and every home had its deathbed scenes. But Christians, it was noticed, "died well." Here's an example. Vermont pastor Daniel Jackson prepared this newspaper obituary of his wife, who passed away on *January 27, 1852*:

> It becomes my painful duty to record the death of Mary Jackson, my beloved consort in life. She expired on Tuesday, the 27th of January, at half-past ten in the evening. Her disease was consumption, which refused to relinquish its hold until the vital powers of life sunk beneath its final grasp. It is not in the power of my pen to depict the agonies of that memorable deathbed scene. I will therefore hasten to present the reader a more inviting phase of this matter.
>
> The triumphant state of her mind softened every agony, hushed every murmur, and completely disarmed the king of terrors. For awhile, she had a sharp conflict with the power of attachment which bound her to family and friends, but by the grace of God she obtained a glorious victory and longed to depart and be with Christ, which is far better.
>
> I will here notice some of her dying words uttered during the last week of her life. Speaking of the happy state into which she was about to enter, she exclaimed, "O glorious day, O blessed hope, my heart leaps forward at the thought." When distressed for breath, she would say, "Blessed Jesus, receive my spirit." When I spake to her about her thirst, she said, "When I have been thirsty I have thought of that river whose streams make glad the city of God."
>
> I am left as a lonely pilgrim with no one to count my sighs nor wipe away the falling tear. But hush, my soul, what means this repining? Couldst thou look beyond the spheres of material worlds, and see the glories of thy departed one, thou wouldst say, "The Lord gave and the Lord hath taken away, blessed be the name of the Lord."

As long as we are in these bodies, we are away from the Lord. But we live by faith, not by what we see. We should be cheerful, because we would rather leave these bodies and be at home with the Lord. But whether we are at home with the Lord or away from him, we still try our best to please him. (2 Corinthians 5:6–9)

Here I Stand

The apostle Paul, having stood alone before the Roman emperor, the most powerful man on earth, said, "When I was first put on trial, no one helped me . . . But the Lord stood beside me. He gave me . . . strength" (2 Tim. 4:16–17). Centuries later, another stood before the greatest ruler on earth making a similar defense—and Luther, too, discovered that God gives unexplained courage at critical moments.

Pope Leo had demanded that Martin Luther retract his teachings. Luther responded by burning the papal orders, and the impasse forced Emperor Charles V to convene an Imperial Congress in Worms, a German city on the Rhine, on *January 28, 1521.*

Leo sent lawyers to discredit Luther, who determined to defend himself even at risk of life. "I will not flee, still less recant," Luther said. "May the Lord Jesus strengthen me." Luther left Wittenberg on the ten-day journey with three friends, riding in a rough two-wheel cart. Crowds gathered along the way, and Luther preached at every stop. But as he grew closer to Worms, suspense grew. His friends warned he would suffer the same fate as John Hus. "Though Hus was burned," Luther replied, "the truth was not burned, and Christ still lives . . . I shall go to Worms, though there were as many devils there as tiles on the roofs."

Luther's arrival in Worms was heralded by city watchmen blowing horns, and thousands gathered. Stepping from his wagon, Luther whispered, "God will be with me." Shortly, he stood before Emperor Charles V and the congress. The tension was thick as fog, and Luther, appearing to lose his nerve, mumbled and seemed near collapse. But the next day, fortified by prayer, he thundered his defense of the sufficiency of Scripture. "I cannot and will not recant!" he reportedly said. "Here I stand. God help me! Amen." The congress erupted in confusion and was abruptly adjourned. Luther's friends quickly spirited him to safety. Luther later said, "I was fearless, I was afraid of nothing; God can make one so desperately bold."

And such is the testimony of all those who stand alone for Christ in perilous times.

The Lord will always keep me from being harmed by evil, and he will bring me safely into his heavenly kingdom. (2 Timothy 4:18)

Saying Too Much

We can sink our own arguments by saying too much, as the French reformers sadly discovered in the 1500s. The Protestant movement initially found fertile ground in France. Several preachers, sympathetic to reform, mounted pulpits in Paris, and the king himself showed interest.

But on October 10, 1533, Nicolas Cop was elected rector of the University of Paris and his inaugural address, prepared by a twenty-four-year-old firebrand named John Calvin, was a declaration of war on the Catholic Church. The speech demanded reformation on the basis of the New Testament and attacked the theologians of the church who "teach nothing of faith, nothing of the love of God, nothing of remission of sins, nothing of grace, nothing of justification."

The speech so inflamed Paris that Cop fled to Basel, and Calvin reportedly escaped his room from a window by means of sheets, fleeing disguised as a vinedresser with a hoe on his shoulder. The ensuing months saw so many posters and tracts on Parisian streets that 1534 became known as "the year of the placards." The tension exploded into violence over a scathing placard by an overzealous Protestant named Feret. He attacked "the horrible, great, intolerable abuses of the popish mass."

On the night of October 18, 1534, Feret's placard was found nailed to the king's bedroom door, and that did it. Protestants soon filled Parisian jails. And on *January 29, 1535*, to purge the city from the defilement caused by Feret's placards, an immense torch-lit procession traveled in silence from the Louvre to Notre Dame. The image of St. Genevieve, patroness of Paris, was accompanied by the royal family, princes, cardinals and church officials, ambassadors, and officers from state and university. Solemn mass was performed in the cathedral. The king declared he would behead even his own children if they embraced the "new heresies."

The day ended with six Protestants being suspended by ropes to a great machine that lowered and raised them into burning flames, slowly roasting them to death. In the coming months, many more Protestants were fined, imprisoned, tortured, and burned.

The French Reformation miscarried.

Make your words good—
you will be glad you did.
Words can bring death or life!
Talk too much, and you will eat
everything you say.
. . . If you are too eager,
you will miss the road. (Proverbs 18:20–21; 19:2)

Eight Englishmen

During the 1970s, vast numbers of Christians were among those who perished violently in Uganda, the so-called *Pearl of Africa.* But they weren't the first. The decade of the 1870s, a full century before Idi Amin, also extracted the church's blood.

Henry Stanley, David Livingstone's convert and biographer, was the first to reach Uganda. When he showed his Bible to King Mutesa, the chieftain told him the Muslims had also brought a book, the Koran. "How do we know which is better?" he asked. "I am like a man in darkness. All I ask is that I be taught how to see."

Stanley published Mutesa's words in London's *Daily Telegraph*, adding, "Oh, that some pious, practical missionary would come. What a harvest ripe for the sickle." His plea aroused such passion that the Church Missionary Society soon appointed a twenty-seven-year-old Scottish bachelor, Alexander Mackay, to lead a party of eight to Uganda. Mackay did not go blindly. "Is it likely that eight Englishmen should start for Central Africa and all be alive six months after?" he asked. "One of us at least will surely fall. When the news comes, do not be cast down, but send someone else immediately to take the vacant place."

Mackay himself was injured in a wagon accident in Zanzibar. Two others defected. Another was murdered. Another contracted fever. The remaining three set out from Zanzibar to Uganda.

On *January 30, 1877*, they reached Mutesa's court, but two of the three were soon killed, leaving C. T. Wilson to begin Sunday services alone. Mackay soon joined him, and the two labored for years before baptizing their first convert.

Just as their work was accelerating, Mutesa was succeeded by his son, a cruel teenager who promptly tortured a group of Mackay's younger converts for refusing his demands. Mackay survived the tyrant's threats only to die of malaria while translating the Gospel of John. He was forty.

But his efforts were not wasted. The church grew faster than it perished and became one of Africa's strongest.

If you belonged to the world, its people would love you. But you don't belong to the world. I have chosen you to leave the world behind, and that is why its people hate you. Remember how I told you that servants are not greater than their master. So if people mistreat me, they will mistreat you. If they do what I say, they will do what you say. (John 15:19–20)

The Waldensians

The Waldensians are among history's first evangelicals, pre-Protestants who sprang up in the 1200s in the Piedmont Alps of Italy. The movement apparently started when Peter Waldo (or Valdes) of Lyons, a wealthy French merchant, became involved in translating the Bible into his own French-Provençal. Jesus' words in Mark 10:22—"Go sell everything you own . . . Then come with me"—so moved him that he did just that. His radical Christianity led to his expulsion from Lyons and his removal to the Italian Alps. There his message of simple discipleship took root among Alpine Christians.

The Waldensians stressed love of Christ and his Word and a life of poverty. But their nonconformity invited the wrath of the church, making them targets for extermination. In 1251, for example, the Waldensians in Toulouse, France, were massacred, their town burned.

Nevertheless by 1600, there were twenty thousand Waldensians, mostly farmers and shepherds, in the French–Italian Alps. During Easter week in 1655, some five thousand soldiers came against them, killing, torturing, raping, looting—1,712 were killed. The survivors escaped into the French mountains and claimed protection under the Edict of Nantes, which granted freedom to French Protestants.

When King Henry XIV revoked the Edict of Nantes on October 18, 1685, the Waldensian communities swelled with Protestant refugees. The villages became armed camps of resistance. They found themselves caught between the Catholic forces of both France and Italy. On *January 31, 1686*, Louis XIV issued an edict to burn Waldensian churches to the ground. Protestant assemblies were forbidden, children were ordered baptized in the Catholic faith, and pastors deposed. The Waldensians were trapped and massacred—two thousand killed, two thousand more "converted" to Catholicism, eight thousand imprisoned, half of whom soon died of starvation and sickness.

But the next several years saw a shifting in European politics, and eventually some of the Waldensians returned to their homeland. Others made their way from the Piedmont mountains of Europe to the Piedmont mountains of North Carolina. They established the town of Valdese, where they live to this day, every summer presenting their story in the open-air drama *From This Day Forward*.

Jesus looked closely at the man. He liked him and said, "There's one thing you still need to do. Go sell everything you own. Give the money to the poor, and you will have riches in heaven. Then come with me." (Mark 10:21)

On This Day in Christian History…

FEBRUARY

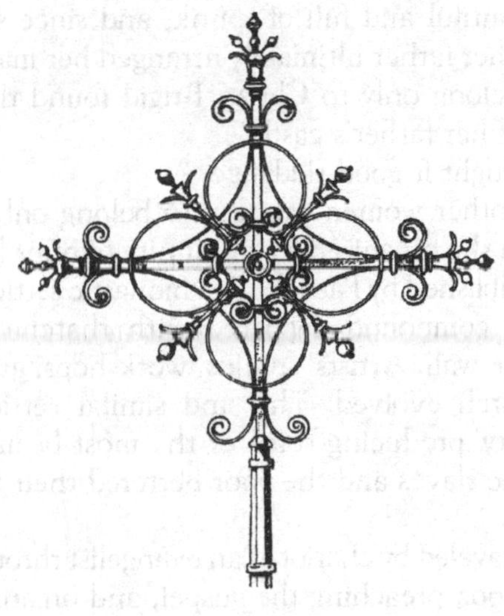

February 1 Stubbornly Generous

In the fifth century, according to Irish church tradition, a king impregnated a slave, and the baby, Brigid, was raised a servant who grew up grinding corn, washing feet, tending livestock—and giving the king's bacon to hungry dogs and his butter to working boys.

Losing patience, he took her to a nearby kingdom, intending to sell her. Finding an interested buyer, he left Brigid in the chariot while he went inside to finalize the arrangements. When a leper passed by, Brigid gave him her father's battle sword from the chariot. The king was enraged, and the prospective husband backed out, saying that he could not afford such a wife.

Brigid was beautiful and full of spunk, and since she loved music and conversation, her father ultimately arranged her marriage to a poet. But resolving to belong only to Christ, Brigid found the man another wife, then deserted her father's castle.

Her father thought it good riddance.

Brigid sought other women wanting to belong only to Christ, and with seven of them she organized a community of nuns like the communities of monks established by Patrick. The monastic settlement at Kildare became a buzzing compound peppered with thatched-roof buildings within a great stone wall. Artists' studios, workshops, guest chambers, a library, and a church evolved. This and similar settlements became beehives of industry, producing some of the most beautiful craftsmanship in Europe. The slaves and the poor bettered their lot by becoming artisans.

Brigid herself traveled by chariot as an evangelist through the countryside, helping the poor, preaching the gospel, and organizing nunneries. By her death on *February 1, ca. 453*, at least thirteen thousand women had escaped from slavery and poverty to Christian service and industry. Throughout ensuing centuries, Christians across Ireland have placed St. Brigid's crosses of woven straw over their doors on February 1, and housekeepers have repeated a rhyme bidding them give a portion of their butter to working boys.

If you forget to bring in a stack of harvested grain, don't go back in the field to get it. Leave it for the poor, including foreigners, orphans, and widows, and the LORD will make you successful in everything you do. (Deuteronomy 24:19)

Two Giants

The son of Pepin the Short rose to power in the eighth century, and there was nothing short about him. Standing seven feet tall, Charlemagne was active, dignified, strong, and intelligent. His continual warfare enlarged his kingdom till it covered most of central Europe, and on Christmas Day, 800, he was crowned king of the Franks by Pope Leo III.

Charlemagne craved education, not only for himself but for his people. He believed that religion and education were the only sure foundations for a healthy state. But he needed a teacher.

Enter Alcuin.

Alcuin, having evidently lost his parents in childhood, had been raised by schoolmasters in York, England. In the vast library of York's Cathedral School, the boy fell in love with Ambrose, Augustine, Bede, Pliny, and the writers of antiquity. He rose from student to teacher, and on *February 2, 767*, Alcuin was made a deacon and the school's headmaster.

Years passed, and the now-famous scholar, traveling in Italy, met Charlemagne. The two hit it off, one a physical giant, the other an intellectual one. Charlemagne asked Alcuin to educate his court, train his clergy, and establish parish schools. So Alcuin resigned at York and began teaching the royal family, the imperial advisors, and the clergy of the palace chapel. He based his curriculum on the seven liberal arts, saying the house of knowledge can only be perfectly built on these seven columns. He collected manuscripts for a royal library. And he began efforts to educate clergy everywhere, then the people. The first thing to learn, Alcuin said, was the Lord's Prayer. Then, the Ten Commandments. He was ever zealous for studying the scriptures and preaching the gospel. People cannot be "christianized" by force, he warned Charlemagne, but brought to Christ by the Word of God.

Ten years later an exhausted Alcuin returned to England, where he spent the rest of his life defending orthodoxy, reorganizing schools, developing curriculum, copying manuscripts, and teaching Scripture. He died unexpectedly on Pentecost Sunday, May 19, 804, but his efforts brought light into the darkness and paved the way for the universities that were soon to rise.

> Wisdom has built her house with its seven columns.
> She has prepared the meat and set out the wine.
> Her feast is ready.
> "Everyone who is ignorant or foolish is invited!
> If you want to live, give up your foolishness
> and let understanding guide your steps." (Proverbs 9:1–2, 4, 6)

February 3 Apostle to the North

In the evangelization of Europe, the Scandinavians were the last Teutonic peoples to accept Christianity. These Vikings from the North threatened Western Christendom, and their raids terrorized Britain and Western Europe. One man wanted to reach them, and his desire for a martyr's crown gave him courage to try.

Anskar, born in France in 801, was schooled from age five at the monastery of Corbey founded by Columba, and he possessed a tender heart. As a young man he was recruited to help establish a new monastery, New Corbey, in Germany.

While there, Anskar heard of a Scandinavian politician, Harald, who was asking for military assistance. The resulting discussions opened a door, albeit dangerous, for a missionary to go to the Danes. Anskar volunteered. His friends tried to dissuade him, but he was ready, he told them, to perish if need be. He didn't die, but little is known of Anskar's resulting trip to Denmark, and when Harald fell from power, Anskar was expelled.

Swedish envoys soon requested missionaries, and Anskar again headed north. This time his ship was attacked by pirates, and he lost his possessions but not his life. Reaching Sweden, he was warmly welcomed by King Björn. But his preaching produced few converts.

Meanwhile, German emperor Louis the Pious, seeing Anskar's work, conceived an ambitious plan for Christianizing the North. He had Anskar appointed archbishop, gave him money, and established a monastery in Flanders as headquarters for the Scandinavian thrust. Anskar did his best, but making headway was difficult. Pirates raided his monastery. He lived in hiding. His missionaries were driven from Sweden. Many of his converts reverted to paganism.

But Anskar prayed and fasted and worked until *February 3, 865*, when he felt the life draining from his body. He gave urgent instructions to his associates, then died peacefully—without gaining his coveted martyr's crown. His efforts failed to establish a permanent Scandinavian base for Christianity, but the seed was planted, and in the tenth century the church there gained a sure foothold. For this reason, Anskar is known in church history as the Apostle to the North.

Father, I don't ask you to take my followers out of the world, but keep them safe from the evil one. They don't belong to this world, and neither do I. Your word is the truth. So let this truth make them completely yours. I am sending them into the world, just as you sent me. (John 17:15–18)

Too Valuable a Man

Some Christian workers, facing the sunset years, may retire from official positions and pace themselves more carefully in ministry. But withdrawing entirely from the Lord's work isn't an option, for Christians don't really retire. They just get transferred.

In 776, Rabanus Maurus was born in Germany with a good brain. His parents educated him in the best schools, and he eventually studied in Tours, France, under the great Christian educator Alcuin, who had advised Charlemagne. Alcuin mentored Rabanus with more than book knowledge; he equipped him to teach others. Back in Germany, Rabanus was appointed principal of the school in Fulda, and under his leadership German youth, both poor and rich, were afforded an education. Rabanus painstakingly developed the library into the best anywhere and made his school Europe's most famous, the mother of scholars and of a score of affiliated institutions. He extended the curriculum to include many sciences, and "reproved superstitions." His graduates were in demand across Europe.

At the heart of Rabanus's educational genius was a passion for God's Word. His academic programs included diligent study of Scripture. He wrote commentaries on almost every book in the Bible, preached regularly, composed hymns, wrote handbooks for ministers, and worked hard for a well-trained clergy—all in an age of darkness, ignorance, and superstition.

Finally in 842, exhausted, he retired. At sixty-six, he longed to spend the rest of his life in quiet study, free from official responsibility. "But he was too valuable a man to be allowed to retire from active life." Appointed archbishop of Mainz, Germany, Rabanus spent his remaining years preaching the gospel and contending for the faith. He didn't lay down his labors until *February* 4, 856, when, at age eighty, the Lord transferred him home. What kept Rabanus going? The Spirit's anointing! In one of his hymns he prayed:

Come from the throne of God above
O Paraclete, O Holy Dove,
Come, Oil of gladness, cleansing Fire,
And Living Spring of pure desire.

Good people will prosper
like palm trees,
and they will grow strong
like the cedars of Lebanon.
They will take root
in your house, LORD God,
and they will do well.
They will be like trees
that stay healthy and fruitful,
even when they are old. (Psalm 92:12–14)

February 5 To God Be the Glory

The hymns "To God Be the Glory," "Blessed Assurance," "All the Way My Savior Leads Me," and "He Hideth My Soul" remind us that it's never too late to begin serving Christ. Some people start as children, others as teens or young adults. But Moses was eighty when God commissioned him, and Paul was middle-aged. So was Fanny Crosby, author of the above hymns.

Fanny was born in a cottage in Southeast, New York, in 1820. Six weeks later, she caught a cold in her eyes, and a visiting doctor prescribed mustard poultices, leaving her virtually blind for life. Growing into childhood, she determined to make the best of it, writing at age eight: "O what a happy soul I am! / Although I cannot see, I am resolved that in this world contented I will be."

Fanny spent many years in New York's Institution for the Blind, first as a student, then as a teacher and writer-in-residence. Her career flourished; her fame swelled. She recited her poems before Congress and became friends with the most powerful people in America, including presidents.

But not until 1851 did Fanny meet her greatest friend, the Lord Jesus. While attending a revival meeting at John Street Methodist Church in New York, she later recalled, a prayer was offered, and "they began to sing the grand old consecration hymn, 'Alas! And Did My Savior Bleed?' and when they reached the line, 'Here, Lord, I give myself away,' my very soul was flooded with celestial light."

Fourteen years later she met the hymnist William Bradbury, who told her, "Fanny, I thank God we have met, for I think you can write hymns." Bradbury suggested an idea for a song he needed, and on *February 5, 1864*, Fanny Crosby, seizing his idea, wrote: "We are going, we are going / To a home beyond the skies / Where the fields are robed in beauty / And the sunlight never dies."

It was her first hymn, and she was forty-four. But by the time she reached her "home beyond the skies" fifty years later, she had written eight thousand more.

I will start playing my harps
before the sun rises.
I will praise you, LORD,
for everyone to hear;
I will sing hymns to you
in every nation.
Your love reaches higher
than the heavens,
and your loyalty extends
beyond the clouds. (Psalm 108:2–4)

Judson

Christian parents often worry about sending their sons and daughters to colleges and universities. Sometimes with good reason. Young people can lose their faith there. But some lose it only to regain it later with added strength.

Adoniram Judson grew up in parsonages around Boston in the 1700s. He entered Brown University at age sixteen and graduated valedictorian of his class. While there he became best friends with Jacob Eames. Jacob was a deist and, in practical terms, an atheist. Ridiculing Judson's faith, he challenged him with the writings of Voltaire and the French philosophers. When Adoniram returned home, he told his parents that he, too, had become an atheist. His mother broke into gentle sobs. His father roared and threatened and pounded the furniture.

Adoniram, at twenty-one years of age, migrated to New York City to establish himself as a playwright. But then, hearing tales from the American frontier, he saddled his horse and headed west. One evening, weary from traveling, he stopped at an inn. The proprietor said, "Forgive me, sir, but the only room left—well, it'll be a bit noisy. There's a young fellow next door awfully sick." Adoniram, too tired to care, took the key.

The night became a nightmare. The tramping of feet coming and going. Muffled voices. Painful groans. Chairs scraping against the floor. Adoniram was troubled by it all, and he wondered what his friend Jacob Eames would say about fear, illness, and death.

The next morning while checking out, he asked about the young man in the next room. The proprietor said, "I thought maybe you'd heard. He died, sir, toward morning. Very young. Not more than your age. Went to that Brown University out East." Adoniram stiffened. The man continued, "His name was Jacob Eames."

The West suddenly lost its lure, and Adoniram turned his horse toward home. Soon he gave his life to Christ, and, shortly afterward, devoted himself to missions. On *February 6, 1812*, Adoniram Judson was commissioned as America's first foreign missionary. He, his wife, and companions sailed for Burma on February 18.

The Scriptures say that the Messiah must suffer, then three days later he will rise from death. They also say that all people of every nation must be told in my name to turn to God, in order to be forgiven. So beginning in Jerusalem, you must tell everything that has happened. (Luke 24:46–48)

A Strong Tower

In 1934, Adolf Hitler summoned German church leaders to his Berlin office to berate them for insufficiently supporting his programs. Pastor Martin Niemoller explained that he was concerned only for the welfare of the church and of the German people. Hitler snapped, "You confine yourself to the church. I'll take care of the German people." Niemoller replied, "You said that 'I will take care of the German people.' But we too, as Christians and churchmen, have a responsibility toward the German people. That responsibility was entrusted to us by God, and neither you nor anyone in this world has the power to take it from us."

Hitler listened in silence, but that evening his Gestapo raided Niemoller's rectory, and a few days later a bomb exploded in his church. During the months and years following, he was closely watched by the secret police, and in June 1937, he preached these words to his church: "We have no more thought of using our own powers to escape the arm of the authorities than had the apostles of old. We must obey God rather than man." He was soon arrested and placed in solitary confinement.

Dr. Niemoller's trial began on *February 7, 1938*. That morning, a green-uniformed guard escorted the minister from his prison cell and through a series of underground passages toward the courtroom. Niemoller was overcome with terror and loneliness. What would become of him? Of his family? His church? What tortures awaited them all?

The guard's face was impassive, and he was silent as stone. But as they exited a tunnel to ascend a final flight of stairs, Niemoller heard a whisper. At first he didn't know where it came from, for the voice was soft as a sigh. Then he realized that the officer was breathing into his ear the words of Proverbs 18:10: "The LORD is a mighty tower where his people can run for safety."

Niemoller's fear fell away, and the power of that verse sustained him through his trial and his years in Nazi concentration camps.

The LORD is a mighty tower
where his people can run
for safety—
the rich think their money
is a wall of protection.
Pride leads to destruction;
humility leads to honor. (Proverbs 18:10–12)

Squalls and Stalls

Just when the apostle Paul intended a Spain-ward thrust of the gospel to evangelize Western Europe, he was detained in Jerusalem, then imprisoned two years in Caesarea. Finally appealing to the imperial court, he was hustled aboard ship for Rome. But a typhoon besieged the vessel; it sank and Paul swam ashore—only to be bitten by a viper. Thus he found himself stranded on the island of Malta for three months.

But careful readers of Acts 27 and 28 are always impressed with Paul's self-possession. He kept his head above water even when his ship was going down. He knew how to remain even tempered, though all the elements of frustration were at hand. Paul's missionary dreams were thwarted. He was imprisoned when he craved freedom and forced into inactivity when he desired action. He was eager to reach Rome, but the winds blew against him. He was a man of progress, making no headway. Wanting to redeem the time, he was beached on an obscure island.

He was stalled.

In due time the sea lanes reopened for the spring, and on *February* 8, 60, Paul boarded ship for the remainder of the trip to Rome.* As for being frustrated, there's no sign of it. Paul's life and ministry were so entrusted to the Lord that he took everything that befell him, both squalls and stalls, as from God. Experience had taught him to trust in the Lord's providence and to lean on the Lord's promises. During the height of the earlier tempest, he had summarized his philosophy for the terrified sailors: "I belong to God, and I worship him . . . Cheer up! I am sure that God will do exactly what he promised" (Acts 27:23–25).

It was not in *due time*—but in *divine time*—that Paul reached Rome. His nerves held steady in the storm. His spirit remained patient in delay.

He knew how to wait on his God.

Three months later we sailed in a ship that had been docked at Malta for the winter . . . We arrived in Syracuse and stayed for three days. From there we sailed to Rhegium. The next day a south wind began to blow, and two days later we arrived in Puteoli. There we found some of the Lord's followers, who begged us to stay with them. A week later we left for the city of Rome. (Acts 28:11–14)

---

*F. F. Bruce, *Commentary on the Book of Acts* (Grand Rapids: Eerdman's Publishing Co., 1977). Bruce quotes Pliny the Elder, who says that navigation begins to be resumed when the west winds start to blow on February 8, and it was "probably about this date that the party set sail from Malta."

February 9 Defending the Faith

Defend," wrote Jude, "the faith that God has once for all given to his people" (1:3). No one has done that better than Athanasius. Born in 296 to Christian parents in Egypt, Athanasius was ordained to the ministry just as a heretic named Arius was teaching that Jesus Christ was not divine. Christ, said Arius and his followers the Arians, was created higher than angels but inferior to the Father.

Emperor Constantine convened a church council in Nicaea in 325 to settle the issue, and Athanasius attended. The young man strongly agreed with the council's decision. Jesus is God. The Father, Son, and Holy Spirit are all divine—one God existing in three names. God, Athanasius believed, became a man and died to provide our forgiveness.

Athanasius soon afterward became bishop of Alexandria. But Constantine, still troubled by the rancor, ordered him to allow Arians to join his church. Athanasius refused, kicking over a hornet's nest of intrigue. Traveling to Constantinople, he planted himself in front of Constantine's horse, grabbed the bridle, and demanded the emperor retract his order. Instead, he found himself deposed.

After Constantine's death, Athanasius returned to Alexandria, but not for long. The Arians had him exiled again in 339, and he spent the next several years in Rome, where his teaching attracted crowds and his writings an eager audience.

He returned to his church in 346. Thousands welcomed him, the city ablaze with torches, and his enemies retreated. But only briefly. On *February 9, 356*, as Athanasius led midnight worship, five thousand soldiers stormed the church and the doors began buckling. Athanasius calmly asked his assistant to read Psalm 136, then slipped out a side door and escaped to the Egyptian desert.

He was later restored to his church, only to be exiled a fourth time. But he soon returned and ministered until his death at age seventy-seven. Seventeen of his forty-five years of ministry had been away from his congregation. But today we owe enormous gratitude to Athanasius. He devoted his difficult life to protecting orthodox doctrine and to defending the faith that God once for all gave to his people.

My dear friends, I really wanted to write you about God's saving power at work in our lives. But instead, I must write and ask you to defend the faith that God has once for all given to his people. (Jude 1:3)

Wesley's Three Nurses

The great evangelist John Wesley was small but well built and handsome. He could charm women at will, and often did—but not always with desired results.

At age thirty-three he met Sophy Hopkey, and she began making daily visits to his cottage for prayer and French lessons. When he became sick, Sophy nursed him, and he fell in love with her. "Her words," he wrote, "her eyes, her air, her every motion and gesture, were full of such a softness! I know not what might have been the consequence had I then but touched her hand. And how I avoided it, I know not." But he hesitated too long, and when Miss Sophy suddenly married another, Wesley was shattered.

Some years later during another illness, he fell in love with nurse Grace Murray. He more or less proposed to her, saying, "If I ever marry, I think you will be the person." She more or less accepted. But when John's brother Charles heard of it, he stormed into Grace's house and burst out, "Grace Murray! You have broken my heart," and fainted. When he recovered, he pelted her with objections, saying she would destroy his brother's ministry. She broke the engagement, leaving John to painfully scribble, "We were torn asunder by a whirlwind."

On *February 10, 1751*, Wesley, now in his late forties, suffered a fall in the middle of ice-coated London Bridge and was carried to the home of nurse Mary Vazeille. This time, he didn't hesitate. They were married within a week.

It was a disaster. Wesley's friend, John Hampson, gave this account of one scene: "Once I went into a room and found Mrs. Wesley foaming with fury. Her husband was on the floor, where she had been trailing him by the hair of his head; and she was still holding in her hand venerable locks, which she had plucked by the roots. I felt as though I could have knocked the soul out of her."

The two spent little time together, and in 1771, we find this curious entry in Wesley's journal: "I came to London, and was informed that my wife died on Monday. This evening she was buried, though I was not informed of it."

A nagging wife goes on and on
like the drip, drip, drip
of the rain.
You may inherit all you own
from your parents,
but a sensible wife
is a gift from the LORD. (Proverbs 19:13–14)

February 11 Four Rules for Dying

When entrusted to God even sickness can become a tool for his glory. Asked why a man was blind, Jesus replied, "This happened so that the work of God might be displayed in his life" (John 9:3 NIV). Paul's illness, though a "thorn" in his flesh, displayed the sufficiency of God's grace. William Sangster's four rules for facing illness show us how that happens.

Sangster was born in London in 1900 and started attending a Methodist church at age nine. At thirteen he became a Christian and immediately began sharing his faith with friends. Three years later he preached his first sermon on *February 11, 1917.* After stints in the army and in college, he began pastoring a circuit of Methodist churches, working himself to exhaustion, frequently saying, "I just can't do enough!" His reputation as a powerful preacher and beloved pastor followed him from church to church.

In 1939, Sangster assumed leadership of Westminster Central Hall, a Methodist church near London's Westminster Abbey. During his first worship service, he announced to his stunned congregation that Britain and Germany were officially at war. He quickly converted the church basement into an air raid shelter, and for 1,688 nights Sangster ministered to the various needs of all kinds of people. At the same time he somehow managed to write, to preach gripping sermons, to earn a PhD, and to lead hundreds to Christ. He became known as Wesley's successor in London and was esteemed as the most beloved British preacher of his era.

After the war, Sangster headed Britain's Methodist home missions department until he was diagnosed with progressive muscular atrophy. For three years he slowly died, becoming progressively more paralyzed, finally able to move only two fingers. But his attitude didn't falter, for when first learning of his illness, Sangster made four rules for himself. Many people have rules for living. Sangster composed four rules for dying: "I will never complain. I will keep the home bright. I will count my blessings. I will try to turn it to gain." He did all those things. And thus the work of God was displayed in his life, and God's strength was made perfect in his weakness.

As Jesus walked along, he saw a man who had been blind since birth. Jesus' disciples asked, "Teacher, why was this man born blind? Was it because he or his parents sinned?" "No, it wasn't!" Jesus answered. "But because of his blindness, you will see God work a miracle for him." (John 9:1–3)

The Sin of Simony

A man named Simon brought money to the apostles (see Acts 8), trying to purchase spiritual power. Peter, ever blunt, replied, "You and your money will both end up in hell if you think you can buy God's gift!" We aren't sure of Simon's outcome, but he unwittingly lent his name to church history. A deplorable practice arose during the Middle Ages—the buying of church offices and positions—and it was called simony.

Simony was so widespread by the eleventh century that the twenty-two-year-old German king, Henry III, grieved for the church. On December 20, 1046, he called a synod in Sutri, twenty-five miles from Rome, to discuss the problem. Pope Gregory VI chaired the proceedings. But Gregory was among the worst simonites, having "bought" the papacy. When Henry reminded the churchmen of the need for integrity and purity among God's leaders, Pope Gregory spoke these remarkable words to the synod: "I, Gregory, bishop, servant of the servants of God, do hereby adjudge myself to be removed from the pontificate of the Holy Roman Church, because of the enormous error which by simoniacal impurity has crept into and vitiated my election."

He asked, "Is it your pleasure that it be so?" The assembled clergymen answered unanimously: "Your pleasure is our pleasure; therefore so let it be." Gregory descended from his throne, removed his pontifical robes, fell to his knees, begged forgiveness, and fled the country.

But now another problem arose: none of the assembled bishops was unstained by simony. They had all bought their positions. After searching the land, an honest man named Suidger, bishop of Bamberg, was elected pope, but he lived less than a year. The next two popes also died quickly. Then Bruno was found, a good-looking, well-educated man of unblemished character and sincerity. Summoned to Rome, he arrived barefoot, dressed as a pilgrim and weeping. The people sang hymns of praise and consecrated him Pope Leo IX on *February 12, 1049.* He battled simony all his days, paving the way for the reforms later enacted under his associate and successor, Hildebrand (Pope Gregory VII).

Simon noticed that the Spirit was given only when the apostles placed their hands on the people. So he brought money and said to Peter and John, "Let me have this power too!" . . . Peter said to him, "You and your money will both end up in hell if you think you can buy God's gift! Get rid of these evil thoughts and ask God to forgive you." (Acts 8:18–20, 22)

But It *Does* Move

Genuine science and correctly taught Scripture are never in conflict, for the same God created both. But endless damage occurs when either is misinterpreted and used to condemn the other. Here is one of church history's saddest, sorriest examples.

Galileo Galilei was an Italian astronomer and physicist who made his first scientific discoveries while a student in Pisa. He dropped out of the university for lack of money, but returned at age twenty-five to teach mathematics. He formulated laws about gravity by conducting novel experiments like dropping weights from the leaning tower at Pisa. He devised the law of the pendulum by watching a lamp swing from the cathedral ceiling. His fame spread across Europe, drawing both students and criticism.

In 1609, he began building telescopes and making spectacular discoveries about the heavenly bodies. Galileo was a Christian who believed that God's world and God's Word were both valid objects for study. Using one of his telescopes, he even showed Pope Paul V some of his findings. But he was nonetheless attacked by the church, for his discoveries contradicted traditional teachings. Some clergymen condemned the whole study of astronomy by quoting Acts 1:11: "Why are you men from Galilee standing here and looking up into the sky?"

In 1632, Galileo was called before the Inquisition to answer charges that his writings violated church teaching. Despite being seventy years old and infirm, he was forced to travel from Florence during the winter, arriving in Rome on a litter on *February 13, 1633*. Historians are unsure whether Galileo, during his trial, was tortured or simply threatened with torture. In any event, the old scientist was forced to read a statement renouncing his views—especially his observation that the earth moves around the sun—confessing them as "errors and heresies." A legend persists that having read his recantation, Galileo muttered, *E pur si muove*—"But it moves after all."

Galileo remained under house arrest, treated badly by church officials, until he became blind and feeble. He died on a winter's day in 1642, in the presence of his son and two of his pupils.

The heavens keep telling
the wonders of God,
and the skies declare
what he has done.
They don't speak a word,
and there is never
the sound of a voice.
Yet their message reaches
all the earth,
and it travels
around the world. (Psalm 19:1, 3–4)

"Your Valentine"

Legends have occasionally crept into Christian history. Stories of some of the early martyrs, for example, handed down orally, have sometimes become embellished and romanticized. Such is the story of St. Valentine.

Two Valentines are actually described in the early church, but they likely refer to the same man—a priest in Rome during the reign of Emperor Claudius II. According to tradition, Valentine, having been imprisoned and beaten, was beheaded on *February 14*, ca. 270, along the Flaminian Way.

Sound romantic to you? How then did his martyrdom become a day for lovers and flowers, candy and little poems reading *Roses are red . . .* ? According to legends handed down, Valentine undercut an edict of Emperor Claudius. Wanting to more easily recruit soldiers for his army, Claudius had tried to weaken family ties by forbidding marriage. Valentine, ignoring the order, secretly married young couples in the underground church. These activities, when uncovered, led to his arrest.

Furthermore, Valentine had a romantic interest of his own. While in prison he became friends with the jailer's daughter, and being deprived of books he amused himself by cutting shapes in paper and writing notes to her. His last note arrived on the morning of his death and ended with the words "Your Valentine."

In 496, February 14 was named in his honor. By this time Christianity had long been legalized in the empire, and many pagan celebrations were being "christianized." One of them, a Roman festival named Lupercalia, was a celebration of love and fertility in which young men put names of girls in a box, drew them out, and celebrated lovemaking. This holiday was replaced by St. Valentine's Day, with its more innocent customs of sending notes and sharing expressions of affection.

Does any real truth lie behind the stories of St. Valentine? Probably. He likely conducted underground weddings and sent notes to the jailer's daughter. He might have even signed them "Your Valentine." And he probably died for his faith in Christ.

But he almost certainly never wrote, "Roses are red, violets are blue . . ."

This is Solomon's
most beautiful song.
Kiss me tenderly!
Your love is better than wine,
and you smell so sweet.
All the young women adore you;
the very mention of your name
is like spreading perfume. (Song of Songs 1:1–3)

February 15 A Prison Bundle

Adoniram Judson, who wanted to become America's first foreign missionary, fell in love with the most beautiful girl in Bradford, Massachusetts. Ann Hasseltine was the daughter of a Congregational deacon, and Judson's letter asking for her hand is among the most emboldened in church history:

> I have now to ask whether you can consent to part with your daughter, whether you can consent to her departure to a heathen land, and her subjection to the hardships and suffering of a missionary life? Whether you can consent to her exposure to the dangers of the ocean, to the fatal influence of the southern climate of India, to every kind of want and distress, to degradation, insult, persecution, and perhaps a violent death.

John Hasseltine did consent, and the couple was married in the Hasseltine home on February 5, 1812. The next day they were commissioned as missionaries and soon left American shores. Their new home, Rangoon, Burma, was a filthy, crowded city. The atmosphere was oppressive, the work discouraging. By 1820, there were ten Burmese converts, but at a cost. One Judson child had been stillborn; another died of tropical fever.

When war broke out between Burma and England, Adoniram was accused of being a spy and placed in a death prison. His dark, dank cell was filled with vermin, and Adoniram was shackled at the ankles. Every evening he was hanged upside down with only his head and shoulders resting on the ground.

Ann, pregnant again, visited one government official after another, urging her husband's release. On *February 15, 1825*, eight months after Adoniram's arrest, she showed up at his prison, carrying a small bundle, their newborn daughter, Maria. No artist can capture the poignancy of that brief union with its intense emotions of sorrow and joy, fear and faith.

Torturous months followed. Adoniram was finally released, but both Ann and Maria soon died of fever. Adoniram suffered a mental breakdown that nearly took both his ministry and his life.

But God wasn't finished with him. America's first foreign missionary still had a world to change.

Unless you are willing to take up your cross and come with me, you are not fit to be my disciples. If you try to save your life, you will lose it. But if you give it up for me, you will surely find it. (Matthew 10:38–39)

Child of Promise

February 16

Andrew and Elizabeth Renwick, a young couple, weavers, lived in the hills of Glencairn, Scotland, in the 1600s. All their children had died. Andrew accepted his grief, but Elizabeth cried to the Lord day and night for another child.

The Lord answered, and little James was taught the Holy Scriptures from infancy. Growing up, his conscience was tender; his mind, sharp. He excelled at the University of Edinburgh, but was denied a degree because he refused to accept Charles II as head of the Scottish church.

Remaining in Edinburgh, James watched with alarm as nonconformists were martyred, their severed heads and hands nailed to the city gates as a warning to others. He left Scotland for training and ordination abroad, but his heart was still in the highlands, and he soon returned to preach, teach, organize, counsel, and wear himself out. "Excessive travel," he told a friend, "night wanderings, unseasonable sleep and diet, and frequent preaching in all seasons of weather, especially in the night, have debilitated me." He trudged with diligence through moors and mountains, in the cold stormy nights and by day. His study was often a cold glen or cave; his pillow, a rock or log. He managed a hundred escapes, but, at length, one winter's night in Edinburgh, he was captured, put in irons, and convicted of treason.

His widowed mother visited him in prison, her heart breaking apart. "O James!" she cried, "How shall I look up to see your head and hands upon the city gate? I shall not be able to endure it." He comforted her as he could, and on *February 16, 1688*, smuggled a message to her, "There is nothing in the world that I am sorry to leave but you . . . Farewell, mother. Farewell, night wanderings, cold, and weariness for Christ. Farewell, sweet Bible and preaching of the gospel. Welcome, crown of glory. Welcome, O Thou blessed Trinity and one God! I commit my soul into Thy eternal rest."

The next morning he embraced his weeping mother once more, then went to the scaffold.

He was twenty-six.

Keep on being faithful to what you were taught and to what you believed. After all, you know who taught you these things. Since childhood, you have known the Holy Scriptures that are able to make you wise enough to have faith in Christ Jesus and be saved. (2 Timothy 3:14–15)

February 17

Modern Martyrs

In 1971, Idi Amin overturned the government of Uganda while President Obote was out of the country. He immediately dissolved Parliament, suspended the constitution, and outlawed political activity. His army began raiding homes and arresting foes. All Asians were expelled. Americans were killed. Robbers were shot on sight. A reign of terror ensued.

On January 30, 1977, Anglican bishop Festo Kivengere preached to a large outdoor crowd, charging, "God entrusts governments with authority. But authority has been misused in our country by force." The audience trembled, for in the crowd were officers of the dreaded State Research Bureau. The following Saturday, soldiers arrested Anglican archbishop Janani Luwum, dragging him from his bed at 1:30 AM. Church leaders immediately sent a letter to Amin, saying, "This is the climax of what has been constantly happening to our Christians. We have buried many who have died as a result of being shot and there are many more whose bodies have not yet been found."

On *February 17*, Uganda Radio announced Luwum's death in a car wreck. The real story was pieced together later. Luwum had been taken to Amin's torture chamber and permitted to hold a brief prayer meeting with other prisoners. Then he was shoved into a Land Rover and driven to a compound near the capital. Amin himself came to the lodge, demanding Luwum sign a prepared confession of plotting to overthrow the government. A war of wills followed, and at length Luwum was forced to strip. He was whipped mercilessly.

Still Luwum refused to sign the confession, praying for his tormentors instead. This sent Amin into a rage. He screamed obscenities, struck the archbishop, and commanded the soldiers to repeatedly molest him. Finally Amin drew his pistol and shot Luwum twice through the heart.

Ironically, Protestants in Uganda had been planning for the one hundredth birthday of Christianity in their country. A group of gifted young Christians was producing a play about the first martyrs in Uganda. A week after Luwum's death, the young people themselves became martyrs, their bodies later found a few miles outside Kampala.

Be on your guard! You will be taken to courts and beaten with whips in their meeting places. And because of me, you will have to stand before rulers and kings to tell about your faith. But before the end comes, the good news must be preached to all nations. (Mark 13:9–10)

The Excellent Map

February 18

As I walked through the wilderness of this world, I lighted on a certain place where was a den, and laid me down in that place to sleep; and as I slept, I dreamed a dream . . .

The dreamer? John Bunyan. The dream? *Pilgrim's Progress*, one of history's bestsellers, published on *February 18, 1678*. Bunyan tells the story of a pilgrim named Christian who encounters many trials, toils, and triumphs while traveling from the City of Destruction to the Celestial City.

Princeton's Dr. Emile Gaillet, who read this book fifty times, said, "Next to the Bible, *The Pilgrim's Progress* rates highest among the classics . . . The reason is that as I proceed along the appointed course, I need not only an authoritative book of instruction; I need a map. Bunyan's masterpiece has provided us with the most excellent map found anywhere."*

In one memorable scene, Christian, finding the pathway difficult, climbed over a stile to walk in a meadowy bypath. Eventually the ground grew soggy and was covered with poisonous vines. The sky became black, and Christian spent the night huddled at the foot of an oak tree, caught in a downpour. The next morning, Giant Despair came upon him, captured him, beat him, and imprisoned him in the dungeon of Doubting Castle with its grim battlements and thick, black walls. Christian tried to sing but couldn't. His mood was dungeon-dark. Giant Despair beat him mercilessly, and he grew weaker each day. At length, he found in his cell a rope, a knife, and a bottle the tools of suicide, and for a moment, he was tempted to end his misery.

But one evening about midnight he began to pray, and . . .

". . . a little before day, good Christian, as one half amazed, brake out into this passionate speech: What a fool am I, thus to lie in a stinking dungeon, when I may as well walk at liberty! I have a key in my bosom, called Promise, that will, I am sure, open any lock in Doubting Castle."

Using the key of God's promises, Christian escaped, never again to fall into the clutches of Giant Despair or Doubting Castle.

> I patiently waited, LORD,
> for you to hear my prayer.
> You listened and pulled me
> from a lonely pit
> full of mud and mire.
> You let me stand on a rock
> with my feet firm,
> and you gave me a new song,
> a song of praise to you. (Psalm 40:1–3)

*Quoted in "From the Publisher," *Christian History* 5, no. 3, (July 1, 1986): 3.

Sickerfoot

James Guthrie was nicknamed *Sickerfoot*, a Scottish term meaning "surefooted." He was unflappable and self-possessed, having a knack for stilling arguments and calming crises. He taught philosophy at the University of St. Andrews for years before becoming a preacher of the gospel in the Scottish town of Stirling.

On *February 19, 1651*, Guthrie was accused of disloyalty, for he had preached that Christ, not the Scottish king, should rule the church. Guthrie answered the accusation, saying that while he respected the monarch's civil authority, he didn't believe the king should control church affairs. In time an indictment was issued, charging that Guthrie "did contrive, complot, counsel, consult, draw up, frame, invent, spread abroad or disperse—speak, preach, declaim or utter—divers and sundry vile seditions tending to the vilifying of His Majesty."

Guthrie was sentenced to be hanged. On the morning of his execution, June 1, 1661, he rose about four in the morning for worship. When asked how he was, Guthrie replied "Very well. This is the day that the Lord hath made; let us rejoice and be glad in it."

His five-year-old son was brought to him. Taking the boy on his knee, he said, "William, the day will come when they will cast up to you that your father was hanged. But be not thou ashamed, lad. It is in a good cause."

Guthrie soon mounted the scaffold and preached for an hour to the assembled multitude. Then he was hanged, after which his head was hacked off and affixed on Netherbow Port. In coming months little William, sneaking away to steal glances at his father's decaying head, would run home crying, "I've seen my father's head! I've seen my father's head!" Its impact wasn't lost, for William learned to lean on Christ, to spend time alone in prayer, and to excel in school. He might have become a powerful minister but for an early death from illness.

Meanwhile Guthrie's bleached skull looked down on the throngs of Netherbow Port for twenty-seven years until a brave student climbed up, removed it, and buried it with reverence.

This day belongs to the LORD!
Let's celebrate
and be glad today.
We'll ask the LORD to save us!
We'll sincerely ask the LORD
to let us win.
God bless the one who comes
in the name of the LORD! (Psalm 118:24–26)

Puritan New England 1698 freezing cold in church.

Wigglesworth's Words

When you're tempted to stay in bed on rainy or cold Sunday mornings, remember the sacrifice of early generations. In Puritan New England, Judge Samuel Sewall once noted in his diary after an unusually frigid Sunday in February, that "the communion bread was frozen pretty hard and rattled sadly in the plates."

Ministers were forced to preach while wrapped in layers of coats, heads covered with caps, and hands cased in heavy mittens. According to Sewall, one Puritan preacher in Kittery, Maine, used to send his servant to the meetinghouse to find out how many had braved the snow. If only six or seven had come, the servant would ask them to return with him to the parsonage and listen to the sermon there.

Another entry in Sewall's diary tells of a bitterly cold day when there was a "Great Coughing" in the meetinghouse, yet a newborn was carried in to be baptized. In harshest weather, mothers brought little footstoves—filled with hot coals—around which their children huddled beneath the church pews. But after several churches burned down because of footstoves left behind, their use grew controversial.

In some communities it was customary on coldest Sundays for worshipers to bring "doggs" to curl at their masters' feet and keep them warm. A few of the men sometimes smuggled another kind of warmth into the church. One such gentleman imbibed too much, and his drunken snores so disrupted the sermon that the deacons dragged him off to the tavern.

In one of his journal entries, Judge Sewall tells of a winter's Sunday when his friend, Rev. Michael Wigglesworth, preached from the verse in Psalm 147 that says, "Who can stand the cold?" By the next Sunday, the entire congregation was so afflicted with illness that services were canceled for three weeks. On *February 20, 1698*, services resumed and Wigglesworth prayed and preached from the words "At his command the ice melts." The very next day, a thaw set in. It was regarded as a direct answer to his prayer.

As soon as God speaks,
the earth obeys.
He covers the ground with snow
like a blanket of wool,
and he scatters frost
like ashes on the ground.
God sends down hailstones
like chips of rocks.
Who can stand the cold? (Psalm 147:15–17)

Jeanne d'Arc

A sorceress or a saint? Spiritual forces were active in her life, but from what source? The French called her a godsend; the English burned her as a witch.

Joan was raised in a poor farming family in Champagne during the Hundred Years' War when England was battling for possession of France. When Joan was thirteen, she had the first of many transcendental experiences, hearing voices accompanied by searing light. The saints, she determined, were commissioning her to save France. She set out to see the Dauphin (prince). He attempted to disguise himself, but Joan wasn't fooled. "The King of Heaven sends word by me," she told him, "that you shall be anointed and crowned in the city of Reims. You are the heir to France, true son of the king."

The young man listened, for he doubted his legitimacy. His father was insane and his mother slept with many men. The Dauphin gave Joan an army just as France was losing the war. She rallied her forces and led them to a remarkable victory, liberating the city of Orleans. Soon she accompanied the Dauphin to Reims, where he was enthroned King Charles VII.

Joan's voices warned her she hadn't long to live, and she returned to battle only to be captured by the English. She stood trial for witchcraft on *February 21, 1431*, before a handpicked English church court. Her visions were pronounced "false and diabolical" and she was declared "heretical and schismatic." On May 30, 1431, she was led to the Place du Vieux-Marche and burned at the stake. Her body was consumed by the flames; all but her heart, which terrified English guards seized from the ashes and threw into the river Seine. But her death inspired the French to recapture Paris and to drive the English from their country.

Prodded by Charles, Pope Callixtus III declared Joan innocent of witchcraft in 1456. She became a patron saint of France.

Saul took one look at the Philistine army and started shaking with fear. Then Saul told his officers, "Find me a woman who can talk to the spirits of the dead . . ." His servants told him, "There's a woman at Endor who can talk to spirits of the dead." That night, Saul put on different clothing so nobody would recognize him. Then he and two of his men went to the woman . . . (1 Samuel 28:5, 7–8)

Gothic Greatness

In Europe at the turn of the thirteenth century, hundreds of great Gothic cathedrals were erected, among them the famous Notre Dame in Paris. A young man, studying at the University of Paris, watched with interest. He listened to reports of crusader armies and discussed theology with his fellow students. They didn't dream he was destined to become the most powerful man in the world.

He was Giovanni Lotario de' Conti, and his interests were law and theology. Then he entered the service of the church. On *February 22, 1198*, at the young age of thirty-seven, he was consecrated pope, and immediately chose the name Innocent III.

The new pope wanted the papacy to reflect the mysterious majesty and Gothic splendor of the new cathedrals like Notre Dame, and he set out at once to become absolute ruler over both church and state. He wrote to kings, princes, scholars, and universities, seeking to influence events in Europe. He organized new crusades to capture the Holy Land. He identified heresy and worked hard to root it out. He massacred dissenters. He expanded papal control of central Italy. He involved himself in the selection of kings and emperors. He forced King Philip II to return to his wife. He brought England's King John to his knees. In one way or another, he dominated the leaders of Europe, insisting that he was their spiritual leader.

Pope Innocent also made his mark on church dogma. In 1215, he convened the Fourth Lateran Council in Rome. The council issued seventy pronouncements, the most significant involving the Lord's Supper. The council decreed that the elements of the Eucharist actually possess the substance of the body and blood of Christ, a doctrine known as transubstantiation.

Pope Innocent died in 1216, at the age of fifty-six. "No other mortal," wrote one historian, "has before or since wielded such power."

He had gained the whole world.

What will you gain, if you own the whole world but destroy yourself? What would you give to get back your soul? (Matthew 16:26)

February 23 Eighty and Six Years

Though Polycarp is not mentioned in the Bible, he was born during the New Testament age, converted early in life, and trained for the ministry by the apostle John himself. Polycarp and John remained friends for twenty years. They worked in churches twenty miles from one another, John in Ephesus and Polycarp at his home church in Smyrna (modern Izmir, Turkey). When John wrote the Revelation, he addressed a portion of it to the believers in Smyrna, and of that church he had no critical words. It may well have been Polycarp who read John's message to the congregation: "I know how much you suffer and how poor you are, but you are rich . . . Don't worry about what you will suffer . . . If you are faithful until you die, I will reward you with a glorious life" (Rev. 2:9–10).

Though Polycarp devoted most of his time to pastoring the church at Smyrna, he also became well-known elsewhere. We still have a letter he wrote to the Philippian church, and in it he quotes extensively from the New Testament. He traveled to Rome to consult with Bishop Anicletus about theological matters. He battled heresy throughout the empire. All in all, he serves as a vital link between the apostles and the rest of church history.

He faced his greatest test in the mid-second century, during the reign of Antoninus Pius. A persecution broke out against Christians, and several of his church members were killed. On *February 23, ca. 155*, a Roman officer publicly demanded that Polycarp renounce Christ. The old pastor's famous reply has echoed through history: "Eighty and six years have I served him and he has done me no wrong. Can I revile my King that saved me?"

"I'll throw you to the beasts!" shouted the Roman. Polycarp told him to bring them on. "Then I'll have you burned," the man warned.

Polycarp replied, "You try to frighten me with fire that burns for an hour and you forget the fire of hell that never goes out."

An hour later his body was ashes, his soul with Christ.

Don't worry about what you will suffer. The devil will throw some of you into jail, and you will be tested and made to suffer for ten days. But if you are faithful until you die, I will reward you with a glorious life. If you have ears, listen to what the Spirit says to the churches. (Revelation 2:10–11)

The Franciscans

On *February 24, 1208*, Francis of Assisi attended Mass in the little church of Saint Mary of the Angels. The priest read from Matthew's Gospel, chapter 10: "Jesus sent out the twelve apostles with these instructions: 'You received without paying, now give without being paid. Don't take along any gold, silver, or copper coins. And don't carry a traveling bag or an extra shirt or sandals'" (vv. 5, 8–10).

Those verses so moved Francis that he resolved to become an itinerant evangelist in the mold of the original apostles. He shared his burden with a few followers, and they devised a simple strategy: to wander through the country as poor men, preaching the gospel and attending those with needs. Francis put his thoughts into writing and traveled to Rome, seeking endorsement from Pope Innocent III. The pope hesitated. "My son," he said, "your plan of life seems too hard and rough." But he eventually acquiesced, and Francis later wrote: "When the Lord entrusted brothers to me, nobody told me how to treat them, but the Most High revealed to me personally that I ought to live according to the norms of the Holy Gospel. I had it all written down in a few simple words, and the lord Pope approved it. And those who wished to embrace the life gave the poor everything they had and contented themselves with a tunic patched inside and out, and a belt and some underclothes. And we did not wish for anything more."

Within eight years Francis's order numbered five thousand men, and by the time he died from tuberculoid leprosy in his mid-forties, he was so beloved that his followers feared the masses would steal his body. So they entombed him beneath the altar of the Basilica of Saint Francis under a slab of granite, gravel, ten welded bands of iron, a 190-pound grill, and a 200-pound rock. They buried him so well, in fact, that his coffin wasn't discovered until the nineteenth century. His followers, however, continued his mission, and today the Franciscan Order in all its branches is the largest religious order in the Roman Catholic Church.

As you go, announce that the kingdom of heaven will soon be here . . . You received without paying, now give without being paid. Don't take along any gold, silver, or copper coins. And don't carry a traveling bag or an extra shirt or sandals or a walking stick. (Matthew 10:7–10)

February 25 Doused with Brandy

"If all the world were like us," wrote a humble hatmaker, "there would be no war." Those simple words cost Jacob Hutter his life.

Hutter was among the first Anabaptists. The term *Anabaptism* means *to baptize again*, originally a term of contempt used by opponents, referring to the Anabaptist belief that state-sponsored baptism of infants was unscriptural. The movement had its beginnings when those impatient with the pace of Zwingli's reformation in Zurich separated from the state church and baptized themselves on January 21, 1525. Persecuted by both Catholics and reformers, many of them fled to Moravia (in modern Czechoslovakia), where government officials seemed more tolerant. They lived in communes, and Jacob Hutter was attracted to their cause.

Hutter was a hatter. His scant education in Prague had been in the trade of hatmaking, and he traveled widely making and selling hats until he had come in contact with Moravian Anabaptists and eventually became their leader. But in 1536, King Ferdinand I ordered the Moravian Anabaptists from homes and communes into the open fields, where they lived under the sky and in caves. Hutter appealed to the governor: "Now we are camping on the heath. We do not want to wrong any human being, not even our worst enemy. Whoever says that we have camped on a field with so many thousands, as if we wanted war or the like, talks like a liar and a rascal. If all the world were like us there would be no war. We can go nowhere. May God himself show us where to go."

Hutter's letter so inflamed the authorities that he and his pregnant wife were captured and taken to a nearby fortress. For three months, Hutter was tortured with rack, whip, and freezing water. He refused to recant, and on this day, *February 25, 1536*, he was tied to a stake, doused with brandy, and set on fire. He was about thirty-six. After Hutter's death, his followers, calling themselves by his name, began spreading their faith. Eighty percent of all Hutterite missionaries died a martyr's death, but today groups of Hutterites still live in pockets of Europe and in several western states in America.

I am sending you like lambs into a pack of wolves. So be as wise as snakes and as innocent as doves. Watch out for people who will take you to court and have you beaten in their meeting places. Because of me, you will be dragged before rulers and kings to tell them and the Gentiles about your faith. (Matthew 10:16–18)

Hair and Helper

od often uses single men and women to do more alone than they could do if encumbered with family obligations. Other times, however, a spouse is needed.

Francois Coillard, born in France in 1834, studied theology in Paris and Strasbourg and sailed to South Africa in 1857 under the Paris Evangelical Missionary Society. He was single, clean shaven, and young. The Africans were perplexed, wondering how this beardless, wifeless youth could teach them anything. "Beards and wives are necessary for respect," they said. "We can't listen to one with neither hair nor helper."

Hearing these whispers, Coillard immediately grew a fine beard. But what could be done about a wife? Yes, he had someone in mind, a young lady in Paris. In fact, he had secretly fallen in love with her while still there but had said nothing about it—not even to the young lady herself. Francois was insecure and afraid and quiet. He had sailed away without a word to Miss Christina Mackintosh.

Now he regretted it, and at length he wrote to a mutual friend, Madame Andre-Walther, asking her to propose marriage for him to Miss Mackintosh. Six months passed; then came the dreaded word: "I don't know you well enough." It wasn't an outright rejection, for Christina remembered the young missionary and had been attracted to him. Nevertheless Coillard was broken by the news. His diary and letters betray intense emotional suffering, and he longed for someone to talk to. But he was in the bush with no one near him but the Lord.

Two years passed. He tried to forget Christina, but without success. Finally he wrote her again, this time in person, bathing his letter in prayer. On July 5, 1860, the answer came. Coillard wrote in his diary, "I cannot believe my own happiness." Christina had accepted.

They were married *February 26, 1861*. "Today," the Africans told him, "you are a man." They listened to him now, and for the next thirty years the Coillards worked hand in hand in Barotseland, establishing churches and planting the gospel.

Our God, you are the one
who rides on the clouds,
and we praise you.
Your name is the LORD,
and we celebrate
as we worship you.
Our God, from your sacred home
you take care of orphans
and protect widows.
You find families
for those who are lonely. (Psalm 68:4–6)

February 27

Heart Palpitations

You can pray when you can do little else.

Robert Murray McCheyne taught himself Greek at age four. He rose to the top of his elementary school at five. He entered high school at eight, and enrolled at Edinburgh University at fourteen.

At age eighteen, he began dreaming of ministry and began the lifelong habit of the morning quiet time, his journal for February 23, 1834, reading, "Rose early to seek God and found Him whom my soul loveth. Who would not rise early to meet such company?" In 1836, he began pastoring St. Peter's church in Dundee, beginning each day reading God's Word and praying.

But McCheyne wasn't well. He experienced "violent palpitations" of the heart, growing so weak and frail that he took an extended trip, seeking to recover. But he missed his church, and on *February 27, 1839*, he wrote them these words in a pastoral letter:

> I wish to be like Epaphras in Colossians 4: "Always laboring fervently for you in prayer." When hindered by God from laboring for you in any other way, it is my heart's joy to labor for you thus. When Dr. Scott of Greenock, a good and holy minister, was laid aside by old age from preaching some years before his death, he used to say, "I can do nothing for my people now but pray for them . . ." This I also feel.

McCheyne only partially recovered, dying in 1843 at age twenty-nine. On the day of his death, nothing was heard in the houses of Dundee but weeping. Men, meeting each other on the streets, burst into sobs. Scottish ministers studied his life and methods for the next hundred years, and his collected letters and sermons are classics. He once said, "If the veil of the world's machinery were lifted off, how much we could find is done in answer to the prayers of God's children."

How much indeed.

We have not stopped praying for you since the first day we heard about you. In fact, we always pray that God will show you everything he wants you to do and that you may have all wisdom and understanding that his Spirit gives. Then you will live a life that honors the Lord. (Colossians 1:9–10)

Opening China

James Morrison, an agriculturist from Scotland, married a young English girl, Hannah Nicholson, and had eight children. The youngest of their children, Robert, born in 1782, was a plodder. His schoolmaster uncle viewed him as an average student with a high degree of determination.

He became a Christian at age fifteen and joined a praying society that met every Monday night in his father's workshop. Robert spent weekends studying the Bible, applying his brand of determination to Christian growth. He redoubled his academic disciplines, moving his bed to a corner in his father's workshop so he could study in solitude through late evenings. He later wrote, "The happiest abode (so far as the house goes) was my father's workshop, swept clean by my own hands of a Saturday evening, and dedicated to prayer and meditation on Sunday. There was my bed, and there was my study."

By 1801, he felt he could only be happy by entering the ministry, and in preparation, he began taking Latin. As it turned out he discovered a gift for languages, and he began thinking about missionary service. His mother, hearing of it, was alarmed. She wasn't well, and felt she couldn't part from him. Robert agreed to stay by her side as long as she lived.

She died the next year, and on November 24, 1802, Robert applied for admission at a preachers' college in London. Two years later he sought duty with the London Missionary Society. His father's protests broke his heart but not his determination. He pursued further training, then boarded ship and sailed from Britain on *February 28, 1807*, becoming the first Protestant missionary to China.

His plodding, viselike determination served him as well in China as it had in England, for he witnessed no breakthroughs for seven years. Finally he baptized his first convert. He persevered another eighteen years, encountering staggering difficulties and seeing fewer than a dozen others follow Christ. At his death there were only three native Christians in the entire Chinese Empire.

But he opened the door, and today there are millions.

Such a large crowd of witnesses is all around us! So we must get rid of everything that slows us down, especially the sin that just won't let go. And we must be determined to run the race that is ahead of us. We must keep our eyes on Jesus, who leads us and makes our faith complete. (Hebrews 12:1–2)

Six Hours

Hamilton, Wishart, and Knox form a chain of names that transformed Scotland. The first man, Patrick Hamilton, was born about 1504 to a wealthy family near Glasgow. His mother told him stories of the Bible, and her lessons lived in his heart till the close of his life. His father, wanting a church career for Patrick, used his influence and money to secure his appointment to a church position when he was but thirteen.

That was in 1517, the year that Luther made his protest.

But Hamilton wanted nothing of church work, and he fled to the Sorbonne, the University of Paris, where he heard the sensational news of Luther's protestation. For an entire year, the Sorbonne studied little but Luther's writings. Hamilton graduated in 1520, returned to Scotland, and continued his studies in the University of St. Andrews, where, in time, he joined the faculty. The Scottish Parliament, meanwhile, condemned Lutheranism and announced that anyone possessing Reformation books or views was in jeopardy.

As it happened, Hamilton had adopted Reformation views. Archbishop David Beaton, rabid foe of Protestants, instantly sought his life. Hamilton fled the country. He traveled to Germany and spent time with Luther and the other Reformation leaders. His faith and courage deepened dramatically, and Hamilton determined to return to Scotland, heedless of danger, and preach salvation by grace through faith alone.

Great crowds flocked to hear him, and many were converted to Christ. Beaton promptly trapped and arrested him, tried him, and sentenced him to death. At high noon on *February 29, 1528*, Hamilton walked to the stake with a quick, firm step. He handed a friend his copy of the Gospels and gave his cap, gown, and upper garments to his servant. The executioner chained him to the post and attempted to set the wood afire. The flame didn't burn well, and Hamilton suffered for six long, torturous hours. Finally when it appeared the fire was at last doing its work, he cried, "How long, O God, shall darkness cover this kingdom?"

His words were not lost on young George Wishart.

Ropes from the world
of the dead
had coiled around me,
and death had set a trap
in my path.
I was in terrible trouble
when I called out to you,
but from your temple
you heard me
and answered my prayer. (Psalm 18:5–7)

On This Day in Christian History...

MARCH

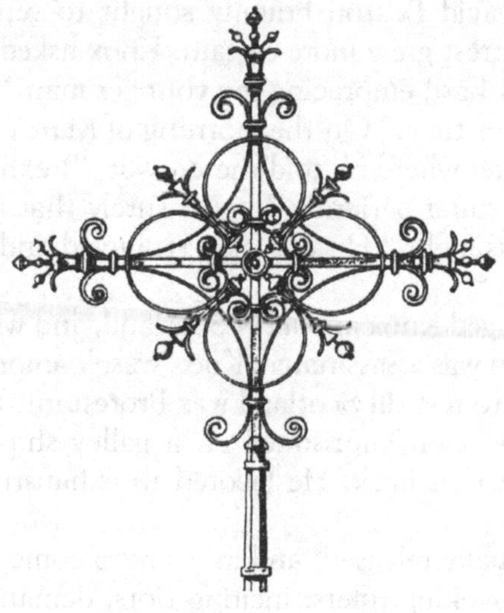

Passing the Flame

How long, O God, shall darkness cover this kingdom?"

Patrick Hamilton's dying words haunted George Wishart, only son of distinguished James Wishart of Pitarrow, Scotland. George was tall, dark haired, good-looking, pleasant, and eager to both learn and teach. He believed that God's way of salvation was through the finished work of Christ alone. Those Reformation beliefs put him at risk. In 1544, he began preaching in Dundee from the book of Romans. Among his listeners was a young man named John Knox. Knox was struck with Wishart and began serving as his bodyguard, carrying a two-handed sword.

Archbishop David Beaton brutally sought to repress Protestants, and as Wishart's arrest grew more certain, Knox asked to remain at his side. "No" said Wishart, embracing the younger man. "One is sufficient for a sacrifice at this time." On the morning of *March 1, 1546*, Wishart was led to the stake, where he told the crowds, "I exhort you, love the Word of God and suffer patiently. I know surely that my soul shall sup with my Savior this night." He was then strangled and his body burned to ashes.

His death enraged Knox and all of Scotland, and within two months Archbishop Beaton was assassinated. Knox wasn't among the murderers, but he vowed not to rest till Scotland was Protestant. It proved a costly vow, for Knox was soon imprisoned on a galley ship, chained to the oars with a whip to his back. He labored to exhaustion with no hope of release.

He *was* eventually released, and in years to come Knox took Scotland by storm, provoking rulers, inciting riots, demanding change. He prayed down the wrath of heaven on his nemesis, Mary, Queen of Scots. He was called the "Thundering Scot," and as he aged, his visage darkened. The years took their toll on both his health and his patience. He died exhausted, perhaps embittered, in 1572.

But his efforts inspired Scots for years to come, and the Reformation triumphed in their land at last.

Elijah prayed: Our LORD, you are the God of Abraham, Isaac, and Israel. Now, prove that you are the God of this nation, . . . Please answer me, so these people will know that you are the LORD God, and that you will turn their hearts back to you. (1 Kings 18:36–37)

Council of Constance

The *Great Schism* is a term describing two events in church history. The first is the breach between the eastern and western churches that occurred in 1054. The second is the sad period from 1378 to 1417, during which time rival popes claimed to rule Christendom. In 1414, one of the three claimants, Pope John XXIII, called together a church council in the city of Constance to end this schism.

John packed the conference with his followers, and he felt he would be affirmed as sole pope. As he approached Constance, he said, "Ha, this is the place where foxes are trapped." He entered the city on a white horse accompanied by sixteen hundred troops. The excitement was breathtaking. Constance swelled with as many as a hundred thousand visitors from across Europe, including princes, musicians, and prostitutes. So many people bathed in the city's lake that five hundred drownings were reported.

But John's smugness quickly faded. The proceedings were dominated by an overriding desire to restore church unity. The council, to John's surprise, wanted to elect a new pope from scratch. When documents began circulating questioning his fitness for office, John became frightened. On *March 2, 1415*, he appeared before the council and said, "I, John XXIII, a pope, promise and obligate myself, vow and swear"—here he dramatically rose from his seat and fell on his knees—"before God, the church, and this holy council to give peace to the Church by abdication, provided the pretenders, Benedict and Gregory, do the same."

Constance erupted in joy, church bells pealing, people weeping and laughing and shouting. John, fearing for his life, fled, but the council tracked him down, returned him to Constance, condemned him for scandalous conduct, and officially deposed him. In time, it successfully ended the Great Schism.

The same assembly also attacked so-called heretics, including John Wycliffe and Jon Hus. When Hus came to Constance under promise of safe conduct, he was imprisoned, condemned, and burned at the stake.

> I did not send these prophets
> or speak to them,
> but they ran to find you
> and to preach their message.
> If they had been in a meeting
> of my council in heaven,
> they would have told
> you people of Judah
> to give up your sins
> and come back to me. (Jeremiah 23:21–22)

The Counterreformation

Churches and denominations, like houses and hearts, need periodic cleaning and occasional renovation. Luther's response to the deterioration of the sixteenth-century church sparked not only the Protestant Reformation, but the Catholic Counterreformation, efforts within the Roman church to repair itself. On December 13, 1545, Pope Paul III convened a council in the northern Italian city of Trent, attended at first by only thirty-four leaders. The several sessions lasted from 1545 to 1563. Participants included Jesuits and scholars, political leaders desiring reunification with Protestants, and clergymen, some desiring reform, others wanting none of it.

The widespread sale of indulgences (which had inflamed Luther) was modified, and many measures were passed to correct and protect the morality of clergymen and church leaders. The doctrines of the church were also reexamined in light of emerging Protestant theology. In most cases, the council reaffirmed traditional medieval doctrines. Protestant views of the Lord's Supper were dismissed, and transubstantiation upheld (the belief that the wine and bread of the Lord's Supper become the very body of Christ). The council affirmed Latin as the proper language for the mass, and it disagreed with Luther on making the Bible available in the common languages. It also rejected the reformer's cry of "Scripture alone." Church tradition, said the council, joins Scripture as a source of divine authority for believers.

On this day in Christian history, *March 3, 1547*, the council began affirming the seven sacraments of the church, all of them, it said, necessary for salvation: baptism, confirmation, the Eucharist, penance, extreme unction, orders, and matrimony. The Protestant view of two divine ordinances—baptism and the Lord's Supper—was rejected.

The Council of Trent is one of the most important events in Reformation history, establishing the tone and doctrine of the Catholic Church for the next four hundred years, and providing a basis for reformation within the Roman church. Not until the 1960s, at Vatican II, did another major reexamination take place.

Look deep into my heart, God,
and find out everything
I am thinking.
Don't let me follow evil ways,
but lead me in the way
that time has proven true. (Psalm 139:23–24)

A Practical Examination

The sailing of the mission ship *Duff* was an event to remember. Thirty missionaries and their families set out from England to the South Pacific in August 1796. The morning was foggy, but the crowds were celebrative, singing hymns and offering prayers. The ship crossed the horizon and seven months later, on Saturday, *March 4, 1797*, the missionaries landed safely on Tahiti. The next day they held a worship service, then set to work.

The *Duff*'s captain, a Christian, was entrusted with the responsibility of seeing the missionaries established on various islands in the region. After several weeks on Tahiti, he felt secure enough to leave some of the workers there and take others to neighboring islands. He planted ten missionaries on Tonga, then proceeded to the islands of the Marquises to deposit two men, William Crook and John Harris.

But an unexpected problem arose, one that their theological and missions training had not equipped the preachers to handle. No sooner had the ship anchored than beautiful naked native women swam out to welcome the missionaries. Crook and Harris nervously bundled their things and went ashore.

Such curious crowds met the two that Crook became separated from Harris and found himself alone with the chief's wife. To his horror, she immediately began seeking his attentions. When he refused, she seemed bewildered. As it turned out, she wondered if he was, in fact, *a man*. Resolving to find out, she and a mob of other women attacked Harris during the night and conducted a practical examination to clear up the matter.

The *Duff*'s crew found Harris sitting on the beach the next morning, suffering from shock, humiliated, and very anxious to leave. The work in the Marquises was abandoned. The work on Tonga proceeded with difficulty. The Tahiti mission showed more promise and eventually led to many conversions.

Joseph was well-built and handsome, and Potiphar's wife soon noticed him. One day, Joseph went to Potiphar's house to do his work, and none of the other servants were there. Potiphar's wife grabbed hold of his coat and said, "Make love to me!" Joseph ran out of the house, leaving her hanging onto his coat. (Genesis 39:6–7, 11–12)

Sam Jones vs. Sam Jones

John J. Jones felt God calling him into the ministry, but he resisted, choosing instead the profession of law. His son followed in his footsteps. Young Sam Jones proved a brilliant attorney at first. But alcoholism quickly ruined his life and reduced him to shoveling coal. He was on a drinking binge when he heard of his father's illness. He rushed home, and the old lawyer became a preacher at last, saying, "My poor, wicked, wayward, reckless boy. You have brought me down in sorrow to my grave. Promise me, my boy, to meet me in heaven."

Sam fell to his knees and promised; then he flew to a bar and begged for a glass of liquor. But as he started to drink it, he saw himself in the mirror. Hair matted. Filth and vomit on his clothes. Lips swollen. He smashed the glass on the floor and gave his life to Jesus Christ. A week later, he preached his first sermon.

Jones became the most famous evangelist of the nineteenth century, save for Moody. He held crusades in major cities throughout America, winning an estimated five hundred thousand people to Christ. His most unusual revival began on *March 5, 1899*, in Toledo, Ohio. The mayor of Toledo was also named Sam Jones. Mayor Jones introduced Evangelist Jones on the revival's opening night. The next mayoral election was only a month away, and he enjoyed the exposure. But he didn't enjoy what Evangelist Jones had to say, for the preacher lost no time in attacking the mayor's policies. There were seven hundred saloons and one hundred fifty gambling dens in Toledo, and city administrators were unconcerned about it. The evangelist said that if the devil were mayor of Toledo, he wouldn't change a thing. He flailed away at alcohol and sin. He lifted high the cross, and preached with the zeal of a lawyer trying to save his client from the gallows. Men wept. Women groaned. Children were spellbound. The seats were packed night after night. Hundreds, perhaps thousands, were converted during the Toledo meetings.

But the mayor won reelection the next month by a huge margin.

Who is always in trouble?
Who argues and fights?
Who has cuts and bruises?
Whose eyes are red?
Everyone who stays up late,
having just one more drink.
Don't even look
at that colorful stuff
bubbling up in the glass! (Proverbs 23:29–31)

The Artist

March 6, 1475, is the birth date of the creator of *David*, *Moses*, the *Pietà*, and the dome of St. Peter's. Michelangelo Buonarroti was born in a small Italian town, nursed in a marble quarry, and raised in nearby Florence. He spent his leisure painting and drawing, and was chosen at age thirteen for admittance to a new art school established by Lorenzo de' Medici in the Medici Gardens. Between lessons, he listened to the mighty Savonarola preaching his fiery gospel nearby.

As a young man Michelangelo gained rapid fame for his *Pietà* (Madonna holding her crucified son), then for carving *David* from an eighteen-foot piece of discarded marble. Pope Julius next put him on his back atop scaffolding, painting the ceiling of the Sistine Chapel. He was called a genius.

But behind Michelangelo's genius resided a tragic figure. He didn't get along with people and frequently burned with jealousy, foul moods, and disdain for others. He wore old clothes that he seldom changed, and he never bathed. Though rich, he lived as a miser. He ate whatever he found, sometimes only crumbs, and he slept in his raiment and boots. He hated small talk and preferred being alone. He disliked women. All his passion went into his work, and he had little need for friends, except for a servant who tended to him for twenty-five years and shared his bed.

Michelangelo's bad temper caused one pope to remark, "He is such an alarming man, and there is no getting on with him." At times the artist was depressed to the edge of insanity, and in his old age he became obsessed with the fear of hell.

But in advancing age his thoughts turned more and more to the Christ he had so frequently painted, and to the sermons he had heard from the martyred Savonarola. Near the end of his life, Michelangelo wrote that "Painting nor sculpture now can lull to rest / My soul, that turns to His great love on high, / Whose arms to clasp us on the cross are spread."

He died in his eighty-ninth year.

Only God gives inward peace . . .
Trust God, my friends,
and always tell him
each one of your concerns.
God is our place of safety.
We humans are only a breath;
none of us are truly great.
All of us together weigh less
than a puff of air. (Psalm 62:5–9)

Perpetua

Human affections, dear as they are, must always yield primary allegiance to Christ. This day in church history belongs to Perpetua, who so inspired the early Christians that Augustine warned against viewing her story as equal to Scripture. Perpetua was born about 176, in Carthage, North Africa, growing up in a well-to-do family. Her father wasn't a Christian, but her brothers and mother were devoted to Christ. Perpetua, bright and attractive, gained a good education and a husband, then a baby boy.

In 202, Emperor Septimus Severius issued an edict against Christians, and presently Perpetua was placed under house arrest. When her father begged her to recant, she pointed to a waterpot and asked, "Father, do you see this vessel? Can it be called by any other name than what it is? So also I cannot call myself by any other name than what I am—a Christian."

She was moved to prison, where her father again visited her, begging her with sobs to renounce her faith. She refused. Perpetua and a handful of other believers were then tried in the marketplace where, again, her father appeared, carrying her infant son and begging her to free herself.

Sentenced to torture and execution, the Christians were dragged back to prison. When she asked to see her baby a final time, she was refused. But on the eve of her death, Perpetua wrote of God's sustaining presence: "I saw that I should not fight with beasts but with the devil; I knew the victory to be mine."

On *March 7, 202*, the Christians were marched into the arena, where Perpetua was gored and thrown by a savage heifer. Surviving the first encounter, she crept to the aid of a companion. Shortly thereafter, a gladiator pierced her with his sword. When the trembling youth came at her again, she helped guide his shaking sword to her throat.

Her devotion to Christ so inspired the Christians in North Africa that she personified Tertullian's famous quote, "The blood of the martyrs is the seed of the church." Indeed, through the power of her witness, her chief jailer, Pudens, committed himself to the Lord Jesus.

My dear friends, I want you to know that what has happened to me has helped to spread the good news. The Roman guards and all the others know that I am here in jail because I serve Christ. Now most of the Lord's followers have become brave and are fearlessly telling the message. (Philippians 1:12–14)

An Evening Sermon

Charles Spurgeon, the Prince of Preachers, read voraciously through the week, but not until Saturday night did he determine and develop his message for the following morning. Only on Sunday afternoon did he prepare his evening address. But it worked. For thirty years, he kept London's Metropolitan Tabernacle packed. On Sunday night, *March 8, 1874*, Spurgeon preached from 1 Corinthians 6:20: "God paid a great price for you. So use your body to honor God." Had you entered Metropolitan Tabernacle that evening, you would have heard Spurgeon's carillon voice pealing these words through the lamplit hall:

> You young men who come to London amidst its vices, shun everything that is akin to lewdness or leads on to unchastity, for your bodies were bought with your Lord's lifeblood, and they are not yours to trifle with. Shun the strange woman, her company, her wine, her glances, her house, her songs, her resorts. Your bodies are not yours to injure by self-indulgence of any sort. Keep them pure and chaste for that heavenly Bridegroom who has bought them with his blood.
>
> And then your soul is bought too. I was obliged to mention the body, because it is mentioned here, and it is so needful it should be kept pure. But keep the soul pure. Christ has not bought these eyes that they should read novels calculated to lead me into vanity and vice, such as are published nowadays. Christ has not bought this brain of mine that I may revel in the perusal of works of blasphemy and filthiness. He has not given me a mind that I may drag it through the mire with the hope of washing it clean again . . .
>
> Your whole manhood belongs to God if you are a Christian. Every faculty, every natural power, every talent, every possibility of your being, every capacity of your spirit . . . It is all bought with blood. Therefore keep the whole for Jesus, for it belongs to him.

Don't be immoral in matters of sex. That is a sin against your own body in a way that no other sin is. You surely know that your body is a temple where the Holy Spirit lives. The Spirit is in you and is a gift from God. You are no longer your own. God paid a great price for you. So use your body to honor God. (1 Corinthians 6:18–20)

The Father of Revivalism

One day a lawyer in Adams, New York, grew disturbed about his soul. He retreated to a nearby forest, climbed a fence, knelt by a log for prayer, and experienced a dramatic conversion. Waves of liquid love, he later said, rolled over him. The next day, Charles Finney resigned from the bar to preach the gospel, saying he was now on retainer for Jesus Christ.

His tall frame, riveting eyes, shaggy brows, beaklike nose, and powerful voice brought many to Christ. His preaching reflected a legal mind, for he presented the case for Christ as if convincing a jury. And he was dramatic. Audiences seemed to smell smoke whenever he spoke of hell, as he frequently did.

The highlight of Finney's career occurred on *March 9, 1831*, when he successfully concluded a six-month series of meetings at the Third Presbyterian Church in Rochester, New York. The city was dramatically transformed by his preaching. One hundred thousand people were reportedly converted, including many of the city's leaders—bankers, lawyers, physicians, judges. Stores in Rochester closed so people could attend Finney's meetings, and the taverns went out of business. The theater became a livery stable, and the crime rate dropped by two-thirds. The city jail was virtually empty for the next two years. The Rochester meetings have been called "the world's greatest single revival campaign," and 1831 is known as the greatest year of spiritual awakening in American history.

Finney pastored for a year in New York City while recovering from cholera. Then, suffering from respiratory problems, he accepted a teaching position at Oberlin College in Ohio, later becoming its president. He left school every year at the end of the term to conduct crusades, and according to some estimates, a half million were converted during his lifetime. His innovative methods (like asking seekers to come forward) paved the way for later evangelists like D. L. Moody, Billy Sunday, and Billy Graham.

We were sent to speak for Christ, and God is begging you to listen to our message. We speak for Christ and sincerely ask you to make peace with God. (2 Corinthians 5:20)

Amazing Grace

It took John Newton to write the hymn "Amazing Grace." "Let me not fail to praise that grace that could pardon," he said, "such sins as mine."

Newton had gone to sea at age eleven, apprenticed on his father's ship. He spent his teen years learning to be profane, irreligious, and indulgent. Female slaves being transported from Africa were at Newton's disposal, and even seasoned sailors were alarmed at his corruption.

Newton's life angered his father and disgusted his friends, and he was finally pressed into service for the British Navy. He deserted, but was arrested, stripped, and flogged. He became the property of a slave trader in Sierra Leone, who gave him to his sadistic mistress. John became a loathsome toy she tormented for over a year.

He finally boarded ship for Britain. On March 9, as he carelessly read a Christian book to pass the time, the thought came to him, "What if these things are true?" He snapped the book closed and shook off the question.

> I went to bed in my usual indifference, but was awakened by a violent sea which broke on us. Much of it came down below and filled the cabin where I lay. This alarm was followed by a cry that the ship was going down. We had immediate recourse to the pumps, but the water increased against all our efforts. Almost every passing wave broke over my head. I expected that every time the vessel descended into the sea, she would rise no more. I dreaded death now, and my heart foreboded the worst, if the Scriptures, which I had long since opposed, were true.

The vessel survived the *March 10, 1748*, storm, and Newton began earnestly studying the Bible. He embraced Christ and eventually entered the ministry, becoming one of England's best-loved preachers and a leader in the fight against slavery. He once recalled, "That tenth of March is a day much remembered by me; and I have never suffered it to pass unnoticed since the year 1748—the Lord came from on high and delivered me out of deep waters."

From a sea of troubles
I call out to you, LORD.
Won't you please listen
as I beg for mercy?
But you forgive us,
and so we will worship you. (Psalm 130:1–2, 4)

Art or Idols?

If we aren't careful, our traditions can become our idols, and rooting them out may be hazardous to the church's health. This was the case in Eastern Christianity's infamous iconoclast controversy.

During medieval times, Christians began worshipping and praying to saints, a practice that gradually led to the prominence of icons—flat pictures representing Christ, Mary, or some other saint. While Christian art has edified believers since the days of the catacombs, the Eastern church began worshipping these images. The pictures were reverently kissed. Incense was offered before them. Prayers were rendered to them. Some icons reputedly possessed miracle-working powers.

The Byzantine emperor Leo III was repelled by the worship of icons, perhaps because his political enemies, the Jews and the Muslims, accused him of heading an empire of idolaters. In 726, he outlawed image worship and soon thereafter ordered the destruction of icons everywhere. But image worship had become so entrenched in the Byzantine church that his edicts were viewed as attacks on Christianity itself. An uprising raged through his empire, and many died. Pope Gregory in Rome ridiculed the emperor and held two synods condemning Leo's iconoclasm (icon breaking).

Leo's son, Constantine V, continued his father's war against icons with vigor. He convened a church council in Constantinople, attended by 360 bishops. The council, citing the second commandment, denounced icons as idols and declared all religious paintings and sculpture as pagan. Their use in public and private worship was forbidden. The council's decree was carried out with intensity, and sacred images were smashed, destroyed, painted over, and burned. Fifty thousand icon-producing monks fled or perished. For the next eighty-nine years, the icon controversy seesawed back and forth, tearing the church, ripping its unity, and providing it with a new crop of dubious martyrs.

The persecution ended only after the death of Emperor Theophilus, the last great iconoclast, in 842. On *March 11, 843*, icons were formally sanctioned and reintroduced in all Eastern Orthodox churches. This day, the so-called *Triumph of Orthodoxy*, has been commemorated in Eastern congregations around the world for more than a thousand years.

People of Israel,
your God is a mystery,
though he alone can save.
Anyone who makes idols
will be confused
and terribly disgraced. (Isaiah 45:15–16)

Resiliency

William Carey, the father of modern missions, wanted to translate the Bible into as many Indian languages as possible. He established a large print shop in Serampore, where translation work was continually being done. Carey spent hours each day translating scripture.

Carey was away from Serampore on March 11, 1832. His associate, William Ward, was working late. Suddenly Ward smelled smoke. He leaped up to discover clouds belching from the printing room. He screamed for help, and workers passed water from the nearby river until 2:00 AM, but everything was destroyed.

On *March 12, 1812*, missionary Joshua Marshman entered a Calcutta classroom where Carey was teaching. "I can think of no easy way to break the news," he said. "The print shop burned to the ground last night." Carey was stunned. Gone were his massive polyglot dictionary, two grammar books, and whole versions of the Bible. Gone were sets of type for fourteen eastern languages, twelve hundred reams of paper, fifty-five thousand printed sheets, and thirty pages of his Bengal dictionary. Gone was his complete library. "The work of years—gone in a moment," he whispered.

He took little time to mourn. "The loss is heavy," he wrote, "but as traveling a road the second time is usually done with greater ease and certainty than the first time, so I trust the work will lose nothing of real value. We are not discouraged; indeed the work is already begun again in every language. We are cast down but not in despair."

When news of the fire reached England, it catapulted Carey to instant fame. Thousands of pounds were raised for the work, and volunteers offered to come help. The enterprise was rebuilt and enlarged. By 1832, complete Bibles, New Testaments, or separate books of scripture had issued from the printing press in forty-four languages and dialects.

The secret of Carey's success is found in his resiliency. "There are grave difficulties on every hand," he once wrote, "and more are looming ahead. Therefore we must go forward."

We often suffer, but we are never crushed. Even when we don't know what to do, we never give up. In times of trouble, God is with us, and when we are knocked down, we get up again. (2 Corinthians 4:8–9)

Gutenberg's Bible

Johann Gutenberg grew up in Mainz, Germany. He devoured books, reading all that his wealthy father ordered. The volumes were outrageously expensive, sometimes costing as much as a farm. Local scribes copied the texts by hand, illuminators decorated the margins, and binders made the covers. Finally the title was stamped into the leather cover by brass punches. It was the punches that suggested an idea to Johann. Why not make separate metal letters and arrange them into words? Why not set up a page and print it using a press?

Johann moved to Strasbourg and set up a secret workshop near an old monastery. Though beset by problems, he toiled for years to get his invention to work. Finally, Johann returned to Mainz, where he was assured an income by inheritance.

He set up a printing shop, and in 1450, after thirty years, he was ready to begin. He chose the Bible as his first book. Such a project required he borrow eight hundred guldens from Johann Fust, but if he wasn't repaid with interest in five years, Fust demanded, all the equipment and materials would revert to him.

It took Johann two years to set up a workshop. He hired workers, had presses built, and taught laborers to grind and mix ink. Then he was ready to begin printing. Two more years went by, and the invention wasn't working well. Another year passed, and two months before the Bible was completed, Fust sued. On November 6, 1455, the judge ruled in his favor.

Gutenberg angrily turned over his presses and almost-completed Bibles to Fust. The Bible was reportedly first published on *March 13, 1456*, and for many years the credit went to Fust and his partner, Peter Schoffer. But after Gutenberg died on February 3, 1469, Schoffer admitted that, after all, Johann Gutenberg had invented printing.*

What God has said isn't only active and alive! It is sharper than any double-edged sword. His word can cut through our spirits and souls and through our joints and marrow, until it discovers the desires and thoughts of our hearts. (Hebrews 4:12)

---

*Information about Gutenberg is notoriously hard to pin down. The above account is based on *Fine Print: A Story About Johann Gutenberg* by Joann Johansen Burch (Minneapolis: Carolrhoda Books, Inc., 1991).

Dr. Livingstone, I Presume

As missionary David Livingstone plunged ever more deeply into the African interior, all the world followed him. He was a hero, an explorer whose every foray was widely discussed. But in the early 1870s, word from him ceased. The world held its breath and waited and wondered. Five years passed. Finally the *New York Herald* sent reporter Henry Stanley to find him, dead or alive. Stanley was an untamed adventure-seeker and journalist. He was also an infidel who viewed Christianity with considerable cynicism. "Spare no expense," his newspaper said. Stanley organized two hundred persons in five caravans and plunged into the jungle.

Stanley finally located Livingstone near Lake Tanganyika. He bowed and uttered his famous words, "Dr. Livingstone, I presume." He arrived just in time, for the old missionary was sick, lonely, and desperate for medicine, supplies, and news from home. Stanley stayed with Livingstone four months, and the two men grew very attached. Stanley later reported, "I went to Africa as prejudiced against religion as the worst infidel in London. But I saw this solitary old man there, and I asked myself, 'What is it that inspires him?' For months I found myself listening to him, wondering at the old man carrying out the words, 'leave all and follow me.' Little by little, seeing his piety, gentleness, zeal, and how he went quietly about his business, I was converted by him."

On their last day together, *March 14, 1872*, the two said little. Stanley lingered as long as he dared; then he said, "Now, my dear doctor, the best friends must part." Livingstone, heart throbbing, replied, "God guide you safe home and bless you, my friend." Stanley went a way then turned for a last look. Livingstone had also turned. Stanley waved his handkerchief, and Livingstone lifted his hat. They would not see each other on earth again. When Stanley heard of Livingstone's death the following year, he determined to follow his footsteps.

Paul . . . knelt down with all of them and prayed. Everyone cried and hugged and kissed him. They were especially sad because Paul had told them, "You will never see me again." (Acts 20:36–38)

March 15 The Money Machine

St. Peter's is one of the most beautiful basilicas in the world, and the most famous. But it was built at a cost.

The church in the early 1500s was beset with sin. Priests by the thousands, finding it impossible to live in celibacy, broke their vows. Monks enjoyed filthy talk, gluttony, and promiscuity; one observer noted that many "convents differ little from public brothels."

But forgiveness of sins, both by priests and laity, was easy to find. It could be purchased. The sale of indulgences—a kind of pardon for sins—was widespread. The chancellor of Oxford noted, "Sinners say nowadays: 'I care not how many evils I do in God's sight, for I can easily get remission of all guilt by the indulgence granted me by the pope.'"

On *March 15, 1517*, Pope Leo X, needing money to rebuild St. Peter's, announced a special sale of indulgences. Johann Tetzel, a middle-aged Dominican friar, became the principal agent of the sale. He took to his new role like P. T. Barnum, traveling through central Europe with a brass-bound chest and a bag of printed receipts. Beside him, an assistant carried Leo's edict on a velvet cushion. The men would enter a village to the ringing of church bells. Crowds gathered and jugglers performed. Tetzel would bark, "I have here the passports to lead the human soul to the celestial joys of Paradise."

Any and every sin could be forgiven, he said. "The Holy Father has the power in heaven and earth to forgive the sin, and if he forgives it, God must do so also." What's more, he said, pardons could be purchased for deceased loved ones. "As soon as the coin rings in the bowl, the soul for whom it is paid will fly out of purgatory and straight to heaven." Tetzel was a virtual money machine, exceeding his quota everywhere . . . until he entered the region of a young monk named Luther.

All of us have sinned and fallen short of God's glory. But God treats us much better than we deserve, and because of Christ Jesus, he freely accepts us and sets us free from our sins. God sent Christ to be our sacrifice. Christ offered his life's blood, so that by faith in him we could come to God. (Romans 3:23–25)

The Fifth Lateran Council

Pope Leo had been born Giovanni de' Medici, second son of Lorenzo the Magnificent. At age eight he was nominated to an archbishopric. By age fourteen he had become a cardinal-deacon, the youngest ever to be so named. His father wrote to him, warning that Rome "was the sink of all iniquities" and that he must live "a virtuous life . . ."

Leo ignored the advice. When he became pope at age thirty-seven, his attitude was "Let's enjoy the papacy, for God has given it to us." He entered Rome on a white horse amid great pageantry and immediately became embroiled in European politics as though in a chess game. He promoted relatives to church positions and imprisoned enemies in deepest dungeons. He was nearly assassinated by poison, and the unfortunate plotters were tortured and strangled. He enjoyed ornate clothing and covered his fingers with gems. He reveled in entertainment and kept a monk able to swallow a pigeon in one mouthful and forty eggs at one sitting. He hunted, aided by seventy dogs. He commissioned artists to elaborate projects and attended pornographic plays.

He exhausted his treasury, and that was one of the concerns of the Fifth Lateran Council. The council, which resumed shortly after Leo's election, made several important decisions. The newly invented printing press was recognized as a gift from heaven, but only books approved by the Vatican could be published. A new crusade against the Turks was approved, and a tax was authorized to pay for it. The Roman pontiff was assured of authority over all church councils, and obedience to the pope was declared necessary for salvation. And to raise money, Pope Leo, aided by the council, lifted the prohibition against usury, took out outrageous loans, and issued his special sale of indulgences.

Having accomplished its work, the council adjourned on *March 16, 1517*, and Leo returned to the pleasures of his office. He once reportedly quipped, "How profitable that fable of Christ has been to us."

Jerusalem's prophets are proud
and not to be trusted.
The priests have disgraced
the place of worship
and abused God's Law.
All who do evil are shameless,
but the LORD does right
and is always fair.
With the dawn of each day,
God brings about justice. (Zephaniah 3:4–5)

St. Patrick's Day

Our greatest misfortune can catapult us into our greatest service for the Lord. Consider Joseph and Daniel, two Old Testament teens whose kidnappings took them to distant countries where they later become God's ambassadors in strange lands.

Saint Patrick died *March 17, 461*, a day that has since borne his name. Patrick was born about 389 in Britain. His father was a deacon and his grandfather a priest. Roman protection of England had deteriorated, and bands of Irish invaders tormented coastal areas, pillaging farms, slaughtering villagers, kidnapping teens. Patrick was taken at age sixteen. The Irish farmer who bought him put him to tending sheep, and somehow through all this Patrick found Christ. "The Lord opened to me a sense of my unbelief, that I might be converted with all my heart unto the Lord."

Following a daring escape at age twenty-two, Patrick returned home to joyous parents who prayed that he would never again leave. But Patrick's heart burned for his erstwhile captors, and one night he dreamed an Irishman was begging him to return and preach. After several years of Bible study, Patrick returned to Ireland as a missionary. The Irish were almost wholly unevangelized at the time, worshipping the elements, seeing evil spirits in trees and stones, and engaging in magic, even in human sacrifice, performed by the druids. "It very much becomes us," he said, "to stretch our nets, that we may take for God a copious and crowded multitude." And so he did, planting two hundred churches and baptizing approximately one hundred thousand converts, despite a dozen attempts against his life and violent opposition from civil authorities. In his *Confessions*, he wrote, "I am greatly a debtor to God, who has bestowed his grace so largely upon me, that multitudes were born again to God through me. The Irish, who had never had the knowledge of God and worshipped only idols and unclean things, have lately become the people of the Lord, and are called sons of God."

Jesus said to them, "You don't need to know the time of those events that only the Father controls. But the Holy Spirit will come upon you and give you power. Then you will tell everyone about me in Jerusalem, in all Judea, in Samaria, and everywhere in the world." After Jesus had said this and while they were watching, he was taken up into a cloud. (Acts 1:7–9)

The Imperfect Vessel

Great men boast of great strengths, but they can also harbor great faults. Charles T. Studd, one of England's most famous cricket players, was converted in 1883 through D. L. Moody's influence. He developed a deep friendship with six other young men, and they offered themselves en masse to Hudson Taylor for missionary service in China. The "Cambridge Seven" sailed from England and arrived in Shanghai on *March 18, 1885*.

Studd set passionately to work, adopting Chinese clothes and customs and laboring to exhaustion for souls. On December 5, he turned twenty-five and legally gained control of a large inheritance. He gave it all to the Lord's work, for he had found a greater wealth. "I cannot tell you," he later said, "what joy it gave me to bring the first soul to the Lord Jesus Christ. I have tasted almost all the pleasures this world can give. Those pleasures were as nothing compared to the joy that the saving of that one soul gave me."

Studd later poured himself into India, then Africa. He once said, "If Jesus Christ be God and died for me, then no sacrifice can be too great for me to make for him." He toiled day and night, eighteen hours at a stretch, with no meals except what he gulped down while working, and no vacations.

But his zeal overwhelmed those around him, leading to stress and broken relationships. His wife, often ill and lonely, was abandoned in England for years at a time while Studd was overseas. He expected his associates to work as he did, and he grew critical of those who didn't. He wrote a book deploring the lethargy he saw among Christians, and its title offended his supporters: *D.C.D.*, standing for "Don't Care a Damn." He began treating his exhaustion and disorders with morphine. And when he died in Africa in 1931, he was broken in body and spirit.

But his fruit remains. The organization he founded, Worldwide Evangelism Crusade, is still sending out missionaries and changing the world. Despite his faults, Studd remains as one of our most passionate missionary heroes.

Try your best to please God and to be like him. Be faithful, loving, dependable, and gentle. Fight a good fight for the faith and claim eternal life . . . Promise to obey completely and fully all that you have been told until our Lord Jesus Christ returns. (1 Timothy 6:11–12, 14)

March 19 Pope vs. Peacemaker

Frederick was only four when his father, Henry VI of Germany, suddenly died, and he was yet a teenager when officially given his father's crown. But in time he became known as the Wonder of the World. Frederick was a cultured man who knew when to negotiate and when to fight. He quarreled with the papacy all his life and remained skeptical of religion till his death. He was repeatedly excommunicated—once, ironically, for being a peacemaker.

It happened during the Sixth Crusade. The deepest passion of Pope Honorius III was wresting Jerusalem from the Muslims. Having no army of his own, he looked to Frederick for help and set a date for the crusading armies to depart. The day came and went. The pope then schemed by hook and crook to nudge Frederick eastward into holy war. Still, the emperor showed little passion for the mission.

The next pope, Gregory IX, was tough as leather and soon secured Frederick's pledge to lead a new crusade. This time Frederick suddenly called off the crusade, saying he felt sick. Gregory angrily excommunicated him and applied every possible pressure. Frederick set off at last, troops in tow.

He reached Palestine on September 7, 1228, and found two Muslim chieftains engaged in conflict. Frederick used their disarray to secure a peace treaty allowing Christians free access to Jerusalem. The crusade was over before the first battle cry. There was no war, no bloodshed. Holy places were reopened to Christians.

Frederick then entered Jerusalem and visited the ancient Church of the Holy Sepulcher. There on *March 19, 1229*, in historic fashion, he crowned himself king according to ancient tradition. But his peace treaty was denounced by devotees of both faiths, and on the same March 19, the Catholic patriarch of Jerusalem pronounced an interdict over the city. Frederick was pelted with offal as he made his way home.

He returned to a furious pope who excommunicated him yet again, this time for making peace rather than war. But of all the latter crusades, only this one was successful in gaining Christian access to holy sites.

> Everything on earth
> has its own time
> and its own season.
> There is a time . . .
> for killing and healing,
> destroying and building,
> for crying and laughing,
> weeping and dancing.
> There is also a time
> for love and hate,
> for war and peace. (Ecclesiastes 3:1–4, 8)

The Last Day

Thomas Cranmer had the misfortune of being archbishop of Canterbury for King Henry VIII, but he survived by bending to the wind. He approved the king's divorces. He condemned the king's wives when necessary. He renounced the pope when expedient. He took no heroic stands.

But Thomas grew as the years passed. He composed and compiled *The Book of Common Prayer* and increasingly loved Reformation theology. When young King Edward died, Thomas sought to deny the throne to fiercely Catholic Mary.

Mary nevertheless assumed rule, and she forced the archbishop to watch as his two best friends, Hugh Latimer and Nicholas Ridley, were burned at the stake. Thomas was imprisoned and subjected to torture. After months of coercion, the old cleric broke down and signed a series of recantations. Queen Mary then planned a spectacle: Cranmer publicly reading his recantations and reaffirming loyalty to the pope and queen at the church of St. Mary's.

On the eve of the spectacle, *March 20, 1556*, Thomas sat wearily at a small desk in an Oxford jail, reading the speech planned for the next morning. His hand slowly gripped a pen, trembled, and started writing a second version.

The next day was cold and rain swept. Thomas was escorted to St. Mary's with the two speeches secretly stowed in his shirt. He rose to speak, saying, "I come to the great thing that troubleth my conscience more than any other thing that I ever said or did in my life, and that is setting abroad of writings contrary to the truth . . ." He declared that his recantations had been signed under duress, and he boldly embraced the pure gospel.

Guards rushed through the aisles. Thomas was pulled from the pulpit and hustled to the stake. As the fire was lit, the old man thrust his arm into the flames, saying that the hand that had signed the recantations should be the first to burn.

Thomas Cranmer had waited till the last day of his life to be heroic. But it was the last day that counted.

When the council members heard Stephen's speech, they were angry and furious. But Stephen was filled with the Holy Spirit. He looked toward heaven, where he saw our glorious God and Jesus standing at his right side. (Acts 7:54–55)

He Is Risen!

Easter is the greatest of Christian holidays. But what does the word *Easter* mean? Where and when was it first celebrated?

The origin of the word is uncertain, but the Venerable Bede claimed that the Christian resurrection festival displaced ancient pagan celebrations involving the Anglo-Saxon spring goddess Eostre. That, he said, occasioned the term. Others believe the word derives from an old German term meaning "sunrise."

Whatever its meaning, it is the oldest celebration of Christianity. The earliest written reference to Easter comes from the mid-second century. A controversy arose about the dating of Easter, causing Polycarp to visit Rome's bishop Anicetus. The two were unable to settle the controversy, and it became a hotly debated issue that threatened to split the church. Believers in Asia celebrated one day, Christians in Europe another. Books, tracts, sermons, and harangues were devoted to the topic. Synods and councils were called. Tempers flared. Clergy excommunicated one another. Irenaeus wrote, "The apostles ordered that we should judge no one in respect to a feast day or a holy day. Whence then these wars? Whence these schisms?"

The issue came to a vote at the famous Council of Nicaea in 325. Easter, declared the council, should be celebrated on the first Sunday following the first full moon after *March 21*, the vernal equinox. Easter then is a "movable feast" that may occur as early as March 22 or as late as April 25. The matter wasn't entirely settled, but believers seemed to realize that it wasn't the date but the significance that gave Easter its magnificence.

A custom arose among early worshippers to keep watch the Saturday night preceding Easter morning, and many believed that Christ would return at the breaking of this day. New converts kept watch and prayed throughout the night, then were baptized at sunrise. Another custom, still widely practiced, finds the pastor addressing the congregation with the glorious words: *He is risen!* The assembled worshippers shout in return: *He is risen indeed!* For two thousand years the foundation of Christianity has rested securely on this simple yet unfathomable truth.

The angel said to the women, "Don't be afraid! I know you are looking for Jesus, who was nailed to a cross. He isn't here! God has raised him to life, just as Jesus said he would." (Matthew 28:5–6)

Little John

England's Reformation, inaugurated by Henry VIII, Elizabeth I, and James I, was largely political. The genuine reformers, the Puritans and Separatists, were oppressed. But then, so were the Roman Catholics.

"Good Queen Bess" used fines, gallows, gibbets, racks, and whips against those who said mass, honored the pope, or harbored a priest. Reputed Catholics had no peace. Often in the middle of the night, thugs would burst in and drag them away to be scourged, fined, or seared with glowing irons.

Nicholas Owen, probably a builder by trade, designed countless hiding places for endangered Catholics. He hid them in secret rooms and between the walls and under the floors. He hid them in stone fences and in underground passages. He designed nooks and crannies that looked like anything but hiding places.

He was a slight man, nicknamed Little John, so the royalists long discounted him of hiding so many. He seemed too small to move stones, break walls, and excavate the earth. But he viewed his work as divine. He always began construction of a hideaway by receiving the Eucharist. He prayed continually during the building, and he committed the spot to God.

He also proved a master at devising getaways for helping Catholics escape prison. He was an escapist himself, having several aliases and disguises. Perhaps no one saved the lives of more Catholics in England during those days than Nicholas Owen.

But Nicholas was at last betrayed. Taken to the Tower of London, his arms were fixed to iron rings and he was hung for hours, his body dangling. Weights added to his feet increased the suffering, yet not a word of information passed his lips. The tortures continued till March 2, 1606, when "his bowels broke in a terrible way" and he passed to his reward. He was canonized by the church and is honored each year on *March 22*, in Catholic tradition the feast day of St. Nicholas Owen.

God will bless you, even if others treat you unfairly for being loyal to him. You don't gain anything by being punished for some wrong you have done. But God will bless you, if you have to suffer for doing something good. After all, God chose you to suffer as you follow in the footsteps of Christ, who set an example by suffering for you. (1 Peter 2:19–21)

S.D.G.

ission statements for organizations and individuals are prevalent today. Johann Sebastian Bach did that two hundred years ago.

The youngest in a family of German musicians, the two-day-old Bach was baptized on *March 23, 1685*, in Eisenach. He excelled at music, and his skills increased when, at age nine, he moved in with an older brother who taught music.

Bach also loved Scripture. He collected a library of eighty-three volumes that included the Bible, Luther's writings, and the works of Luther's followers. He soon combined his love of music and Scripture, penning this note in the margin of 1 Chronicles 25, the chapter in which King David commissioned the temple musicians: "This chapter is the true foundation for all God-pleasing music."

Bach would travel any distance to hear good music. Often he tramped thirty miles to Hamburg or sixty miles to Celle to hear famous organists. At age twenty, hearing that a renowned organist would perform in Lubeck, he persuaded his superiors to give him a month's leave of absence, and he made the two-hundred-mile trip by foot.

Three years later he announced his life's purpose: to create "well-regulated church music to the glory of God." He believed music should exist only for God's glory, and when he sat down to compose, he often scribbled *J.J.* on his blank pages: *Jesu Juva* ("Help me, Jesus"). At the manuscript's end, he jotted *S.D.G., Soli Deo Gloria* ("To God alone the glory").

Bach served as court musician at Weimar and Cothen, then taught music in Leipzig until his death. He fathered twenty children during his life and hundreds of compositions.

He received little fame during his lifetime and died in relative obscurity. His grave was not marked. After his death, his music was largely forgotten until Mendelssohn rediscovered it. Bach himself had remained modest. When a friend once praised his skill as an organist, he shrugged and smiled. "There is nothing very wonderful about it," he said. "You have only to hit the right notes at the right moment and the instrument does the rest."

David and the temple officials chose the descendants of Asaph, Heman, and Jeduthun to be in charge of music. They were to praise the LORD by playing cymbals, harps and other stringed instruments. (1 Chronicles 25:1)

"By the Teeth of God" March 24

Christians should respect those in authority, pray for our leaders, and be lights in the world. Seems simple enough. But relations between church and state have vexed believers from the time of Constantine to the days of the Christian Coalition. And never were they more complicated than during the days of Lotario de' Conti, who was born to aristocratic parents near Rome in 1161. Lotario was brilliant. Though he was short of stature, his keen eyes and dark face were magnetic. He was blessed with social ease, excellent speech, a warm smile, and a flare for poetry and song. He was religious.

He was elected Pope Innocent III at age thirty-seven.

The young man immediately asserted that Christ had given the successors of Peter the right of ruling the whole world as well as the church. "The state should be related to the church as the moon is to the sun."

But when Innocent appointed Stephen Langton as England's archbishop of Canterbury, King John defied him. An irreligious man, John forbade Langton to set foot in Britain and swore "by the teeth of God" to banish every clergyman from the land, to put out their eyes and cut off their noses.

On *March 24, 1208*, Innocent placed England under an interdict, a religious ban. All religious services were cancelled, churches were closed, church bells silenced. The dead were not given Christian burials and the mass was not celebrated. Innocent released the British people from loyalty to John and nudged France to prepare to invade England.

Brought to his knees by the ensuing public outrage, John acknowledged Innocent the victor; and his surrender so weakened him before the English people that shortly afterward at Runnymede on the Thames, he signed the most famous document in English history, the Magna Carta. The first article affirms "That the Church of England shall be free . . ."

Innocent III raised the papacy to its zenith, but the pressures of it led to premature death. "I have no leisure," he mourned. "Scarce can I breathe." He died from exhaustion at age fifty-five, finding the task of ruling both church and state too much for mortal man, even one of his skill and brilliance.

Be strong and brave! Be careful to do everything my servant Moses taught you. Never stop reading *The Book of the Law* he gave you. Day and night you must think about what it says. If you obey it completely, you and Israel will be able to take this land. I've commanded you to be strong and brave. (Joshua 1:6–9)

Black Easter

Some one thousand missionary personnel under the China Inland Mission were trapped in China when the Communists took over in the 1940s. CIM ordered a total evacuation in January 1951, but was it too late? Communists are not averse to killing.

Arthur and Wilda Mathews applied for exit visas on January 3. Their living conditions had deteriorated to a bare kitchen, where, in the corner, Wilda had converted a footlocker into a prayer nook. Days passed with no action on their requests. Meanwhile citizens were executed every day, and from her kitchen Wilda could hear the shots. The strain grew unbearable. "The imagination is what jumps around into all sorts of places it ought to keep out of," Arthur wrote to his parents.

He was told at last that his wife and child could leave if he would secretly work for the Communists. Arthur refused. Day after day he was summoned and grilled. Day after day he said good-bye to Wilda, wondering if he would ever see her again. Finally Arthur bluntly told the authorities, "I am not a Judas. If you expect me or anyone else in the China Inland Mission to do that kind of thing, you had better not try because we cannot do it."

Wilda was utterly overcome by fear and doubt. Sunday, *March 25, 1951*, was, as she recalled it later, Black Easter. Wilda sneaked into an Easter church service, but when she opened her mouth to sing "He Lives!" no words came out. Returning home, she fell at the trunk and her trembling fingers found 2 Chronicles 20:17: "You won't even have to fight. Just take your position and watch the LORD rescue you from your enemy. Don't be afraid." Wilda clamped onto that verse, and two weeks later she wrote, "The conflict has been terrible, but peace and quiet reign now."

It was two years before she exited the country and even longer for Arthur, who became the last CIM missionary to leave China. But miraculously, all of them got out without a single one being martyred. It was the greatest exodus in missionary history.

You won't even have to fight. Just take your positions and watch the LORD rescue you from your enemy. Don't be afraid. Just do as you're told. And as you march out tomorrow, the LORD will be there with you. Jehoshaphat bowed low to the ground and everyone worshiped the LORD. (2 Chronicles 20:17–18)

Cuthbert

Cuthbert was born to a shepherding family in Northumbria in the early 630s, but we know little of him until he entered the Scottish monastery in Melrose at about age twenty. His faithfulness and piety resulted in his being named prior of Melrose ten years later. He found himself caught in the struggle between the Roman and the Celtic Christians, and he eventually retired to complete solitude in 676, traveling to a deserted island six miles off the British coast to live among the birds and seals.

By 684, his reputation for holiness had become widespread, and King Ecgfrith of Northumbria traveled to plead with him to become bishop of Hexham. Cuthbert refused at first, not wanting to leave his tranquil retreat. The king persuaded him at last, and on *March 26, 685*, Cuthbert was consecrated bishop. He spent his remaining days in public ministry, traveling around the diocese, preaching, converting sheep farmers in the Northumbrian hills, and distributing alms.

He returned to his island after Christmas in 686, believing he was dying. When he passed away on March 20, 687, monks spread the news by lighted torches, and on the following morning carried his body to Lindisfarne for burial in the monastic church.

The burial habits were odd. It was the custom to bury holy men long enough for the flesh to rot in an earthen grave. The bones would then be raised, washed, wrapped in silks, and placed in a shrine. This ceremony was called the *elevation of the relics*. The elevation of Cuthbert's relics occurred on March 20, 698, the eleventh anniversary of his death. According to church tradition, however, when Cuthbert's relics were raised, it was found that his body had not decayed. It was solemnly placed in a shrine on the floor of the church. Miracles were soon reported there, and by the time the Venerable Bede penned Cuthbert's biography in 720, thousands of pilgrims were traveling to the shrine. Cuthbert became the most beloved Christian in the north of England.

My friends, I want you to know that our bodies of flesh and blood will decay . . . but we will all be changed. It will happen suddenly, quicker than the blink of an eye. At the sound of the last trumpet the dead will be raised . . . Our dead and decaying bodies will be changed into bodies that won't die or decay. (1 Corinthians 15:50–53)

Old Jeffrey

In 1697, Samuel and Susanna Wesley assumed responsibility for the church in Epworth, England, and they soon filled the parsonage with children. Susanna gave birth to nineteen in all—among them was John, the future founder of Methodism. The Epworth years were hard, days of poverty, disagreement, and discouragement. The difficulties increased in December 1716, when an unexpected visitor arrived—a ghost. The parsonage came alive with mysterious sounds. Groaning. Loud knockings. Feet on the stairs. Bottles breaking. Chains rattling. The house sometimes shook from top to bottom. No explanation could be found, but strange apparitions were occasionally seen.

The ghost (or demon or whatever it was) became most agitated during family devotions when Rev. Wesley prayed for the royal family. Terrible poundings came from upstairs, which so provoked the minister that he prayed with increasing defiance and volume. Losing all patience, he once shouted, "Thou deaf and dumb devil, why dost thou frighten the children? Come to me in my study that am a man." Afterward, it constantly annoyed Wesley in his study.

At first, Susanna had attributed the noises to rats. But when strange horns began blaring throughout the house, she grew convinced that no human or animal could make such sounds. On *March 27, 1717*, she wrote to her skeptical son Samuel, away at school, "I cannot imagine how you should be so curious about our unwelcome guest. For my part, I am tired with hearing or speaking of it; but if you come, you will find enough to satisfy all your scruples, and perhaps you may hear or see it yourself."

The family eventually named their ghost Old Jeffrey. The children grew accustomed to him, finding they could tease and anger him with personal remarks. His antics finally died down, but years later John, then a world-famous evangelist, wrote an account of him for a magazine. It seems the devil had overplayed his hand. Seeking to frighten or destroy the future evangelist, Old Jeffrey had, instead, convinced John that the battle was not against flesh and blood but against rulers of darkness and powers in the spiritual world.

We are not fighting against humans. We are fighting against forces and authorities and against rulers of darkness and powers in the spiritual world. So put on all the armor that God gives. Then when that evil day comes, you will be able to defend yourself. And when the battle is over, you will still be standing firm. (Ephesians 6:12–13)

William's Sermon

Rev. John Minder, the college dean, was concerned for his students. But he had his hands full with William. On the day William arrived, he took out a big scout knife, played around with it, and took off running all over the adjacent golf course like an overgrown schoolboy. Shortly thereafter he and his roommate went canoeing in their best clothes on a Sunday afternoon. William stood up in the canoe, raised his oar, and said, "I see an Indian—bang!" He leaned backward, and both boys fell into the river. William wrestled under the beds, knocked down bullies, wore bright bow ties, and charmed the girls.

But Dean Minder, a big, ginger-haired man with sparkling eyes, had endless patience, and he knew potential when he saw it. On Easter Sunday, *March 28, 1937*, he took William with him to evening services at a small Baptist church in a nearby town. Minder was to fill in for the church's part-time pastor, who doubled as an interior decorator. But Minder had no intention of preaching that evening. On the way there he informed William, "*You're* preaching tonight."

"No, sir!" said the horrified young man. "I've never preached before."

"Well," replied Dean Minder, "you are preaching tonight. When you run out, I'll take over."

As it happened, William had secretly been practicing four messages taken from a book of sermons by the Baptist preacher Lee Scarborough. Now he frantically tried to remember them. The men arrived at the small, clapboard church, finding it surrounded by men with hunting dogs. The hunters and ranchers and their families went inside for worship, making an audience of twenty-five or thirty. The song leader led the group in a series of fast-paced hymns, pausing occasionally to spit tobacco juice into the boiler.

When time came for the sermon, William rose, looked at the crowd, and grew so nervous that his knees knocked and his face glistened with perspiration. He preached all four sermons in eight minutes, then collapsed back into his seat.

Such was the beginning of the preaching ministry of William Franklin Graham—better known as Billy.

I don't have any reason to brag about preaching the good news. Preaching is something God told me to do, and if I don't do it, I am doomed . . . It is . . . something God has sent me to do . . . I have become a slave to everyone, so that I can win as many people as possible. (1 Corinthians 9:16–17, 19)

March 29

The Welsh Revival

Evan Roberts was a coal miner, tall, blue-eyed, young, and thin. His dark hair curled over his forehead and ears. He harbored a deep burden for souls, and he prayed earnestly for revival. At age twenty-five, having just begun studying for the ministry, he asked his pastor for permission to hold some evening meetings. Only a few people came at first, but within days village shops were closing early for the services. People left work to secure seats at church. The building was packed and roadways clogged with would-be attenders. Services often lasted until 4:30 AM. Sins were confessed, sinners converted, homes restored.

In neighboring towns Roberts saw similar results. All across Wales theaters closed, jails emptied, churches filled, and soccer matches were canceled to avoid conflicting with the revival. Welsh miners were so converted that their pit ponies had to be retrained to work without the prodding of curse words.

On *March 29, 1905*, Roberts opened a series of meetings at Shaw Street Chapel in Liverpool—out of Wales into England, out of the country into the city. Thousands thronged around the church from all parts of England, Scotland, Ireland, the Continent, and America. Multitudes were converted or found new joy in Christ. Often Roberts didn't even preach. The very sight o[illegible] sent rivers of emotion flowing through the crowds. Whe[illegible] his message was quiet and simple: "obedience to Je[illegible]ration to his service, receiving the Holy Spirit, an[illegible] be ruled by him."

The Liverpool me[illegible]usted, needing weeks to recover. On his next pr[illegible]d of revival again swirled around him, and again [illegible]ome exhausted. Roberts spoke four times more; [illegible]d's home for a week's recovery. He stayed sev[illegible]ched again. He spent his remaining forty-five [illegible]nd prayer, here and there, with friends. He [illegible]

His public ministry [illegible] months, but it had shaken Wales and England to the fou[illegible]s.

You are wrong to think that these people are drunk. After all, it is only nine o'clock in the morning. But this is what God had the prophet Joel say,

"When the last days come,
I will give my Spirit
to everyone.
Your sons and daughters
will prophesy.
Your young men
will see visions,
and your old men
will have dreams." (Acts 2:15–17)

Stand Up for Jesus

Dudley Tyng served as his father's assistant at Philadelphia's Church of the Epiphany and was elected its pastor when his father retired in 1854. He was only twenty-nine when he succeeded his father at the large Episcopal church, and at first it seemed a great fit. But the honeymoon ended when Dudley began vigorously preaching against slavery. Loud complaints rose from the more conservative members, resulting in Dudley's resignation in 1856.

He and his followers organized the Church of the Covenant elsewhere in the city, and his reputation grew. He began noontime Bible studies at the YMCA, and his ministry reached far beyond his own church walls. Dudley had a burden for leading husbands and fathers to Christ, and he helped organize a great rally to reach them. On Tuesday, *March 30, 1858*, five thousand men gathered. Dudley looked over the sea of faces and declared, "I would rather this right arm were amputated at the trunk than that I should come short of my duty to you in delivering God's message." More than a thousand men were converted that day.

Two weeks later Dudley was visiting in the countryside, watching a corn thrasher in the barn. His hand moved too close to the machine and his sleeve was snared. His arm was ripped from its socket, the main artery severed. Four days later his right arm was amputated close to the shoulder. When it appeared he was dying, Dudley told his aged father: "Stand up for Jesus, Father, and tell my brethren of the ministry to stand up for Jesus."

Rev. George Duffield of Philadelphia's Temple Presbyterian Church was deeply stirred by Dudley's funeral, and the following Sunday he preached from Ephesians 6 about standing firm for Christ. He read a poem he had written, inspired by Dudley's words: "Stand up, stand up for Jesus, / Ye soldiers of the cross; / Lift high His royal banner, / It must not suffer loss."

The editor of a hymnal heard the poem, found appropriate music, and published it. "Stand Up, Stand Up for Jesus" soon became one of America's favorite hymns, extending Dudley's dying words to millions.

Your desire to tell the good news about peace should be like shoes on your feet. Let your faith be like a shield, and you will be able to stop all the flaming arrows of the evil one. Let God's saving power be like a helmet, and for a sword use God's message that comes from the Spirit. (Ephesians 6:15–17)

My Heart's Desire

The apostle Paul loved his people, the Jews, enough to have wished himself cursed and cut off from Christ for their sake. "My greatest wish and my prayer to God is for the people of Israel," he said, "to be saved" (Rom. 10:1). But not everyone shared his concern. Roman forces soon afterward destroyed Jerusalem, and many of the beleaguered survivors fled to Europe as refugees. Eventually Spain became a great center of Jewish learning, arts, science, and finance. Maimonides, the "second Moses," helped establish in Spain a Golden Age of Jewish life. But during the fourteenth and fifteenth centuries, sentiment again turned against the Jews.

The marriage of Ferdinand of Aragon and Isabella of Castile in 1469 established a state church with little sympathy for Jews. Isabella wielded great power. She was active in government, strict in morality, and devout in formal religion. Vowing to rid her land of unbelievers, Isabella established the Spanish Inquisition. Heretics and Jews were rounded up, interrogated, and tortured without mercy.

When the Inquisition failed to forcibly convert Jews, Ferdinand and Isabella determined to expel them, and on *March 31, 1492*, the royal couple signed an edict giving Jews three months to leave Spain. At least one hundred fifty thousand Jews, stripped of homes and possessions, left the land that had been their home for almost fifteen hundred years. The last Jew reportedly left Spain on August 2, the traditional anniversary of the destruction of the first and second temples, the saddest day in Jewish history. Ironically, the very next day, August 3, 1492, Christopher Columbus sailed from Spain to discover the New World.

Not everything done in the name of Christianity is Christian. Genuine believers resort to prayer and preaching and love, not persecution, to fulfill the Great Commission. And genuine believers harbor a deep love for the Jewish people, remembering that Jesus Christ himself was Jewish. Like Paul, our heart's desire and prayer for the Israelites is that they might be saved.

I am a follower of Christ, and the Holy Spirit is a witness to my conscience . . . I would gladly be placed under God's curse and be separated from Christ for the good of my own people. They are the descendants of Israel . . . (Romans 9:1, 3–4)

On This Day in Christian History…

APRIL

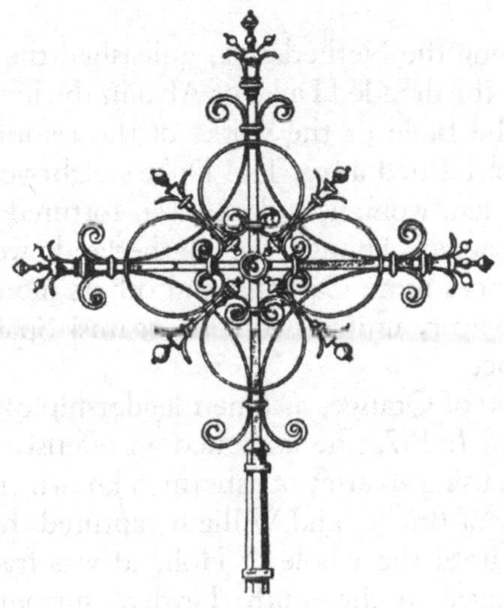

William of Orange

Philip II, king of Spain, born during the days of Luther, despised the Reformation. His object in life was to destroy Protestants and see Catholicism entrenched throughout Europe. It was Philip whose Spanish Inquisition snuffed out Reformation fires in Spain and Portugal. He sent his Spanish Armada against Queen Elizabeth in an attempt to reclaim England for Catholicism. And it was Philip who sent the Duke of Alva against the Dutch.

The Netherlands had long been a hotbed of Reformation ideas. The Bible was freely available there, and teachers from Germany, France, and England spread Reformation ideas, especially Calvinism, throughout the land.

Philip, occupying the Netherlands, unleashed the Spanish Inquisition and stationed the dreaded Duke of Alva in the lowlands. Hundreds who dared read the Bible or the works of the reformers were seized, strangled, killed, or burned alive. The Duke's eight-year reign of terror left thousands of men, women, and children tortured and slain. Entire villages were massacred. Though the Netherlands were internally divided, some provinces more Catholic and others more Protestant, the Duke of Alva's savagery united everyone against Spain and sparked a war of independence.

William, Prince of Orange, assumed leadership of the Dutch resistance, and on *April 1, 1572*, he launched an offensive against Spanish forces in the north, using an army of fishermen known as the Sea Beggars. They took the city of Brielle, and William captured the northern provinces one by one until the whole of Holland was freed from Spanish power. The war raged in the south. Leyden, surrounded by Spanish troops, was desperate. Inhabitants were reduced to living on cats, dogs, and rats. The king and pope promised full pardon if the city would surrender, but the citizens refused. William proposed they open the floodgates, break the dikes, and flood the plains around the city. It was harvesttime, and the city's crops would be ruined, but the people consented. The dikes were broken, the sea swept in, and William's Sea Beggars sailed into the city. The Spanish fled in terror, and the city, liberated and grateful, gathered in the cathedral to give thanks to God.

I, the LORD God of Israel,
will come to their rescue.
I won't forget them.
I will make rivers flow
on mountain peaks.
I will send streams
to fill the valleys. (Isaiah 41:17–18)

His Ideal Idelette

Churchmen had been celibate for centuries, and John Calvin wondered if he, a first-generation Protestant, should break tradition. "I am not yet married," he wrote. "Whether I shall ever marry I do not know. In any case, if I take a wife it will be that, freed from cares, I can consecrate myself to the Lord."

He fell in love at age thirty, but the marriage was called off. His friend William Farel suggested another woman, but Calvin was unimpressed. A third prospect looked promising, but Calvin was cautious. "I will look very foolish if my hope again falls through."

It did. "I have not found a wife," he lamented, "and frequently hesitate as to whether I ought any more to seek one." Suddenly he noticed a widow in his congregation, Idelette de Bure, who had been converted through his preaching. He made frequent pastoral visits to her, and was smitten. They quickly married.

Idelette proved an ideal pastor's wife. She visited the sick, poor, and distressed. She entertained visitors who came consulting her famous husband. She furnished her table with vegetables from her own garden. She bore patiently the loss of the couple's three infants. She softened Calvin's hard edge and provided him joy.

When Idelette fell ill, Calvin anguished. As the hour of death drew near, they talked about "the grace of Christ, the hope of everlasting life, our marriage, and her approaching departure." Then he turned aside to pray. Idelette suddenly cried, "O glorious resurrection! O God of Abraham and of all our fathers, the believers of all the ages have trusted on Thee and none has hoped in vain. And now I fix my hope on Thee." Having thus spoken, she died. Calvin wrote to Farel on *April 2, 1549*, "Intelligence of my wife's death has perhaps reached you. I do what I can to keep myself from being overwhelmed with grief. My friends also leave nothing undone that may administer relief to my mental suffering."

John and Idelette enjoyed nine years together. Never again did John Calvin seek a wife, for no one could replace his ideal Idelette.

There are three or four things
I cannot understand:
How eagles fly so high
or snakes crawl on rocks,
how ships sail the ocean
or people fall in love. (Proverbs 30:18–19)

Politician to Preacher

Ambrose was born in Gaul, where his father was governor. His family shortly moved to Rome, where Ambrose was raised to be a skilled poet, orator, and lawyer. After practicing law in the Roman courts for a time, he was named governor of an Italian province and headquartered in Milan. There a crisis arose when Bishop Auxentius died in 374. The city was divided over who should replace him, and tensions were high. Ambrose assembled the people and used his oratorical powers to appeal for unity. But while he was speaking, a child cried out: "Let Ambrose be bishop!" The crowd took up the chant, and the thirty-five-year-old governor, to his dismay, was elected the city's pastor.

He set himself to study theology, soon becoming a great preacher and a deft defender of orthodox doctrine. He combated paganism and heresy with diligence, maintained the independence of the church against civil powers, and championed morality. He confronted political leaders, even emperors, when necessary. He wrote books and treatises, sermons, hymns, and letters. He tended Milan like a shepherd.

Perhaps none of that was more important than his influence on a hot-blooded infidel who slipped into town one Sunday to hear him preach. The skeptical Augustine found himself deeply impressed by the power of Ambrose's sermons, and he sought personal counseling from the bishop. But Ambrose was too busy. Visitors were allowed into his room, but he paid scant attention to them. He just went ahead reading. Several times Augustine sat watching him, but Ambrose remained unaware of it. His preaching, however, reached the prodigal, and shortly afterward Augustine was converted.

Ambrose continued preaching until he fell sick in 397. When distressed friends prayed for his healing, he said, "I have so lived among you that I cannot be ashamed to live longer, but neither do I fear to die; for we have a good Lord." On Good Friday, *April 3, 397*, Ambrose lay with his hands extended in the form of the cross, moving his lips in prayer. His friends huddled in sadness and watched. Sometime past midnight their beloved bishop passed to his good Lord.

Church officials are in charge of God's work, and so they must also have a good reputation. They must not be bossy, quick-tempered, heavy drinkers, bullies, or dishonest in business. They must stick to the true message they were taught, so that their good teaching can help others and correct everyone who opposes it. (Titus 1:7, 9)

Another Brilliant Bishop

Isidore was born about 560, in Seville, Spain, into a noble Christian family. He was the youngest child and was personally educated by his much-older brother, Leander, the close friend of Pope Gregory the Great. Though severe in his methods, Leander managed to furnish his little brother with both a brilliant mind and a tender heart.

When Isidore became pastor in Seville, he concerned himself with establishing schools for the young, converting false teachers to orthodoxy and evangelizing Jews. He established seminaries in every Spanish diocese for training young ministers.

But he did more. He compiled history's first encyclopedia, the *Etymologiae*. It became the most used textbook of the Middle Ages, containing entries on medicine, arithmetic, grammar, history, science, and theology. Isidore also developed a dictionary of synonyms, a book on astronomy, a summary of world history, a set of biographies of illustrious men, books on biblical characters, and many books of sermons and theological studies. He became known as the greatest teacher in Spain.

The highlight of his career came late in his thirty-seven-year ministry. He presided over the great Spanish church council of Toledo, which opened on December 5, 633. At this council it was determined that baptismal candidates should be plunged into water only once, not three times. The council also approved the singing of hymns, not just the words of Scripture. And it forbade the compulsory conversion of Jews.

Two years later when he sensed he was dying, Isidore began distributing his goods to the poor. Four days before his death he asked two friends to carry him to the church of St. Vincent the Martyr. Once there he had one of them cover him with sackcloth and the other put ashes on his head. The old scholar then raised his hands to heaven and prayed loudly, confessing his sins and pleading for grace. A crowd assembled, and Isidore requested their prayers and forgave his debtors. He preached to the people about love, then distributed his remaining possessions. Returning home, he took to his bed and died peacefully on Thursday, *April 4, 636.*

God told us,
"Wisdom means
that you respect me, the Lord,
and turn from sin." (Job 28:28)

April 5 Norway's Pious Preacher

Lutheranism was born of Martin Luther's mighty zeal in the 1500s, but a century later it had sunk into cold and weary formalism. In the 1600s, God raised up other giants to rekindle the flames and extend the Reformation into a new phase.

P. J. Spener, burdened for his church, opened his home for prayer and Bible reading. That simple act sparked a spiritual renewal across Germany, since called Pietism. The Pietist movement swept over continental Europe, emphasizing inner spirituality, home meetings, mission involvement, hymn singing, and social work (particularly with orphans). Reaching into Scandinavia, Pietism touched twenty-five-year-old Hans Nielsen Hague.

Hans had grown up in rural Norway, learning many crafts from his industrious parents. He was a skilled cabinetmaker, carpenter, blacksmith, and beekeeper. He had also known the words of Scripture and the songs of the hymnbook since infancy. On *April 5, 1796*, as he worked outdoors and sang the hymn "Jesus, I Long for Thy Blessed Communion," he was abruptly caught up in a dramatic experience. His mind felt suddenly exalted and his heart overflowed with God's Spirit. The love of Christ blazed in his soul. He sensed a deep hunger for Bible study and a compelling urge to proclaim the gospel.

Hans ran home and shared his experience with his family, then with his church. He then set out to tell others, traveling for eight years and ten thousand miles throughout Norway by foot, ski, and horse. He preached to crowds large and small, emphasizing repentance, conversion, and true revival. His message sparked renewal everywhere. Occasionally local pastors, fearing his zeal and popularity, opposed him, and he was arrested ten times. But most bishops and pastors eventually thanked God for his ministry.

Having finished his preaching tour, Hans applied himself to commerce and became the owner of paper mills, a salt factory, a trading company, and a fleet of ships. He used his position in the business world to spread his message there. He passed away at age fifty-three, using his final breaths to exhort his wife, "Follow Jesus." He is today called the Father of Scandinavian Pietism.

I felt the LORD's power take control of me, and his Spirit carried me to a valley full of bones. He then told me to say: Dry bones, listen to what the LORD is saying to you, "I, the LORD God, will put breath in you, and once again you will live . . . Then you will know that I am the LORD." (Ezekiel 37:1, 4–6)

The Flying Scotsman

Eric Liddell was a missionary kid born in China. At age seven his parents enrolled him in a boarding school in Britain, and he spent most of his childhood separated from them. But school officials encouraged him to devote himself to sports, and young Eric soon developed an athlete's physique. He also began flexing his spiritual muscles, rising early each day to meet the Lord in prayer and Bible study.

When Eric entered the university, he broke one record after another in sporting events. His sister wrote their parents in China, saying, "Every week he brings home prizes. We've nowhere to put them all." As his fame grew, an innovative Scottish evangelist named D. P. Thomson eyed him as an intriguing prospect for the ministry. He invited Eric to share his testimony with a group of men in Armadale, and on *April 6, 1923*, Liddell made his debut in public evangelism. By the time he arrived at the Paris Olympics that summer, Eric was known worldwide as a powerful athlete and as an outspoken Christian who, despite refusing to race on Sundays, could win the gold.

But fame didn't stop him from following his parents to China. He arrived there as a missionary in 1925. When the Japanese invaded in 1937, he remained; and in 1943, he found himself interned in a camp outside Peking. Conditions were horrible. Eric ministered day by day, praying with the sick, coaching the children, witnessing to the lost. At times, though, his head throbbed. He began visibly weakening. On February 21, 1945, he died. An autopsy revealed a massive brain tumor.

A camp survivor was asked the reason for Liddell's influence at the camp. She replied that every morning at six he would rise and light the peanut-oil lantern on the little dormitory table, just enough to illumine his Bible and notebook. There he would silently meet God at the start of each new day. It was the Flying Scotsman's lifelong habit, she said, and the secret of his power.

I have not yet reached my goal, and I am not perfect. But Christ has taken hold of me. So I keep on running and struggling to take hold of the prize . . . I forget what is behind, and I struggle for what is ahead. I run toward the goal, so that I can win the prize of being called to heaven. (Philippians 3:12–14)

Ordeal by Fire

How could the crowd that cheered Jesus on Palm Sunday crucify him on Friday? How can public opinion turn so quickly? That's what Jerome Savonarola asked on *April 7, 1498.* He lived in Florence during the height of the Italian Renaissance. His flashing dark eyes and blazing sermons electrified the city. Throngs waited for hours for cathedral doors to open, and thousands clung to his every word. "I preach the regeneration of the church," he thundered, "taking the Scriptures as my sole guide."

Eventually Savonarola became city manager and made Florence a republic. He initiated tax reforms, aided the poor, cleaned up the courts, and changed the city to a virtual monastery. He inspired the populace to build bonfires for burning pornographic books and gambling equipment. Having reformed Florence, he rebuked the clergy, denouncing papal corruptions. When Pope Alexander VI excommunicated him, he demanded the pope's dismissal.

A Franciscan proposed an "ordeal by fire" to settle the matter. In this medieval custom a man was forced to walk between walls of fire, and his survival or death was deemed to indicate God's favor or disfavor. Savonarola's close friend Fra Domenico agreed to walk through the fire, and the ordeal was set for April 7. Great preparations were made as the news spread across Italy. Two rows of wood, laid out for sixty feet, were soaked with oil. The two feet between them was just wide enough for a man to pass. The excitement was tremendous, and people began to arrive the night before. Windows and roofs adjoining the square overflowed with people. The ordeal was set for 11:00 AM.

But the hour came and went. The impatience of the crowds increased as Savonarola delayed sending Domenico out. A storm rose and fell. Evening came, and the crowd rioted when the ordeal was called off. Savonarola's power was gone. He was arrested, tortured, and shortly afterward executed on the same public square where the ordeal was to have occurred. The crowd who honored him as a prophet and appointed him a statesman made him, in the end, a martyr.

These unfaithful prophets claim that I have given them a dream . . . Their dreams and my truth are as different as straw and wheat. But when prophets speak for me, they must say only what I have told them. My words are like a powerful fire; they are a hammer that shatters rocks. (Jeremiah 23:25, 28–29)

A Mystery of Providence *April 8*

James Chalmers was a carefree, high-spirited Scottish boy. "I dearly loved adventure," he later said, "and a dangerous position was exhilarating." Perhaps that's why he listened carefully one Sunday when his minister read a letter from missionaries in Fiji. The preacher, tears in his eyes, added, "I wonder if there is a boy here who will by and by bring the gospel to the cannibals." Young James said quietly, "I will!"—and he wasn't even yet converted.

In 1866, having been converted and trained, he sailed for the South Pacific as a Presbyterian missionary. Chalmers had a way with people. "It was in his presence, his carriage, his eye, his voice," a friend wrote. "There was something almost hypnotic about him. His perfect composure, his judgment and tact and fearlessness brought him through a hundred difficulties." Robert Louis Stevenson, who didn't like missionaries until he met Chalmers, said, "He is a rowdy, but he is a hero. You can't weary me of that fellow. He took me fairly by storm."

In 1877, Chalmers sailed on to New Guinea. His ministry was successful there. Packed churches replaced feasts of human flesh. But as the years passed he grew lonely. He was delighted when young Oliver Tomkins came to join him in 1901. The two men decided to explore a new part of the islands, and on Easter Sunday they sailed alongside a new village. The next morning, *April 8, 1901*, Chalmers and Tomkins went ashore. They were never seen again. A rescue party soon learned that the men had been clubbed to death, chopped to pieces, cooked, and eaten.

News flashed around the world. "I cannot believe it!" exclaimed Dr. Joseph Parker from the pulpit of London's famous City Temple. "I do not want to believe it! Such a mystery of Providence makes it hard for our strained faith to recover. Yet Jesus was murdered. Paul was murdered. Many missionaries have been murdered. When I think of that side of the case, I cannot but feel that [illegible] and nobleminded friend has joined a great assembly."

These are the ones
who have gone through
the great suffering.
They have washed their robes
in the blood of the Lamb
and have made them white.
And so they stand
before the throne of God. (Revelation 7:14–15)

The Azusa Street Revival

Don't destroy yourself by getting drunk," warns Ephesians 5:18, "but let the Spirit fill your life." That's a divine command, but just how do we let the Spirit fill us? That question has occasioned a century of debate.

From rural Iowa, Rev. Charles Fox Parham brought a message of holiness to Midwestern towns at the close of the 1800s. In October of 1900, spurred by his success as a preacher and healer, Parham opened a small Bible school in Topeka. He was intrigued by the "baptism of the Holy Spirit." In December he left for meetings in Kansas City, instructing his students to investigate the subject in his absence. Upon his return, December 31, his forty pupils had unanimously concluded from their studies that speaking in tongues was the "indisputable proof" of spiritual baptism.

That night as they gathered for New Year's Eve services, the students began to pray. The next day, January 1, 1901, student Agnes Ozman began speaking in tongues, and a sense of revival swept through the group.

The school soon closed as its professor and students fanned out as evangelists of their new discovery. In Texas, Parham's message reached a Baptist Holiness minister named William Seymour, a one-eyed descendant of African slaves. Seymour traveled to Los Angeles and set up shop at 312 Azusa Street in an abandoned livery stable. There he began preaching. On *April 9, 1906*, Seymour and several others had an experience they claimed as the "baptism of the Spirit." Excitement spread, and a *Los Angeles Times* reporter visited their meeting, writing, "The night is made hideous . . . by the howlings of the worshippers."

Large crowds came from across the nation and around the world, and three years of nonstop prayer meetings followed. Seymour usually sat at the front of the room behind two empty boxes, one on top of the other. During meetings, he kept his head inside the boxes, earnestly praying.

The Azusa Street Revival is commonly regarded as the beginning of modern Pentecostalism, which has mushroomed into one of the largest Christian movements of the twentieth century.

Don't destroy yourself by getting drunk, but let the Spirit fill your life. When you meet together, sing psalms, hymns, and spiritual songs, as you praise the Lord with all your heart. Always use the name of our Lord Jesus Christ to thank God the Father for everything. (Ephesians 5:18–20)

Christmas in April

On December 25, 1766, a son was born to an impoverished Welsh shoemaker and his wife. They considered naming him Vasover, but chose instead to name him for the day of his birth. When Christmas Evans was nine, his father died in his cobbler stall, awl in hand. His mother farmed out the children, and Christmas went to live with an alcoholic uncle. The boy ran with rough gangs, fighting and drinking and endangering his life. He was unable to read a word.

But then Christmas heard the Welsh evangelist David Davies. He soon gave his life to Christ, and Davies began teaching him by candlelight in a barn at Penyralltfawr. Within a month Christmas was able to read from his Bible, and he expressed a desire to preach. His old gang, however, was annoyed. One night they attacked him on a mountain road, beating him and gouging out his right eye.

The young man resolved nonetheless to preach, and preach he did. Wherever he went—churches, coal mines, open fields—crowds gathered and a spirit of revival swept over the listeners. Unable to afford a horse, he started across Wales by foot, preaching in towns and villages with great effect.

But Christmas Evans eventually lost the joy of ministry. His health broke, and he seemed to have used up his spiritual zeal. On *April 10, 1802*, he climbed into the Welsh mountains, determined to wrestle with God until his passion returned. The struggle lasted for hours, but finally tears began to flow, and Christmas felt the joy of his salvation returning. He made a covenant with God that day, writing down thirteen items, initialing each one. The fourth said, "Grant that I may not be left to any foolish act that may occasion my gifts to wither . . ." And the eighth said, "Grant that I may experience the power of thy word before I deliver it."

The burly, one-eyed preacher left the mountaintop that day with a power that shook Wales and the neighboring island of Anglesea until his death thirty-six years later. He is called the *Bunyan of Wales*.

Create pure thoughts in me
and make me faithful again.
Make me as happy as you did
when you saved me; . . .
Then I will shout and sing
about your power to save. (Psalm 51:10, 12, 14)

Fifty Thousand Answers to Prayer

George Mueller, born into a German tax collector's family, was often in trouble. He learned early to steal and gamble and drink. As a teenager he learned how to stay in expensive hotels, then sneak out without paying the bill. But at length he was caught and jailed. Prison did him little good, for upon release he continued his crime spree until, on a Saturday night in 1825, he met Jesus Christ.

Mueller married and settled down in Bristol, England, growing daily in faith and developing a burden for the homeless children running wild and ragged through the streets. At a public meeting in Bristol on December 9, 1835, he presented a plan for an orphanage. Several contributions came in. Mueller rented Number 6 Wilson Street, and on *April 11, 1836*, the doors of the orphanage opened. Twenty-six children were immediately taken in. A second house soon opened, then a third.

From the beginning, Mueller refused to ask for funds or even to speak of the ministry's financial needs. He believed in praying earnestly and trusting the Lord to provide. And the Lord *did* provide, though sometimes at the last moment. The best-known story involves a morning when the plates and bowls and cups were set on the tables, but there was no food or milk. The children sat waiting for breakfast while Mueller led in prayer for their daily bread. A knock sounded at the door. It was the baker. "Mr. Mueller," he said, "I couldn't sleep last night. Somehow I felt you didn't have bread for breakfast, so I got up at 2:00 AM and baked some fresh bread." A second knock sounded. The milkman had broken down right in front of the orphanage, and he wanted to give the children his milk so he could empty his wagon and repair it.

Such stories became the norm for Mueller's work. During the course of his ninety-three years, Mueller housed more than ten thousand orphans, "prayed in" millions of dollars, traveled to scores of countries preaching the gospel, and recorded fifty thousand answers to prayer.

Don't worship foreign gods
or bow down to gods
you know nothing about.
I am the LORD your God.
I rescued you from Egypt.
Just ask, and I will give you
whatever you need. (Psalm 81:9–10)

Calvin's Mentor

Few assume greatness by themselves. Behind the scenes often lies an older mentor, watching with pride. John Calvin exists as a hero in church history because of Guillaume Farel.

Farel was a traveling evangelist in France, full of fire and fury. He was likened to Elijah and was called the *scourge of priests*. He considered the pope the Antichrist and viewed the mass as nothing but idolatry. Priests, wishing him dead, carried weapons under their cloaks to assassinate him. After one attempt on his life, he whirled around and faced the priest who had fired the errant bullet. "I am not afraid of your shots," he roared.

He was small, sunburned, fiery, and powerful. His sermons were cannon blasts, and his oratory captivated the nation. He often said too much, and one friend cautioned him, "Your mission is to evangelize, not to curse."

On *April 12, 1523*, Farel was forbidden to preach in France. He fled to Switzerland and wandered from town to town, turning stumps and stones into pulpits. When he entered Geneva, the city fathers and priests tried to make him leave. "Who invited you?" they demanded. Farel replied:

> I have been baptized in the name of the Father, the Son, and the Holy Ghost, and am not a devil. I go about preaching Christ, who died for our sins and rose for our justification. Whoever believes in him will be saved; unbelievers will be lost. I am bound to preach to all who will hear. I am ready to dispute with you, to give an account of my faith and ministry. Elijah said to King Ahab, "It is thou, and not I, who disturbest Israel." So I say, it is you and yours, who trouble the world by your traditions, your human inventions, and your dissolute lives.

He was ridiculed, beaten, shot at, and abused. But he wouldn't give up on Geneva. Several years later when young John Calvin came passing through, Farel spotted him and gave him a place to minister—and, as it turns out, a place in church history.

Ahab went to meet Elijah, and when he saw him, Ahab shouted, "There you are, the biggest troublemaker in Israel!" Elijah answered: "You're the troublemaker—not me! You and your family have disobeyed the LORD's commands by worshipping Baal." (1 Kings 18:16–18)

The Edict of Nantes

In 1516, Pope Leo X gave Francis I, king of France, the privilege of appointing church leaders in his own country. This agreement, the Concordant of Bologna, turned the French church into a political circus, and succeeding French kings feared the Reformation, for they were unwilling to lose control over the church as granted by the concordant.

Geneva, however, was on the French border, and Geneva was a strong center of Reformation energy. Many French university students, lawyers, and professionals were attracted to its teaching. French Protestants, called *Huguenots*, grew in number and influence, and during the time of King Henry II (1547–1559), they mushroomed from four hundred thousand to two million. When the French crown sought to suppress the Huguenots, a series of eight wars between Protestant and Catholic forces ravaged France. The climax of these conflicts occurred on August 24, 1572, St. Bartholomew's Day, when some twenty thousand Protestants were massacred.

Following the St. Bartholomew's Day massacre, Henry of Navarre, who could switch from Protestantism to Catholicism and back at will depending on his political needs, reconverted back to Catholicism. This allowed him to claim the throne. "Paris is well worth a mass," his advisers said. Henry was denounced on all sides as a hypocrite, but he remained sympathetic to the Huguenots and he badly wanted to heal his war-torn nation. After being crowned Henry IV, he signed an edict in the French city of Nantes, granting toleration to the Huguenots. It allowed them the right to worship, to publish literature, to hold public office, and to educate their children as they wished. The Edict of Nantes, signed on *April 13, 1598*, was the first document in any nation that attempted to provide a degree of religious toleration.

Not everyone was pleased. Pope Clement VIII condemned it as "the most accursed that can be imagined, whereby liberty of conscience is granted to everybody, which is the worst thing in the world." But the Edict of Nantes provided protection and toleration for Huguenots for nearly a century, until it was revoked in 1685 by King Louis XIV.

God is always honest and fair,
and his laws can be trusted.
They are true and right
and will stand forever.
God rescued his people,
and he will never break
his agreement with them.
He is fearsome and holy. (Psalm 111:7–9)

Old Wrapping Paper

Ancient Israel comprised twelve tribes camping around the tabernacle. In the same way, Christianity has always contained various camps, tribes, and denominations, often closely related and working together for the kingdom. One of the fastest-growing in early America was the Freewill Baptists of New England, started when New Hampshire's Benjamin Randall was converted in 1770. Freewill Baptists aggressively pursued evangelism and education in northeastern America and were among the loudest voices against slavery.

The extension of the movement overseas was ignited by a handful of old wrapping paper.

The General Baptists of England had sent Amos Sutton to India in 1830 as a missionary doctor. The load was too great, and his American wife, worried about his health, suggested he write to Freewill Baptists, appealing for help. Sutton immediately penned a long letter ending with, "Come, then, my American brethren, come over and help us."

Unfortunately, Sutton had no address for the Freewill Baptists, so his letter rested in his desk many months. One day he received a package and, opening it, saw a fragile item wrapped in discarded newspaper. The paper proved more valuable than the gift, for it was the *Morningstar*, publication of the Freewill Baptists. Dr. Sutton immediately posted his letter to the listed address. The Freewill Baptist Foreign Mission Society was soon established, and Sutton made a dramatic visit to New Hampshire. Pale and emaciated, he told three thousand assembled Christians, "As I arise to speak, I seem to see the millions in India with bended knees and tearful eyes, saying, 'Sir, plead our cause—plead it effectually!'" He did, returning to India with twenty-one workers. Many of them died, others suffered greatly, but still more followed. And on *April 14, 1839*, the first small Freewill Baptist chapel in India was dedicated to Christ to accommodate the new converts.

"Could the friends of missions have witnessed our little assembly quietly seated on their mats, listening to the Word of eternal life with serious attention," wrote a missionary, "they would have rejoiced with us, and would have praised the name of that God who had here made room for us."

Tell everyone of every nation,
"Praise the glorious power
of the LORD.
He is wonderful! Praise him
and bring an offering
into his temple." (Psalm 96:7–8)

Jerome of Prague

Jerome loved travel, college life, and the Bible. He was born in Prague and excelled at the university there. Following graduation he traveled to England to study at Oxford, where he ran across the teachings of John Wycliffe, the "Morning Star of the Reformation." The more he read, the more thrilled he became, and he returned to Prague with a heart full of new ideas. His zeal soon took him to other cities. He traveled to Jerusalem in 1403, Paris in 1404, Heidelberg in 1405, and Cologne in 1406. He visited the universities of Europe, sharing the good news of justification by faith. He met King Sigismund of Hungary in 1410, discussing the vices of the clergy, trying to interest him in pre-Reformation ideas. He was in Moravia in 1412, then back in Prague. He traveled to Russia in 1413, and to Lithuania. Then in 1415, he came to the aid of his friend John Hus.

Hus, another pre-reformer, had been hauled before the Council of Constance and condemned for his faith. Hus warned Jerome to stay away, but Jerome traveled to Constance anyway. He was seized on *April 15, 1415*, put in chains, and imprisoned. Hus, meanwhile, was burned at the stake.

Under great pressure Jerome temporarily wavered, reading a document on September 11, 1415, accepting the authority of the pope. Hoping to gain as much publicity as possible, the church placed him on trial at the Cathedral of Constance. They wanted all Bohemia to hear his recantation. Jerome, however, recomposed himself and defended his views with powerful eloquence. He renounced his recantation and proclaimed the innocence of Hus and his own adherence to the teachings of Wycliffe.

The enraged authorities proclaimed him a "cast off and withered branch." They stuffed a paper cap, painted with red devils, on his head and led him to the very spot where Hus had been burned. A cheerful expression flooded Jerome's face, and he sang Easter hymns as the wood was piled around him. The fire consumed him slowly, and his ashes were tossed into the Rhine.

Be ready to give an answer when someone asks you about your hope. Give a kind and respectful answer and keep your conscience clear. This way you will make people ashamed for saying bad things about your good conduct as a follower of Christ. You are better off to obey God and suffer for doing right than to suffer for doing wrong. (1 Peter 3:15–17)

Even There . . .

A monument in Westminster Abbey honors a man, born on *April 16, 1786*, whose grave has never been found. He was an Englishman who shipped to sea at age fifteen with Admiral Nelson. He survived the Battle of Copenhagen, then returned to England only to leave again, this time on a voyage to chart Australia. He next joined the Battle of Trafalgar, then the attack on New Orleans repulsed by General Andrew Jackson.

His name was John Franklin, and six years after the attack on New Orleans, he joined an expedition trying to cross the Polar Sea. He fell in love with Arctic exploration, and when the ships were forced to return to England, he joined another expedition to chart the northern coasts of Canada.

John was blessed with optimism and never allowed himself to sink into depression or loneliness. Everyone he met became his friend. His secret, he said, was Christ. "If a man should inquire 'How can I be saved?' " he wrote his sister from an ice-bound camp, "would it not be joy for him to find that the gospel points the way? Christ who died for the salvation of sinners is the Way, the Truth, and the Life."

One of his crew wrote, "He is quite a bishop! We have church morning and evening on Sunday. The men say they would rather have him than half the parsons of England."

On May 19, 1845, he sailed from England to look for the Northwest Passage and to explore the Arctic. Two cheering letters came from him; then news ceased. Years passed, and the fate of John Franklin was unknown to family or country. His wife spent a fortune searching for him. Finally a boat was found frozen in the north. In it were two skeletons and Sir John Franklin's Bible. Psalm 139:9–10 was underlined: "If I . . . dwell in the uttermost parts of the sea; even there shall thy hand lead me, and thy right hand shall hold me" (KJV).

John Franklin has since been credited with discovering the Northwest Passage, and his Arctic explorations resulted in his being knighted and given an honorary degree from Oxford.

You notice everything I do
and everywhere I go.
Suppose I had wings
like the dawning day
and flew across the ocean.
Even then your powerful arm
would guide and protect me. (Psalm 139:3, 9–10)

Acts Revisited

There are more than sixty references to Ethiopia in the Bible, and Christianity there goes back to the days of Philip (Acts 8). But the modern story of the Ethiopian church also sounds like readings from the book of Acts, especially among the Wallamos. In 1927, the Sudan Interior Mission ("SIM")sent missionaries to evangelize this wild tribe, worshippers of Satan. During its annual "passover," the Wallamos sacrificed a bull to Satan, sprinkling its blood on the doorposts of their houses and serving its raw flesh to every member of their families. The atmosphere smelled of demons.

After several years, a small church was established, but missionary labor was interrupted when Mussolini invaded Ethiopia in 1935. When Italian troops reached tribal areas, they demanded SIM to leave. The missionaries met a final time with Wallamos believers. When they had arrived, not a single Wallamo had known of Christ. Now after nine years, forty-eight native believers gathered around them. The little church worshipped, wept, and shared the Lord's Supper. Then the twenty-six SIM missionaries boarded army trucks for evacuation. On *April 17, 1937*, their first day without missionary support, the little Wallamo church found itself having to stand on its own feet. "We knew God was faithful," wrote missionary Raymond Davis, "that he was able to preserve what he had begun among the Wallamos. But still we wondered—if we ever come back, what will we find?"

The invasion of Ethiopia marked the beginnings of World War II, and it wasn't until July 4, 1943, that the missionaries returned. What they found almost defies belief. The Italian soldiers had tried to stamp out the small church. Church leaders were given one hundred lashes, and one was given four hundred. They were unable to lie on their backs for months. Several had died. One of them, Wandaro, was beaten in public and preached to the crowds between lashes. Another, Toro, stripped in the marketplace and flogged with a hippo-hide whip, bravely shouted out the gospel. Conversions multiplied, and tribal villages began sending missionaries to other villages.

Instead of forty-eight believers, the returning missionaries now found—eighteen thousand.

The Lord's angel said to Philip, "Go south along the desert road that leads from Jerusalem to Gaza." So Philip left. An important Ethiopian official happened to be going along that road in his chariot . . . Philip ran up close and heard the man reading aloud from the book of Isaiah . . . So Philip began at this place in the Scriptures and explained the good news about Jesus. (Acts 8:26–27, 30, 35)

Book of Martyrs

John Foxe entered Oxford still a boy. He was eventually elected a fellow of Magdalen College, and from 1539 to 1545, he studied church history. He converted to Protestantism and was forced to resign his academic position as a result. In 1550, he was ordained by Nicholas Ridley, Bishop of London, and he became friends with Hugh Latimer, William Tyndale, and Thomas Cranmer. But when Queen Mary ascended the throne, tilting England back into Catholicism, Foxe fled. In Switzerland he heard horrible news filtering from England. Latimer, Ridley, Cranmer, and countless others were being captured and burned.

An idea formed in Foxe's mind, soon obsessing him. He would compile a record of the persecution of God's people. Living on the edge of poverty, Foxe spent every spare moment on his project. He labored by day in a printing shop to support his family, but by night he pored over his manuscript. He wrote vividly, giving details, painting word pictures. In 1559, Foxe published his book on the continent—732 pages in Latin. Returning to England under Protestant Elizabeth, he resumed pastoral work and translated his book into English. John Day published it in London in 1563, under the title *Acts and Monuments of These Latter and Perilous Days Touching Matters of the Church.*

But Foxe wasn't finished. He spent four years interviewing witnesses, tracking down documents, finding letters. After long days of church ministry, he sat by flickering candlelight, continuing his writing. In 1570, a second edition appeared—two large volumes totaling 2,315 pages—then a third and a fourth. Foxe's *Book of Martyrs* was one of the most important publications in Elizabeth's reign, having an extraordinary impact. It was in every cathedral alongside the Bible. Vicars read from it during Sunday services. Francis Drake read it aloud on the Western seas. It inspired the Puritans. It took the world by storm.

But it also took a toll on Foxe's personal health, and he never recovered. He died from weariness on *April 18, 1587.* But he had given us his life's crowning achievement.

At that time the church in Jerusalem suffered terribly. All of the Lord's followers, except the apostles, were scattered everywhere in Judea and Samaria . . . The Lord's followers who had been scattered went from place to place, telling the good news. (Acts 8:1–4)

Archbishop Alphege

Alphege, an Englishman born in 954, entered a monastery in Gloucestershire as a young man and quickly fell in love with Jesus Christ. Some years later he became a church leader in Bath, and when he was thirty he was chosen by St. Dustin to become bishop of the city of Winchester. At first Alphege refused the bishopric, considering himself too young for such responsibility. But he was keen, saintly, and well liked, and Dustin persuaded him to serve.

Burdened for Winchester's poor, Alphege soon began organizing ministries of food and provision. Presently no beggars were reported anywhere in his diocese. In the process, however, Alphege nearly starved himself to death, becoming so thin that worshippers declared they could see through his hands when he uplifted them at mass. They loved him all the more, and Alphege served as their pastor for twenty-two years.

When Aelfric, archbishop of Canterbury, died, Pope John XVIII chose Alphege as his successor. England was, at the time, in the throes of an invasion by the warring Danes, and shortly after Alphege became archbishop, Danish forces, assisted by the rebel earl, Edric, marched into Kent and attacked Canterbury. The city was trapped, and its leaders begged Alphege to escape for the good of England. The archbishop chose to remain with his encircled people.

The Danes breached the walls, burst upon the populace, and began plowing down young and old. Alphege rushed to the center of the carnage. Confronting the Danish commander, he demanded that the massacre cease. Instead, he was seized, roughly handled, and thrown into a dungeon.

The Danes demanded a ransom from England for his release, but Alphege refused to be freed, declaring that his country was too poor to pay such a sum. He was taken to Greenwich, where the invaders again sought a ransom. Alphege, again adamantly refusing, was murdered by the Danes during a drunken feast in 1012.

His body was later recovered and buried in St. Paul's Cathedral in London, then moved to Canterbury in 1023. Every year England remembers its faithful Christian martyr on *April 19*, feast day of St. Alphege, archbishop of Canterbury.

I know that my Savior lives, and at the end
he will stand on this earth.
My flesh may be destroyed,
yet from this body
I will see God.
Yes, I will see him for myself,
and I long for that moment. (Job 19:25–27)

The Devil's Dungeons

Paul rightly warned of those who only pretend to be apostles of Christ. Some of them, wrapped in religious robes, have been diabolical beyond belief. Take the Inquisitors, for example. The word *inquisition*, akin to *inquire* and *inquest*, refers to the judicial machinery authorized by the medieval church to uproot heresy. In earlier centuries the church had excommunicated heretics, but most church leaders had opposed physical punishment. But as bureaucracy grew and heresy flourished, attitudes changed.

During the 1100s and early 1200s, stronger measures evolved; and on *April 20, 1233*, Pope Gregory IX issued two edicts, delegating the prosecution of heresy to the Dominican order. The Inquisitors roamed the countryside, admonishing heretics to confess. Those who didn't were brought to trial, the Inquisition serving as a special court with broad and frightening powers.

In 1252, Pope Innocent IV allowed the use of torture, and the Inquisition soon became the most "terrible engine of oppression that the mind of man or devil ever conceived." Suspects were flogged, burned, slashed, frozen, stretched, and suspended by their limbs. Their feet were slowly roasted over fiery coals. Devilish inventions filled the dungeons and dens of the church: thumbscrews for crushing thumbs, boots for slowly crushing feet, and the dreaded *Jungfer* or "iron maid." This device enfolded the victim with metal arms, crushed him in a spiked hug, then opened and let him fall, bleeding from countless stab wounds, bones all broken, to die slowly in an underground hole of revolving knives and spears.

Children and the elderly could be "lightly" tortured, and only pregnant women were exempt—until after delivery. The Inquisition operated in Germany, thrived in France and Italy, and reached its zenith in Spain. It wrought its destruction against Jews, Waldensians, Protestants, and anyone with black skin. It made a show of being religious, but in its grim dungeons was the very enemy of the One in whose robes it was wrapped.

They are no more than false apostles and dishonest workers. They only pretend to be apostles of Christ. And it is no wonder. Even Satan tries to make himself look like an angel of light. So why does it seem strange for Satan's servants to pretend to do what is right? Someday they will get exactly what they deserve. (2 Corinthians 11:13–15)

God in the Alps

"God's eternal power and character cannot be seen. But from the beginning of creation, God has shown what these are like by all he has made" (Rom. 1:20). Many miss the majesty of God's creation, but one boy on the Swiss-Italian border got the message.

Anselm grew up in the breathtaking St. Bernard Pass. His mother frequently reminded him of the Creator, and Anselm imagined God living among the Alps. In his mid-teens Anselm, quarreling with his father, entered a French monastery, where he expanded his knowledge of God through study of Scripture. His keen mind and mature faith led to repeated calls from England, and eventually Anselm crossed the channel to become archbishop of Canterbury.

His life and teaching breathed of Christ. Belief in God, Anselm felt, was rational and logical, not a blind leap of mindless faith. The beauty of creation evidenced God's existence; and furthermore, the very fact that our minds could imagine an infinite, loving God gave evidence that he existed. Anselm's famous argument for God's existence said that if God could exist in our minds, he could exist in reality.

But Anselm's deepest writings were on the atonement, which he defined as Christ's blood being a "satisfaction" made to God by the Lord Jesus. Love of Christ's atonement brought Anselm comfort when he found himself in the crossfire between the pope and English king. The redheaded King William Rufus (Rufus the Red) was profane and violent. He reputedly arose a worse man every morning and went to bed a worse man every night. He enjoyed seeing animals and men tortured while Anselm would go out of his way to save a hare.

Banished and recalled, exiled and returned, Anselm bore his trials with strength until *April 21, 1109*, when, surrounded by friends, he passed away at age seventy-six as morning was breaking. Friends lifted his dying body from the bed and placed it on ashes in the floor. Thus he met his Creator face-to-face, whom he had first recognized in the beauty of the Alps and in the pages of the Holy Bible.

I look to the hills!
Where will I find help?
It will come from the LORD,
who created the heavens
and the earth.
The LORD is your protector,
and he won't go to sleep
or let you stumble.
The protector of Israel
doesn't doze
or ever get drowsy. (Psalm 121:1–4)

Clouds over Geneva

John Calvin arrived in Geneva in July 1536, intending only to stop for the night. But Pastor John Farel found him and wouldn't let him leave, threatening to curse him "with the curse of Almighty God" if he didn't remain as his assistant. Geneva, population twelve thousand, seemed ripe for reformation.

Calvin began his labors in September, and Farel trusted him with many responsibilities, confident of the young man's industry and genius. Calvin, in turn, remained respectful and affectionate toward Farel. No jealousy ever clouded their relationship.

Other clouds, however, were forming. Geneva wasn't ready for the sobriety Calvin and Farel sought to impose. It was a lighthearted city, full of singing and dancing. It also brimmed with gambling, adultery, prostitution, and vice. Farel and Calvin led the city council to issue laws prohibiting immorality, gambling, Sabbath-breaking, and foolish singing. The council further ordered all citizens to embrace the Confession of Faith, and on November 12, 1537, it voted to banish everyone who didn't.

Unrest formed over the city like storm clouds, and loud complaints rocked a November 15 meeting of the general assembly. In local elections the following February, the Libertine party gained ground. Calvin and Farel, continuing to thunder from their pulpits, were warned not to meddle in politics. They meddled anyway.

The storm struck on Easter Sunday, April 21, 1538. Calvin preached in one church, Farel in another. Both refused to administer the Lord's Supper, saying the city could not possibly partake of communion under such conditions. Pandemonium broke out, men drawing their swords, women gasping, children crying. The preachers were hustled home under protection of friends. The next day, *April 22, 1538*, the city council met, fired both ministers, and ordered them to leave town within three days.

"Very well," said Calvin, "it is better to serve God than man." He fled to Strasburg, married Idelette, and pastored a group of French evangelicals until the tide again shifted in Geneva. By 1541, the time was ripe for Calvin and the Reformation to return, this time for good.

I pray to you, LORD.
So when the time is right,
answer me and help me
with your wonderful love.
. . . save me from my enemies
and from the deep water.
Don't let me be
swept away by a flood
or drowned in the ocean
or swallowed by death. (Psalm 69:13–15)

April 23 The Dragon Slayer

Medieval Christianity, growing up amid superstitious people without widespread access to Scripture, began worshipping its heroes, the saints of earlier days. God seemed unapproachable. The almighty Father was feared. The Holy Spirit was neglected. Jesus seemed less threatening, but he, too, was God, and many people thought it wiser to lay their prayers before saints, asking them to present the requests to Christ's throne. So every day had its saint, and every nation, city, and group its patron.

By the tenth century, twenty-five thousand saints had been canonized by the church. France had St. Denis. St. Bartholomew was patron of tanners, having been skinned alive. St. John was invoked by candle-makers, for he had been plunged into a caldron of burning oil. The Council of Oxford in 1222, established April 23 as St. George's Day to honor the Protector of the Kingdom of England.

But who was George? Each year, according to a familiar legend, a swamp-dwelling dragon threatened to poison a nearby village unless a youth, chosen by lot, was given him to eat. By and by, the lot fell to the daughter of the king. Walking toward the swamp, she was intercepted by George. "Fear not," he said, "I will help you in the name of Christ." When the dragon emerged, George made the sign of the cross and plunged his lance into the beast.

Years later in 1189, when English troops under Richard *Coeur de Lion* went forth in the Crusades, they went under the protection of St. George.

In truth, our knowledge of George is slight. He was evidently born into a noble family in Cappadocia and martyred during the Great Persecution of Emperor Diocletian, reportedly on *April 23, ca. 304.* One version says George was tied to a cross, where his skin was scraped with iron combs. But it is his fabled tryst with the dragon for which he is best remembered in the hearts—and in the art—of medieval Christians.

And after all, perhaps he did, in a sense, slay the dragon.

Michael and his angels were fighting against the dragon and its angels. But the dragon lost the battle. It and its angels were forced out of their places in heaven and were thrown down to the earth. Yes, that old snake and his angels were thrown out of heaven! That snake, who fools everyone on earth, is known as the devil and Satan. (Revelation 12:7, 9)

Monica's Prayers

He was born in 354, in a North African town set among the woods near the Mediterranean. His father was a pagan, but his mother, Monica, was of devout Christian stock. Augustine was an undisciplined child, idle, and truant, despite frequent beatings. He loved sports and pranks and soon discovered a host of adolescent pleasures. When he was fifteen, his father saw him in the public baths and realized his son was a man. He was. He later wished that "the high tides of my youth had spent their foam upon the shore of marriage."

Augustine was also brilliant, and he soon moved to Carthage to further both his studies and his fun. Monica warned him against fornication, but "I ran headlong with blindness." At about eighteen he found himself the father of a son. At the same time, he joined a cult.

Years passed, and Monica, praying ceaselessly, heard that Augustine was planning to leave Africa for Rome. She begged him not to go. When he refused to stay, she determined to go with him. Using deception, he left her praying in a chapel and sailed without her, but she took a later boat and intercepted him. They traveled to Milan, where she persuaded him to listen to the great Bishop Ambrose. The bishop's razor-sharp sermons penetrated Augustine's head, if not yet his heart. Monica continued praying, confiding her struggles to Ambrose. He told her not to worry: "It isn't possible for the son of such prayers to be lost."

One day as Augustine sat in a friend's garden, he heard a child singing, "Take up and read!" He opened the Bible near him and read from Romans 13: "Don't go to wild parties or get drunk or be vulgar or indecent . . . Let the Lord Jesus Christ be as near to you as the clothes you wear" (vv. 13–14). By the time he finished the sentence, he later said, he was converted.

On the eve of Easter, *April 24, 387*, Augustine and his son, Adeodatus were baptized by Ambrose as Monica watched. Her lifetime of prayer was answered, and a church father was born.

So behave properly, as people do in the day. Don't go to wild parties or get drunk or be vulgar or indecent. Don't quarrel or be jealous. Let the Lord Jesus Christ be as near to you as the clothes you wear. Then you won't try to satisfy your selfish desires. (Romans 13:13–14)

April 25 The Combative Bishop

No generation is without its Christian heroes, but they were scarce in the tenth century. Ratherius might have been one but for his headstrong style. He was brilliant and religious but opinionated and envious.

Ratherius was born near Verona, Italy. He excelled in school and eventually became a monk. In 931, he was consecrated Bishop of Verona. His tenure was turbulent, for he railed against the sins of the clergy. "The cohabitation of clergy with women," he wrote, "is so customary, so public, that they think it lawful." It wasn't just immoral relationships that Ratherius had in mind but wedded ones. He was merciless on priests who married, calling their unions "adulteries."

The concept of a celibate clergy reaches early into church history. In the Eastern Church, the early councils approved marriage for clergymen. But the Western Church wasn't so sure. At the Council of Nicaea, an idea arose for ministers to leave their wives and devote themselves to the single life. The scheme was rejected, but a few years later Pope Siricius ordered celibacy for priests. Later, Pope Leo decreed that if a married man entered the ministry, he was not to "put away" his wife, but to live with her "as brother and sister."

The issue was being vigorously debated during the days of Ratherius, and the Bishop of Verona knew what he believed—that the single life allows full devotion to Christ. But his aggressive stance on that and other issues provoked backlash. He was deposed and imprisoned for two years, during which time, being without books, he wrote one entitled *The Combat.* He escaped to Southern France and supported himself by tutoring rich children. Being restored to his bishopric, he was soon deposed again. This time he became abbot of Alna, but he argued with his monks about the Eucharist. They sighed with relief when he returned a third time to Verona. Once again he was exiled, returning to the abbotship of Alna. He stayed there awhile then moved to other positions here and there before dying on *April 25, 974.*

Love each other as brothers and sisters and honor others more than you do yourself. Never give up. Eagerly follow the Holy Spirit and serve the Lord. Let your hope make you glad. Be patient in time of trouble and never stop praying. And do your best to live at peace with everyone. (Romans 12:10–12, 18)

Mass Murder

Under Pope Sixtus IV, builder of the Sistine Chapel, the nepotism of the Renaissance papacy reached its worst. The Vatican was a flurry with his sixteen nephews, two brothers, and three sisters who continually injected themselves into Italian and church affairs. They became the leading figures of Rome. They traveled with vast retinues, feasted at banquets, dressed in pearl-embroidered clothes, and slept with endless partners in luxuriant beds.

But they soon clashed with their rivals in pleasure and power, the Medici family, based in Florence. The Medici banking firm had been the traditional Vatican bankers. But when conflicts arose, Sixtus transferred the vast papal fortunes to another family of bankers, the Pazzi. The Medici counterattacked, tempers flared, and in 1478, with the pope's knowledge, his nephews and bankers hatched a plan to murder Lorenzo and Julian Medici.

On Sunday, *April 26, 1478*, the two Medici brothers entered the cathedral in Florence for Easter mass. They were, according to their custom, unarmed and unguarded. The service began. Suddenly, as the priest lifted the bread of the Eucharist into the air, Julian felt a stabbing pain pierce his chest. The dagger was withdrawn, then thrust again and again. He died quickly. Lorenzo was attacked at the same instant. He instinctively flung his cape around his arm, forming a shield, and fought off his attackers.

His rage was unquenchable. He tracked down the conspirators and had them hung or thrown from palace windows. Their ears and noses were cut off, and they were hacked to pieces, dragged through the streets, and thrown into the river Arno.

Sixtus retaliated by excommunicating Lorenzo, suspending all religious services in Florence, and launching a futile two-year war against the city. The two men remained enemies till 1484, when Sixtus died. Lorenzo the Magnificent, as he was called, lived eight years longer, then died at age forty-three after drinking a mixture of jewels prescribed by physicians for his stomach pains.

We know what love is because Jesus gave his life for us. That's why we must give our lives for each other. (1 John 3:16)

April 27 Two Men, Two Martyrs

April 27 belongs to two martyrs. They never knew one another, never met, and indeed, lived centuries apart. One was married on this day, then killed shortly afterward. The other marks this as the day of his death. The latter was a Christian named Pollio in the town of Gibalea (modern Vinkovce, Hungary). On *April 27, 304*, he was hauled before a judge who demanded his name. "Pollio," he said.

"Are you a Christian?"

"Yes."

"What office do you hold?" Pollio replied that he was chief of the readers in his church, one whose duty it was to read God's Word to the congregation. For that offense, Pollio was promptly burned to death.

Sixteen hundred years later, another Christian named Roy Orpin, a New Zealander, considered missionary service. He had been deeply moved by the martyrdom of John and Betty Stam in China. He went to Thailand, and there, on *April 27, 1961*, married an Englishwoman named Gillian. She was also a missionary in that country. At the reception the two sang a duet, the hymn "Calvary."

The couple moved into a shanty in a Thai village and spent their first year of marriage amid growing danger. Violence was escalating in Southeast Asia. Gillian became pregnant, and Roy became afraid. "I had no peace," he wrote friends, "until I remembered 2 Corinthians 10:5." Gillian moved to a regional town having a missionary hospital while Roy stayed in the village of Bitter Bamboo to work with a small band of Christians. Suddenly three robbers appeared, demanded his valuables, and shot him.

He was taken to a government hospital, and Gillian rushed to his side. He lingered four days. His dying wish was for his wife to join him in singing a favorite hymn. The two lovers raised faltering voices and sang, "Jesus! I am resting, resting / In the joy of what Thou art; / I am finding out the greatness / Of thy loving heart." Then Roy, at age twenty-six, passed away. They had been married less than thirteen months.

We live in this world, but we don't act like its people or fight our battles with the weapons of this world. Instead, we use God's power that can destroy fortresses. We destroy arguments and every bit of pride that keeps anyone from knowing God. We capture people's thoughts and make them obey Christ. (2 Corinthians 10:3–5)

The *Bounty* Bible

The English ship *Bounty*, commanded by Lieutenant William Bligh, journeyed to the South Pacific in 1787, to collect plants of the breadfruit tree. Sailors signed on gladly, considering the voyage a trip to paradise. Having no second-in-command, Captain Bligh appointed his young friend Fletcher Christian to the post. The *Bounty* stayed in Tahiti six months, and the sailors, led by happy-go-lucky Fletcher Christian, enjoyed paradise to the full. When time came for departure, some of the men wanted to stay behind with their island girls. Three men, trying to desert, were flogged. The mood on ship darkened, and on *April 28, 1789*, Fletcher Christian staged the most famous mutiny in history. Bligh and his supporters were set adrift in an overloaded lifeboat (which they miraculously navigated thirty-seven hundred miles to Timor).

The mutineers aboard the *Bounty* began quarreling about what to do next. Christian returned to Tahiti, where he left some of the mutineers, kidnapped some women, took some slaves, and traveled a thousand miles to uninhabited Pitcairn Island. There the little group quickly unraveled. They distilled whiskey from a native plant. Drunkenness and fighting marked their colony. Disease and murder eventually took the lives of all the men except for one, Alexander Smith, who found himself the only man on the island, surrounded by an assortment of women and children.

Then an amazing change occurred. Smith found the *Bounty's* neglected Bible. As he read it, he took its message to heart, then began instructing the little community. He taught the colonists the Scriptures and helped them obey its instructions. The message of Christ so transformed their lives that twenty years later in 1808, when the *Topaz* landed on the island, it found a happy society of Christians, living in prosperity and peace, free from crime, disease, murder—and mutiny. Later the Bible fell into the hands of a visiting whaler who brought it to America. In 1950, it was returned to the island. It now resides on display in the church in Pitcairn as a monument to its transforming message.

People of Israel, what does the LORD your God want from you? The LORD wants you to respect and follow him, to love and serve him with all your heart and soul, and to obey his laws and teachings that I am giving you today. Do this, and all will go well for you. (Deuteronomy 10:12–13)

April 29 Death by Exhaustion

Giacomo Benincasa, dyer of fabrics in Siena, Italy, named his twenty-third child Catherine. Their house sat on a hillside, the basement containing dye rooms. Atop the hill sat the church of St. Dominic over which, when Catherine was seven, she saw a vision of Jesus. From that day she yearned to serve Christ.

At age twelve she so resisted her father's pressure to marry that he said, "May God preserve us, dearest daughter, from trying to set ourselves against the will of God. We have long seen that it was no childish whim of thine, and now we know clearly that it is the Spirit of God." He gave her a room near his dye quarters, and there Catherine made herself a chapel.

Catherine's personality burned like a knife, and she soon inserted herself without invitation into community and church affairs, becoming the most outspoken Italian woman of the Middle Ages. She railed against the death sentence of a young man convicted of criticizing the government, and she accompanied him to his execution, snapping up his decapitated head and arousing public protest. She cared for prisoners. When the Black Death swept Italy, Catherine was everywhere giving aid.

Catherine fumed and stormed about corruption in the church. She denounced materialism and immorality in the monasteries. "Those who should be the temples of God," she wrote, "are the stables of swine." She fired letters like missiles, keeping three secretaries busy at a time. She told Pope Gregory it would be better for him to resign than to founder, and "Do not be a boy, but a man!" She negotiated peace treaties. She was instrumental in moving the papacy from France back to Rome.

It's no wonder that on *April 29, 1380*, she died at age thirty-two of exhaustion from these and other labors. Her last words: "Dear children, let not my death sadden you; rather rejoice that I am leaving a place of many suffering to be united forever with my most sweet and loving Bridegroom."

Next to St. Francis, Catherine of Siena is the most celebrated of the Italian saints.

Don't get tired of helping others. You will be rewarded when the time is right, if you don't give up. We should help people whenever we can, especially if they are followers of the Lord. (Galatians 6:9–10)

The Tempest

During its first three centuries, the church met persecution in sporadic intervals around the empire. But nothing compared with the tempest that befell it during the days of Roman emperor Diocletian. Diocletian, seizing power in a coup, appointed fellow-soldier Maximian as coemperor and two other men as assistants, Constantius and Galerius. The four ruled the empire, east and west, conservatively and with a philosophy of traditional values.

"Traditional values," for ancient Rome, excluded Christianity. Though Diocletian himself seemed tolerant at first of Christians (his wife and daughter were believers), Galerius was strongly anti-Christian. His military prowess and battlefield victories gave him increasing influence. Slowly and methodically he painted Christians as enemies. He pushed through a series of persecutions against Christians, beginning with the destruction of a church in Nicomedia on February 23, 303. In rapid fire, several edicts were issued against the church, the last and worst being published on *April 30, 304*.

No one can describe the carnage. Christians were dismissed from their positions, their civil rights suspended. Church buildings were set afire. Copies of the Scriptures were burned in the marketplaces. Pastors and church leaders were caught and executed, many by lions in the coliseums. In Phrygia one whole community was wiped out. Other Christians were thrown into squalid prisons or sent to dreaded mines. All former persecutions were forgotten in the horror of this last and greatest storm.

But the empire gradually grew sick of the killing. Executioners were exhausted, and even the lions, it is said, grew tired of Christian flesh. Galerius, meanwhile, found he was dying of a disease commonly known as "being eaten with worms." On *April 30, 311*, anniversary of the earlier edict, he issued another in which he suspended persecution against Christians if they would pray for his recovery. From a thousand prisons, mines, and labor camps, the scarred warriors of Christ streamed home.

Many of them no doubt prayed for Galerius, but he did not recover. Some five days after he signed the edict, the worms finished their work.

Herod . . . sat down on his throne and made a speech. The people shouted, "You speak more like a god than a man!" At once an angel from the Lord struck him down because he took the honor that belonged to God. Later, Herod was eaten by worms and died. God's message kept spreading. (Acts 12:21, 24)

On This Day in Christian History...

MAY

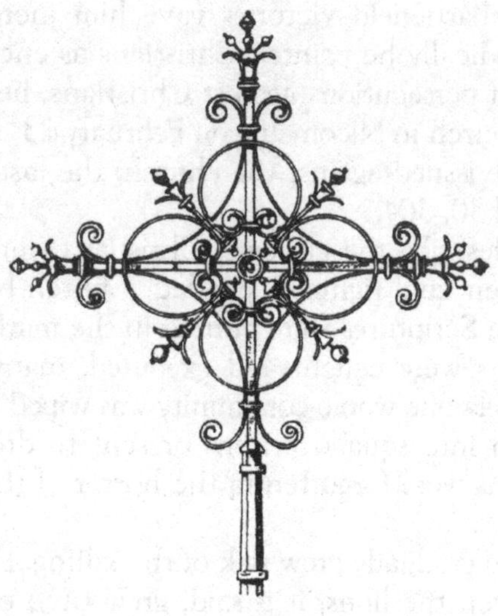

1680's Scotland - Soldiers killed Scottish Presbyterians at will.

John Brown Finds a Wife

May 1

The mid-1680s is remembered as the "Killing Time" in Scotland. Royal regiments martyred Scottish Presbyterians at will. Despite the danger, Presbyterian John Brown fell in love with Isabell Weir. He proposed to her but warned that he would one day seal his testimony with blood. Isabell replied, "If it be so, I will be your comfort. The Lord has promised me grace." They were married in a secret glen by the outlawed minister Alexander Peden. "These witnesses of your vows," said Peden, beginning the illegal ceremony, "have come at risk of their lives to hear God's word and his ordinance of marriage." The vows were spoken; then Peden drew Isabell aside, saying, "You have got a good husband. Keep linen for a winding-sheet beside you; for in a day when you least expect it, thy master shall be taken."

The Brown home soon included two children. It was happy, filled with prayer and godly conversation. Fugitive preachers were hidden and cared for there. But on *May 1, 1685*, John rose at dawn, singing Psalm 27, to find the house surrounded by soldiers. The family filed onto the lawn. The commander, Claverhouse, shouted to John, "Go to your prayers; you shall immediately die." Kneeling, John prayed earnestly for his wife, pregnant again, and for his children. Then he rose, embraced Isabell, and said, "The day is come of which I told you when I first proposed to you."

"Indeed, John. If it must be so, I can willingly part with you."

"This is all I desire," replied John. "I have no more to do but to die." He kissed his children; then Claverhouse ordered his men to shoot. The soldiers hesitated. Snatching a pistol, Claverhouse placed it to John's head and blew out his brains. "What thinkest thou of thy husband now, woman?" he snarled. Isabell, fixing Claverhouse in her gaze, told him she had never been so proud of him. Claverhouse mounted his horse and sped away, troops in tow. Isabell tied John's head in a napkin and sat on the ground weeping with her children until friends arrived to comfort them.

Armies may surround me,
but I won't be afraid;
war may break out,
but I will trust you.
I ask only one thing, LORD:
Let me live in your house
every day of my life
to see how wonderful you are
and to pray in your temple. (Psalm 27:3–4)

May 2

A Trumpet's Voice

Giffordgate, Scotland, outside Haddington, was an ardently Catholic village containing several churches, two monasteries, an abbey, and a farming couple named Knox who reared a child named John. The lad excelled at Haddington Grammar School, where his teacher proclaimed him the most brilliant pupil he had ever had. John entered the University of Glasgow, then St. Andrews University, where the gusts of the Reformation tugged at his Catholic heart.

Knox spent the next twenty years as a village priest and college lecturer. Then one day, listening to a Mr. Williams preach Reformation truth, he was struck as with an arrow. Soon thereafter he "cast anchor" by faith in Christ alone. His Reformation ideas put him at risk, and for years he alternated between flight and imprisonment (once chained to the oars of a galley ship). He finally settled down in relative safety on the Continent where he studied, wrote, discussed, and kept an eye on his native land.

In 1559, he sensed it was time to return. England's Queen Mary had been replaced by the more Protestant Elizabeth, and the groups of Protestant refugees in Europe were abuzz with excitement. Protestants began streaming back into England, and in late April, Knox himself set sail for Scotland, determined to "blow the Lord's trumpet" gallantly.

He landed on *May 2, 1559*, to find a nation on the knife edge of chaos. Mary of Guise, queen regent and mother of young Mary, Queen of Scots, was railing against Protestants. Civil war was threatening. Knox's presence and preachments so inspired the people that the English ambassador reported, "The voice of one man is able in one hour to put more life in us than five hundred trumpets continually blustering in our ears."

The government fought Protestants tooth and nail until June 10, 1560, when the queen regent died. The Treaty of Edinburgh temporarily ended the conflict, and the Reformation took hold. More storms lay ahead, and the aging Knox grew surly. But he managed to lead a bloodless revolution in Scotland and establish the faith of a nation.

Sound the trumpet on Zion!
Call the people together.
Show your sorrow
by going without food.
Make sure that everyone
is fit to worship me. (Joel 2:15–16)

To Serve the Armies

May 3

Before the Civil War, few chaplains served with American armies. But on *May 3, 1861*, the Southern Congress approved Bill 102, stating, "There shall be appointed by the President chaplains to serve the armies of the Confederate States during the existing war." The following year on *May 3*, Rev. A. C. Hopkins, Presbyterian pastor from Martinsburg, West Virginia, joined them, commissioned as chaplain of the Second Virginia Regiment.

Hopkins wasted no time. On May 16, he led the men in a day of fasting and prayer. Two days later he conducted Sunday services at Mossy Creek. The ensuing week found him consumed by the wounded, dying, and dead.

During the Seven Days' Battle near Richmond, he marched all day in the hot sun and spent a sleepless night, ministering to the wounded and dying. The next morning, attempting to preach to his men on the line, he collapsed, strength gone. He was carried to the rear to recover, but when he returned to the front ten days later, he learned that his best friends were dead. Hopkins sank into despondency. Heavy losses at Malvern Hill further drained him, and Hopkins felt he could no longer continue.

He retreated for a season of intense prayer, and soon Bible classes were organized and flourished. Evangelists visited the brigade, and religious services were followed by group discussions, prayer meetings, and baptisms. Large sums were raised to provide Christian literature for ravaged cities. Generals and officers were saved, and prayer meetings were conducted three times daily.

Between 100,000 and 200,000 Union soldiers and approximately 150,000 Southern troops were converted during the Civil War revivals. Whole armies on both sides became vast fields, ready for harvest. With the Civil War, chaplains such as A. C. Hopkins, who continued hard in service until the bitter end, earned a lasting place with American troops around the world.

Don't be afraid! I am with you.
From both east and west
I will bring you together.
I will say to the north
and to the south,
"Free my sons and daughters!
Let them return
from distant lands.
They are my people—
I created each of them
to bring honor to me." (Isaiah 43:5–7)

Weak Lungs

Sickness proved a blessing for W. Robertson Nicoll, for it determined his career and ministry. He was born with weak lungs in 1851. His mother, brother, and sister died from tuberculosis. He was raised by his father, Pastor Harry Nicoll, whose church numbered a hundred souls—but whose library numbered seventeen thousand books.

Inheriting his dad's love for literature, Robertson began a weekly column for the Aberdeen *Journal*. He started pastoring, but doctors told him his lungs were too weak for preaching. He contracted typhoid and pleurisy, resigned his church, and retreated to his books. Here Robertson found his calling.

He was already editing a magazine called the *Expositor.* In 1886, he began the *British Weekly.* It became a leading Christian journal in Britain. He then started the *Bookman*, and two years later the *Woman at Home* appeared in magazine stalls. While editing his four periodicals, Robertson began publishing books (he read two books a day throughout his life). *The Expositor's Bible*, a series of fifty volumes, was released between 1888 and 1905. Then *The Expositor's Greek New Testament* appeared. Robertson persuaded Alexander Maclaren to issue his expositions; then he found and developed other writers. In all, Robertson edited hundreds of titles and wrote forty books of his own. He became the most prolific and respected Christian journalist in the English-speaking world.

In 1909, while being knighted, he said, "I never contemplated a literary career. I had expected to go on as a minister, doing literary work in leisure times, but my fate was sealed for me." His illness forced him to do much of his work propped in bed amid the clutter of newspapers, books, pipes, and cigarette ashes. His cats purred nearby, and he always kept a fire burning, claiming that fresh air was the devil's invention. His library contained twenty-five thousand volumes, including five thousand biographies. "I have read every biography I could lay my hands on," he said, "and not one has failed to teach me something."

Sir W. Robertson Nicoll died on *May 4, 1923.* Among his last words were, "I believe everything I have written about immortality!"

"Rain and snow fall from the sky.
But they don't return
without watering the earth
that produces seeds to plant
and grain to eat.
That's how it is with my words.
They don't return to me
without doing everything
I send them to do." (Isaiah 55:10–11)

Justinian and Jesus

The fourth, fifth, and sixth centuries rumbled with prolonged controversy about the nature of Christ, and numerous councils convened to grapple with this issue. The Council of Nicaea, in 325, said that Christ was fully divine. Fifty years later the Council of Constantinople proclaimed Christ fully human. The Council of Chalcedon, in 451, formulated the famous creed that Christ is "truly God and truly man . . . two natures without confusion, without change, without division, or without separation . . ."

On this day in Christian history, *May 5, 553*, another council was convoked, this one by Emperor Justinian in Constantinople. Justinian, brilliant and tireless, longed to be religious. He spent many nights in prayer and fasting and endless days in theological study. He built the fabulous cathedral of Hagia Sophia and spoke longingly of a unified church.

But Justinian was also vain, ambitious, ostentatious, and easily influenced. His beautiful wife, Theodora, daughter of a bear trainer, was ruthless, and she controlled him like a marionette. Unable to understand the two natures of Christ, she held the Monophysite view—that Jesus had no human nature but possessed only a divine nature, clothed somehow in human flesh. At the Council of Constantinople, Justinian, manipulated by his wife, issued a decree favorable to the Monophysites.

Pope Vigilius had refused to attend the council due to fear for his safety and because of the preponderance of Eastern bishops. In Rome he received news of the council's actions with disdain but eventually accepted its decisions as unimportant. Monophysite views, however, continue to this day in Abyssinia, Syria, and in the Coptic church of Egypt.

And Justinian? He eventually became a full-fledged heretic, preaching that the body of Christ, being incorruptible, could not have experienced suffering and death. He died in 565, unrepentant, at age eighty-three, his later years darkened by perpetual disasters.

Healthy Christianity demands both a correct theological knowledge of Christ and a personal knowledge of the Savior through faith and obedience. Justinian grappled with the former, never arrived at the latter, and makes us wonder what the Lord thinks of his title in history—Justinian the Great.

In the beginning was the one
who is called the Word.
The Word was with God
and was truly God.
From the very beginning
the Word was with God.
And with this Word,
God created all things. (John 1:1–3)

Sacked Again

In 1523, Giulio de' Medici became Pope Clement VII. Martin Luther was causing problems at the time, but portents soon appeared of greater distresses to come. On April 8, 1527, as Clement blessed a crowd of ten thousand, a fanatic in leather loincloth mounted a nearby statue, shouting, "Thou bastard of Sodom! For thy sins Rome shall be destroyed. Repent and turn thee!" Not quite a month later on fog-shrouded *May 6, 1527*, a vast army of barbarians burst through Rome's walls. They had been sent—but were no longer controlled—by Emperor Charles V. The troops were hungry, unpaid, reduced to tatters, and rabid.

The defending Roman and Swiss guards were annihilated. The barbarians pillaged, plundered, and burned with abandon. They entered hospitals and orphanages, slaughtering the occupants. Women of every age were attacked; nuns were herded into bordellos; priests were molested. The banks and treasuries were looted, the rich flogged until they turned over their last coin. Children were flung from high windows. Tombs were plundered, churches stripped, libraries and archives burned. Priceless manuscripts became bedding for horses. Drunken soldiers strutted around in papal garments, parodying holy rites. Within a week two thousand bodies were floating in the Tiber, and nearly ten thousand more awaited burial. Rats and dogs eviscerated the bloating, fetid corpses that piled up in the city.

Pope Clement had barely made it into the safety of the Castle of St. Angelo, and from its towers he helplessly watched the ravaging of his city. "Why did you take me from the womb?" he wailed. "Would that I had been consumed."

As news spread over Europe, Protestants interpreted the sack of Rome as divine retribution, and even some Catholics agreed. "We who should have been the salt of the earth decayed until we were good for nothing," wrote Cardinal Cajetan, Luther's contestant at Augsburg. "Everyone is convinced that all this has happened as a judgment of God on the great tyranny and disorders of the papal court."

My people are being wiped out,
and children lie helpless
in the streets of the city.
Those who pass by
shake their heads and sneer
as they make fun and shout,
"What a lovely city you were,
the happiest on earth,
but look at you now!" (Lamentations 2:11, 15)

I Must Tell Jesus

Many New Testament promises have corresponding verses in the Old Testament that reinforce their power. For example, when Peter said, "God cares for you, so turn all your worries over to him" (1 Peter 5:7), he was but restating David's words in Psalm 55:22: "Our LORD, we belong to you. We tell you what worries us, and you won't let us fall."

Elisha A. Hoffman loved those verses. He was born *May 7, 1839*, in Orwigsburg, Pennsylvania. His father was a minister, and Elisha followed Christ at a young age. He attended Philadelphia public schools, studied science, then pursued the classics at Union Seminary of the Evangelical Association. He worked for eleven years with the association's publishing house in Cleveland, Ohio. Then, following the death of his young wife, he returned to Pennsylvania and devoted thirty-three years to pastoring Benton Harbor Presbyterian Church.

Hoffman's pastime was writing hymns, many of which were inspired by pastoral incidents. One day, for example, while calling on the destitute of Lebanon, Pennsylvania, he met a woman whose depression seemed beyond cure. She opened her heart and poured on him her pent-up sorrows. Wringing her hands, she cried, "What shall I do? Oh, what shall I do?" Hoffman knew what she should do, for he had himself learned the deeper lessons of God's comfort. He said to the woman, "You cannot do better than to take all your sorrows to Jesus. You must tell Jesus."

Suddenly the lady's face lighted up. "Yes!" she cried, "That's it! I must tell Jesus." Her words echoed in Hoffman's ears, and he mulled them over as he returned home. He drew out his pen and started writing, "I must tell Jesus! I must tell Jesus! / I cannot bear my burdens alone; / I must tell Jesus! I must tell Jesus! / Jesus can help me, Jesus alone."

Hoffman lived to be ninety, telling Jesus his burdens and giving the church such hymns as "What a Wonderful Savior," "Down at the Cross," "Are You Washed in the Blood?," "Leaning on the Everlasting Arms," and a thousand more.

The Scriptures say,
"God opposes proud people,
but he helps everyone
who is humble."
Be humble in the presence of God's mighty power, and he will honor you when the time comes. God cares for you, so turn all your worries over to him. (1 Peter 5:5–7)

Fighting Fundamentalist

When theological liberalism invaded America in the early 1900s, an army of fundamentalists rose to defend the faith. Many were wise soldiers of the cross, but some were . . . well, overzealous.

J. Frank Norris grew up in a dilapidated shack in Texas. His father, an alcoholic sharecropper, beat him. He was converted as a teen, his mother telling him he was "someone of great worth who would be a leader of men." Entering Baylor University, he dismayed classmates by predicting he would one day "preach in the greatest pulpit in the world."

He was contentious. One day prankish students released a howling dog during chapel, and President O. H. Cooper, losing his temper, hurled the animal from the third-floor window. Norris notified the Society for the Prevention of Cruelty to Animals and led a student protest, resulting in Cooper's resignation.

Following graduation, Norris pastored Fort Worth's First Baptist Church, soon making it the largest Protestant church in America. In 1935, he accepted Temple Baptist Church in Detroit and pastored both churches simultaneously, shuttling twelve hundred miles between them for the rest of his life. He became one of America's best-known preachers, his voice flooding airwaves, his articles filling publications. He was everywhere.

And he was contentious everywhere. Once from his pulpit he censured Fort Worth's Catholic mayor. The following Saturday while Norris was preparing his sermon, a friend of the mayor called on him. Soon four shots rang out, and the visitor fell dead. Norris was released on bond that afternoon. He immediately revised his sermon, and the next day all Fort Worth came to hear him preach from Romans 8:1: "If you belong to Christ Jesus, you won't be punished." His trial preoccupied the nation, the jury finally declaring he had shot in self-defense.

Norris continued his combative ministry, winning souls, defending orthodoxy, fighting vice, attracting and repelling listeners. On *May 8, 1947*, editor Ralph McGill of the *Atlanta Constitution* wrote, "The Rev. J. Frank Norris and others like him, is one good, sound reason why there are fifty million Americans who do not belong to any church at all."

Norris died of heart failure shortly afterward, and only heaven knows whether he did more harm or good.

I am not trying to please people. I want to please God. Do you think I am trying to please people? If I were doing that, I would not be a servant of Christ. (Galatians 1:10)

A Formidable Caravan

Count Nikolaus Ludwig von Zinzendorf has been called the *rich young ruler who said* yes." Born into one of Europe's leading families, he gave his life to Christ, established a Christian community at his Herrnhut estate and oversaw the sending of the first missionaries in Protestant history. Then late in life, Zinzendorf married his beloved Anna.

Three years later his strength ebbed. He pushed himself to finish some writing projects, but he noticed that Anna, too, was growing weaker. On Sunday, May 4, 1760, they attended church together but with difficulty. Anna returned to her bed. The next day Nikolaus was unable to eat much lunch, and he complained of thirst. He visited Anna's sickbed, then fell into bed himself. Speech became difficult, and it grew apparent he and Anna were both dying in rooms next to each other.

On May 8, David Nitshmann visited them. Nikolaus roused himself, reminisced, and said, "Did you suppose in the beginning, that the Savior would do as much as we now really see in the various Moravian settlements, amongst other denominations, and amongst the heathen? I only entreated of him a few firstfruits, but there are now thousands. Nitshmann, what a formidable caravan from our church already stands around the Lamb."

At midnight he was seized by a coughing spasm, and at nine o'clock the next morning, *May 9, 1760*, he told his son-in-law, John Watteville: "My dear John, I am about to go to the Savior. I am ready. I am resigned to his will, and he is satisfied with me . . . I am ready to go to him. Nothing more stands in my way." His eyes lingered another hour; then they closed. Watteville began praying, "Lord, now lettest thou thy servant depart in peace. The Lord bless thee, and keep thee . . . The Lord lift up his countenance upon thee and give thee peace." At the word *peace* Zinzendorf stopped breathing.

When Anna was told, she said, "I have the happiest prospect of you all. I will soon be going to him." She watched his burial from her window, then thirteen days later joined him.

Now the time has come for me to die. My life is like a drink offering being poured out on the altar. I have fought well. I have finished the race, and I have been faithful. So a crown will be given to me for pleasing the Lord. (2 Timothy 4:6–8)

May 10 Knights of the Temple

When the Crusades made it possible for medieval Christians to again visit the Holy Land, the question of security arose. How could pilgrims be safe from banditry? In 1118, Hugh de Payens, a knight of Campagne, joined eight others in a solemn vow to protect European travelers, thus organizing the Knights of Christ and of the Temple of Solomon. Hugh obtained church sanction, and the Templars, as they were called, grew quickly in influence and wealth. They purchased property and set up an organization across Christendom. They acquired castles and became an elite military force coveted and often hired by rulers. As their wealth increased, they established financial institutions in Paris and London.

In 1305, Philip the Fair of France, eyeing their wealth, used a disgruntled knight to bring charges against the order. The initiation rites involved blasphemy and homosexuality, it was claimed. The Templars, it was alleged, in secret admission ceremonies forced recruits to deny Christ, to spit on the cross, and to kiss the posteriors and navels of fellow knights. On the night of October 13, 1307 ("the accursed day"), all the Templars in France were rounded up and arrested. Philip used torture to obtain confessions, and many died in agony. Pope Clement was persuaded to disband the Templars and expand the persecution across Europe.

But Paris remained the center of suffering, and on *May 10, 1310*, fifty-four knights were burned alive in one mass inferno. Thirty-six more died under torture, four more were burned a week later, and hundreds perished in prison. The twenty-second (and last) grand master of the order, Jacques de Molay, was reserved for burning another day. On the eve of March 12, 1314, he was led in front of Notre Dame and tied to the stake. According to sources, while the flames were shooting around him, he summoned the pope and king to meet him at the judgment within a year.

Pope Clement died a few weeks later of a loathsome disease, and Philip, at age forty-six, perished in a hunting accident within six months.

I saw a great white throne with someone sitting on it . . . I also saw all the dead people standing in front of that throne. Every one of them was there, no matter who they had once been. Several books were opened, and then the book of life was opened. The dead were judged by what those books said they had done.
(Revelation 20:11–12)

The New Rome

Early Christianity developed several centers of gravity. The first was Rome, home of Catholic Christianity (and from it, Protestantism). Another came to be Constantinople, source of the Eastern or Orthodox branches of the church.

Constantinople was born in 324, when Emperor Constantine, believing the future lay in the East rather than the West, decided to move his capital from Rome to Byzantium, a site on the eastern flank of Europe, astride the Bosporus. He led his aides, engineers, and priests on a march around its harbor and hills, tracing the boundaries of his envisioned capital. He imported thousands of workers and artisans to build its walls, buildings, palaces, squares, streets, and porticoes. He placed sculptures in the parks and fountains in the forums. Before long there was a fabulous hippodrome, a prized university, 5 imperial palaces, 9 palaces for dignitaries, 4,388 mansions, 322 streets, 1,000 shops, 100 places of amusement, splendid baths, magnificent churches, and a swelling population. It was a city that shimmered in the sunshine.

The New Rome was dedicated as capital of the Eastern Empire on *May 11, 330*. Paganism was officially ended, Christianity was embraced, and the bishop (or patriarch) of Constantinople rivaled the bishop of Rome. Here the world's most beautiful church was built—the Church of Holy Wisdom, St. Sophia.

For a thousand years, Constantinople preserved the Eastern Roman Empire (also called the Byzantine Empire). Christianity moved along parallel tracks, Catholic and Orthodox. The pope and the patriarch rivaled each other, then rejected each other. The greatest division in Christianity was not the Reformation in 1517, splitting Catholics from Protestants, but the Great Schism in 1054, splitting apart the Eastern and Western branches of Christianity. From Constantinople came great Eastern Orthodox families of the church, such as the Russian and Greek Orthodox traditions.

In 1453, Constantinople fell to the Ottomans. The Church of St. Sophia was converted to a mosque, then to a museum. Constantinople is now Istanbul, and Turkey, once the bastion of Christianity, is the largest "unreached" nation on earth.

All of you nations,
come praise the LORD!
Let everyone praise him.
His love for us is wonderful;
his faithfulness never ends.
Shout praises to the LORD! (Psalm 117:1–2)

May 12 The Shoemaker's Book

William Carey was born in a forgotten village in the dullest period of the dullest of all centuries. His family was poor, and he was poorly educated. A skin affliction made him sensitive to outdoor work, so he apprenticed to a nearby shoemaker. When he didn't do well at cobbling, he opened a school to supplement his income. That didn't go well either. He married, but his marriage proved unhappy. A terrible disease took the life of his baby daughter and left Carey bald for life. He was called to pastor a small church, but he had trouble being ordained because of his boring sermons.

Not a likely prospect to become the Father of Modern Missions.

But when Carey borrowed a copy of Captain Cook's *Voyages*, the famous sailor's journals gripped him, and he started thinking of overseas evangelism. On the wall of his cobbler's shop, he hung a homemade map of the world, jotting down facts and figures beside the countries. And he began to feel that something should be done to reach the world for Christ.

Until then most Protestants believed the Great Commission had been given only to the original apostles. Carey insisted it was binding on all succeeding generations of Christians, an idea that brought scorn from many preachers. He was called a "miserable enthusiast," and at one Baptist meeting Dr. John C. Ryland, the man who had baptized him, said, "Young man, sit down! When God pleases to convert the heathen, he'll do it without consulting you or me."

The rebuke moved Carey to write a book, published on *May 12, 1792*: *An Enquiry into the Obligations of Christians, to use means for the Conversion of the Heathens in which the Religious State of the Different Nations of the World, the Success of Former Undertakings, and the Practicability of Further Undertakings, are Considered.*

Despite its unwieldy title, this eighty-seven-page book became a classic in Christian history that deserves a place alongside Luther's *Ninety-five Theses* in its influence on subsequent church history. It led to the formation of a missionary society, funds being collected in a snuff box. The proceeds were used to send Carey to India, launching the modern era of missions.

Go to the people of all nations and make them my disciples. Baptize them in the name of the Father, the Son, and the Holy Spirit, and teach them to do everything I have told you. I will be with you always, even until the end of the world. (Matthew 28:9–20)

The Boy Preacher

Fifteen-year-old David Marks, eyes blurred with tears, left home with a dollar in his pocket to preach the gospel. The "boy preacher" soon created a stir in the American Northeast, and he kept going for the next twenty-five years. He rode one horse nineteen thousand miles, preached to thousands, organized churches throughout New England, published books, wrote articles, taught school, and worked diligently in opposition to slavery and in support of foreign missions. Then he died from sheer exhaustion at age forty.

Just before sunset on *May 13, 1828*, Marks rode into the little town of Ancaster, Ontario, announcing he would preach in seven minutes in the park. A small crowd gathered, and he asked if anyone had a text he would like to hear preached. A man mockingly said, "Nothing!"

Marks immediately began preaching on *nothing.* God created the world from nothing, he said. God gave us laws in which there is nothing unjust. But, Marks continued, we have broken God's law, and there is nothing in us to justify us. There will be nothing to comfort sinners in death or hell. But while Christians have nothing of their own in which to boast, we have Christ. And in him, we have nothing to cause us grief, nothing to disturb our peace, and nothing to fear in eternity.

Finishing his sermon, Marks mounted his horse and traveled to the next village. But some time later, he returned to Ancaster. This time a larger group assembled, and the meeting house was opened to him. Marks preached *something* to them. He said there is something above all things. There is something in man designed to live forever, but there is also something in us that makes us unhappy. There is something about the gospel that reverses our unhappiness, something that gives us hope. There is something that will disturb the impenitent in death, but something resides in Christians that the world can't understand, and something in eternity to give us everlasting joy.

All that from an uneducated young circuit rider, his mind filled with Scripture and his heart full of Christ, who had *something* to say—and *nothing* to fear.

I am sure that nothing can separate us from God's love . . . Nothing in all creation can separate us from God's love for us in Christ Jesus our Lord! (Romans 8:38–39)

May 14 A Light to the Gentiles

John Berridge expected to follow his father into livestock, but he could never learn the ropes. His frustrated dad finally said, "John, I find you cannot form any idea of the price of cattle, and I shall have to send you to college to be a light to the Gentiles." Thus John went to Cambridge, then entered church work, but without personally experiencing the gospel.

His preaching was striking, his life upright, his energy boundless, his ministry worthless. His message, devoid of the death and resurrection of Christ, was like a solar system without the sun. For years he thrashed around brilliantly but fruitlessly.

In 1755, he became vicar in out-of-the-way Everton, and there at age forty-two he finally agonized about his own soul. "Lord," he began crying, "if I am right, keep me so; if I am not right, make me so, and lead me to the knowledge of the truth in Jesus." One morning as he sat before an open Bible, these words flashed to mind: "Cease from thine own works; only believe." He immediately started preaching salvation by grace through faith alone. Soon one of his parishioners visited him. "Why, Sarah," he said, "what is the matter?"

"I don't know," said the woman. "Those new sermons! I find we are all lost now. I can neither eat, drink, nor sleep. I don't know what will become of me." Others echoed the same cry. Berridge's church soon swelled with villagers giving their lives to Christ. People flocked from all parts, and the buildings proved too small. On *May 14, 1759*, Berridge began preaching outdoors. "On Monday," he wrote, "we called at a farm-house. After dinner I went into the yard, and seeing nearly 150 people, I called for a table and preached for the first time in the open air. We then went to Meldred, where I preached in a field to about 4,000 people."

His remaining thirty years found him preaching the gospel in season and out, indoors and out. He never married, always resided alone, and remained in rural parishes until his death at age seventy-seven in 1793. He was the Whitefield of the English countryside.

God treated me with kindness. His power worked in me, and it became my job to spread the good news. I am the least important of all God's people. But God was kind and chose me to tell the Gentiles that because of Christ there are blessings that cannot be measured. (Ephesians 3:7–8)

The Prodigal

"The Law of the LORD is perfect," says Psalm 19:7. "It gives us new life"—and sometimes in unexpected ways.

One of the most powerful personal evangelists of the nineteenth century was "Uncle" John Vassar, who grew up in his family's brewery in Poughkeepsie, New York. Following his conversion to Christ, he abandoned beer-making for soul-winning, and on *May 15, 1850*, he was commissioned as an agent for the American Tract Society of New York. Vassar took off across the country, never resting in his mission of selling Christian literature and asking everyone he met about their relationship with Christ.

On one occasion, traveling in the West, he visited the home of a praying wife whose husband was an infidel. She begged for a Bible, and Vassar gave her one and went his way. He had no sooner left when the husband, coming home, saw the book and was enraged. Seizing the Bible with one hand and the ax with the other, he hurried to the woodpile, where he placed it on the chopping block and hacked it crosswise in two. Returning to the house, he threw half of the destroyed Bible at his wife, saying, "As you claim a part of all the property around here, there is your share of this."

The other half he tossed into his tool shed.

Months later on a wet winter's day, the man, wanting to get away from his Christian wife, retreated to his shed. The time passed slowly, and in boredom he looked around for something to read. Thumbing through the mutilated Bible, his attention was caught by the story of the prodigal son in Luke 15. He became absorbed in the parable only to discover that its ending belonged to his wife's section. He crept into the house and secretly searched for the bottom half of the book, but was unable to find where his wife had hidden it.

Finally he broke down, asked her for it, and read the story again and again. In the process he came to the heavenly Father like a penitent prodigal returning home.

The son said, "Father, I have sinned against God in heaven and against you. I am no longer good enough to be called your son." But his father said to the servants, "Hurry and bring the best clothes and put them on him . . . This son of mine was dead, but has now come back to life. He was lost and has now been found." And they began to celebrate. (Luke 15:21–22, 24)

Swallowed Up

Henry Martyn was born in Cornwall, England, in 1781. His father was a well-to-do businessman, and Henry grew up amid comforts. He proved intelligent, excelled in school, and went on to Cambridge, graduating with honors in mathematics. The writings of missionary David Brainard helped bring Martyn to Christian surrender, and he soon contemplated foreign missions. "Let me forget the world," he said, "and be swallowed up in a desire to glorify God."

But he couldn't forget Lydia Grenfell. Henry was deeply in love with Lydia though she had no desire for Asian missionary service. A vicious war tore the young man apart. Should he go to India with God or remain in England with Lydia? He awakened throughout the night, his mind full of Lydia. He called her his "beloved idol." But, determined to do God's will, he said a final good-bye, and set sail.

At daybreak on *May 16, 1805*, Martyn went ashore at Calcutta and was met by William Carey, who soon nudged him into translation work. Martyn lost himself in ministry, preaching, establishing schools, and translating the Bible into three Asian languages. All the while he brooded over Lydia. On July 30, 1806, after much deliberation, he wrote, proposing marriage. Letters traveled slowly, and a year passed before he received a reply. Lydia's rejection hit the young man like a thunderbolt, and his health, always frail, began to falter. He wrote asking her to reconsider. She would not though she agreed to correspond friend to friend.

In 1810, his Hindustani New Testament ready for the printer, Martyn traveled to Persia hoping to recover his health. By 1812, he had grown so weak that an overland trip to England seemed the only solution. It would also, he knew, bring him to Lydia. He set out but didn't make it, dying en route at age thirty-one. When his journal was opened, the name Lydia, like the droning of sad music, was found on almost every page. But Henry Martyn had fulfilled his objective in coming to India. He had been swallowed up in a desire to glorify God, and the New Testament was read in three new languages.

Please listen, God, and answer my prayer!
I feel hopeless,
and I cry out to you from a faraway land.
Lead me to the mighty rock high above me.
Let me live with you forever
and find protection under your wings, my God. (Psalm 61:1–2, 4)

How About "Hallelujah!"

William Grimshaw was born in rural England in 1708, educated at Cambridge, and ordained to the ministry in 1731, without knowing Christ. Three years later while pastoring in Todmorden, he felt deep concern about his soul. He ceased his hunting, fishing, card-playing, and merrymaking, and began pleading with God for light. After several more years, the scales completely fell from his eyes. The gospel became real, and the Bible came alive. He told a friend that "if God had drawn up his Bible to heaven and sent me down another, it could not have been newer to me."

He moved to Haworth in Yorkshire and began a twenty-one-year ministry. Had he been in London, claim his biographers, he would have become one of the most famous preachers of the eighteenth century. As it was, Haworth was rough and uncivilized, a long, narrow village of brown stone. The main street was so steep that carriages traveled it at their own risk. Here Grimshaw labored in obscurity, but with great zeal. He gathered listeners wherever he could, in barns, fields, quarries, and pressed on them the gospel.

He once said, "When I die I shall then have my greatest grief and my greatest joy—my greatest grief that I have done so little for Jesus, and my greatest joy that Jesus has done so much for me."

But William Grimshaw's heart was broken by his son John, who, rejecting Christ, lived a careless, intemperate life. When William lay dying, John visited him. "Take care what you do," said William, "for you are not fit to die." Those words evidently haunted the young man, for one day he met a Haworth inhabitant who said, "I see you are riding the old parson's horse."

"Yes," replied John. "Once he carried a great saint, and now he carries a great sinner." But not for long, for John soon heeded his father's dying pleas and gave his heart to Christ. He died shortly afterward on *May 17, 1766*, saying, "What will my old father say when he sees I have got to heaven?"

How about *Hallelujah!*

If any of you has a hundred sheep, and one of them gets lost, what will you do? Won't you leave the ninety-nine in the field and go look for the lost sheep until you find it? Jesus said, "In the same way there is more happiness in heaven because of one sinner who turns to God than over ninety-nine good people who don't need to." (Luke 15:4, 7)

He Just Persisted

We often *rush* when we should *plod*, forgetting that we usually accomplish more by persisting than by hurrying. Sheldon Jackson was born on *May 18, 1834*, in the Mohawk Valley of New York. When he was four his parents dedicated him to God's service, and his ambition from youth was to be a missionary.

After graduating from Princeton Theological Seminary, he joined the thousands trekking to the American West. Most were searching for gold, land, and open skies. Wagon trains were leaving St. Louis daily. The golden spike tied East to West in 1866, as the Union Pacific Railway opened. Boom towns arose. Cowboys and mining camps, rowdy saloons and gunfighters filled the frontier. Jackson was everywhere, searching for souls with the fervor of a prairie fire. He once organized seven churches in fifteen days.

He stood just over five feet tall, but his size, he said, allowed him to sleep anywhere. His bed was a stagecoach floor, a saloon loft, a hollow log, a teepee, a canoe. Someone described him as "short, bewhiskered, bespectacled but a giant." And his field was immense. He served as superintendent of Presbyterian missions from New Mexico to Minnesota.

When the United States purchased Alaska, he headed there at once, and the North soon became his passion. He explored the dangerous, uncharted fog-hidden coasts of the Bering Sea and the Arctic Ocean. He established schools for the young and placed missionaries in the hamlets. He evangelized, established churches, and brought Bibles to the Eskimos. He worried that explorers and exploiters were slaughtering whales and seals, depriving Eskimos of their natural food supplies. So, braving criticism and ridicule, Sheldon raised two thousand dollars and brought reindeer from Siberia. Soon great herds were providing transportation, food, clothing, and livelihood for the people.

Sheldon made twenty-six trips to Alaska, and during fifty years of ministry he traveled a million miles through the West and North. He oversaw the establishing of 886 churches. Few men have ever so planted the Christian faith over such a wide area. His secret? His friends simply explained, "He never hurried. He just persisted."

A messenger you can trust
is just as refreshing
as cool water in summer.
Broken promises
are worse than rain clouds
that don't bring rain.
Patience and gentle talk
can convince a ruler
and overcome any problem. (Proverbs 25:13–15)

The Earthquake Synod

God is our . . . fortress," says Psalm 46. "And so, we won't be afraid! Let the earth tremble" (vv. 1–2). The trembling of the earth may even reassure God's children of his power, as happened on this day, St. Dunstan's Day, *May 19, 1382*. St. Dunstan's Day is named for the British politician who, having slighted the king, found himself banished to a monastery in Belgium. There he committed himself to Christ's cause, eventually returning to England and becoming archbishop of Canterbury. Dunstan died *May 19, 988*.

Three hundred years later another archbishop of Canterbury, William Courtenay, held sway. Courtenay, powerful and headstrong, raged against Oxford professor John Wycliffe, who criticized church teaching. Wycliffe believed the head of the church to be Christ, not the pope. He opposed selling indulgences and warned against superstitions associated with the mass. We are saved, he said, by faith in Christ, Scripture alone being our authority. He pre-Luthered Luther, and thus is called the *Morning Star of the Reformation*.

Courtenay tried repeatedly to convict Wycliffe, but the popular professor always bested him. Finally Courtenay summoned a special committee to examine Wycliffe's teachings, to condemn and destroy the Bible teacher. John Foxe tells the story: "Here is not to be passed over the great miracle of God . . . for when the archbishop with other doctors of divinity and lawyers, with a great company of babbling friars and religious persons, were gathered together to consult touching Wycliffe's books, when they were gathered in London to begin their business on St. Dunstan's day, after dinner, about two of the clock, the very hour and instant that they should go forward, a wonderful and terrible earthquake fell throughout all England: whereupon divers of them, being affrighted, thought it good to leave off from their determinate purpose."

Wycliffe later declared that the Lord sent the earthquake "because the friars had put heresy upon Christ. The earth trembled as it did when Christ was damned to bodily death." Wycliffe, however, didn't tremble when the earth did, for God was his fortress. But the archbishop's meeting has ever since been known in English history as the Earthquake Synod.

God is our mighty fortress,
always ready to help
in times of trouble.
And so, we won't be afraid!
Let the earth tremble
and the mountains tumble
into the deepest sea. (Psalm 46:1–2)

Tortured

God's grace arrives just as we need it, appropriate for every challenge. Even if we're lonely? Even if we're ill? Yes. Even if we're tortured? Even then.

Michael Sattler, born in Germany around 1490, became a Benedictine monk. As he studied Paul's letters, he grew dissatisfied, left the monastery, married, and became a Lutheran. Sometime later he became convinced of believer's baptism and became an Anabaptist of growing renown whose ministry attracted both converts and enemies.

Sattler, his wife, and a handful of associates were arrested in the mid-1520s, and imprisoned in the tower of Binsdorf, where he wrote a letter to his flock: "The brethren have doubtless informed you that some of us are in prison. Numerous accusations were preferred against us by our adversaries; at one time they threatened us with the gallows; at another with fire and sword. In this extremity, I surrendered myself entirely to the Lord's will, and prepared myself, together with all brethren and wife, to die for his testimony's sake."

On *May 20, 1527*, his torture, a prelude to execution, began at the city center, where his tongue was sliced. Chunks of flesh were torn from his body with red-hot tongs, and he was forged to a cart. On the way to the stake execution, the tongs were applied five times again. Still able to speak, the unshakable Sattler prayed for his persecutors. After being bound to a ladder with ropes and pushed into the fire, he admonished the people, the judges, and the mayor to repent and be converted. "Almighty, eternal God," he prayed, "Thou art the way and the truth: because I have not been shown to be in error, I will with Thy help to this day testify to the truth and seal it with my blood." As soon as the ropes on his wrists were burned, Sattler raised the two forefingers of his hand, giving the promised signal to his brothers that a martyr's death was bearable. Then the assembled crowd heard coming from his seared lips, "Father, I commend my spirit into Thy hands."

Sattler's wife was executed by drowning eight days later.

Others were made fun of and beaten with whips, and some were chained in jail. Still others were stoned to death or sawed in two or killed with swords. Some had nothing but sheep skins or goat skins to wear. They were poor, mistreated, and tortured. The world did not deserve these good people. (Hebrews 11:36–38)

Infinite Wisdom

Isaac Watts, called the "Father of English Hymns," wrote such classics as "O God Our Help in Ages Past," "Joy to the World," "At the Cross," and six hundred others. He was a small, odd man whose life was shaped by his father, Isaac senior. The elder Watts was repeatedly imprisoned for his Nonconformist beliefs. On *May 21, 1685*, he wrote this letter to his family from prison, addressing his comments especially to eleven-year-old Isaac: "We must endeavor by patient waiting to submit to His will without murmuring; and not to think amiss of His chastening us, knowing that all His works are the products of infinite wisdom." Watts then gave several charges to his son:

- Frequently read the Holy Scriptures, and that not as a task but as a delight.
- Understand the sinful state and begin betimes to be a praying Christian, remembering that prayer is the best weapon of a saint's defense.
- Remember the hope of salvation founded on Jesus Christ.
- Keep perpetually in mind that God is our Creator, and serve Him with a willing mind.
- Worship God in God's own way, that is, according to the rules in the Gospel and not according to the inventions or traditions of men.
- Do not entertain in your heart any popish doctrines, particularly that of praying to the saints or to the Virgin Mary or any other mere creature. Pray instead that God will give you knowledge of His truth, for it is a very dangerous time that you are like to live in.
- Do not entertain hard thoughts of God or of His ways because His people are persecuted, for Jesus Christ Himself was persecuted to death by wicked men for preaching the truth and doing good.
- Be dutiful and obedient to all superiors—to your grandfather, both grandmothers, and in a special manner to your mother.

Watts was soon afterward released from prison and lived to be eighty-five. It was he who planted the music of the gospel in his son's heart and who encouraged him to pursue it.

> Shout praises to the LORD,
> everyone on this earth.
> Be joyful and sing
> as you come in
> to worship the LORD!
> You know the LORD is God!
> He created us,
> and we belong to him. (Psalm 100:1–3)

The Forgotten Basin

The last half of our Lord's ministry was marred by envy and infighting among his followers. The disciples plotted against each other even on the eve of Christ's crucifixion, prompting him to wrap himself in a towel and wash their feet in a servant's basin.

The lesson was lost on many bishops during the ensuing centuries. As churches spread across the Roman world, the bishops of Antioch, Alexandria, and Rome assumed particular leadership. Antioch and Rome were, after all, prominent in the New Testament records, and the Alexandrian church traced its origin through the evangelist Mark to Peter. The Council of Nicaea placed these three bishops on more or less equal footing.

The bishop of Jerusalem, arguing his city deserved recognition, became the fourth world center of Christianity. Soon there was a fifth. Emperor Constantine decided to move the Roman capital to his new city on the Bosporus, and the bishop of Constantinople instantly assumed prominence. The ecumenical council, held in Constantinople in 381, said that the patriarch of Constantinople deserved honor "next to the bishop of Rome."

A low-grade rivalry arose between the two. It worsened in 451, when the Council of Chalcedon issued this decree, extending the authority of the bishop of Constantinople: "With reason did the fathers confer prerogatives on the throne of ancient Rome on account of her character as the imperial city; and moved by the same consideration, the bishops recognize the same prerogatives also in the most holy throne of New Rome."

Papal delegates from Rome protested on the spot, and on *May 22, 452*, Pope Leo launched three angry letters like warheads, addressed to the emperor, the empress, and the patriarch of Constantinople. Leo declared that the elevation of Constantinople was: (1) a work of pride, (2) an attack on the other centers of Christianity, (3) a violation of the rights given Rome by earlier councils, and (4) destructive to church unity. His letters only aggravated the situation. Eastern and Western Christianity drifted further apart until a complete schism occurred in 1054.

They had all, it seems, forgotten the basin and the towel.

And if your Lord and teacher has washed your feet, you should do the same for each other. I have set the example. (John 13:14–15)

The Thirty Years' War

Seventeenth-century Bohemia was a beautiful area at the center of Europe, encircled by mountains and highlands, home of the Moravians. It was the land of John Hus, who died for the Reformation before Luther even launched it. And it was filled with Hussites longing for freedom of worship.

But Bohemia was ruled by the Hapsburg king, Ferdinand II, a dedicated Catholic. He unleashed a campaign to re-Catholicize Bohemia, and on *May 23, 1618*, Bohemian rebels shouting the Protestant cause stormed the palace. They literally threw Ferdinand's governors out the window. The governors landed in a pile of manure (just where the rebels thought they belonged), and Ferdinand sent troops against the Protestants, defeating them soundly in January 1620, at the Battle of White Mountain. Protestants throughout Bohemia were endangered.

Jan Amos Comenius, pastor and Christian educator, lost his family to the war, and he himself barely escaped a burning house. His church members became fugitives; then they became refugees, having to flee their homeland. They packed their few belongings, left home and country, and plodded through bitter snows toward Poland. Arriving at the border, they turned and gazed a final time on their land. In a scene that later became a favorite of Christian artists, Comenius led his shivering flock in prayer for God to preserve in Bohemia "a hidden seed to glorify thy name." Finishing their prayer, the little flock trudged on.

Comenius never returned, never found a home, and when he died in 1670, he owned virtually nothing but a sack of tattered clothes. But he left the world 154 books that laid a foundation for modern Christian education.

Meanwhile, White Mountain wasn't the end of the war, but its beginning. Denmark entered the fray, then Sweden, then France. Europe was ravaged, and half of all Germans perished. Not until 1648 was the Treaty of Westphalia signed—thirty years after the initial revolt in Bohemia.

As for Comenius's prayer, it was answered a hundred years later when Count Zinzendorf gave the Bohemian offspring refuge at Herrnhut. It was the descendants of Comenius and his followers, gathered safely by Zinzendorf, who became the forerunners of the modern missionary movement.

Along the way someone said to Jesus, "I'll go anywhere with you!" Jesus said, "Foxes have dens, and birds have nests, but the Son of Man doesn't have a place to call his own." (Luke 9:57–58)

Storm Greater: Afraid!

Even when I am afraid," said the psalmist, "I keep on trusting you" (Ps. 56:3). John Wesley had never been so frightened as on January 25, 1736. He was aboard a small sailing ship somewhere in the mid-Atlantic in midwinter, en route to Georgia as a missionary to the native Indians, though as yet he himself had never been saved. A group of Moravian missionaries from Germany had booked passage on the same ship. The voyage was treacherous. Three storms had already battered the boat, and a fourth was brewing. Wesley scribbled in his journal, "Storm greater: afraid!" But the Moravians, showing no fear, persevered in their plans for a worship service. In the middle of their singing, a gigantic wave rose over the side of the vessel, splitting the mainsail, covering the ship, pouring water like Niagara between decks "as if the great deep had already swallowed us up."

The English passengers screamed as the ship lurched and pitched between towering waves. Wesley clung on for dear life. But the German missionaries didn't miss a note. Wesley, awestruck by their composure, went to the leader and asked, "Weren't you afraid?"

"I thank God, no."

"Were not your women and children afraid?"

"No," replied the man. "Our women and children are not afraid."

John Wesley's missionary labors in Georgia failed, and he returned to England saying, "I went to America to convert the Indians, but, oh, who shall convert me?" The Moravians, that's who. Back in London, Wesley attended a Moravian meeting in Aldersgate Street, *May 24, 1738*, and listened to someone reading from Luther's preface to Romans. He later said, "I felt my heart strangely warmed. I felt I did trust in Christ, Christ alone for salvation; and an assurance was given to me that he had taken away my sins, even mine."

Wesley became a famous evangelist and social reformer, with the world as his parish. But he himself was won to Christ by the power of a small group whose commitment to Christ was strong enough to keep them unflappable in a storm.

Have pity, God Most High!
My enemies chase me all day.
Many of them are pursuing
and attacking me,
but even when I am afraid,
I keep on trusting you.
I praise your promises!
I trust you and am not afraid. (Psalm 56:1–4)

The Eccentric Preacher

Charles Spurgeon once wrote a little book entitled *Eccentric Preachers.* He described eleven peculiar ministers, his concluding example being Billy Bray of Cornwall, England. Billy, an alcoholic miner, found the Lord at age twenty-nine. "In an instant the Lord made me so happy I cannot express what I felt," said Billy. "I shouted for joy. Everything looked new to me; the people, the fields, the cattle, the trees. I was like a man in a new world." Billy joined the Methodists and set out immediately to win others. His bursting, driving energy made some people call him a madman.

"But they meant 'glad man'!" said Billy.

He took Cornwall by storm. On meeting strangers, Billy would inquire about their souls; and he would shout "Glory!" whenever hearing of anyone being saved. Sometimes he would pick people up and spin them around the room. "I can't help praising God," he said. "As I go along the street I lift one foot and it seems to say 'Glory!' and I lift the other, and it seems to say, 'Amen!' And they keep on like that all the time I'm walking."

From age twenty-nine to his death at seventy-three, he danced and leaped and shouted his way through each day. He preached and built chapels and took orphans into his home. He fasted Saturday afternoon till Sunday night each week. When pressed to eat, he would say, "On Sunday I get my breakfast and dinner from the King's table, two good meals too."

When his wife died, Billy jumped around the room in excitement, shouting, "Bless the Lord! My dear Joey is gone up with the bright ones! Glory! Glory! Glory!" And when his doctor told him he, too, was dying, he shouted, "Glory! Glory to God! I shall soon be in heaven." Then lowering his voice, he added, "When I get up there, shall I give them your compliments doctor, and tell them you will be coming, too?"

His dying word as he fell asleep on *May 25, 1868*, was "Glory!"

"It does not seem so very horrible after all," commented Spurgeon, "that a man should be eccentric."

Shout praises to the LORD!
With all that I am,
I will shout his praises.
I will sing
and praise
the LORD God
for as long as I live. (Psalm 146:1–2)

A Quiet Life

Some lives crackle with adventure—great answers to prayers, narrow escapes, dramatic conversions, broad travel. But Christians with quieter lives often cast longer shadows. The life of Venerable Bede was so uneventful that little can be said about him. Yet few have left such a record of scholarship and faithfulness.

Bede was born about 672, in north England. At seven, probably orphaned, he went to live at a nearby monastery. The boy took to books, studying Scripture, biography, literature, music, and history. He pored over manuscripts—the church fathers, the Vulgate, the classics. He learned Latin, Greek, and Hebrew. By age thirty, he was adding to early literature with books of his own. "I always took delight," he said, "in learning, teaching, and writing." His *Ecclesiastical History of the English Nation* is meticulously accurate, setting a standard for historians. He became the greatest scholar of his era, the father of English history and theology.

In the spring of 735, Bede labored on his crowning work, translating the Gospel of John into Anglo-Saxon. On May 25, he told his assistant, "Go on quickly; I know not how long I shall hold out, and whether my Maker will not soon take me away." By early morning, *May 26, 735*, only one chapter remained, and Bede said, "Take your pen and write fast." He told a friend, "I have some little articles of value in my chest—pepper, napkins, and incense: Quickly bring the priests to me that I may distribute among them the gifts God has bestowed on me." He spoke to each priest, and they wept. "I have lived long," he said. "I desire to die and be with Christ."

Bede spent the day joyfully, and near evening his helper said that only one sentence remained to be translated. "Write quickly," Bede replied with satisfaction. The work finished, Bede sat on the floor of his small room and began singing, "Glory be to the Father, and to the Son, and to the Holy Ghost," and, finishing the hymn, passed quietly into the presence of the Lord.

If I live, it will be for Christ, and if I die, I will gain even more. I don't know what to choose. I could keep on living and doing something useful. It is a hard choice to make. I want to die and be with Christ, because that would be much better. But I know that all of you still need me. (Philippians 1:21–24)

Sunset

If a beautiful death authenticates a holy life, then we can feel good about John Calvin. On February 6, 1564, Calvin, fifty-five years old, stood for the last time in his pulpit at Saint Pierre in Geneva. In mid-sermon he was seized by a coughing fit and his mouth filled with blood. He slowly forced his way down the circular staircase from the pulpit, his sermon unfinished.

On Easter Sunday, April 2, he was carried back to Saint Pierre's and sat near the pulpit, listening as Theodore Beza preached. At the end of the service, Calvin joined the congregation in singing a final hymn, "Now lettest thou thy servant depart in peace." He was taken to his bed, still working feverishly on his papers. When friends begged him to rest, he replied, "What! Would you have the Lord find me idle when he comes?" On April 30, the Geneva Council gathered around him. He spoke to them, prayed for them, and gave his right hand to each one. The men left the bedroom weeping like children. Two days later Geneva's ministers paid a similar visit. Calvin asked pardon for his failings, pointed the men to Christ, and grasped their hands tenderly. They, too, parted with anguished tears.

When it appeared the end was near, his friend and mentor, eighty-year-old William Farel, set out on foot, walking a long distance, hoping to make it in time. He arrived, covered with dust, to join others who had gathered at the deathwatch. Calvin lingered, quoting Scripture and praying continually, until Saturday, *May 27, 1564*, just as the sun was setting. He passed from one life to another very quietly, without twitch or gasp or even a deeper sigh. "On this day with the setting sun," said Beza, "the brightest light in the Church of God on earth was taken to heaven!" Geneva mourned deeply.

Calvin had instructed that his body be laid in a common cemetery with no tombstone. He didn't want his grave becoming a shrine as tombs of earlier saints had become. It didn't—today his grave site is unknown.

"Lord, I am your servant,
and now I can die in peace,
because you have kept
your promise to me.
With my own eyes I have seen
what you have done
to save your people,
and foreign nations
will also see this.
Your mighty power is a light
for all nations
and it will bring honor
to your people Israel." (Luke 2:29–32)

Alleine's Alarm

While a chaplain at Oxford, Joseph Alleine often neglected his friends for his studies. "It is better they should wonder at my rudeness," he explained, "than that I should lose time; for only a few will notice the rudeness, but many will feel my loss of time." Though barely twenty-one, he was already "infinitely and insatiably greedy for the conversion of souls," devoting every moment to studying, preaching, and evangelizing.

In 1655, Joseph was called to a church in the west of England. He soon married, and his wife, Theodosia, later claimed his only fault was not spending more time with her. "Ah, my dear," he would say, "I know thy soul is safe; but how many that are perishing have I to look after?"

Joseph habitually rose at 4:00 in the morning, praying and studying his Bible until 8:00 AM. His afternoons were spent calling on the unconverted. He kept a list of the inhabitants of each street and knew the condition of each soul. "Give me a Christian that counts his time more precious than gold," he said. At the beginning of the week, he would remark, "Another week is now before us; let us spend this week for God." Each morning he said, "Now let us live this one day well!"

But his time was nonetheless cut short. The restoration of England's monarchy in 1662, resulting in the Act of Uniformity, removed two thousand preachers from their pulpits in a single day. Most preached their farewell sermons August 17, 1662. Joseph, however, continued preaching. The authorities descended, and on *May 28, 1663*, he was thrown into prison. His health soon declined.

"Now we have one day more," he told Theodosia when he was finally released. "Let us live well, work hard for souls, lay up much treasure in heaven this day, for we have but a few to live." He spoke truthfully. He died on November 17, 1668, at age thirty-four. But he had spent his years well, outliving himself not only in the souls he saved but in the book he left, a Puritan classic entitled *Alleine's Alarm*.

Act like people with good sense and not like fools. These are evil times, so make every minute count. Don't be stupid. Instead, find out what the Lord wants you to do. (Ephesians 5:15–17)

The Restoration

Joseph Alleine's imprisonment was occasioned by the restoration of the English monarchy and the laws passed by England's government in the 1660s. For years England had seesawed between Catholic and Protestant mandates, depending on the monarch in power. When the king was Catholic, Protestants were burned. When Protestant, Catholics died. In both situations, Puritans and non-Anglicans (Dissenters) were hunted down with such vengeance that they finally rebelled. King Charles I was beheaded, his young son fled to France, and a Puritan government was installed.

But the people missed their monarchy, and in 1658, young Charles II headed home from France, promising religious liberty. He entered London on his thirtieth birthday, *May 29, 1660.* Twenty thousand soldiers escorted the young king through flower-strewn streets. Trumpets blared, crowds cheered, and bells pealed from every tower. His love life and his dubious faith in God made him the most scandalous leader of his time. But his easy smile and approachability caused few to dislike him.

Some did. In 1661, a pack of religious fanatics known as Fifth Monarchy Men tried to overthrow him and set up a kingdom awaiting the return of Christ. They failed, but the experience left Charles more suspicious of Dissenters than ever. Such preachers as John Bunyan found themselves languishing in prison, and a series of laws put the screws to Dissenters.

Five different acts were passed: (1) the Corporation Act of 1661 excluded all Dissenters from local government; (2) the Act of Uniformity in 1662 required all ministers to use *The Book of Common Prayer* as a format for their services (it was this act that drove two thousand preachers from their pulpits in a single day); (3) the Conventicle Act of 1664 aimed primarily at Baptists, forbade religious meetings by Dissenters; (4) the Five Mile Act of 1665 prohibited dissenting ministers from coming within five miles of any city or town in which they had ministered; and (5) the Test Act of 1673 excluded Catholics from civil and military positions.

Baptists, Catholics, Quakers, Presbyterians, and Congregationalists all found themselves again under the lash. In the jail. At the stake. So much for religious liberty.

We don't want any of you to be discouraged by all these troubles. (1 Thessalonians 3:3)

May 30 The Cautious Reformer

Desiderius Erasmus, born in 1466, in Rotterdam, Holland, was the illegitimate son of a priest. He was orphaned in childhood, swindled out of his inheritance, and forced into a monastery that he hated—except for its library. Reaching adulthood, Erasmus approached theology with freshness, sought out scholars, then eclipsed them. He became the most cultivated man of his age.

In appearance, his skin was fair, hair blond, eyes blue, voice pleasant. His manners were polished. In temper, he could be irritable. He repeatedly visited England (though complaining of its "bad beer and inhospitable weather") where John Colet urged him to master the original language of the New Testament. He did, and in 1516, Erasmus published his Greek New Testament. "Would that these were translated into every language," he said. In studying Erasmus's New Testament, ministers found themselves returning to the truth of the Bible. Erasmus's translation became Luther's fodder, and the primary source for his German translation of the Bible (and later, of Tyndale's English version).

But Erasmus, having spent his first years advocating reform, spent his latter ones resisting it. He initially supported Luther, but retreated when he saw the church splitting. On *May 30, 1519*, he wrote Luther, suggesting that it "might be wiser of you to denounce those who misuse the Pope's authority than to censure the Pope himself . . . Old institutions cannot be uprooted in an instant. Quiet argument may do more than wholesale condemnation. Keep cool. Do not get angry."

Erasmus neither supported nor flatly condemned the Protestants. As a result, he lost friends on both sides. "Men of learning," he wrote, "who were once warmly attached to me, and old friends, are the most dangerous of foes."

Erasmus had expected the new wine to ferment in old skins. It wouldn't and couldn't, to his dismay. But never mind, he did his part. In giving the church back its Greek New Testament, he had, in effect, squeezed the grapes.

No one pours new wine into old wineskins. The wine would swell and burst the old skins. Then the wine would be lost, and the skins would be ruined. New wine must be put into new wineskins. Both the skins and the wine will then be safe. (Matthew 9:17)

Concordance

Half-Crazy Cruden

Christians of many generations have located verses of Scripture by pulling their *Cruden's Concordance* off its shelf. Spurgeon wrote in the flyleaf of his, "For ten years this has been at my left hand when the Word of God has been at my right."

Here's the rest of the story: Alexander Cruden was born in Scotland on *May 31, 1699*. His father, a strict Puritan, forbade games on the Lord's Day, and Alexander entertained himself by tracing words through the Bible. He enrolled in college at thirteen, graduated at nineteen, and fell in love. The girl's father forbade him in the house, and when the girl became pregnant, she was sent away. Alexander, his nerves broken, entered an asylum.

In 1726, he was hired to read books for Lord Derby of Sussex. Alexander began reading the way he always did—spelling out each word letter by letter. He was quickly fired, but he refused to leave the grounds. For months, he followed Lord Derby around, creating one scene after another. He eventually moved to London and began working on his *Concordance*. It was published in 1737, and became an immediate success.

Alexander fell in love again, was rejected again, and went to such extremes to attract the woman's affection that he was seized, taken to a private asylum, and chained to a bed for ten weeks. He finally managed to escape by cutting off the bed leg, then began traveling around calling himself *Alexander the Corrector*, trying to reform morals. One evening, wanting to stop a man from swearing, he hit him over the head with a shovel. A riot ensued, and Alexander endured a third stay in an asylum. Being released, he fell in love again, was rejected again, and badgered the king to appoint him *Alexander the Corrector*.

People thought him crazy—but they loved his *Concordance*. Alexander spent his final days giving out tracts and studying the Bible. One morning in 1770, a servant found him on his knees, his head on the open Bible, dead. "This half crazy Cruden," said Spurgeon, "did better service to the church than half the D.D.'s and L.L.D.'s of all time."

If we seem out of our minds, it is between God and us. But if we are in our right minds, it is for your good. We are ruled by Christ's love for us. We are certain that if one person died for everyone else, then all of us have died. And Christ did die for all of us. (2 Corinthians 5:13–15)

On This Day in Christian History...

JUNE

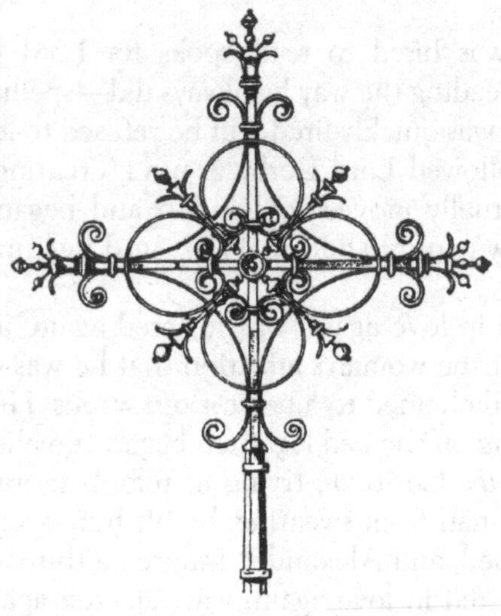

The Christian Atheist

He was about thirty when, walking along the shore, he listened to the liquid thunder of sea and surf. Solomon's words in Ecclesiastes 1:2 described his mood: "Nothing makes sense! Everything is nonsense. I have seen it all—nothing makes sense!" He had pursued every philosophy, and none of them made sense to him. He had studied the Stoics but wasn't satisfied. Aristotelianism didn't fulfill him, nor Pythagoreanism. He found Platonism empty of power. But by the ocean that day, he met an old man who gave him a message of profound simplicity: Jesus Christ is Lord. Justin's life was never again the same.

Justin came from Palestine, born soon after the death of the apostle John. His wealthy, pagan parents had given him a splendid education, and Justin proved brilliant. But though his mind was filled with philosophy, nothing filled his heart. That is, not until he met the old man by the sea sharing the gospel.

Justin immediately began telling everyone that Christ can satisfy both mind and heart. He presented his case for Christianity clearly, defending the gospel so effectively that he is known as one of the church's first and finest apologists (defenders of the faith). He became a teacher in Ephesus, then moved to Rome and opened a Christian school. He wrote books advancing the Christian message, three of which still survive, including a remarkable dialogue with a Jew in Ephesus named Trypho, a survivor of the Bar Kochba War. Justin skillfully explained the reasons Trypho should consider Christianity as a sound and reasonable faith.

In the mid-160s, while teaching in Rome, he debated a cynic named Crescentius who held that virtue alone was the goal of life. Justin won the contest so decisively that Crescentius, enraged, apparently reported Justin to the Roman prefect and brought him before the court on charges of atheism—that is, of not believing in the gods of Rome. Justin and several others were condemned, flogged, and beheaded.

He has since been known as Justin Martyr, and his life is remembered every year by the church in both East and West on his feast day, *June 1*.

> Everything you were taught can be put into a few words:
> Respect and obey God!
> This is what life
> is all about.
> God will judge
> everything we do,
> even what is done is secret,
> whether good or bad. (Ecclesiastes 12:13–14)

June 2

Let Them Become Angels

The British Isles were evangelized perhaps as early as the first century, but the decline of the Roman Empire allowed the Anglo-Saxons to eventually overrun the islands. Christians were massacred, churches destroyed, the gospel nearly extinguished. The years passed, and one day in Rome an abbot named Gregory saw three blond, blue-eyed British boys being sold in the slave market. His heart went out to them. Being told their nationality he reportedly said, "They are Anglos; let them become angels." He set out as a missionary, longing to reintroduce Christianity to the British, but the pope called him back before he had reached England. Shortly afterward, being named pope himself, Gregory dispatched a group of thirty or forty missionaries led by a monk named Augustin.

The group landed near the mouth of the Thames in the spring of 597. They discovered that Queen Bertha of Kent had previously heard the gospel in her native France and had been converted. With her help, King Ethelbert agreed to see Augustin though he insisted their meeting be conducted in the open air where he thought Augustin's "magic" wouldn't affect him. But it did. Hearing Augustin preach, Ethelbert acknowledged Christ as Lord on this day, *June 2, 597*. Later that year the king and ten thousand of his subjects were baptized. The message of Christ spread throughout neighboring Anglo-Saxon kingdoms, and as the church grew, Augustin was named archbishop. King Ethelbert gave his own castle to the new archbishop, thus establishing the archbishopric of Canterbury as the episcopal center of England.

Augustin, refusing to compromise on points like the dating of Easter and modes of baptism, sowed much discord, marring his record. When he died on May 26, 604, he was buried in the cathedral of Canterbury with these words on his tomb: "Here rests Augustin, first archbishop of Canterbury, who being sent hither by Gregory, bishop of Rome, reduced King Ethelbert and his nation from the worship of idols to the faith of Christ."

Paul went there to worship, and on three Sabbaths he spoke to the people. He used the Scriptures to show them that the Messiah had to suffer, but that he would rise from death. Paul also told them that Jesus is the Messiah he was preaching about. Some of them believed. (Acts 17:2–4)

Curse Ye Woodchuck

***June* 3**

If you often have trouble sleeping, try reading Psalms 3 and 4. David, running for his life and surrounded by Absalom's rebellious army, wrote in Psalm 3:5, "I sleep and wake up refreshed because you, LORD, protect me." Psalm 4:8 indicates the promises of God make good pillows for those who rest in him: "I can lie down and sleep soundly, because you, LORD, will keep me safe."

But not during the preacher's sermons.

At least, not in early American church history.

The Puritans of colonial New England appointed "tithingmen" to stroll among the pews on Sunday mornings, alert for anyone nodding off during the long, sometimes ponderous sermons. They carried long poles with feathers on one end and knobs or thorns on the other. Worshippers napped at their own peril, and the results were unpredictable—as noted by Obadiah Turner of Lynn, Massachusetts, in his journal for *June 3, 1646*:

> Allen Bridges hath bin chose to wake ye sleepers in meeting. And being much proude of his place, must needs have a fox taile fixed to ye ende of a long staff wherewith he may brush ye faces of them yt will have napps in time of discourse, likewise a sharpe thorne whereby he may pricke such as be most sound. On ye last Lord his day, as hee strutted about ye meetinghouse, he did spy Mr. Tomlins sleeping with much comfort, hys head kept steadie by being in ye corner, and his hand grasping ye rail. And soe spying, Allen did quickly thrust his staff behind Dame Ballard and give him a grievous prick upon ye hand. Whereupon Mr. Tomlins did spring vpp mch above ye floore, and with terrible force strike hys hand against ye wall; and also, to ye great wonder of all, prophanlie exclaim in a loud voice, curse ye wood-chuck, he dreaming so it seemed yt a wood-chuck had seized and bit his hand. But on coming to know where he was, and ye greate scandall he had committed, he seemed much abashed, but did not speak. And I think he will not soon again goe to sleepe in meeting.

There are some who ask,
"Who will be good to us?"
Let your kindness, LORD,
shine brightly on us.
You brought me more happiness
than a rich harvest
of grain and grapes.
I can lie down
and sleep soundly
because you, LORD,
will keep me safe. (Psalm 4:6–8)

***June* 4**

Wireless Witness

Invisible beams of evangelism flash day and night across sky and sea, penetrating nations and hearts where missionaries cannot go. Such are the shortwave ministries of ventures like HCJB, TransWorld Radio, and Far East Broadcasting Company.

The FEBC began in 1945, when three Christians pooled their resources and formed a nonprofit corporation to broadcast the gospel through the Orient. One of the men, John Broger, set out for Shanghai searching for a spot for a transmitter. He sailed to Manila to explore the possibility of locating the transmitter in the Philippines.

While completing paperwork for the Philippine government, Broger requested permission for ten thousand watts. Imagine his thrill when officials marked out the amount and wrote: *Unlimited Power.*

But the Philippine government insisted the station go on the air by June 4 or not at all. Meanwhile in the U.S. the founders frantically tried to raise funds as bills came due. One delay after another tore at the project, but government officials refused to extend the timetable. Nail-biting difficulties arose, and three days before the deadline, transmission problems developed. When June 4 dawned, high-voltage wires crisscrossed the station, and workers stepped through ankle-deep water from heavy rains. Broger rushed downtown to make a final plea for an extension. He was refused.

He had no choice but to rush back through cart-congested streets, weaving through traffic jams, racing against the clock. He came to a screeching halt in front of the station, rushed in and shouted, "We'll test on the air." The switch was flipped, the transmitters hummed with power, and the winded staff began singing "All Hail the Power of Jesus' Name." It was 6:00 PM, *June 4, 1948*, and FEBC was on the air. Almost immediately reports arrived of barbers, atheists, thieves, housewives, and teenagers being saved. Today FEBC is still on the air, serving every country in Asia with local and/or international services in more than one hundred fifty languages.

Praise God! He can make you strong by means of my good news, which is the message about Jesus Christ. For ages and ages this message was kept secret, but now at last it has been told. And now, because of Jesus Christ, we can praise the only wise God forever! Amen. (Romans 16:25, 27)

The Ax of the Apostle

June 5

He is called the apostle to the Germans and was perhaps the greatest missionary of the Dark Ages.

Boniface was an Englishman, born in 680. He entered a monastery and at age thirty was ordained. His abilities guaranteed a rising career in the English church, but Boniface had a missions call on his life that would not be denied. About 716, he sailed to Holland on his first missionary endeavor, but he met strong political opposition and returned to England discouraged.

He recovered and left again for the Continent, going to Rome in 718, then, with the pope's sanction, to Germany. For the next twelve years he worked there (with occasional forays back to Holland), and he soon began seeing great numbers of pagans converted. His boldness knew no bounds. In one village he could win no converts because the local populace was convinced that a massive tree, the sacred oak of Thundergod, held supernatural powers over them. Boniface took an ax and felled it in full view of the horrified citizens. He then proceeded to build a church with the wood. News spread across central Europe, and thousands confessed Christ as Lord. Boniface traveled from village to village, smashing idols, destroying temples, and preaching the gospel.

But he soon reconsidered his smash-and-burn evangelism and began building churches, training and organizing an indigenous clergy. Women became actively involved in his work. In 744, he established the important monastery of Fulda, to this day the center of Roman Catholicism in Germany. Boniface's converts fanned out as missionaries throughout central Europe.

Everywhere he went, it was with papal sanction and authority, and he became one of the most powerful churchmen of the eighth century. Some have criticized him for emphasizing the church over the gospel. He was back in Holland for a preaching tour, and thousands of converts were being baptized. On *June 5, 755*, a band of hostile pagans fell upon him as he camped by the river Borne. He was slain while clutching a Bible in his hand.

The Lord has given us this command, "I have placed you here as a light for the Gentiles. You are to take the saving power of God to people everywhere on earth." . . . Everyone who had been chosen for eternal life then put their faith in the Lord. (Acts 13:47–48)

June 6

The Yellow Enemy

Central America was conquered by Spain in the 1500s, and held in the grip of Catholicism for three hundred years. Non-Catholic holdouts were subjected to dripping water torture while bound in straitjackets. Others were hung from rings in the ceilings or roasted alive in huge ovens. When the Spanish Empire broke apart in 1838, several new nations emerged, including Honduras, El Salvador, Nicaragua, and Costa Rica. The entrance of evangelical missionaries then became possible but hazardous.

The first to come were German Moravians, followed by Presbyterians. Then in the late 1880s, C. I. Scofield established the Central American Mission (CAM). One of these early missionaries, Miss Eleanor Blackmore, wrote to her supporters: "I'm stoned and cursed and hooted in every street. I don't know one road in the whole city where I can walk in which there are not houses where they lie in wait to stone me . . . We don't want pity. We count it an honor thus to be trusted to suffer, but we do covet your prayers."

The first CAM missionaries went to Costa Rica, but soon a team of three headed toward El Salvador. They didn't make it, but it wasn't sticks and stones that struck them down. Mr. and Mrs. H. C. Dillon and Clarence Wilber were traversing Nicaragua in 1894, headed to El Salvador, when they became ill with fever, chills, and congestion of eyes and mouth. Clarence died vomiting black blood and was buried in a makeshift grave. The Dillons reached ship and started for home, but Mrs. Dillon died en route. Mr. Dillon survived and soon remarried.

He and his new wife, Margaret, returned to Central America, where Dillon again contracted yellow fever and soon died. Margaret remained in Honduras, living in a small shack, sleeping on a straw mat, and training Honduran evangelists. Fifteen years passed without a furlough; then she planned a trip home. She was stricken with yellow fever while packing and was carried thirty-six miles in a hammock to a missions station, arriving on *June 6, 1913.* She died two days later.

These graves were but seed-plots for a harvest of souls that continues to this day.

My friends, we want you to understand how it will be for those followers who have already died. Then you won't grieve over them and be like people who don't have any hope. We believe that Jesus died and was raised to life. We also believe that when God brings Jesus back again, he will bring with him all who had faith in Jesus before they died. (1 Thessalonians 4:13–14)

The Banner of Jesus

***June* 7**

London's Metropolitan Tabernacle sits across from a run-down subway station in the south of London, surrounded by housing projects, bars, and abandoned shops. It is off the tourist path, and average Sunday attendance hovers at three hundred. Its successful ministry attracts young people and serves a vital need in the inner city.

Looked at another way, the Metropolitan Tabernacle has never been the same since Sunday morning, *June 7, 1891*, when Charles Spurgeon preached there for the last time. He was exhausted in ministry and broken down by denominational conflict. His hair was white, his face lined, his heavy frame weak. He ended his sermon without knowing these would be his last words in the pulpit: "These forty years and more have I served him, blessed be his name! And I have had nothing but love from him. I would be glad to continue yet another forty years in the same dear service here below if so it pleased him. His service is life, peace, joy. Oh, that you would enter on it at once! God help you to enlist under the banner of Jesus even this day! Amen!"

That afternoon his congregation was alarmed to hear that Spurgeon had fallen ill. He lay in bed for over a month, most of the time unconscious, sometimes delirious. London clung to every bulletin, and prayer meetings were held continually at the tabernacle. Months passed. Spurgeon rallied enough in late summer for a trip to the south of France, and hope for his recovery soared. Workers at the tabernacle installed a lift to save him the exertion of the stairs.

But about midnight, January 31, 1892, Spurgeon breathed his last breath, surrounded by his wife and a few friends in his room at the Hotel Beau Rivage in Menton, France. England was numbed by the news, and twelve days later his funeral cortege was surrounded by a hundred thousand mourners as it entered Upper Norwood Cemetery in London.

He was fifty-seven. He had worn himself out under the banner of Jesus.

These are the last words
of David the son of Jesse.
The Spirit of the LORD
has told me what to say.
Our Mighty Rock, the God of Jacob, told me,
"A ruler who obeys God
and does right
is like the sunrise
on a cloudless day,
or like rain that sparkles
on the grass." (2 Samuel 23:1–4)

June 8

A New Trinity

The French Revolution was not a crusade for religious freedom but an effort to replace religion with reason and rationalism. France, boasting the largest population in Europe, had trouble feeding its masses. Multitudes, including local clergy, lived in direst poverty while royalty and high church officials—cardinals, archbishops, bishops, and abbots—lived richly.

On *June 8*, 1794, a disciple of Rousseau named Robespierre and the French National Convention formally inaugurated a new religion. It was a form of deism, the belief that there is a God who, having created the universe, more or less disappeared. The convention ordered people to recognize the existence of a supreme being and the immortality of the soul but to reject the "superstition" of Christianity. The seven-day Christian week was exchanged for a ten-day week, and new holidays were commissioned celebrating the great events of the Revolution. Saints were replaced with political heroes. Churches were designated "temples of reason." A statue called the Goddess of Reason was erected in Notre Dame. The salaries of Catholic clergy were stopped, and priests were forbidden to teach. June 8 became France's holy day, the Festival of the Supreme Being. The revolutionaries vowed to replace the Father, Son, and Holy Ghost with a new trinity—Liberty, Equality, and Fraternity.

It didn't work. Liberty, equality, and fraternity deteriorated into fear, bloodshed, and the guillotine. The weeks following June 8, 1794, saw the heads of fourteen hundred people fall "like slates from a roof." Chaos paved the way for Napoleon Bonaparte, who, on May 18, 1804, recognized the church once again. He planned to be consecrated by Pope Pius VII. But at the last moment the little dictator took the crown from the pope and set it on his own head. Pius excommunicated Napoleon, and Napoleon imprisoned Pius.

Liberty, equality, and fraternity proved inadequate gods, as did Rousseau, Robespierre, and the Revolution—and Napoleon himself. In the end they offered only misery.

Be silent! I am the LORD God, . . .
. . . I will punish
national leaders
and sons of the king,
along with all who follow
foreign customs. I will punish worshipers
of pagan gods and cruel palace officials
who abuse their power. (Zephaniah 1:7–9)

Hot Head, Strong Heart *June* 9

Hotheaded people can become strong-hearted saints, for the same passions that drive our tempers can be harnessed by the Spirit for good. We learn this from Columba, born in Ulster, Ireland, on December 7, 521. His grandfather had been baptized by St. Patrick himself, and Columba's parents were believers of royal stock. Though he had a yearning for learning and for the Lord, Columba was strong-willed and combative. He possessed a powerful presence, with strong features and an authoritative voice, but his fiery temper and iron will lingered, even after becoming a home missionary to his fellow Irish. One day Columba copied the contents of a book without permission, and when the owner requested the copy, Columba refused. The argument took on a life of its own, involving more and more people. Eventually a war erupted in which three thousand men lost their lives.

Full of remorse Columba committed himself to win as many to Christ as had died in the war. Thus he left Ireland at age forty-two to become a missionary to Scotland. With twelve companions he established himself on Iona, a bleak, foggy island just off the Scottish coast, three miles long and a mile and a half wide. He built a crude monastery that soon became a training center for missionaries, one of the most venerable and interesting spots in the history of Christian missions. It was a lighthouse against heathenism.

From Iona Columba made missionary forays into Scotland, converting large numbers. An entire tribe of pagans, the Picts, were won to the faith. He confronted the druids, contesting with them over their alleged magical arts and demonic powers. Legend suggests he performed miracles to counter theirs, convincing the populace of the gospel's superior power. He spent the rest of his life as the apostle to Scotland and as a trainer of missionaries.

On June 8, 597, Columba, seventy-five years old, spent the day transcribing the Psalms, then joined his brothers for midnight devotions. He collapsed at the altar and died peacefully during the wee hours of *June* 9, 597, his face bearing an expression of seeing holy angels coming to meet him.

People with bad tempers
are always in trouble,
and they need help
over and over again. Pay attention to advice
and accept correction,
so you can live sensibly.
We may make a lot of plans,
but the LORD will do
what he has decided. (Proverbs 19:19–21)

June 10

What Grace!

John Hus, born in a peasant's home about 1373, worked his way through school and began teaching theology at the University of Prague. He was exposed to Wycliffe's writings, and in 1402, when he was appointed preacher at Prague's influential Bethlehem Chapel, his powerful sermons about justification by faith stirred all Bohemia. Church officials grew alarmed by the ferment, and in 1414, Hus was summoned to Constance on charges of heresy. Though promised safe conduct, he was quickly arrested. On *June 10, 1415*, he wrote to his followers in Bohemia:

> Master John Hus, a servant of God in hope, to all the faithful Bohemians who love and will love God, praying that God may grant them to live and die in his grace, and dwell forever in the heavenly joy. Amen. Faithful and beloved of God, lords and ladies, rich and poor! I entreat you and exhort you to love God, to spread abroad his word, and to hear and observe it more willingly. I entreat you to hold fast the truth of God, which I have written and preached to you from the holy Scriptures . . .
>
> I write this letter to you in prison, bound with chains and expecting on the morrow the sentence of death, yet fully trusting in God that I shall not swerve from his truth nor swear denial of the errors, whereof I have been charged by false witnesses. What grace God hath shown me, and how he helps me in the midst of strange temptations, you will know when by his mercy we meet in joy in his presence. Of Master Jerome, my beloved friend, I hear nothing except that he too, like myself, is in a noisome prison waiting for death, and that on account of his faith which he showed so earnestly to the Bohemians . . .
>
> I entreat this too of you, that ye love one another, defend good men from violent oppression, and give every one an opportunity of hearing the truth. I am writing this with the help of a good angel on Monday night before St. Vitus's Day.

Twenty-six days later, John Hus died at the stake.

God blesses those people
who are treated badly
for doing right.
They belong to the kingdom
of heaven. God will bless you when people insult you, mistreat you, and tell all kinds of evil lies about you because of me. Be happy and excited! You will have a great reward in heaven. (Matthew 5:10–12)

Parents' Footprints

June 11

In 1907, missionary Jesse Brand, young and unmarried, left for India, settling in the disease-ridden Chat Mountains. His friends shuddered at his descriptions of flea-covered rats swarming through the hills and spreading plagues with abandon. But one supporter longed to join him—Evelyn Harris, belle of a fashionable London suburb. She journeyed to India and married him in 1913.

The Brands labored tirelessly, giving medical aid to thousands. Jesse organized economic assistance and cooperative programs so farmers could get ahead. He negotiated with government officials to use unemployed workers for labor. He took every opportunity to share Christ, preaching four thousand times in ninety villages in one year. Churches were established. Congregations grew.

And so did the Brand family. Son Paul was born and taught by his mother under a tamarind tree. His nature-loving dad showed him the wonders of nature. At age nine Paul was sent to England for formal education, and his parents pressed on alone.

In the spring of 1928, Jesse contracted blackwater fever. His condition worsened, but he continued working. In early June his fever reached 104 degrees. On June 9, he preached from Isaiah 60: "Stand up! Shine! Your new day is dawning." On *June 11, 1928*, his temperature reached 106 degrees, and he was forced to bed. Evelyn sat by him day after day, watching his skin parch, his color yellow, and his life drain away. Local Indians wrapped his body in a mat and carried it on their shoulders to a hillside grave.

Word was flashed to fourteen-year-old Paul. Two days later Paul received a letter from his dad, mailed by boat before his death. It ended: ". . . and always be looking to God with thankfulness and worship for having placed you in such a delightful corner of the universe as the planet Earth."

Evelyn remained in India, becoming a legend, hiking over the mountains with her walking stick, doing the Lord's work. "Granny Brand" lived to see her son, Dr. Paul Brand, become a famed missionary physician, excelling in the treatment of leprosy.

Stand up! Shine!
Your new day is dawning.
The glory of the LORD
shines brightly on you.
The earth and its people
are covered with darkness,
but the glory of the LORD
is shining upon you.
Nations and kings
will come to the light
of your dawning day. (Isaiah 60:1–3)

June 12

I Can Plod

At nine o'clock on Thursday night, *June 12, 1806*, pioneer missionary William Carey, weary from the day's labors, sat at his desk and wrote this letter in the flickering light of his oil lamp:

> I rose this day at a quarter before six, read a chapter in the Hebrew Bible, and spent the time till seven in private addresses to God and then attended family prayer with the servants in Bengalee. While tea was pouring out, I read a little in Persian with a Moonshi [a native assistant] who was waiting when I left my bedroom. Read also before breakfast a portion of the Scriptures in Hindoosthanee. The moment breakfast was over sat down to the translation of the Ramayuna [an Indian epic] from Sangskrit, with a Pundit . . . continued this translation till ten o'clock, at which time I went to College (Fort William), and attended the duties there (teaching Bengali, Sanskrit, and Marathi) till between one and two o'clock—When I returned home I examined a proof sheet of the Bengalee translation of Jeremiah, which took till dinner time . . . After dinner translated with the assistance of the chief Pundit of the College, greatest part of the 8th Chap. of Matthew, into Sangskrit—this employed me till six o'clock, after six sat down with a Tilingua Pundit . . . to learn that Language. Mr. Thomas (son of the Rev. Tho. Thomas of London) called in the evening; I began to collect a few previous thoughts into the form of a Sermon, at seven o'clock, and preached in English at half past seven . . . The Congregation was gone by nine o'clock. I then sat down to write to you, after this I conclude the Evening by reading a Chapter in the Greek testament, and commending myself to God. I have never more time in a day than this, though the exercises vary.

Eustace Carey said that her uncle never displayed resentment at interruptions. He could give visitors his undivided attention then return immediately to his work. And he never took a furlough from missionary service, living and working in India for nearly forty-one years.

"I can plod," he once said. "To this I owe everything."

Teach us to use wisely all the time we have. (Psalm 90:12)

Luther's Wedding Night

June 13

Katherine von Bora found herself virtually imprisoned as a nun at Cistercian Convent of Nimbschem, Germany, in the sixteenth century. Relatives were unable to speak to her except through a latticed window, and she was even forbidden to talk to her fellow nuns. Silence was the rule at Cistercian Convent.

Katherine managed to smuggle in reading material—the writings of a man named Martin Luther—and she began hoping for new life. In 1523, she and several other nuns hatched an escape plan, and they sneaked word to Luther. He recruited a merchant who sold smoked herring. The man made a delivery to the convent, and when he left, the nuns were stowed away in the empty herring barrels.

Luther succeeded in finding husbands for all the women except Katherine, a strong-willed, twemty-six-year-old redhead. At length he proposed to her. The account of their wedding night by Luther's biographer, Richard Friedenthal, leaves us . . . well, curious:

> On the evening of *13 June 1525*, according to the custom of the day, (Luther) appeared with his bride before a number of his friends as witnesses. The Pomeranian [Johann] Bugenhagen blessed the couple, who consummated the marriage in front of the witnesses, [Justus] Jonas reported the next day: "Luther has taken Katharina von Bora to wife. I was present yesterday and saw the couple on their marriage bed. As I watched this spectacle I could not hold back my tears."*

The marriage created a storm of criticism in church circles across Europe. Erasmus called it a comedy, and Henry VIII called it a crime (as if he should talk!). But Luther said, "I would not change my Katie for France and Venice, because God has given her to me." She proved equal to her role as Protestantism's first pastor's wife, becoming known as First Lady of the Reformation.

> Her words are sensible,
> and her advice
> is thoughtful.
> . . . Her husband says,
> "There are many good women,
> but you are the best!" (Proverbs 31:26, 28–29)

---

*Richard Friedenthal, *Luther: His Life and Times*, trans. John Nowell (New York: Harcourt Brace Jovanovich, 1970), p. 438, quoted in Ruth A. Tucker and Walter Liefeld, *Daughters of the Church* (Grand Rapids: Zondervan Publishing House, 1987), p. 180.

Entombed Alive

Methodius was born in Syracuse, Sicily, an island off the Italian coast famous for its olives, wine, and marble. The schools there afforded him a good education, and he developed political ambitions. The capital of the surviving Roman Empire was Constantinople, so Methodius packed his bags and traveled there, hoping for a post at court. Instead he met a monk who persuaded him to abandon secular pursuits and to enter the ministry. Methodius was eventually noticed by Patriarch Nicephorus, who gave him ecclesiastical responsibilities.

The iconoclastic controversy was tearing the church apart at the time. Should icons and images of Christ and the saints be worshipped? Methodius vigorously argued in the affirmative, but he found himself on the losing side. Patriarch Nicephorus was deposed, and Methodius was condemned, flogged, and imprisoned in a tomb with two thieves. When one of the thieves died, officials refused to remove the body, leaving it to rot where it had fallen. Methodius suffered in this putrid confinement for seven years, and he was little more than a skeleton when released.

But he immediately resumed his crusade for the worship of idols and relics in the Eastern church. He was summoned before Emperor Theophilus and charged with heresy, but he threw the charges back in the ruler's face: "If an image is so worthless in your eyes," he reportedly thundered, "how is it you do not also condemn the veneration paid to representations of yourself? You are continually causing them to be multiplied."

Emperor Theophilus died soon thereafter, and his widow, Theodora, took Methodius's side. Icon worshippers returned to the churches, exiled clergy returned to the empire, and within thirty days icons had been reinstated in all the churches of the capital.

Methodius was named Patriarch of Constantinople and soon called a council of Eastern churches to endorse his decrees about icons and to institute the Feast of Orthodoxy, celebrating the return of images to the churches. He ruled as patriarch for four years until he died of dropsy on *June 14, 847.*

What is an idol worth?
It's merely a false god.
Why trust a speechless image
made from wood or metal
by human hands?
What can you learn from idols
covered with silver or gold?
They can't even breathe . . .
Let all the world be silent—
the LORD is present
in his holy temple. (Habakkuk 2:18–20)

A Mob and a Boy

England's John Wycliffe embodied Protestantism long before Luther, and the Reformation could have broken out in England one hundred thirty years before it began in Germany. It was aborted, however, by a mob and a boy.

During Wycliffe's day, England was an unhealthy place. Few reached age forty. There was little public sanitation, and the stench of latrines, tanneries, and livestock sullied the air. The plague struck with frightening regularity—in 1361, 1368, 1375, 1382, and 1390—taking one in three and nearly half the clergy. The population grew angry, and social order deteriorated. In 1380, a poll tax sparked violence, and Wycliffe, finding himself quoted by rebel leaders, tried to distance himself from the revolt. But many felt his reformer's message had contributed to the uprising.

On June 10, 1381, mobs swarmed through Canterbury, sacking the palace of Archbishop Sudbury. On June 11, revolutionaries rolled like a flood toward London. "Now," they said, "the reign of Christian democracy will begin, and every man will be a king."

King Richard II hid in the Tower of London as the horde stormed the capital. The next morning he agreed to meet with the insurgents in North London. Rebel leaders, unsatisfied with his answers, rushed back to the tower, seized Archbishop Sudbury while he was singing mass in the chapel, forced his neck on a log, and hacked off his head (which required eight strokes to do the job). Mobs pillaged and murdered at will. The shaken king retired to his mother's apartments near St. Paul's Cathedral.

The next morning, *June 15, 1381*, Richard took the sacrament and rode out to face the rebels. When a skirmish erupted, he rode bravely toward the masses, shouting, "Sirs, will you shoot your king? I will be your captain; you shall have from me that which you seek." The rebels hesitated, and the people sided with Richard. The tide turned. The king, his state, and the official Church of England were preserved; the revolt was crushed; William Courtnay, who hated Wycliffe, was named archbishop; and the Reformation was deferred until another day.

King Richard II, incredibly, was only fourteen years old.

Who makes these things happen?
Who controls human events?
I do! I am the LORD.
I was there at the beginning;
I will be there at the end.
Islands and foreign nations
saw what I did
and trembled
as they came near. (Isaiah 41:4–5)

June 16 William and Catherine

Abraham believed that angels help us find our mates. "The LORD will send his angel ahead of you," he told his servant, "to help you find a wife for my son" (Gen. 24:7). Many years later the heavenly matchmakers (assisted by a London businessman) also brought together William Booth and Catherine Mumford, who became one of the finest tag teams in church history, founding the Salvation Army and helping hundreds of thousands of England's poorest. Of the two, Catherine was smarter—and the better preacher. "It was she," wrote Constance Coltman, "who turned an energetic, rather vulgar dyspeptic into one of the great religious leaders in the world."*

William was born in 1829, in Nottingham. Catherine arrived the following year in a nearby county, growing up in a Puritan-like home. She had read the Bible through eight times before age twelve, and she excelled in studies. But at fourteen Catherine developed curvature of the spine, making her bedfast. She was also diagnosed with tuberculosis. But her sickbed became a study where she devoured theology and church history. She slowly grew strong enough to start thinking of marriage. "I could be most useful to God," she said, "as a minister's wife." She wanted a man dark and tall, and she thought he should be a William.

Several years later businessman Edward Rabbits, knowing both William's and Catherine's people, invited them to a meeting on Good Friday. Afterward he encouraged William to escort Catherine home. She later wrote, "That little journey will never be forgotten by either of us. Before we reached my home, we both felt as though we had been made for each other."

For a few weeks the romance wavered. Despite a growing reputation as evangelist to the poor, William had no job, no income, and no home. Catherine's mother viewed him unfavorably. Nevertheless they persevered and were married in London on *June 16, 1855*.

William preached a revival meeting on their honeymoon. The angels were smiling. The Salvation Army was about to be born.

Charm can be deceiving,
and beauty fades away,
but a woman
who honors the LORD
deserves to be praised.
Show her respect—
praise her in public
for what she has done. (Proverbs 31:30–31)

---

*Quoted by Norman H. Murdoch in "The Army Mother," *Christian History* 9, no. 26 (1990): 5.

Links in the Chain

Edward Kimball was determined to win his Sunday school class to Christ. A teenager named Dwight Moody tended to fall asleep on Sundays, but Kimball, undeterred, set out to reach him at work. His heart was pounding as he entered the store where the young man worked. "I put my hand on his shoulder, and as I leaned over I placed my foot upon a shoebox. I asked him to come to Christ." But Kimball left thinking he had botched the job. Moody, however, left the store that day a new person and eventually became the most prominent evangelist in America.

On *June 17, 1873*, Moody arrived in Liverpool, England, for a series of crusades. The meetings went poorly at first, but then the dam burst, and blessings began flowing. Moody visited a Baptist chapel pastored by a scholarly man named F. B. Meyer, who at first disdained the American's unlettered preaching. But Meyer was soon transfixed and transformed by Moody's message.

At Moody's invitation, Meyer toured America. At Northfield Bible Conference, he challenged the crowds saying, "If you are not willing to give up everything for Christ, are you willing to be made willing?" That remark changed the life of a struggling young minister named J. Wilber Chapman.

Chapman proceeded to become a powerful traveling evangelist in the early 1900s, and he recruited a converted baseball player named Billy Sunday. Under Chapman's eye, Sunday became one of the most spectacular evangelists in American history. His campaign in Charlotte, North Carolina, produced a group of converts who continued praying for another such visitation of the Spirit. In 1934, they invited evangelist Mordecai Ham to conduct a citywide crusade. On October 8, Ham, discouraged, wrote a prayer to God on the stationery of his Charlotte hotel: "Lord, give us a Pentecost here . . . Pour out thy Spirit tomorrow . . ."

His prayer was answered beyond his dreams when a Central High School student named Billy Graham gave his heart to Jesus.

And Edward Kimball thought he had botched the job!

I am not praying just for these followers. I am also praying for everyone else who will have faith because of what my followers will say about me. I want all of them to be one with each other, just as I am one with you and you are one with me. (John 17:20–21)

June 18

Heretic or Heroic?

Thomas Kyme kicked his wife, Anne Askew, out of the house when she became a Protestant. The loss of home, husband, and two children was only the beginning of sorrows, for she soon faced trial for denying the doctrine of the mass—that the bread and wine change into the body and blood of Christ. "Thou foolish woman," said her accuser, "sayest thou that priests cannot make the body of Christ?"

"I say so, my Lord. I have read that God made man; but that man can make God, I never yet read, nor, I suppose, shall ever read. That which you call your God is a piece of bread; for proof thereof let it lie in a box three months, and it will be moldy."

She was taken to the Tower of London. "Then they did put me on the rack . . . a long time; and because I lay still and did not cry, my Lord Chancellor and Master Rich took pains to rack me with their own hands, till I was nigh dead." Despite being so crippled that she could never walk again, she refused to recant. "I sent word," she said, "that I would rather die than break my faith." Anne then composed this prayer:

> O Lord! I have more enemies now than hairs on my head; yet Lord, let them never overcome me with vain words, but fight Thou, Lord, in my stead; for on Thee I cast my care. With all the spite they can imagine, they fall upon me, who am Thy poor creature. Yet, sweet Lord, I heartily desire of Thee, that Thou wilt of Thy merciful goodness forgive them that violence they do. Open also their blind hearts, that they may hereafter do that thing in Thy sight which is only acceptable before Thee. So be it, Lord.

On *June 18, 1546*, she was officially condemned. A month later she was carried to Smithfield, chained to the stake, and burned as a heretic. Others, however, such as John Foxe, thought her heroic, "leaving behind a singular example of Christian constancy for all men to follow."

Even my bones are in pain,
while all day long
my enemies sneer and ask,
"Where is your God?"
Why am I discouraged?
Why am I restless?
I trust you!
And I will praise you again
because you help me,
and you are my God. (Psalm 42:10–11)

The Nicene Creed

During the first three centuries of its life, the church suffered waves of persecution—the shackles, the lash, the sword, the teeth of lions. With the conversion of Emperor Constantine in 312, the persecution ended, and the church considered a problem worse than persecution—heresy. A teacher named Arius from North Africa was denying that Jesus was both fully man and fully God. "There was a time when the Son was not," taught Arius. He claimed that Jesus is not eternal, not divine, not God. The heresy grew, alarming Constantine. The emperor didn't understand the debate, but he desired unity in the church. "These questions are the idle cobwebs of contention, spun by curious wits," he said.

Constantine called a general council of the church in the small town of Nicaea. Eighteen hundred bishops were invited from across the empire, and each bishop was allowed to bring two other church leaders and three slaves. Traveling conditions were difficult, and fewer than four hundred bishops assembled, most from the eastern realm. Many bore marks of persecution. Some were scholars; some were shepherds. Into this motley crew stepped Emperor Constantine, wearing high-heeled scarlet boots, a purple robe, long hair, and a short beard.

The delegates were soon at each other's throats. Arius presented his views. Alexander and Athanasius retaliated with orthodox teaching. Finally Hosius, a bishop from Cordova, suggested drawing up a creed. The statement of faith was developed, and Hosius announced it on *June 19, 325*. It described Jesus Christ as "God from very God, begotten not made, of the same substance as the Father, through whom all things were made . . . who for us men, and for our salvation, came down and was made flesh, was made man, suffered and rose again . . ."

The creed was adopted, and the doctrine of Christ's divine nature—a belief both essential and unique to Christianity—was formally affirmed for the first time.

Christ is exactly like God,
who cannot be seen.
He is the first-born Son,
superior to all creation.
Everything was created by him,
everything in heaven
and on earth, everything seen and unseen,
including all forces
and powers,
and all rulers
and authorities . . .
He is the head of his body
which is the church. (Colossians 1:15–16, 18)

Have Pity on Me

Not even the most powerful on earth can face the last enemy alone. Power, riches, fame, and fortune vanish like a dream, leaving the naked soul groping for comfort. Too many wait too long before preparing to face God.

Marie Antoinette symbolized the extravagance and decadence of French society immediately before the Revolution. She and her dithering husband, King Louis XVI, lived in the grand mansions of Versailles, taxed their subjects into poverty, and spent the money lavishly. But Marie smelled impending danger long before Louis, and she sensed their days were numbered. For months she begged Louis to flee France. He vacillated and hesitated. Then on October 5, 1789, hundreds of women descended on Versailles brandishing kitchen knives and brooms. The terrified royals were forced to Paris and placed under guard.

Louis belatedly schemed to escape the country. Plot after plot was hatched and discarded. Finally at darkest midnight, *June 20, 1791*, the royal family slipped through the shadows, entered a carriage, and bolted out of town disguised as the Korff family. They traveled in unbearable suspense night and day toward the Austrian border. Just shy of safety, they were stopped and arrested by peasants armed with pitchforks.

Marie Antoinette aged overnight into an old woman—gaunt, white-haired, stooped, and tottering. Back in Paris she was locked in an airless dark room. She hemorrhaged uncontrollably; wept for her husband, who perished; and worried endlessly for her young son, who had been torn from her arms.

Antoinette now turned to God. She observed mass in her cell, and in her prayer book she wrote, "My God have pity on me! My eyes have no more tears to shed for you, my poor children. Adieu, adieu!" When the executioner came on October 16, 1793, she was on her knees praying. At the Place de la Revolution, she was tied down and a wooden collar was snapped around her neck. The drums rolled, the blade fell, and a soldier held the head by its ghostly white hair before the multitude. She was not yet forty.

Now, Israel, I myself
will deal with you.
Get ready to face your God!
I created the mountains
and the wind.
I let humans know
what I am thinking. I bring darkness at dawn
and step over hills.
I am the LORD God All-Powerful! (Amos 4:12–13)

A New Heart

John Livingstone was a preacher's kid, born in Scotland in 1603. He continued living with his father when grown, and that caused problems. John wanted to move to France and study medicine. His father forbade him. The old man instead proposed that John marry, settle down nearby, and farm. John refused. They remained at loggerheads until the young man set aside a day to seek God's direction for his life. He retreated to the woods and after much agony surrendered himself to preach the gospel. His father acquiesced.

On January 2, 1625, John Livingstone preached his first sermon in his father's pulpit. He remained in his father's house for over a year, carefully writing out his sermons word for word. One day he was asked to preach to a crowd he had addressed just the previous day, and having written no new sermon, he jotted down a few notes and preached with greater power than he had yet experienced. He never again wrote out his sermons.

He was soon in demand, and in June of 1630, he was asked to preach at the Kirk of Shots. On Sunday night he gathered with Christian brothers and spent the night "in prayer and conference." The next morning he was seized by such feelings of inadequacy and unworthiness that he wondered if he could ever preach again. But that evening, Monday night, *June 21, 1630*, he rose to preach from Ezekiel 36:26–27: "I will take away your stubborn heart and give you a new heart and a desire to be faithful. You will have only pure thoughts, because I will put my Spirit in you."

Livingstone preached for an hour and a half, experiencing "the presence of God in preaching" as at no other moment in his life. The power of the Spirit fell on the meeting, and five hundred people later dated their conversion from that message.

His mighty preaching brought both fame and friction throughout Scotland, and he was eventually banished to Holland on account of his Nonconformist views. Many Scots had already fled to Rotterdam, and Livingstone ministered there among them until his death in 1672.

I will take away your stubborn heart and give you a new heart and a desire to be faithful. You will have only pure thoughts, because I will put my Spirit in you and make you eager to obey my laws and teachings. (Ezekiel 36:26–27)

A Simpler Lifestyle

J*une 22* on the church calendar honors the memory of Paulinus: a wealthy man who gave away his money, a married man who became a priest, and a lawyer who became a poet.

Paulinus was born in Bordeaux, Gaul (France), into a noble and wealthy family. His mind was good, his education advanced, and his future bright. He was admitted to the bar at a young age and entered political life in his twenties. He traveled widely and acquired homes in Gaul, Italy, and Spain. The empire's most prominent people sought his friendship, and he was one of Europe's most eligible bachelors. He fell in love with a Spanish lady named Theresia. They were married and retired to private life on their French estate.

Theresia, a Christian, shared the gospel freely with her new husband. He listened and sought out the local bishop with whom he became friends. As Paulinus investigated Christianity, he was impressed with its truthfulness and relevance. At age thirty-four, he gave his life to Christ and was baptized alongside his brother about the year 393.

Then tragedy made a visit. After years of childlessness, Theresia became pregnant and bore a son. When the baby died within a week, the couple was heartbroken. They reconsidered their values and decided on a far simpler lifestyle. Most of their possessions were sold, the money going to the poor.

The couple moved to Nola, a small town near Naples, and purchased a long, two-story building. They devoted the lower floor to the homeless and turned the upper floor into an informal monastery where they lived, taught Scripture, and encouraged God's people. Paulinus built a church for the community and funded a needed aqueduct. In time Paulinus was chosen to lead the church. He spent the rest of his life preaching there, overseeing the ministry, writing poetry, penning prayers, and corresponding with the most famous Christians of his generation. He encouraged Christian art as a tool for understanding Scripture. And according to tradition he was the first to introduce bells into Christian worship.

Warn the rich people of this world not to be proud or to trust in wealth that is easily lost. Tell them to have faith in God, who is rich and blesses us with everything we need to enjoy life. Instruct them to do as many good deeds as they can and to help everyone. Remind the rich to be generous and share what they have. This will lay a solid foundation for the future, so that they will know what true life is like. (1 Timothy 6:17–19)

The Augsburg Confession

You are better off to have a friend than to be all alone," said Solomon in Ecclesiastes 4:9. Martin Luther had Philipp Melanchthon. Melanchthon was younger, calmer, and smarter than Luther. Born in Germany in 1494, Melanchthon entered the University of Heidelberg at age thirteen, excelling in Greek. He became professor of Greek at the University of Wittenberg, where, in a stammering inaugural lecture, he appeared nervous. But Luther, professor of theology, listened with interest as the young man called students "back to the sources, back to the Holy Scriptures."

Soon the two were allies, as perfectly matched as David and Jonathan. Melanchthon, cautious and moderate, provided balance to Luther's impulsiveness. He was a peacemaker, as contrasted to Luther's contentiousness. Melanchthon tempered his friend's ideas and calmly drafted the theology and organization of Luther's movement. He became the formulating genius of the Reformation, casting Luther's teachings in proper, systematic form. Luther loved his younger associate, admitting that without Melanchthon's organizational skills his own work would have been lost.

Melanchthon also directed the publishing and educational side of the Reformation, and his work in developing German schools earned him the title "the teacher of Germany." He became involved in training clergy and wrote commentaries, theologies, and ministerial manuals for that purpose.

In 1529, Emperor Charles V, in a final effort to unify the church, called a meeting in Augsburg. Luther wasn't invited. The emperor hoped Melanchthon's gentler spirit might calm the storm and pacify the debate. But Melanchthon's beliefs were as deep as Luther's. On this night, *June 23, 1530*, being told a position paper was required quickly, Melanchthon worked into the wee hours, writing and rewriting and formulating Protestant doctrines. His paper was read on June 25, while delegates stood listening for two hours.

Its rejection by the largely Catholic assembly marked the final break between Protestants and Catholics. But the Augsburg Confession, with its definitive expression of Lutheran beliefs, has become the basis of Lutheran theology to this day.

You are better off to have a friend than to be all alone, because then you will get more enjoyment out of what you earn. If you fall, your friend can help you up. But if you fall without having a friend nearby, you are really in trouble. (Ecclesiastes 4:9–10)

June 24

Bones in the Rafters

Movements often suffer more from friends than from foes, and the devil often slips his extremists among God's servants. The Anabaptists, for example, were a peaceful people who believed in baptism as a symbol of salvation and opposed the baptism of infants. They originated the idea of the free church—a church separate from the state. And they provided the roots for such groups today as the Mennonites, the Amish, and the Brethren in Christ. But the Anabaptist movement itself never recovered from a fanatic named Jan van Leiden.

It happened in Munster, Germany. In the 1530s, Munster attracted many with Anabaptist sentiments, and in a series of elections Anabaptists gained control of the city council. Into the picture emerged twenty-eight-year-old Jan van Leiden. Charismatic and zealous, he seized power and stirred up the citizenry with soaring visions, calling Munster the New Jerusalem and himself King David. He took multiple wives and passed laws permitting polygamy, there being six times as many women as men in the city.

Jan predicted the world would soon end but that his followers would be spared. He forced people to be baptized and introduced communization of property. The Catholic world was shocked by his hedonistic orgies. The whole city was jolted when, in a fit of frenzy, he beheaded one of his four wives with his own hands in the marketplace.

On *June 24, 1535*, after twenty-four months of chaos and corruption, the besieged city fell to Francis of Waldeck, and Anabaptists were butchered. "King David" was captured and tortured, red-hot pinchers clawing every inch of his body. Then he was hung in a cage in the tower of the Church of St. Lambert in Munster's chief marketplace. His remains swung in the cage from the church rafters for four hundred years until finally removed in the twentieth century.

The Munster fiasco was the most serious aberration of sixteenth-century Anabaptism, and it strengthened the position of those wanting to persecute the Anabaptist cause. Rulers determined to rid Europe of every vestige of Anabaptism, and multitudes of good people suffered endlessly because of a handful of extremists.

You were doing so well until someone made you turn from the truth. And that person was certainly not sent by the one who chose you. A little yeast can change a whole batch of dough. (Galatians 5:7–9)

"Gipsy" Smith

Audiences never tired of hearing Rodney Smith tell his story: "I was born on the thirty-first of March, 1860, in a gipsy tent, the son of Cornelius Smith. When I got old enough to ask questions about my birth my mother was dead, but my father told me the place, though not the date. It was only recently that I knew the date. I discovered I was a year younger than I took myself to be."

It was while imprisoned for debts that Cornelius heard the gospel. Later he took his children to Latimer Road Mission where, as worshippers sang "There Is a Fountain Filled with Blood," he suddenly fell unconscious to the floor. Soon he jumped up, shouting, "I am converted! Children, God has made a new man of me!" Rodney ran from the church terrified.

But at age sixteen Rodney attended a Methodist meeting, went forward, and prayed for Christ to come into his own heart. Someone nearby whispered, "Oh, it's only a gipsy boy." But Rodney, undeterred, acquired a Bible, taught himself to read, and began preaching. His efforts came to the attention of General William Booth, and on *June 25, 1877*, Rodney attended a Salvation Army meeting. The general recognized him and said, "The next speaker will be the gipsy boy."

"Trembling, I took my way to the platform, which, luckily, was only five or six steps off. When I reached it, I shook in every limb. Mr. Booth saw I was in a predicament and said, 'Will you sing us a solo?' I said, 'I will try, sir'; and that night I sang my first solo at a big public meeting."

After his solo Rodney coughed nervously and said, "I am only a gipsy boy. I do not know what you know about many things, but I know Jesus. I know that He has saved me. I cannot read as you do; I do not live in a house as you do; I live in a tent. But I have got a great house up yonder, and some day I am going to live in it. My great desire is to live for Christ."

Thus began seventy years of remarkable, world-renowned evangelistic work.

Nothing is as wonderful as knowing Christ Jesus my Lord. I have given up everything else and count it all as garbage. All I want is Christ. All I want is to know Christ and the power that raised him to life. (Philippians 3:8, 10)

A Great Love Story

Few couples have worked with greater harmony of heart and aim than Francis and Edith Schaeffer, missionaries to the intellectuals of the twentieth century. The Schaeffers set out as overseas evangelists right after World War II, and they were soon attracting hoards of university students to their chalet in the village of Huemoz in the Swiss Alps. From this came L'Abri Fellowship, founded in 1955, a study center and refuge for students and skeptics seeking answers to the great philosophical questions of life.

How the Lord brought Francis and Edith together makes a great love story. Francis grew up in Germantown in northwest Philadelphia. His parents weren't believers, and he had little exposure to Christianity. But at age seventeen he began teaching English to a Russian immigrant, and he went to a bookstore to purchase an English grammar book. When he returned home, he found the salesclerk had wrapped the wrong book, an introduction to Greek philosophy. As Francis studied the book, he discovered the basic philosophical questions about the meaning of life. But he found no answers until he decided to read the Bible straight through. The Scripture brought him to faith in Christ.

On Sunday night, *June 26, 1932*, he attended a service at a nearby Presbyterian church. A Unitarian came to speak on why he denied the Bible and its teachings about God, Christ, and other vital truths. A young lady in the audience had prepared herself in advance to stand and refute the man's comments. When he finished his talk, Edith gripped her notes and prepared to challenge him. Before she could rise to her feet, Francis jumped up and began shredding the speaker's arguments. Edith listened in amazement. Until that moment she had not known of anyone else in the church who believed as she did. When Francis finished, she rose and made her comments. Francis was equally impressed. After the service, he insisted on accompanying Edith home.

Thus began a lifelong partnership in taking the gospel of Jesus Christ to students and scholars in America, Europe, and among the nations.

People will come to you
from distant nations and say,
"Our ancestors worshiped
false and useless gods,
worthless idols
made by human hands."
Then the LORD replied,
"That's why I will teach them
about my power,
and they will know
that I am the true God." (Jeremiah 16:19–21)

Abiding, Not Striving

Hudson Taylor envisioned a missionary task greater than any since the days of Paul—the evangelization of China. Toward that end he established the China Inland Mission (CIM) on *June 27, 1865*. It was the dream of his life, for even before age five he had told friends he wished to be a missionary to the Orient.

He wasn't actually converted to Christ, however, until years later. His mother long prayed for his conversion but with no apparent results. One day while a hundred miles from home, she felt unusually burdened for him. She withdrew to her room, locked the door, and began to pray earnestly. She didn't stop until convinced he had been saved.

Meanwhile the seventeen-year-old Taylor Hudson was at home with nothing to do. He wandered into his father's library, shuffled through some papers, and came to a leaflet that began with an interesting story. He read the story, then kept reading. It was a gospel tract, and as Taylor later put it, "Light was flashed into my soul by the Holy Spirit. There was nothing in the world to be done but to fall down on one's knees and [pray for salvation]."

After a stint in medical school, Taylor sailed for China. He was immediately engulfed in financial crises, language difficulties, homesickness, and personality conflicts with other missionaries. Trying to dye his hair black (to blend in with the Chinese), he was injured when the top blew off the ammonia bottle. More troubles followed, and over the next years Taylor grew bitterly depressed.

Then he received a letter from his friend John McCarthy, who told him to try "abiding, not striving nor struggling." Christ himself is "the only power for service; the only ground for unchanging joy."

Taylor said, "As I read, I saw it all. I looked to Jesus; and when I saw, oh, how the joy flowed. As to work, mine was never so plentiful or so difficult; but the weight and strain are gone." New voltage surged through his life and ministry as though he were connected to a heavenly power plant. By the time Hudson Taylor died, CIM had eight hundred missionaries in China.

I am the vine, and you are the branches. If you stay joined to me, and I stay joined to you, then you will produce lots of fruit. But you cannot do anything without me. (John 15:5)

June 28

Grumpy Old Man

Martin Luther, always stormy, became a virtual tempest in his latter days. His dogmatic outbursts and inflexible positions damaged the unity of the Reformation and troubled his friends, especially coworker Philipp Melanchthon. On *June 28, 1545*, John Calvin wrote Melanchthon, asking him to take Luther in hand:

> [Martin] allows himself to be carried beyond all bounds with his love of thunder. We all of us acknowledge that we are much indebted to him. But in the Church we must always be upon our guard, lest we pay too great a deference to men. It is all over when a single individual has more authority than all the rest. Where there is so much division and separation as we now see, it is indeed no easy matter to still the troubled waters and bring about composure. You will say that [Luther] has a vehement disposition and ungovernable impetuosity. Let us, therefore, bewail the calamity of the Church and not devour our grief in silence. While you dread to meddle with this question, you are leaving in perplexity and suspense very many persons who require from you somewhat a more certain sound on which they can repose.

But Melanchthon was seldom able to restrain Luther, and Luther's revered name was sullied by his obstinacy, his criticisms of other reformers, and his inexcusable tirades against Jews.

Hard times should never make us hardened people, and adversity should never make us abrasive. Psalm 92 teaches that aging saints are like palm trees and cedars—tall, stately, majestic, evergreen. Robertson McQuilkin has suggested that God planned the strength and beauty of youth to be physical, and the strength and beauty of age to be spiritual. We gradually lose the strength and beauty that is temporary so we'll be sure to concentrate on the strength and beauty that is forever.

That's a blessing that Luther, for all his merits, missed.

Our bodies are gradually dying, but we ourselves are being made stronger each day. These little troubles are getting us ready for an eternal glory that will make all our troubles seem like nothing. Things that are seen don't last forever, but things that are not seen are eternal. That's why we keep our minds on things that cannot be seen. (2 Corinthians 4:16–18)

The Fluttering Heart

David Hackston was a "Scottish Worthy"—one of those stalwart Calvinists who suffered terribly for his beliefs between the restoration of Charles II and the reign of William III.

Hackston was a well-off gentlemen who, wandering among the Scottish hills one day, heard some of the outlawed Presbyterian preachers. He returned home a new man in Christ. His life was immediately in jeopardy, and he became a fugitive, running from house and home, taking up arms against the crown. At length, he was captured, stripped ("not even having shoes on his feet"), and set backwards on a barebacked horse. His hands were tied behind him, and his feet were fastened under the horse's belly. Arriving in Edinburgh, he stood trial and gave this defense: "Now I stand here before you as a prisoner of Jesus Christ for adhering to his cause and interest, which has been sealed with the blood of many worthies who have suffered in these lands. I do own all the testimonies given by them, and desire to put in my mite among theirs, and am not only willing to seal it with my blood, but also to seal it with the sharpest tortures you can imagine."

They took him at his word. He was condemned on *June 29, 1662*, and the next day taken to an execution site. His right hand was stretched out and hacked off. The executioner took so long to do it that Hackston asked if the left hand could be severed at the joint. This was done. He was then pulled to the top of the gallows, allowed to choke awhile, then dropped with his whole weight. This was repeated twice. Then the hangman with a sharp knife sliced open his chest and pulled out his heart, still beating. It fell on the scaffold, and the hangman picked it up on the point of his knife and said, "Here is the heart of a traitor." Witnesses claim that it fluttered on the knife. Hackston's body was disemboweled, drawn, quartered, and burned. His head and hands were nailed to the top of a nearby bridge.

Give a kind and respectful answer and keep your conscience clear. This way you will make people ashamed for saying bad things about your good conduct as a follower of Christ. You are better off to obey God and suffer for doing right than to suffer for doing wrong. (1 Peter 3:16–17)

June 30 Eroticism to Evangelism

The best missionaries are often those saved from vilest lifestyles. Raymond Lull, for example, grew up self-indulged on the island of Majorca off the Spanish coast in the Mediterranean. His father was wealthy and powerful, a friend of the king. Lull, sexually indulgent, slept with many women, even following his marriage and the birth of two children. But one day at age thirty-two, writing some erotic poetry, he was stricken with guilt. He envisioned Christ suffering on the cross. He was converted.

Majorca was controlled by Muslims, and gradually the young man felt a desire to reach the Islamic world. After providing for his wife and children, Lull gave away the rest of his possessions. He studied extensively for several years, learning the Arabic language and all he could about both Christianity and Islam. With the king's help, he established a school on Majorca for the training of missionaries. He met repeatedly with popes and cardinals, trying to persuade them to establish similar schools across Europe for missionary training and language study. He lectured, wrote, and preached extensively. Then he began his actual missionary work at age fifty-five, targeting North Africa.

It began unsteadily. Having announced his departure for Tunis, Lull was joined by well-wishers at the port at Genoa. But he was suddenly overwhelmed by the terror of possible martyrdom. His belongings were unloaded, and the ship sailed without him. He quickly recovered and caught the next ship for Tunis. His fears were valid. He found himself in constant danger, living a fugitive's life. He was eventually arrested, deported, and stoned on his way to the boat. But he couldn't stay away, and he made repeated forays into North Africa, always at risk of life and limb. Throughout his seventies and into his eighties, Lull was preaching to Muslims. Finally on *June 30, 1314*, Lull was seized, dragged out of town, and stoned. He died shortly afterward. But he advanced Christian missions like no one else in his age and paved the way for everyone since with a burden for the Muslims.

What offering should I bring
when I bow down to worship
the LORD God Most High?
Should I try to please him by sacrificing
calves a year old?
The LORD God has told us
what is right
and what he demands:
"See that justice is done,
let mercy be your first concern,
and humbly obey your God." (Micah 6:6, 8)

On This Day in Christian History…

JULY

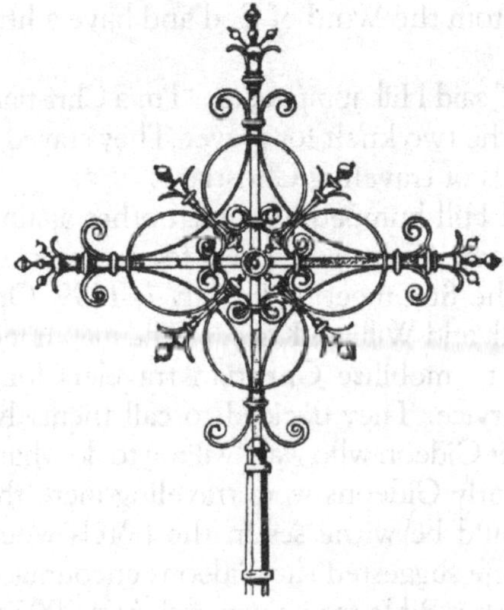

No Vacancy

A snug, private hotel room is a welcome site for traveling salesmen after a long day. But imagine arriving at your hotel only to find it so full that rooms had to be shared. That happened on September 14, 1898, at the Central Hotel of Boscobel, Wisconsin. John Nicholson arrived at 9:00 PM to find every room taken. The clerk suggested he share room 19 with a stranger, Samuel Hill.

Before crawling into bed, Nicholson opened his Bible. At age nineteen he had promised his dying mother he would read the Bible every night. Hill, asleep in the next bed, awoke. "Mr. Hill," said Nicholson, "you will pardon me if I keep the light on just a little longer; I make it a practice to read from the Word of God and have a little chat with him before I retire."

"Read it aloud," said Hill, jumping up. "I'm a Christian too." Nicholson read John 15, and the two knelt for prayer. They stayed up until 2:00 AM discussing the needs of traveling Christians.

Nicholson and Hill bumped into each other again in Beaver Dam, Wisconsin. They soon announced plans for an association of Christian salesmen, setting the first meeting for *July 1, 1899*. Only three showed up—Nicholson, Hill, and William Knights. The men nonetheless launched their organization to mobilize Christian travelers for encouragement, evangelism, and service. They decided to call themselves after the Old Testament character Gideon who was "willing to do whatever God asked."

Since all the early Gideons were traveling men, the question arose as to how they could be witnesses in the hotels where they spent so much time. Someone suggested the Gideons encourage every hotel they patronized to furnish a Bible for its patrons. At a 1907 Chicago meeting someone went so far as to suggest Gideons place Bibles in all the rooms of the hotels. The idea was adopted, the first distribution of Bibles occurring at the Superior Hotel in Iron Mountain, Montana, in 1908. Since then more than 750 million copies of Scripture have been distributed in more than 170 nations.

Gideon said, "When we get to the enemy camp, spread out and surround it. Then wait for me to blow a signal on my trumpet. As soon as you hear it, blow your trumpets and shout, 'Fight for the LORD! Fight for Gideon!'" (Judges 7:17–18)

"That Part of Publick Worship Called Singing"

From the records of the First Church of Windsor, Connecticut, for Sunday, *July 2, 1736*:

Society meeting, Capt. Pelatiah Allyn Moderator. The business of the meeting proceeded in the following manner: The Moderator proposed consideration of what should be done respecting that part of publick Worship called Singing, whether in their Publick meetings on Sabbath day, they would sing the way Deacon Marshall usually sung in his lifetime commonly called the "Old Way" or whether they would sing the way taught by Mr. Beal commonly called "Singing by Rule," and when the Society had discoursed the matter the Moderator proposed to vote. But when the vote was passed there being many voters it was difficult to take the exact number of votes in order to determine on which side the major vote was; whereupon the Moderator ordered all the voters to go out of the seats and stand in the alleys and then those that were for Deacon Marshalls way should go into the men's seats and those that were for Mr. Beals way should go into the women's seats. The Moderator asked me how many there was (for Deacon Marshall's way). I answered 42 and he said there was 63 or 64.

Then the Moderator proceeded and desired that those who were for singing in Publick the way that Mr. Beal taught would draw out of their seats and pass out of the door and be counted. They replied they were ready to show their minds in any proper way where they were if they might be directed thereto but would not go out the door to do the same and desired that they might be led to a vote where they were and they were ready to show their minds which the Moderator refused to do and thereupon declared that it was voted that Deacon Marshall's way of singing called the "Old Way" should be sung in Publick for the future and ordered me to record the same which I refused to do under the circumstances thereof and have recorded the facts and proceedings.

Then they sang a new song, "You are worthy . . .
And with your own blood
you bought for God
people of every tribe,
language, nation, and race.
Praise, honor, glory,
and strength
forever and ever
to the one who sits
on the throne
and to the Lamb!" (Revelation 5:9, 13)

July 3 The Trial of Faith

It's possible to love our families more than we love God, a sin that turns our children into idols. The Lord once tested two men along these lines—the patriarch Abraham with his son and the philanthropist George Mueller with his daughter. Mueller's ministry was primarily to orphans, but it was his own child who most tested his faith. His journal says:

> My beloved daughter and only child, and a believer since 1846, was taken ill on June 20, 1853. This illness, at first a low fever, turned to typhus. On *July 3rd* there seemed no hope of her recovery. Now was the trial of faith. But faith triumphed. My beloved wife and I were enabled to give her up into the hands of the Lord. He sustained us both exceedingly. Though my only and beloved child was brought near the grave, yet was my soul in perfect peace, satisfied with the will of my Heavenly Father, being assured that He would only do that for her and her parents, which in the end would be best. She continued very ill till about July 20th, when restoration began.
>
> Parents know what an only child, a beloved child, is. Well, the Father in Heaven said, as it were, "Art thou willing to give up this child to me?" My heart responded, "As it seems good to Thee, my Heavenly Father. Thy will be done." But as our hearts were made willing to give back our child to Him, so He was ready to leave her to us, and she lived.
>
> Of all the trials of faith that as yet I have had to pass through, this was the greatest; and by God's abundant mercy, I own it to His praise, I was enabled to delight myself in the will of God; for I felt perfectly sure, that, if the Lord took this beloved daughter, it would be best for her parents, best for herself, and more for the glory of God than if she lived. This better part I was satisfied with; and thus my heart had peace, perfect peace.

"Don't hurt the boy or harm him in any way!" the angel said. "Now I know that you truly obey God, because you were willing to offer him your only son." Abraham looked up and saw a ram caught by its horns in the bushes. So he took the ram and sacrificed it in place of his son." Abraham named that place "The LORD Will Provide." (Genesis 22:12–14)

The Investment

Martha Scarborough celebrated Independence Day, *July 4, 1870*, by giving birth to a son, Lee. When the boy was eight, Martha and her husband George, a part-time Baptist preacher, moved to Texas to raise cattle and share Christ. A dugout shelter first served as home, then a log cabin near Clear Fork Creek. George and Martha dreamed of a beautiful house atop a nearby hill. They saved frugally, but times were lean, and years passed before they accumulated enough to proceed with the long-discussed house. Lee, meanwhile, grew into a brawny sixteen-year-old cowboy.

One day, their work behind them, George said to Martha, "Let's go up the hill and select a suitable place for the home. We have saved money for that purpose, so we had as well begin plans to build." Arm in arm the couple strolled to the grassy crest of the hill behind their cabin. This was a moment long anticipated. At the top of the hill, he said, "Here is the place. This is the most suitable location we can find." But Martha turned toward him, her eyes filling with tears. "My dear," she said, "I do appreciate your desire to build me a new, comfortable home on this place of beauty, but there is another call for our money which is far greater. Let's live on in the old house and put this money in the head and heart of our boy. I fear that if we use this money to build a home we shall never be able to send Lee to college. I would rather a thousand times that we should never build this house if we can invest the money in our boy."

George was disappointed, and he said little for several days. Finally one evening past midnight he yielded. The house was never built, but Lee Scarborough left home on January 8, 1888, for Baylor College in Waco, Texas. He eventually became a powerhouse for Christ, a Southern Baptist leader, a writer, a seminary president, a pastor, an evangelist, and a business leader who built colleges, seminaries, churches, hospitals, and mission stations around the world.

Invest in truth and wisdom,
discipline and good sense,
and don't part with them.
Make your father truly happy
by living right
and showing
sound judgment.
Make your parents proud,
especially your mother. (Proverbs 23:23–25)

Bread and Book

When parents grow exasperated with their children, they often need to remember that God frames us all differently, giving each child a unique perspective and personality.

George Borrow was born on *July 5, 1803*, during the age of Napoleon, and George's soldier-father expected a disciplined and eager son. Instead, George was moody and introspective with a penchant for running away. He was bored with the conventional and intrigued by the odd. He hated school but possessed an insatiable curiosity about herbalists, fortune-tellers, snakes, and dwarfs. He picked up languages with remarkable ease yet adopted a gypsy life, eventually becoming a tinker with cart and pony, selling pots and pans.

One evening while sleeping under the stars, George was awakened by a muffled voice saying, "Cut the rope; this is his pony." By the faint glow of smoking embers, George saw two figures stealing his rig. He leaped on them, and for two hours the men fought and wrestled. Then one of the thieves smashed George's head with a rock, and the rogues threw his body into the underbrush.

The next morning two traveling Welsh evangelists saw a pair of feet sticking from a thicket. They dragged George to a clearing and attended his cuts with a damp cloth. The men gave him some bread and a book before going their way. George sat in the grass for hours, devouring both the bread and the book, a Bible—the Bread of Life. His brilliant mind soon discovered the Lord.

In coming years George learned dozens of languages and became a Bible translator. His autobiography, telling his adventures as a colporteur for the British and Foreign Bible Society, is full of breathtaking perils, narrow escapes, imprisonments, and gypsy-like journeys, especially in Spain.

This odd man and his remarkable ministry captured the imagination of England and greatly advanced the cause of European Bible distribution.

Don't forget how the LORD your God has led you through the desert for the past forty years. He wanted to find out if you were truly willing to obey him and depend on him, so he made you go hungry. Then he gave you manna, a kind of food that you and your ancestors had never even heard about. The LORD was teaching you that people need more than food to live—they need every word that the LORD has spoken. (Deuteronomy 8:2–3)

Brief Reunion

On November 17, 1417, Cardinal Oddone Colonna was elected Pope Martin V in Constance, and when he later arrived in Rome, he was shocked by the conditions he saw. Both buildings and people were dilapidated, and the capital of Christendom had deteriorated into perhaps the least civilized city in Europe. Italy was in turmoil. Warlords ruled the cities, and bandits terrorized the countryside. The pope's treasuries were empty, and his enemies legion.

Martin restored order in Rome, cleared out nests of bandits along roadways, and named men of intellect to office. He was more a political than a spiritual leader, but he ate sparingly, drank only water, slept little, worked hard, and earned the respect of the people and the wrath of his foes.

Meanwhile the patriarch of Constantinople, Martin's counterpart in the Eastern Church, was having problems of his own. The Ottomans were advancing on Constantinople, and Eastern leaders, who had torn apart from Rome in 1054, now needed military help. News that Christendom might reunite stirred all Europe. On February 8, 1438, Patriarch Joseph of Constantinople arrived in Venice with a delegation of seven hundred to meet Pope Martin. A joint council convened in Ferrara, then in Florence. Committees formulated ways to reconcile the divergences between the two churches, tackling issues like the relationship between pope and patriarch, the use of unleavened bread, the nature of purgatory, and the role of the Holy Spirit. Debates raged for months; then compromises were struck. On *July 6, 1439*, in the great cathedral of Florence, the council read a decree uniting the two churches. The leaders kissed, and all present bent the knee and celebrated.

Their joy was brief. The people of Constantinople flatly rejected the decisions. The Turkish Ottomans took the city and decreed it Islamic. And back in Florence, the Renaissance broke out partly because of the impact made by the influx of Eastern Greeks to the council that had been hosted by Cosimo de' Medici. The Ferrara/Florence Council, one might argue, contributed to losing the church in the East to the Muslims and the church in the West to the humanists.

My dear friends, remember the warning you were given by the apostles of our Lord Jesus Christ. They told you that near the end of time, selfish and godless people would start making fun of God. And now these people are already making you turn against each other. They think only about this life, and they don't have God's Spirit. (Jude 17–19)

July 7 Christ's Withered Garden

Samuel Rutherford was born in Scotland in 1600. He lived a careless life as a youth, but after graduating from the university in Edinburgh, he became serious about following Christ. He studied theology and was licensed to preach. The Scottish village of Anwoth, Kirkcudbrightshire, called him to pastor its church. Rutherford's wife and two of his children died shortly after arrival. But Samuel busied himself with ministry and pressed on.

Rutherford's vision encompassed the entire Scottish church, suffering at the time from weak theology. He wrote a book entitled *An Apology for Divine Grace*, which so attacked the clergy that he was withdrawn from his church and exiled in Aberdeen, forbidden to preach. He felt like a half-blind man whose one eye had just been plucked out. There, suffering mentally and spiritually, he wrote a letter on *July 7, 1627*, to his similarly beleaguered friend, James Hamilton:

> For your ensuing and feared trial, my dearest in our Lord Jesus, alas! What am I, to speak comfort to a soldier of Christ who hath done a hundred times more for that worthy cause than I can do! But I know, those of whom the world was not worthy wandered up and down in deserts and in mountains and in dens and caves of the earth; and while there is one member of mystical Christ out of heaven, that member must suffer strokes, till our Lord Jesus draw in that member within the gates of the New Jerusalem.
>
> My one joy, next to Christ, was to preach my sweetest, sweetest Master and the glory of his Kingdom; and it seemed no cruelty to them to put out the poor man's one eye. I cannot be delivered. None here will have my Master. Alas! what aileth them? (But) fear not. Christ's withered garden shall grow green again in Scotland. My Lord Jesus hath a word hid in heaven for Scotland, not yet brought out.

Rutherford didn't realize that the Lord's hidden word for Scotland included his own collected letters from Aberdeen, published after his death and destined to become one of the classics of Christian literature.

I am badly injured
and in constant pain.
Are you going to disappoint me,
like a stream that goes dry
in the heat of summer?
Then the LORD told me:
Stop talking like a fool! . . .
I am making you strong,
like a bronze wall.
They are evil and violent,
but when they attack,
I will be there to rescue you. (Jeremiah 15:18–21)

Spiders over the Fire

Jonathan Edwards, a New England pastor of the 1700s,is often identified as America's greatest theologian. Edwards was brilliant. At six he studied Latin. He entered Yale when not quite thirteen and graduated when barely fifteen. He was ordained at age nineteen, taught at Yale by age twenty, and later became president of Princeton. Harvard granted him both a bachelor's and a master's degree on the same day. But he is best known for his "Sinners in the Hands of an Angry God"—the most famous sermon in American history.

He preached it on Sunday, *July 8, 1741*, while ministering in tiny Enfield, Connecticut. A group of women had spent the previous night praying for revival. When Edwards rose to speak, he quietly announced that his text was Deuteronomy 32:35, "Their foot shall slip in due time" (NKJV). This "hellfire and brimstone" approach was somewhat a departure for Edwards. Of his one thousand written sermons, fewer than a dozen are of this type.

Edwards spoke softly and simply, warning the unconverted that they were dangling over hell like a spider over the fire. "O sinner! consider the fearful danger. The unconverted are now walking over the pit of hell on a rotten covering, and there are innumerable places in this covering so weak that it will not bear their weight, and these places are not seen."

Edwards's voice was suddenly lost amid cries and commotion from the crowd. He paused, appealing for calm. Then he concluded: "Let everyone that is out of Christ, now awake and fly from the wrath to come. The wrath of Almighty God is now undoubtedly hanging over a great part of this congregation. Let every one fly out of Sodom."

Strong men held to pews and posts, feeling they were sliding into hell. Others shook uncontrollably and rolled on the floor. Cries of men and women were heard throughout the village, begging God to save them. Five hundred were converted that evening, sparking a revival that swept thousands into the kingdom.

The Great Awakening had come.

> Soon our enemies will get
> what they deserve—suddenly they will slip,
> and total disaster
> will quickly follow.
> When only a few
> of the LORD's people remain,
> when their strength is gone,
> and some of them are slaves,
> the LORD will feel sorry for them
> and give them justice. (Deuteronomy 32:35–36)

Ora et Labora

A group of frightened children huddled around their mother's bed in a dark little room in Germany. Among them was a bewildered four-year-old boy about to become an orphan. As he listened, his sinking mother whispered, "My dear children, I have a great treasure for you."

"What is it, Mother?" asked an older sister.

The woman pointed to the Bible. "Seek it in the Bible; there you will find great treasure. I have watered every page with my tears." With that she died. The family was broken up, and little Bartholomew Ziegenbalg went to live with sympathetic friends in Halle. He never forgot his mother's words, and at age twelve, he claimed Christ as his Savior. At eighteen he graduated from the university in Halle with honors.

Lutheranism in Germany had been rekindled by a revival known as Pietism, and King Ferdinard of Denmark had been stirred. He appealed for missionaries for the Danish possession of Tranquebar on the southern tip of India. Ziegenbalg heard the call and presented himself. Scarcely anyone saw him off at the dock, and the trip to India was long—seven months, twenty days. He arrived in India on *July 9, 1706*, and was promptly imprisoned.

Ziegenbalg, however, had a motto: *Ora et Labora*—Pray and Work! He would not be denied. Even in prison, he labored at learning the Tamil language, and as soon as he gained freedom, he began sharing Christ. Within a year he baptized five slaves in the first Protestant baptismal service ever held in India, and soon the first Protestant church for nationals in India was dedicated. By 1711, Ziegenbalg completed the translation of the New Testament into Tamil, along with Luther's catechism, a Danish liturgy, and some German hymns.

His health failed after thirteen years, and he died at Tranquebar in 1719, at age thirty-five, leaving 350 converts to mourn his death and continue his work. If William Carey is the Father of Modern Missions, perhaps Ziegenbalg should be called its grandfather, for he served faithfully in India almost a generation before the Moravian missionaries left Herrnhut and approximately one hundred years before Carey.

Because of Christ Jesus, I can take pride in my service for God. In fact, all I will talk about is how Christ let me speak and work, so that the Gentiles would obey him. I have always tried to preach where people have never heard about Christ. I am like a builder who doesn't build on anyone else's foundation. (Romans 15:17–18, 20)

A Little Relief

During the days of Emperor Trajan, John the apostle, the last surviving of the twelve disciples, passed away of natural causes. Then Trajan himself fell ill, suffered a stroke, developed dropsy, and died in 117, at the age of sixty-four. His widow conspired with Hadrian to bring him to the throne. He was tall and elegant, his hair curly, and he sported a beard to hide the blemishes on his face.

During 124–125, Emperor Hadrian provided a little relief for suffering Christians. Anti-Christian riots had broken out in Asia Minor, and the governor had written Hadrian for advice. The emperor, whose nod against the church might well have led to a Christian holocaust, proved neutral. He ordered cases against Christians tried, but he decreed that the defendants had to be proven guilty before they could be condemned. Slanderous attacks on them were forbidden.

> Now, if our subjects of the provinces are able to sustain by evidence their charges against the Christians I have no objection. But I do not allow them to have recourse to mere clamorous demands and outcries to this end. If therefore anyone accuses and proves that the aforesaid men do anything contrary to the laws, you will pass sentences corresponding to their offenses. On the other hand, I emphatically insist that if anyone demand a writ of summons against any of these Christians merely as a slanderous accusation, you proceed against that man with heavier penalties, in proportion to the gravity of his offense.

But while Hadrian was indifferent toward Christianity, he was bitterly opposed to Judaism. He ordered Jerusalem rebuilt as a Roman colony and renamed Aelia Capitolina. He erected pagan altars on the temple site, leading to another Jewish uprising and bloodbath. It was during that same year, 135, that Hadrian, fifty-nine, fell sick with a painful, wasting illness. He begged for hemlock. No one would oblige him, and he suffered three years before dying on *July 10, 138.*

Children, this is the last hour. You heard that the enemy of Christ would appear at this time, and many of Christ's enemies have already appeared. So we know that the last hour is here. Keep thinking about the message you first heard, and you will always be one in your heart with the Son and with the Father. (1 John 2:18, 24)

The Homemade Rope

The growth of the Korean Church, one of the greatest legacies of modern Christianity, came at a cost. The first Catholic missionaries were persecuted in the 1700s, and the first Protestant missionary, Carl Gutzlaff, stayed only a month in 1832. The next, Robert Thomas, arrived in 1876 to become the first Protestant martyr there. Then on *July 11, 1886*, missionary Horace Underwood secretly administered the first Protestant baptism on Korean soil to Mr. Toh Sa No.

But was Mr. No really the first convert?

In his book *What in the World Is God Doing?* Dr. Ted Engstrom relates a story told him by a veteran Korean Christian. In the early 1880s, three Korean workmen, laboring in China, heard the gospel and embraced the Lord Jesus. The three soon conspired about getting the message of Christ into their own country, an action forbidden by the government. Since the Korean and Chinese alphabets were similar, they decided to smuggle in a copy of the Chinese Bible. They drew straws to see who would have the privilege of bringing the gospel into Korea.

The first man buried the Bible in his belongings and headed toward the border, a journey of many days by footpath. There he was searched, found out, and killed. Word reached the others that their friend was dead. The second man tore pages from his Bible and hid the separate pages throughout his luggage. He, too, made the long trip to the border only to be searched and beheaded.

The third man grew more determined than ever to succeed. He ingeniously tore his Bible apart page by page, folding each page into a tiny strip. He wove the strips into a rope and wrapped his baggage in his homemade rope. When he came to the border, the guards asked him to unwrap his belongings. Finding nothing amiss, they admitted him.

The man arrived home, untied the rope, and ironed out each page. He reassembled his Bible and began to preach Christ wherever he went. And when the missionaries of the 1880s fanned into the country, they found the seed already sown and the firstfruits appearing.

> Our LORD, you are eternal!
> Your word will last as long
> as the heavens. You remain faithful
> in every generation,
> and the earth you created
> will keep standing firm.
> Brutal enemies are waiting
> to ambush and destroy me,
> but I obey your rules. (Psalm 119:89–90, 95)

Scotland's Preacher

Thomas Guthrie was born on *July 12, 1803*, to a prosperous merchant and his devout wife. He entered the University of Edinburgh at age twelve, devoured the physical sciences, and graduated at sixteen. He followed his inclinations toward theological studies, and in 1830, assumed the pastorate of a small congregation of farmers and weavers in Arbirlot, Scotland. He started with a rush, forming cottage prayer meetings, Sunday schools, and a parish library. His preaching was relentless, warm, and well received.

After seven years, Guthrie was made minister of Old Gray Friars Church in Edinburgh, then of St. John's Church in Edinburgh's slums. He established ministries to the poor, whom he frequently visited, talking with them about their feelings and needs. He continually innovated. His best-known program was the Ragged Schools for juvenile delinquents. He fiercely promoted total abstinence, seeing daily the effects of alcohol on the unfortunate. The poor loved him. Yet his outgoing personality, intense passion, and colorful sermons appealed to the higher classes of society, and Guthrie soon became the most popular minister in Scotland.

When his health failed, he turned from pastoring to spend his remaining years editing a Christian magazine. On February 24, 1873, while resting in the arms of his son, he looked up and said, "I am as helpless now in your arms as you were in mine when you were a baby." With that, he died. His funeral procession wound through a crowd of thirty thousand spectators, which included 230 children from the original Ragged School.

The success of his preaching is best explained in his own words:

> When I went to Arbirlot I knew pretty well how to speak sermons, but very little about how to compose them; so I set myself vigorously to study how to illustrate the great truths of the gospel, so that there should be no sleepers in the church, no wandering eyes; but everywhere an eager attention. To convert my hearers was not within my power; but to command their attention, to awaken their interest, to touch their feelings and instruct their minds, was—and I determined to do it.

Be pleasant and hold their interest when you speak the message. Choose your words carefully and be ready to give answers to anyone who asks questions. (Colossians 4:6)

Domini Canes

Dominic and Francis lived at the same time, and both founded an order of preachers—the Dominicans and the Franciscans. Francis grew up amid great wealth, repudiated it all, and established an order stressing manual labor and preaching. Dominic grew up in libraries and study cells, embraced it all, and founded an order stressing study and preaching.

Dominic was born in Spain in 1170. His mother, Juana, raised him until he reached seven then passed him to the priestly instruction of his uncle. The young man loved his studies, especially philosophy and theology. In 1202, while accompanying a Spanish bishop to France on a mission to secure a wife for a Spanish prince, he was greatly moved by the need he saw. Theology in France was weak, doctrine was faulty, and heresy was rampant.

Dominic organized a preaching tour especially aimed at converting those who had fallen into error. Death threats and danger imperiled him on every side, but he pressed on, using persuasion rather than persecution to convert the heretics. By 1215, he was recruiting other preachers to the task. The order quickly took root in Paris, Bologna, Rome, Madrid, and Seville. Dominican preachers went into Germany, where chapters were established in Cologne, Worms, Strasburg, and Basel. In 1221, the order was introduced into England and settled in Oxford.

Dominic preached throughout Europe until he fell ill and returned to Bologna, where he died on August 6, 1221. He was canonized on *July 13, 1234*. At the time of his death, his preaching friars had sixty monasteries scattered from England to Eastern Europe.

But even a good cause can take a wrong turn. The symbol of the Dominicans eventually became a watchdog carrying a flaming torch—the *Domini Canes*. Their zeal for orthodoxy led to their being named chief agents of the Inquisition. They loaded up suspected heretics by the wagonful and took them to grim dungeons to be tortured. The devil, having created the disease of heresy, managed also to corrupt the cure.

Don't let the errors of evil people lead you down the wrong path and make you lose your balance. Let the wonderful kindness and the understanding that come from our Lord and Savior Jesus Christ help you to keep on growing. Praise Jesus now and forever! Amen. (2 Peter 3:17–18)

The Gambler

Gambling can take a man's shirt off his back, but Christ can clothe him with hope. Camillus de Lellis learned both lessons. He was an Italian, born in 1550, to a mother who was almost sixty years old. By the age of seventeen Camillus stood six and a half feet, big boned, well muscled, quick-tempered, and unchaste. He enlisted in the army, was sent to war, and on the battlefield contracted a leg disease that afflicted him the rest of his life.

The hospital for incurables in Rome, San Giacomo, admitted him, but he was soon ejected for quarreling. That wasn't his worst fault. Camillus relished betting, and by 1574, his addiction had taken his last penny. That autumn in the streets of Naples, he gambled with his last possession, the shirt on his back. Losing the wager, he stripped it off and limped away both broke and broken.

Camillus secured a construction job, and one day a friar came along preaching. The message hit home, and Camillus fell to his knees, crying to God for mercy. He was twenty-five when he became a Christian. He returned to San Giacomo and offered himself as a volunteer. He ministered intently to the suffering, and in time he was promoted, then promoted again. He eventually became hospital superintendent.

With a friend's endowment, he organized a small army of male nurses to serve the sick in Christ's name. He also mobilized volunteers to travel with troops in Hungary and Croatia, thus forming the first military field ambulance. He sent nurses aboard galley ships to attend slaves suffering from pestilence. In all Camillus organized eight hospitals, pioneered medical hygiene and diet, and successfully opposed the prevailing practice of burying patients alive.

All the while Camillus's leg was worsening, and he began suffering ruptures elsewhere on his body. Sometimes on his rounds, he crawled from sickbed to sickbed. On *July 14, 1614*, after a final tour of his works, Camillus de Lellis died at age sixty-four. He was canonized in 1746, and declared patron saint of the sick by Pope Leo XIII, and of nurses and nursing by Pope Pius XI. In Catholic tradition he is remembered every year on this day.

> If you don't confess your sins,
> you will be a failure.
> But God will be merciful
> if you confess your sins
> and give them up.
> The LORD blesses everyone
> who is afraid to do evil,
> but if you are cruel,
> you will end up in trouble. (Proverbs 28:13–14)

July 15

The First Crusade

In 1095, Pope Urban II preached an electrifying sermon before a great multitude. He described the plight of the Eastern church, inundated by Turkish Muslims. Infidels controlled the Holy Land, Urban thundered, and Jerusalem's Church of the Holy Sepulcher, the holiest spot in Christendom, lay in Islamic hands.

All Europe set out to liberate Jerusalem. Colorful hordes of militant lords and ladies, knights, and peasants marched two thousand miles across Europe.

Their numbers were soon depleted, however, by the realities of war. By the time the crusaders reached Jerusalem, only about twenty thousand remained. Meanwhile the Islamic governor of Jerusalem readied for siege. Wells outside city walls were poisoned. Flocks were driven into the city, and Christian inhabitants expelled. Jerusalem's ancient towers were reinforced.

A lunar eclipse on June 5 seemed to augur success for the pilgrims, and on the evening of June 7, the main army reached the Holy City. On June 12, a hermit on the Mount of Olives promised, "If you will attack the city tomorrow, the Lord will deliver it into your hands."

When the sun rose over the city the next day, trumpets blared, and the armies melted into attacking hoards assailing the walls. Ladders were thrown up, and knights scaled the ramparts only to be repelled by sticks, stones, and boiling oil. The assault failed. Thirst set in. Temperatures reached a hundred degrees, and the wind blew hot. Rotting corpses of horses sullied the air. Quarrels broke out. Rumors of advancing Muslim forces frightened the troops.

On Wednesday, July 13, another assault was mounted. The city finally fell on Friday, *July 15, 1099*, at three o'clock—the day and hour of the Savior's death, it was noted. Crusaders slaughtered the inhabitants until streets were choked with the dead. None were spared. Jews perished in burning synagogues, and the blood of Muslims flowed up to the ankles. Jubilant crusaders sang hymns as they waded through a sea of bodies to the holiest spot in Christendom.

Jerusalem, we pray
that you will have peace,
and that all will go well
for those who love you.
May there be peace
inside your city walls
and in your palaces.
Let's pray for peace in Israel! (Psalm 122:6–7; 128:6)

I Will Still Celebrate

The London plague of 1665 was terrible. Most shops closed, orphans roamed the streets, parents wailed, and the dead were borne out daily. On *July 16, 1665*, businessman Walter Petherick, a widower with four children, took his family to the parish church. The sun was brilliant, the Thames smooth. But the heart of London was sad, and the somber church was packed. The minister read from Habakkuk 3: "Fig trees may no longer bloom, or vineyards produce grapes; olive trees may be fruitless, and harvest time a failure; sheep pens may be empty, and cattle stalls vacant—but I will still [rejoice in the Lord]."

That evening a horror fell over Petherick. He feared his children would die. He called them together, read Habakkuk 3, sent them to bed, then knelt and prayed earnestly for the first time in years. He cried over each child, saying, "If my children were snatched from me—my fine boys and lovely girls—the treasures that *she* left me—how could I rejoice in the Lord?" He continued praying in anguish, "Spare him, oh, spare him. Spare her, O Lord; have pity!"

As he prayed he realized he had long neglected prayer and the Lord. He had been more concerned for figs and olives and cattle and harvest than for the things of Christ. He wept, confessed, prayed on—and found peace.

The next year as the Great Fire consumed London, it threatened Petherick's warehouse containing practically all his earthly substance. This time, however, there was no anguish, just simple trust in God's will. He later wrote, "Lord, thou hast been pleased by pestilence and fire to redeem my soul from destruction. Thou didst threaten me with the loss of thy choicest gifts that I might set my heart's affections once more upon the Giver. But the fig tree did not wither; the vines did not perish; the olive not fail. The pestilence did not touch my children; the flames did not destroy my goods. Accept the thanks of thy servant this day and help him, all his days, to rejoice in the Lord."

Fig trees may no longer bloom,
or vineyards produce grapes;
olive trees may be fruitless,
and harvest time a failure;
sheep pens may be empty,
and cattle stalls vacant—
but I will still celebrate
because the LORD God
saves me.
The LORD gives me strength.
He makes my feet as sure
as those of a deer. (Habbakkuk 3:17–19)

July 17

The Martyrs of Scilli

The northern shores of Africa teemed with Christians during the second century, but all were at risk. In 180, seven men and five women were captured carrying "the sacred books, and the letters of Paul, a just man." On *July 17, 180*, they appeared before the Roman proconsul Saturninus in Carthage. Charges against them were read: "Whereas Speratus, Nartzalus, Cittinus, Donata, Vestia, Secunda, and the rest have confessed they live in accordance with the religious rites of the Christians, and when an opportunity was given them of returning to the usage of the Romans they persevered in their obstinacy, it is our pleasure they should suffer the sword."

Speratus, hearing the charges, shouted, "Thanks be to God!"

Nartzalus said, "Today we are martyrs in heaven. Thanks be to God!"

The proconsul was bewildered by their reaction and by their claim that Christianity was the only true religion. "We, too, have a religion," he said, "and ours is a simple one. We swear by the fortune of the emperor. You should do the same."

Speratus replied, "I do not recognize an empire in this world. I serve that God whom no man has seen or can see. The Lord I acknowledge is the Emperor of all kings and all nations."

Donata added, "Honor to Caesar, but reverence to God alone."

"We reverence no one except our God in heaven," said another.

Saturninus, still perplexed, asked, "Would you like time to think it over?"

"What is the use?" replied Speratus. "The matter is as plain as can be."

And it was. The early Christians expected persecution. The Savior had died on the cross, the Twelve had suffered for their faith, and no generation since had escaped pain and bloodshed. In 95, Domitian executed his own family members who espoused Christianity. In 107, Simeon, Bishop of Jerusalem, was killed. In 110, Ignatius died. Polycarp was martyred in 155. In 165, Justin Martyr was scourged and killed. In 177, forty-eight Christians perished in France.

And in 180, the twelve from Scilli were marched out and beheaded.

It is exactly as the Scriptures say, "For you we face death
all day long.
We are like sheep
on their way
to be butchered."
In everything we have won more than a victory because of Christ who loves us.
(Romans 8:36–37)

Exquisite Cruelty

The sickening crackle of flames attracted the attention of residents near the Circus Maximus in Rome *July 18, 64.* Trumpets sounded the alarm, but winds whipped the fire into an inferno that spread across the Eternal City, roaring unchecked for a week. Thousands died, and hundreds of thousands became homeless. Rumors circulated that the fire had been started by the emperor himself—twenty-six-year-old Nero.

Nero had become emperor ten years before, and almost from the beginning, the teenage emperor had gorged himself with eroticism. He arranged the murders of his mother, wives, rivals, and enemies. At the same time, he won praise for his artistic and athletic pursuits. He began thinking himself a god, though he was actually "a degenerate with swollen paunch, weak and slender limbs, fat face, blotched skin, curly yellow hair, and dull gray eyes."

The arson rumors began because Nero had been wanting to raze and rebuild large portions of Rome, planning to rename the city for himself. A fire, people assumed, was just what the emperor had ordered. To divert blame, Nero pointed a finger at Christians. Tacitus wrote that the followers of Christ "were put to death with exquisite cruelty, and to their sufferings Nero added mockery and derision. Some were covered with skins of wild beasts, left to be devoured by dogs; others were nailed to crosses; numbers of them were burned alive; many, covered with inflammable matter, were set on fire to serve as torches during the night." Peter and Paul, according to tradition, were among the martyrs.

But what of the young emperor himself? Four years later he died, too, trembling and terrified in a cold cellar four miles from Rome while hiding from his own army. Trying repeatedly to commit suicide, he faltered and failed until a friend helped him plunge a dagger into his throat.

But within a short time the church in Rome was stronger than ever, and St. Peter's Cathedral stands today on the very spot where Christians were tortured in Nero's Circus.

You have faith in God, whose power will protect you until the last day. Then he will save you, just as he has always planned to do . . . Your faith will be like gold that has been tested in a fire. (1 Peter 1:5, 7)

July 19 A Tender Conscience

Samuel Ward stuffed himself with plums one evening. In his journal the next morning, *July 19, 1596*, he confessed his sin—"my gluttony in eating plums and raisins and drinking so much after supper." It was one of many such confessions.

Samuel was a Puritan, born in 1577, who attended St. John's College, Cambridge, and was a fellow at Sidney College. In 1603, he became town preacher at St. Mary's in Ipswich. He married Deborah Bolton, a widow from Cambridgeshire, the following year. When King James approved a new translation of the Bible, Samuel was selected as part of the New Testament translating team. Samuel, known as the youngest of the King James translators, is better known for his diary in which he daily confessed his sins:

May 13—My desire of preferment over much. Thy [he often addressed himself in the second person] wandering regard in the chapel at prayer time.
May 17—Thy gluttony the night before.
May 23—My sleeping without remembering my last thought, which should have been of God.
May 26—Thy dullness this day in hearing God's word . . . thy by-thoughts at prayer time same evening.
June 12—My too much drinking after supper.
June 14—My negligence . . . in sleeping immediately after dinner.
June 22—My immoderate diet of eating cheese.
June 27—My going to drink wine and that in the tavern, before I called upon God.
July 8—My immoderate laughter in the hall.
July 15—My incontinent thoughts at Hobsons.
July 23—For eating so many plums, although thou heard that many died of surfeits (intemperance).
August 13—My intemperate eating of damsons, also my intemperate eating of cheese after supper.
August 21—My long sleeping in the morning.

Despite his vices (and perhaps because of his diligence in confessing them, being tender of conscience) he did a great work for Christ and helped translate the most beautiful version of the Bible in history.

Let's come near God with pure hearts and a confidence that comes from having faith. Let's keep our hearts pure, our consciences free from evil, and our bodies washed with clean water. (Hebrews 10:22)

The East-West Schism

During the first millennium of Christianity, two centers of gravity emerged—Rome and Constantinople. As the centuries passed, differences in theology developed and a rivalry emerged between the pope in Rome and the patriarch in Constantinople. The two camps differed on issues such as whether priests could marry, the makeup of Eucharistic bread, days of fasting, and whether the Holy Spirit proceeds from the Father and the Son or just from the Father.

In 1043, a rigid, ambitious churchman named Michael Cerularius was named patriarch of Constantinople, and five years later in Rome a French bishop rose to the papacy under the name Leo IX. During those days Norman armies overran southern Italy and replaced Eastern (Orthodox) bishops from Constantinople with Western (Catholic) bishops from Rome. The new bishops started changing forms of worship, and when Michael Cerularius heard it, he retaliated by closing Roman churches in the Eastern regions.

Leo sent three men to Constantinople to deal with the problem. They were led by Humbert, a pompous, tactless man, who arrived in the imperial city denouncing, decrying, berating, and condemning the Orthodox leaders. The legates were housed in the imperial palace, but the patriarch ignored them, refusing even to see them. On July 16, 1054, as afternoon prayers were about to begin at Constantinople's Hagia Sophia, Humbert marched through the cathedral and deposited on the high altar a parchment reading *Videat Deus et Judicet*, excommunicating Michael Cerularius. Humbert then tromped out, shook the dust off his feet, and left the city. Four days later, on *July 20, 1054*, at the same place, Cerularius responded in kind and excommunicated the pope and his followers. He was supported by the patriarchs of Alexandria, Antioch, and Jerusalem.

The Great Schism had finally occurred. From that point each side typically looked at the other not as brothers but as enemies or as heathen who needed to be converted. Today the Western church is represented largely by the Catholic and Protestant bodies and the Eastern church by the Greek and Russian Orthodox faiths.

Whether we live or die, it must be for the Lord. Alive or dead, we still belong to the Lord. This is because Christ died and rose to life, so that he would be the Lord of the dead and of the living. Why do you criticize other followers of the Lord? Why do you look down on them? The day is coming when God will judge all of us. (Romans 14:8–10)

O Susanna

What a difficult life. She was the twenty-fifth child in a Dissenter's family. Though brilliant, she procured little education. Though strong-willed, she lived in a male-dominated age. She married an older man and bore him nineteen children. Nine of them died. Her house burned up, her barn fell down, her health failed, and she lived with a wolf at the door.

She was Susanna Wesley.

Samuel and Susanna, married in 1689, began pastoring in dreary little Epworth in 1697. They served there forty years, enduring hardships like these:

- Samuel's salary was so small (and he was so incapable of managing it) that he was thrown into debtor's prison, leaving Susanna to fend for herself.
- The two were strong-willed and argumentative. Samuel once prayed for the king and waited for Susanna's "Amen." She didn't say it. "I do not believe the prince of Orange to be the king," she said spiritedly. "Then you and I must part," replied Samuel, "for if we have two kings we must have two beds." They separated, to be reunited only after the king's death.
- They also disagreed about Susanna's ministry, for her Bible lessons drew more listeners than his sermons.
- Susanna gave birth to a daughter during the election of 1705. The nurse, exhausted by overnight revelry, slept so heavily the next morning that she rolled on the baby and smothered it.
- Susanna herself was often bedfast, having to delegate home duties to the children. But several of her children were so wayward that she called them "a constant affliction."
- Her brother, having promised her a sizable gift, disappeared mysteriously and was never heard from again.
- Finally on *July 21, 1731*, Susanna described an accident in which her horses stampeded, throwing Samuel from their wagon and injuring him so that he was never well from that day.

A difficult life. And yet . . .

And yet the parsonage at Epworth was destined to become the most celebrated in English history, for from it came two of the greatest evangelists of all time, John and Charles Wesley. And the mother who raised them shook the world.

It looks like nothing. But cheer up! Because I, the LORD All-Powerful, will be here to help you with the work, just as I promised your ancestors when I brought them out of Egypt. Don't worry. My Spirit is right here with you. (Haggai 2:3–5)

The *Mayflower*

Many nations originate amid heathenism and are slowly converted to Christ. America is uniquely different. Of all the nations of history, it alone began as a Christian venture and has slowly sunk into heathenism.

It began during the reign of King James. The Puritans weren't happy with mere political reform in the church in England; they wanted genuine spiritual reform. James rejected their demands (except for approving a new translation of the Bible), and this left the Puritans unsettled. Some, believing the Church of England beyond help, separated from it into independent congregations of their own. These people became known as Separatists, and King James, viewing them as traitors, "harried them out of the land."

In 1607 and 1608, two groups fled to Holland. One of them, while studying Scripture, concluded that baptism was a rite for believers only (rather than for infants), and the Baptist movement was born. The other group, led by William Brewster and John Robinson, remained in Holland until *July 22, 1620*, when with packed bags and children in tow, its members sailed back to England and there boarded the *Mayflower* for the trip of their lives.

The Pilgrims arrived off the coast of Cape Cod in November of that year and paused long enough to draw up an organizing charter, the Mayflower Compact, the first written agreement for self-government ever put in force in America.

Its words plainly stated the purpose of the first government on American shores: "In ye name of God Amen. We whose names are underwritten, the loyall subjects of our dread soveraigne Lord King James, by ye grace of God, of Great Britaine, Franc, & Ireland king, defender of ye faith. Haveing undertaken, for ye glories of God, and advancemente of ye Christian faith and honour of our king & countrie, a voyage to plant ye first colonie in ye Northerne parts of Virginia, doe by these presents solemnly & covenant, & combine ourselves togeather into a Civill body politick; for our better ordering, & preservation & furtherance of ye ends aforesaid . . ."

If I promise to make a nation strong, but its people start disobeying me and doing evil, then I will change my mind and not help them at all. So listen to me. (Jeremiah 18:9–11)

Arise, It Is Day!

Protestantism came of age amid the perils and persecutions of sixteenth-century England partly because of a brave man who was neither preacher nor politician—printer John Day. He was born during the reign of Henry VIII and entered his profession at age twenty-two during Edward's brief Protestant rule. He became the most prominent publisher of Protestant materials in London and was appointed at age thirty by King Edward to publish Poynet's Protestant catechism. It was a feather in his cap. But when the king was succeeded by his Catholic half sister, "Bloody" Mary, the feather in his cap became a stone around his neck. His best authors perished at the stake, and he himself was imprisoned before somehow escaping abroad.

John Day spent his European exile traveling around, learning all he could of new printing methods, meeting young apprentices, and planning future work. When Protestant Elizabeth became queen, Day returned to London better equipped than ever. He was the first to print music; to cut, cast, and use Anglo-Saxon type; to introduce mathematical signs; and the first to make Roman and italic types used on the same line as regular print. He included pictures (woodcuts) in his books. And he was the first to print smaller sections of the Bible, which he advertised like this: "Printed in sundry parts for these poor, that they which are not able to bie the hole, may bie a part."

After settling securely back into England, Day published all of Latimer's sermons, then Ridley's "Friendly Farewell." But his most famous book was John Foxe's *Book of Martyrs*, which went through repeated printings and became the most important book of its . . . well, of its day. Business soared, forcing him into larger quarters near St. Paul's Cathedral. The sign in front of his new shop featured a man pointing to the sun, saying, "Arise, For It Is Day."

And many more Days followed. John had thirteen children by his first wife and another thirteen by his second. When he died on *July 23, 1583*, his son Richard carried on the family business of publishing quality Bibles and Christian materials for England and the world.

The Law of the LORD is perfect;
it gives us new life.
His teachings last forever,
and they give wisdom
to ordinary people.
The LORD's instruction is right;
it makes our hearts glad.
His commands shine brightly,
and they give us light. (Psalm 19:7–8)

Making Waves, Winning Souls

Charles Bowles's father was African; his mother was the daughter of a Revolutionary War hero. He was converted as a youth and called to the Freewill Baptist ministry. On *July 24, 1816*, he preached his first sermon, and his ministry soon resulted in both converts and controversy. He was a black preacher in the far north, making waves and winning souls. In Huntington, Vermont, a mob secretly plotted to attack him at his next worship service. They intended to tie him to a wooden horse and plunge him in the lake to sink or swim as he would. Bowles, however, heard of the plot.

> The time arrived for the meeting; and while the enemy was preparing the weapons of their warfare, he is fitting himself. Behold him in yonder grove, bowed low before the throne of the Redeemer. What a noble sight to behold that despised servant of God, bowed alone in the grove, seeking only a preparation of heart! What a contrast with that band preparing by whiskey and oaths.

The service began, and the mob seated before him awaited its signal. Bowles read Matthew 23:33: "You are nothing but snakes . . . ! How can you escape going to hell?" He preached with such fervor that no one dared move. He finished by saying, "I am informed there are persons here who have agreed to put me on a wooden horse, carry me to the pond, and throw me in; and now, dear creatures, I make no resistance." But he had one request—that on the way to the lake the assembly sing hymns. "Glory be to God! Yes, we will have music. Glory to God!"

> This was said with his powerful voice with such confidence in God that it went like an electric shock through the congregation, and produced an effect upon the mob that could scarcely have been equaled had a bolt from heaven fallen; so completely were they overcome, that they fell prostrate upon the floor.

Shortly afterward, the troublemakers did meet Bowles at the lake—where *he* plunged *them* into its chilly waters, baptizing them as followers of his Lord Jesus.

You must stay calm and be willing to suffer. You must work hard to tell the good news and to do your job well. (2 Timothy 4:5)

Man of Habit

William Romaine was a safe and predictable minister in eighteenth-century England—until he sat under the preaching of George Whitefield. For the rest of his life, Romaine was a fiery evangelical in the Church of England. His zeal confounded church leaders, and he lost both friends and positions. In at least one church, officials refused to light the building where he spoke, forcing him to preach by the light of a single candle held in his hand. But Romaine's revivalistic preaching drew larger and larger audiences until all of London was affected.

While Whitefield traveled around the world and Wesley throughout Britain, Romaine held down the fort in London. That was his citadel, and he became the rallying point for London's Anglicans who loved the evangelical truth.

Romaine was a man of habit. He took breakfast each day at six, reading from the book of Psalms as he ate. Dinner was at half past one, supper at seven in the evening, after which he took a walk. He conducted family prayer at nine in the morning and at nine at night. Bedtime was ten.

He lived to be eighty-one, working unabated until his final illness. On Saturday, *July 25, 1795*, Romaine found himself unable to go down the stairs. He settled on an upstairs couch in great weakness, "giving glory to God." In late afternoon he was heard to whisper, "Though I walk through the valley of the shadow of death I will fear no evil, for thou art with me." A little later a friend bent over and said, "I hope, my dear sir, you now find the salvation of Jesus Christ precious, dear, and valuable to you." Romaine replied, "He is a precious Savior to me now." A little later, as though seeing the Lord, he cried, "Holy! Holy! Holy! Blessed Jesus! To thee be endless praise." And about midnight "as the Sabbath began," he took his final breath. His friends planned a private funeral, but thousands showed up. Fifty coaches followed the hearse and multitudes on foot. His critics had long since folded their tents. The city loved him, and it loved his truth.

You are true to your name,
and you lead me
along right paths.
I may walk through valleys
as dark as death,
but I won't be afraid.
You are with me,
and your shepherd's rod makes me feel safe. (Psalm 23:3–4)

Wilberforce

In the 1700s, an exclusive little hamlet outside London called Clapham became home to a number of prominent evangelicals and evangelical causes. Historians call these Christians the Clapham Sect. The most famous member of the Clapham Sect was a politician who stood five feet four inches tall, named William Wilberforce, who had come to Christ at age twenty-five. Wilberforce gathered his Clapham friends into regular "Cabinet Councils" to discuss national trends and to establish Christian strategies for dealing with them, making the Clapham Sect one of the most unusual fraternities in British public life. Out of it sprang the Church Missionary Society, the British and Foreign Bible Society, the Society for Bettering the Condition of the Poor, the Society for the Reformation of Prison Discipline and most of all, Wilberforce's history-changing crusade against slavery.

In 1789, Wilberforce first spoke against slavery in the House of Commons. Two years later in another speech he said: "Never, never will we desist till we have wiped away this scandal from the Christian name, released ourselves from the load of guilt, and extinguished every trace of this bloody traffic."

The Clapham Sect went to work mobilizing opinion and helping Wilberforce marshal his arguments. They lectured on public platforms, wrote books, posted billboards, and lobbied leaders. Finally in 1807, after nearly twenty years of work, Wilberforce sat bent in his chair, head in his hands, weeping, as the parliament outlawed the trading of slaves in the British Empire. Later that night a beaming Wilberforce turned to a friend and said, "Well, Henry, what do we abolish next?"

Slavery itself, that's what. Wilberforce pressed on for another twenty years for complete emancipation of all slaves in the British Empire. He was a virtual one-man nonstop crusade until his health broke and he became a dying man. His friends finished the fight. On *July 26, 1833*, the Bill for the Abolition of Slavery passed in the House of Commons. News was rushed to the bedfast Wilberforce, who raised himself on one elbow, smiled quietly, and said, "Thank God that I have lived to witness [this] day."

He died three days later, his life's work finished.

The Spirit of the LORD God
has taken control of me!
The LORD has chosen and sent me
to tell the oppressed
the good news,
to heal the brokenhearted,
and to announce freedom
for prisoners and captives. (Isaiah 61:1)

Bond of Blood

Donald Cargill was a Scottish Presbyterian when such were outlawed. One listener said his sermons "came *from* his heart and went *to* the heart. He spake as never man spake, and his words went through us." People often complained his messages were too short. But his life proved almost as short as his sermons. His arrest being imminent, he gathered his people and spoke from Isaiah 26. The final words of his last sermon were recorded thus: "He exhorted us earnestly to dwell in the clefts of the rock, to hide ourselves in the wounds of Christ, to wrap ourselves in God's promises, and to make our refuge under the shadow of his wings until these sad calamities pass over."

On July 10, 1681, Scottish troops burst into the house where Cargill, James Boig, and Walter Smith were sleeping. The men were rousted from bed, tied to barebacked horses, and taken to prison. Soon two others joined them. All were condemned.

At the scaffold Cargill put his foot on the ladder, turned, blessed the Lord with uplifted hands, and said, "The Lord knows I go up this ladder with less fear, confusion or perturbation of mind than ever I entered a pulpit to preach."

After watching Cargill die, Walter Smith ascended the executioner's block. A hood was placed over his head, but he lifted it and said, "I have one more word to say, and that is that all who love God and his righteous cause would set time apart and sing a song of praise to the Lord for what he has done for my soul. To him be praise." The hood was replaced, he was forced against the decapitated corpse of his friend, and his head, too, fell.

James Boig was next. He shouted praise to God, saying he was as calm at the scaffold as he would be at the marriage altar.

The next to die was William Cuthill and finally William Thomson—five good men all martyred in Edinburgh on "that never-to-be-forgotten bloody day—*27 July, 1681.* The hangman hashed and hagged off all their heads with an axe."

The LORD gives perfect peace
to those whose faith is firm.
So always trust the LORD
because he is forever
our mighty rock. (Isaiah 26:3–4)

Never on Sunday

Jonathan Edwards fell in love with Sarah Pierrepont when she was thirteen. He was moody and stiff; she was as vivacious as a songbird. He could think of nothing else, and one day studying Greek, he scribbled in the cover of his textbook that Sarah goes "from place to place, singing sweetly, full of joy. She loves to be alone, walking in the fields and groves, and seems to have someone invisible always conversing with her."

They married on *July 28, 1727*, the bride (then seventeen) wore a green dress. Jonathan was hired by a Massachusetts church. But parishioners often criticized the young couple. Jonathan was too strict for some, Sarah too extravagant for others.

Even worse, they evidently were intimate on the Lord's Day. Colonial New Englanders believed that babies were born on the same day of the week as conceived. When six of the Edwards's eleven children arrived on Sundays, it sent tongues wagging. Such intimacy was not appropriate Sunday behavior.

But through all the hardships, the couple nurtured their love. They cherished afternoon horseback rides along forest trails. They had nightly devotions, and Jonathan read Sarah his compositions daily. He devoted an hour each day to the children and took them on trips one at a time.

George Whitefield wrote: "A sweeter couple I have not seen. Their children were not dressed in silks and satins but plain, examples of Christian simplicity. Mrs. Edwards is adorned with a meek, quiet spirit; she talked solidly of the things of God, and seemed to be such a helpmeet for her husband, that she caused me to renew those prayers, I have put up to God, [for] a wife."

Jonathan's last words were, "Give my love to my dear wife, and tell her that the uncommon union which has long subsisted between us has been of such a nature as I trust is spiritual and therefore will continue forever."

Years later a reporter tracked down fourteen hundred descendants of Jonathan and Sarah, finding among them eighty college presidents, professors, and deans; a hundred lawyers; sixty-six physicians; eighty political leaders, three senators, and three governors; countless preachers and missionaries—and one traitor, Aaron Burr.

A woman's family
is held together by her wisdom . . .
If you respect the LORD,
you and your children
have
a strong fortress. (Proverbs 14:1, 26)

Stokeley's Slave

Richard Allen grew up in slavery, toiling alongside parents and siblings on Stokeley Sturgis's Delaware farm. The family was broken up before Richard became an adult. Sturgis sold Richard's mother and three of his siblings, and Richard never saw them again. Heavyhearted, he followed a crowd into the fields one day to hear a Methodist preacher. "I was brought to see myself, poor, wretched, and undone," he wrote. "Shortly after, I obtained mercy through the blood of Christ."

Allen soon purchased his freedom and commenced as an itinerant Methodist evangelist. In 1786, he joined the staff of Philadelphia's St. George's Methodist Episcopal Church, the founding church of American Methodism. He conducted the 5:00 AM Sunday services. When his powerful preaching brought many blacks to St. George's, white parishioners felt uneasy, and African-American worshippers were gradually denied seating, being forced to stand along the walls during services.

Still the church grew, and a building expansion became necessary. On the first morning in the refurbished auditorium, Allen took his seat in the new balcony. As the congregation knelt for prayer, he heard a scuffle. A church trustee was pulling blacks to their feet, trying to force them from the gallery. "Wait until the prayer is over," whispered a disturbed worshipper, "and we'll trouble you no more." But the trustee only increased his efforts. Allen and his friends left, vowing never to return to St. George's.

They were without a church, and Allen had no job. He hired out as a chimney sweep, then opened a shoemaker's shop. But his spare time was devoted to preaching the gospel and serving the black community. His heroic efforts during the yellow fever epidemic of 1793 so impressed the Philadelphians that tensions eased with St. George's. With the church's blessing Allen assembled a group of black Christians on *July 29, 1794*, in a converted blacksmith's shop. The Bethel African Methodist Episcopal Church was formed, the mother church of the African Methodist Episcopal Church, now known throughout the world. Allen became the first consecrated bishop in the growing movement today that is among the largest Methodist groups on earth.

Live in harmony by showing love for each other. Be united in what you think, as if you were only one person. Don't be jealous or proud, but be humble and consider others more important than yourselves. Care about them as much as you care about yourselves and think the same way that Christ Jesus thought. (Philippians 2:2–5)

The Lame Man

Luther's Reformation swept over Europe like a flash flood. Most of Germany and Scandinavia became Protestant. England broke with Rome. Switzerland and the Netherlands were largely Protestant, and the Reformation tide rose in France, Austria, Hungary, and Poland. Some expected Spain and Italy to be next.

The Vatican responded in several ways. The Council of Trent addressed church problems. The Inquisition was unleashed. Military and diplomatic efforts were employed. But perhaps the most effective counteroffensive was a religious order established in 1540, by a crippled Spanish nobleman named Ignatius Loyola.

Loyola was born among the Basques of Spain, the youngest of twelve children. He was a reckless youth, frequently in trouble with the law. While serving in the Spanish army, he was crippled for life when a cannonball crashed into his leg. The doctors repeatedly broke and reset the leg without anesthesia but to little avail. While recovering, Ignatius began reading books about Christ and the saints. *What if I should do great things for God like St. Francis and St. Dominic?* he asked himself in excitement. A new passion rose in his heart, and he fasted, prayed, scourged himself, and experienced hundreds of strange visions.

Out of his experiences came a manual, *Spiritual Exercises*; and book in hand he limped to the University of Paris. He was thirty-eight, barely five feet tall, and unwell. But he recruited six students (including Francis Xavier) to the Society of Jesus—the Jesuits.

The Jesuits emphasized knowledge and displayed great intelligence. Loyola lived to see a thousand men in his order and one hundred colleges and seminaries established. The Jesuits became the greatest force in the Catholic Reformation. His work ended, Loyola was seized by a violent gallbladder attack. On *July 30, 1556*, in intense suffering, he devoted the evening to prayer, then died. But he left behind arguably the most powerful religious order in the Catholic Church.

Peter said, "I don't have any silver or gold! But I will give you what I do have. In the name of Jesus Christ from Nazareth, get up and start walking." Peter then took him by the right hand and helped him up . . . Everyone saw him walking around and praising God. (Acts 3:6–7, 9)

The Blessed Tie

John Fawcett was converted as a teenager listening to George Whitefield. He joined the Baptists and was ordained on *July 31, 1765*. He began pastoring a poor church in Wainsgate, finding time here and there for writing. His writings spread abroad, and the little church feared they would lose their pastor to a larger place. Fawcett wondered the same thing, lamenting in his diary that his family was growing faster than his income.

The call came from London's famous Carter's Lane Church. "Think of it!" Fawcett told his wife. "They want us in London to take the place of the late Dr. Gill at that great church! It's almost unbelievable!" The following Sunday he broke the news to his church, then began packing. Books, dishes, pictures, and furniture were crated for the overland journey to the world's largest city. When the day of departure came, church members assembled and bravely tried to hold their tears. Finally everything was loaded but one box, and Fawcett entered the house to retrieve it. There he found his wife deep in thought. "John," she said, voice breaking, "do you think we're doing the right thing? Will we ever find a congregation to love us and help us with the Lord's work like this group here?"

"Do you think we've been too hasty in this?" John asked.

"Yes. I think we should stay right here and serve these people."

John was silent a moment, for his heart, too, had been breaking. He nodded. "I was so overjoyed when the call came that I never really prayed about it like a minister should."

They walked onto the porch, called the people together, revealed their change of heart, and amid joyous tears unloaded their wagons. Fawcett stayed at Wainsgate the rest of his life. But not in obscurity. Out of this experience, he wrote the world-famous hymn:

Blest be the tie that binds
Our hearts in Christian love.
The fellowship of kindred minds
Is like to that above.

I pray that your love will keep on growing and that you will fully know and understand how to make the right choices. Then you will still be pure and innocent when Christ returns. And until that day, Jesus Christ will keep you busy doing good deeds that bring glory and praise to God. (Philippians 1:9–10)

On This Day in Christian History…

AUGUST

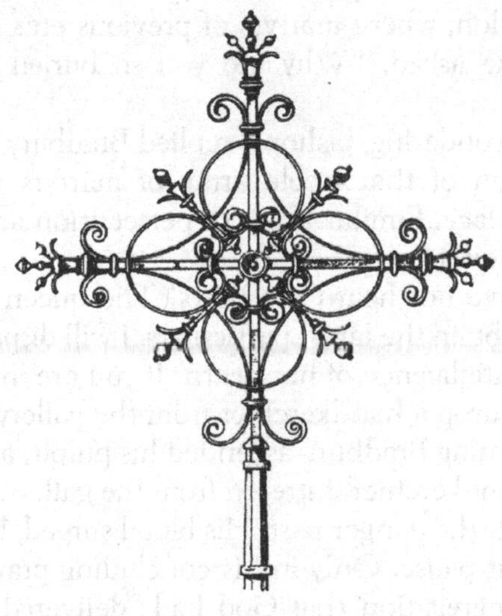

August 1 The Protestant Passover

We can't blame churchmen in England for agonizing every time a new monarch was crowned, for the religious persuasion of the kings determined who would be burned. Anxiety continued even in the days of Isaac Watts and his fellow pastor, Thomas Bradbury. During their day Queen Anne and the parliament passed the Schism Bill, to take effect *August 1, 1714*. Many predicted it would reestablish Catholicism in England "with mighty gust," and that Baptists and other Dissenters would again be racked and burned. A terrible storm gathered, and even the stalwart Bradbury grew anxious.

In the early hours of August 1, Bishop Burnet was passing through Smithfield in London, where martyrs of previous eras had died. Seeing Bradbury there, he asked, "Why are you so buried in thought, Mr. Bradbury?"

"I have been wondering, bishop," replied Bradbury, "whether I shall have the resolution of that noble army of martyrs whose ashes are deposited in this place. Similar times of persecution are at hand, and I shall be called to suffer."

"Then you have not heard the news! The queen is seriously ill. I am on my way to obtain the latest particulars. I will dispatch a messenger with the earliest intelligence of her death. If you are in the pulpit when he arrives, he will drop a handkerchief from the gallery."

Later that morning Bradbury ascended his pulpit, and in the middle of his sermon, a handkerchief fluttered from the gallery. Anne was dead, the Schism bill lost, the danger past. His blood surged, but he continued his sermon without pause. Only in his concluding prayer did he reveal to his stunned congregation that God had "delivered these kingdoms from evil counsels." He prayed for "His Majesty, King George," then quoted Psalm 89.

For years Dissenters regarded August 1, 1714, as a day of deliverance, the Protestant Passover. And the commemoration continues every time we sing the anthem Watts wrote on that occasion: "O God Our Help in Ages Past, Our Hope for Years to Come."

Our LORD, I will sing
of your love forever.
Everyone yet to be born
will hear me praise
your faithfulness.
I will tell them,
"God's love
can always be trusted,
and his faithfulness lasts
as long as the heavens." (Psalm 89:1–2)

Arrow from Nowhere

William the Conqueror may have conquered England during the Norman Invasion of 1066, but he never conquered his own appetites. He was ruthless, harsh, wrathful—and always hungry. He grew so stout that his coffin proved too small for him, and on his death attendants had trouble stuffing the corpse into place. It burst open during the effort.

His son Rufus moved quickly to seize the throne. He inherited all his father's vices, none of his virtues, and is remembered as one of history's worst men. He was officially William II, but commonly called Rufus because of his red hair or, some say, his red face. He had reason to be red faced. His cruelty was sadistic, and he derived perverse pleasure by watching animals tortured and innocent men subjected to screaming degrees of pain.

Rufus was incorrigible. Once while recovering from a severe illness, he vowed never to become a good man. His sexual appetite was unquenchable. It was said he rose a worse man every morning and lay down a worse man every night.

Rufus passionately hated Christ, Christianity, and the clergy. His profane and blasphemous words continually shocked his contemporaries. He plundered churches, robbing them of their offerings and treasuries. He sold church positions to the highest bidder. He kept the archbishopric of Canterbury vacant before finally appointing good Anselm to the office. And he converted sacred cemeteries into royal parks to satisfy his thirst for hunting.

It was this last indiscretion that took his life. He had seized land for a hunter's paradise called New Forest. On *August 2, 1100*, while hot on the chase, he was struck by a powerful arrow that flew from nowhere. He died quickly, and to no one's sorrow. No church bells tolled, no prayers were said for him, no alms given in his memory, no monuments built to his name. His eternal damnation was taken for granted by England, and his younger brother Henry reigned in his stead.

Send your sharp arrows
through enemy hearts
and make all nations fall
at your feet. (Psalm 45:5)

August 3 The Boxer Rebellion

Between 1830 and 1949, China became the largest Protestant mission field in the world, occupying up to eight thousand missionaries at any one time. It also became the scene of Protestant mission's largest massacre when, in 1900, a rabidly anti-Christian group known as the Society of Harmonious Fists (or the Boxers) waged a virtual war against believers. Nearly two hundred missionary adults and children and thirty thousand national Chinese Christians perished. Among them was missionary Lizzie Atwater, who wrote her family on *August 3, 1900:*

> Dear ones, I long for a sight of your dear faces, but I fear we shall not meet on earth. I am preparing for the end very quietly and calmly. The Lord is wonderfully near, and he will not fail me. I was very restless and excited while there seemed a chance of life, but God has taken away that feeling, and now I just pray for grace to meet the terrible end bravely. The pain will soon be over, and oh the sweetness of the welcome above!
>
> My little baby will go with me. I think God will give it to me in Heaven, and my dear mother will be so glad to see us. I cannot imagine the Savior's welcome. Oh, that will compensate for all these days of suspense. Dear ones, live near God and cling less closely to earth. There is no other way by which we can receive that peace from God which passeth understanding . . .
>
> . . . I just keep calm these hours. I do not regret coming to China, but am sorry I have done so little. My married life, two precious years, has been so very full of happiness. We will die together, my dear husband and I. I send my love to you all, the dear friends who remember me.

Twelve days later the Atwaters perished. But it was not for nothing. When tensions subsided, the missionary army returned, remaining until expelled by the Communists in 1949. The number of Chinese Christians grew to about five to seven million by 1980, and has since mushroomed to an estimated fifty million—and counting.

Our people defeated Satan
because of the blood of the Lamb
and the message of God.
They were willing
to give up their lives. (Revelation 12:11)

Three Loves and a Fourth

Our passions can often be channeled for God's glory. Wilfred Grenfell developed three loves, the first being sports. He swam in cold rivers and sailed the Irish Sea. At eighteen he found another passion when a doctor showed him a human brain chemically preserved. Grenfell decided at once to become a physician.

One evening while still a medical student, Grenfell was passing a large tent and thinking it a circus, he ducked in. It was a revival meeting, and an aged man was droning on in prayer. Grenfell started to leave when another man leaped up and announced a hymn "while our brother continues his prayer." The man, D. L. Moody, proceeded to preach so effectively that Grenfell was converted on the spot. He found his third love—the Lord.

Those passions—sports, medicine, and God—led Grenfell to volunteer with an organization called Mission to Deep Sea Fishermen. The mission sponsored a mercy ship that ministered to thousands living on boats and along the North Atlantic coastline. The work spread to Newfoundland, and on *August 4, 1892*, Grenfell sailed into the waters of Labrador to begin a lifetime of ministry.

Grenfell soon saw that two hospitals were needed there, an onshore clinic for coastal residents and a floating hospital for fishing fleets. He raised money, established the hospitals, and the work soon included numerous hospitals and dispensaries throughout the cold, bitter land. He started schools and orphanages for the young. He organized cooperative stores for Labradorians to barter their furs and fish for supplies. He spent his life sailing along northern shores and traveling by dogsled across frozen landscapes, caring for the sick, teaching the young, preaching the gospel. His whole life was a glorious indulgence in his three loves.

He found a fourth love as well. One day aboard a ship he met a beautiful woman, a total stranger, fell violently in love with her, and proposed without even asking her name. She accepted. The two ministered side by side for the rest of their lives.

Trust the LORD and live right!
The land will be yours,
and you will be safe.
Do what the LORD wants,
and he will give you
your heart's desire. (Psalm 37:3–4)

August 5 Only One Missionary

Mary Slessor's childhood was marred by a drinking father. Every Saturday his paycheck turned into alcohol, leaving the family destitute for another week. By age eleven Mary was putting in twelve-hour shifts in the mills, from six in the morning until six at night. She hid her earnings from her father, incurring his wrath but keeping the family fed. In her spare time Mary taught herself to read and found she could prop books on her loom and read while working. There Mary learned of Calabar (Nigeria), an "unhealthy, mysterious, terrible land ruled by witchcraft and secret societies." She was convinced she should go there as a missionary.

For several years Mary worked in mission halls near her home in the slums of Dundee, Scotland. She learned to face down gangs, to pray down blessings, and to break down hardened hearts. Her work finally led to her being appointed missionary to Calabar, and on *August 5, 1876*, she sailed for West Africa aboard the SS *Ethiopia*. She was dismayed to find the ship loaded with hundreds of barrels of whiskey. Remembering how alcohol had ruined her own family, she frowned. "Scores of barrels of whisky," she muttered, "and only one missionary."

But what a missionary! In the years that followed she single-handedly tamed and transformed three pagan areas by preaching the gospel, teaching the children, defending the abused, and rescuing the mistreated. She was feisty. She didn't mind living in mud huts and sleeping amid sweating bodies. She was a combination circuit preacher, village teacher, nurse, nanny, and negotiator. She diverted tribal wars and rescued women and children by the hundreds. Often babies filled her home by the dozens. (Mary learned to tie a string to each little hammock, lie in bed at night, and pull the strings as each baby needed soothing.)

She so won the respect of Europe and Africa that she became the first woman vice consul of Britain, using her position to further her missions. For forty years she pioneered the gospel in areas that had proved the graveyard of other missionaries.

How can they hear, unless someone tells them? And how can anyone tell them without being sent by the Lord? The Scriptures say it is a beautiful sight to see even the feet of someone coming to preach the good news. (Romans 10:14–15)

Death in the Catacombs

The leaders of the early church included two men named Sixtus. The first served as bishop of Rome from about 117 to 127. Sixtus II occupied the same office in 257 and 258.

The latter rose to the position during the unfortunate reign of Emperor Valerian, when the empire was ravaged by plagues, droughts, earthquakes, tornadoes, and tidal waves. Valerian was initially tolerant toward Christians, but as natural disasters rocked his realm, he superstitiously began to blame the church. Edicts were issued against bishops and priests, and decrees forbade the gathering of Christians for worship. Churches were closed to the living Christians, and cemeteries were closed to the dead ones.

The followers of Christ, however, were not daunted, and within a year Valerian realized his edicts were failing. In July 258, he ordered bishops, priests, and deacons executed. He confiscated church property and denied civil privileges to believers. Members of the royal court who espoused Christianity were made slaves on imperial estates. One prominent church leader was tied to a bull and driven up and down the streets until his brains were dashed out.

Sixtus II had become bishop of Rome just as Valerian was issuing his orders. He created a small chapel in the catacombs, and there he met secretly with his faithful flock. One day as he taught the people, imperial soldiers burst in and seized him. He was rushed before a judge, condemned, and taken back to the catacombs where, on *August* 6, 258, he was put to death in his episcopal chair. Several of his deacons also perished.

Three weeks later in North Africa, Bishop Cyprian of Carthage was brought before another imperial judge. When challenged he declared, "I am a Christian bishop. I know no gods but the only true God."

"Have you made up your mind to that?" asked the Roman.

"A good mind," replied Cyprian, "cannot alter." He was soon escorted to a natural amphitheater, where his head was severed. In many parts of the empire, the persecution of 258–259 was the bloodiest the church had yet endured.

Be brave when you face your enemies. Your courage will show them that they are going to be destroyed, and it will show you that you will be saved. (Philippians 1:28)

A Bathroom, a Leg, and $1.50

What would you expect from a baby whose father abandoned her at birth and whose mother died when she was three? Taken in by impoverished neighbors, Eleanor Chestnut was an unhappy child, lonely and hungry for a mother's love. She didn't get it. Nor was she offered much of an education. But she was stubborn, and when she discovered a school where she could earn her way through both the academy and college, she enrolled and did just that. She developed a yen for medicine. While in school she also joined a Presbyterian church and acquired a corresponding interest in missions.

In 1888, Eleanor entered Woman's Medical College in Chicago, where she completed the programs for both doctors and nurses while living in an attic and eating mostly oatmeal. Following that she did a stint at Moody Bible Institute.

On *August 7, 1893*, Eleanor was appointed a medical missionary and assigned to south China. Her work there was complicated by a poor grasp of the language and by impoverished conditions, and she continually found herself in arduous straits. On one occasion she became responsible for a demented patient who had ruined his brain with opium. "He thinks he is continually being pursued by demons," she wrote a friend. "I have no place for him but my study. He is sometimes violent and has to be carefully watched. So I am sitting here on guard now."

But her affection for the people of Lien-chou was boundless. She used her own bathroom as an operating room and once used skin from her own leg as a graft for a coolie whose own leg was healing poorly following surgery. She established a women's hospital in Lien-chou, living on $1.50 a month so the rest of her salary could be used to buy bricks.

She served China selflessly for ten years; then on October 29, 1905, her missions compound was attacked by an antiforeign mob. Eleanor might have escaped had she not returned to aid her colleagues. Her final act of service was ripping a piece from her dress to bind a child's wound.

Then Jesus asked, "Which one of these three people was a real neighbor to the man who was beaten up by robbers?" The teacher answered, "The one who showed pity." Jesus said, "Go and do the same!" (Luke 10:36–37)

Winds of Providence

King Philip II of Spain, a Catholic, wanted to topple Queen Elizabeth of England, a Protestant. In 1586, he conspired to assassinate her. When that failed, he readied his navy, the largest and strongest on earth, to invade her land. It was a critical hour for Protestantism. Elizabeth's defeat would mean ultimate disaster for Protestants in England and everywhere in Europe.

Philip was trusting God, he said, to send him favorable weather as he would be fighting a divine cause. On May 30, 1588, he fell to his knees before his *Invincible* Armada, prayed for victory, and watched it disappear over the horizon.

But providence sided with the English. The Spanish Armada was quickly hurled in every direction by a violent storm. The beleaguered fleet regrouped, pressed on, and was spotted by the British on July 19. Winds turned against the Armada, slowing its progress. When the battle was joined on July 21, weather again aided the English. Heavy winds favored their smaller, more manageable ships, and they were able to outmaneuver the Spanish. At just the right moment, the weather always shifted in England's favor.

By July 31, the Duke of Parma had informed Philip of likely defeat: "God knows how grieved I am at this news at a time when I hoped to send Your Majesty congratulations. I will only say that this must come from the hand of the Lord, who knows well what He does . . ."

On *August 8, 1588*, Elizabeth visited her military headquarters at Tilbury and was told there that the danger of invasion was past. The relieved queen addressed her forces, saying: "I know that I have the body of a weak and feeble woman, but I have the heart and stomach of a king."

Philip's tattered ships, limping back to Spain, were caught in another deadly squall. Less than half the vessels and a third of the troops survived the storms and battles. But back in London the queen went to St. Paul's Cathedral and "with her own princely voice, she most christianly urged the people to give thanks unto God."

England and Protestantism were saved.

Have you been to the places
where I keep snow and hail,
until I use them to punish
and conquer nations?
From where does lightning leap,
or the east wind blow?
Who carves out a path
for thunderstorms?
Who sends torrents of rain? (Job 38:22–25)

The Cane Ridge Revival

Christianity fell away following the American Revolution. A Scotsman traveling through the South saw "few religious people." Francis Asbury found "not one in a hundred" concerned about religion. Alcoholism was rampant, and universalism and deism captivated the infant nation.

But in 1800, scattered revivals erupted like geysers in the backlands of Kentucky. People gathered under makeshift arbors while the gospel was preached, sometimes accompanied by emotional outbursts. Barton Stone, pastor of the Presbyterian church at Cane Ridge (near Lexington), hearing of the camp meetings, witnessed one for himself: "The scene was passing strange. Many fell down as slain in battle and continued for hours in an apparently motionless state—sometimes for a few moments reviving and exhibiting symptoms of life by a deep groan or by a prayer for mercy most fervently uttered."

His church at Cane Ridge immediately planned a camp meeting for the first weekend of August 1801. The church could hold five hundred; but workers, fearing an oversized crowd, threw up a large tent. Church families opened homes, barns, and cabins to the expected visitors.

But they didn't expect twenty thousand! Hordes arrived by horse, carriage, and wagon. Prayer and preaching continued around the clock on Friday, Saturday, and Sunday. Excitement mounted; cries and screams pierced the hazy summer air; men swooned; women were seized by spasms; children fell into ecstasy; so many fainted that the ground was covered with bodies like a battlefield. Then the "jerks" broke out: "Their heads would jerk back suddenly, frequently causing them to yelp. I have seen their heads fly back and forward so quickly that the hair of females would crack like a whip."

On Monday, *August 9, 1801*, food and supplies were exhausted, and so were the worshippers. Many left, but others came to take their places. Four more days of singing, preaching, shrieking, and jerking continued before the geyser died down. Between one thousand and three thousand had been converted, and the news was the buzz of the region. People across the new nation began discussing the revival of Christianity, and the Cane Ridge Revival is considered one of the most important religious gatherings in American history.

Always be joyful and never stop praying. Whatever happens, keep thanking God because of Jesus Christ. This is what God wants you to do. (1 Thessalonians 5:16–18)

The Fall of Jerusalem

Jesus warned of a time when Herod's beautiful temple would be destroyed, but the disciples could hardly believe him. The temple was arguably the most magnificent structure in the world, and its glow in the setting sun seemed as eternal as Jerusalem itself.

But a generation later Jewish zealots revolted against Rome. The rebellion began at the fortress of Masada then spread throughout Judea and Galilee. Romans were slaughtered; Jewish defenders battled bravely, and Emperor Nero sent General Vespasian to quell the uprising.

When Nero died, the general left for Rome, placing his son Titus in charge of the eighty thousand troops. The siege began in April 70, immediately after the Passover when Jerusalem was filled with strangers. Within city walls the Jews splintered into various factions, fighting each other at the very time they needed solidarity. Food supplies ran out, and the population began dying from starvation. The high priest's wife, accustomed to living in luxury, begged for crumbs like a street urchin. Captured Jews were crucified at a rate of five hundred a day, crosses encircling the city. Daily temple sacrifices ceased July 17, all hands being needed for defense.

The Romans, using catapults and battering rams, finally broke through the walls. The Jews streamed into the temple. Titus had reportedly wanted to spare the edifice, but his soldiers would not be restrained. A firebrand was hurled through the golden gate and exploded like a bomb. The temple became an ocean of fire. It was *August 10, 70*, the same day of the year, it was said, in which Solomon's earlier temple had been destroyed by Babylon.

This and the subsequent fall of Masada extinguished Israel as a nation until its rebirth in the twentieth century. Most Christians had fled Jerusalem before its final hour, but the city's destruction remains a defining event in Christian history. It further severed the young church from its Jewish roots, making it a global entity distinct from Israel and destined to develop its own identity among the Gentiles, bearing a message for all the world.

As Jesus was leaving the temple, one of his disciples said to him, "Teacher, look at these beautiful stones and wonderful buildings!" Jesus replied, "Do you see these huge buildings? They will certainly be torn down! Not one stone will be left in place." (Mark 13:1–2)

August 11 A Curious Romance

Theirs was a curious romance, spiritual but not sexual, ministerial but not marital. Francis and Clare were celibates, evidently in love but unable to marry, who joined forces for Christ.

Clare was born in Assisi, Italy, in 1194, growing up in a palace. When sixteen, she heard St. Francis preach and was deeply moved. She sought him out, and he spoke to her of spiritual things. For two years he visited often in her home.

On Palm Sunday 1211, Clare pulled off her beautiful clothes, donned an ash-colored robe, and slipped from an unused gate on her parent's estate. She found her way through the darkening woods to a spot where Francis awaited her. There she joined a group of Benedictine nuns. Francis prepared a home for her in the Chapel of St. Damian just outside Assisi, and according to some biographers, Clare never left the cloister for the remaining forty years of her life, entertaining those seeking spiritual help. Francis, too, visited often.

She grieved deeply at his death but lived another thirty years, confined to a bench from a leg disease. But from that bench, she taught, counseled, and prayed while sewing linens for churches.

In 1249, her cloister was attacked by marauders intent on ransacking and burning it. Showing no fear, she had herself carried to the door, where she prayed resolutely for protection. The invaders scrambled from the walls and retreated.

Another tradition, an odd one, developed from her deathbed. From her room in San Damiano, she reportedly saw and heard solemn midnight mass being conducted in a basilica miles away. In 1958, citing this ability to receive images and sound over distance, Pope Pius XII proclaimed her the patron saint of television.

Her more common title has been the Little Flower of St. Francis.

She died on *August 11, 1253*, but her sisters, the Poor Clares, are serving the needy to this day.

God blesses those people who depend only on him. They belong to the kingdom of heaven! God blesses those people who grieve. They will find comfort! God blesses those people who are humble. The earth will belong to them! (Matthew 5:3–5)

I Am a Christian!

The firestorm against the early Christians created a belief that martyrdom was the norm, something to be expected and even desired. When Emperor Diocletian forbade possession of Scriptures, Euplius, a Christian in Sicily, who was a deacon and a Bible owner, worried that he might escape persecution. To forestall such a calamity, he stood outside the governor's office one day shouting, "I am a Christian! I desire to die for the name of Christ."

When ushered before the governor, he was found to have a manuscript of the Gospels. "Where did these come from?" he was asked. "Did you bring them from your home?"

"I have no home, as my Lord Jesus Christ knows," replied Euplius.

"Read them," said the prosecutor. So Euplius began reading the words: "Blessed are they which are persecuted for righteousness' sake: for theirs is the kingdom of heaven" (Matt. 5:10 KJV). He turned to another passage: "Whosoever will come after me, let him . . . take up his cross, and follow me" (Mark 8:34 KJV).

The judge interrupted him. "Why haven't you surrendered these books?" Euplius replied that it was better to die than to give them up. "In these is eternal life," he said, "and whoever gives them up loses eternal life." The governor signaled that he had heard enough, and Euplius got what he wanted. He was subjected to a series of horrible tortures, then executed *August 12, 304*, with his Gospels tied around his neck. His last words, repeatedly uttered, were "Thanks be to Thee, O Christ. O Christ, help. It is for Thee that I suffer."

The Bible nowhere tells us to deliberately seek persecution, and some of the early Christians undoubtedly overglorified the pursuit of martyrdom. Yet given the choice it is surely better to shout, "I am a Christian!" than to hide our testimony from those around us in this world.

I am proud of the good news! It is God's powerful way of saving all people who have faith, whether they are Jews or Gentiles. The good news tells how God accepts everyone who has faith, but only those who have faith. It is just as the Scriptures say, "The people God accepts because of their faith will live." (Romans 1:16–17)

Maximus

Maximus Confessor was born in Constantinople about 580. His family belonged to the old Byzantine aristocracy, and Maximus was afforded a good education. He proved an able leader and became imperial secretary under Emperor Heraclius. But he resigned. Driven by spiritual passion, he entered a monastery and eventually became the abbot. His theological and literary skills blossomed. The Greek church was inundated with his writings, and men as brilliant as John Scotus Erigena in the West and John of Damascus in the East drew wisdom from his pen.

In the course of time Maximus led the fight against a heresy called Monothelitism—the teaching that Christ had a divine but no human will. This became the fight of his life. For many years Maximus in the East and Pope Martinus I in the Western church held the line for orthodoxy—that Christ has two natures (human and divine) and two wills (not separated or mixed but in harmony).

The emperor, unimpressed, advanced Monothelitism. Pope Martinus was deposed, imprisoned with common criminals, exposed to cold and hunger, and finally banished to a cavern on the Black Sea, where he died in 655. Maximus was treated even worse. Though now a feeble seventy-three-year-old man, he was seized, dragged across the empire, placed on trial in Constantinople, and banished to a remote spot where he suffered greatly from cold and hunger. After several months a commission was sent to interview him; it was headed by Theodosius, Bishop of Caesarea, a Monothelitist. Maximus so eloquently defended the two natures of Christ that Theodosius left a converted man.

Another delegation was sent, and the emperor offered Maximus great rewards to convert to Monothelitism and great suffering if he refused. He refused and was beaten, spat on, robbed of his possessions, imprisoned for six years, then flogged. His tongue and right hand were whacked off. He was displayed at a pillory in each of the twelve quarters of the city, then imprisoned for the rest of his life—which proved only a few weeks. He died *August 13, 662*, at age eighty-two. But his sufferings paved the way for the triumph of his doctrine.

The Word became
a human being
and lived here with us.
We saw his true glory,
the glory of the only Son
of the Father.
From him all the kindness
and all the truth of God
have come down to us. (John 1:14)

And to Die Is Gain

On a sizzling summer's day in 1925, seventeen-year-old Bill Wallace sat in a garage, working on a dismantled Ford, but his thoughts were on the future. Putting down his wrench, he reached for his New Testament and scrawled a decision on its grease-stained flyleaf. He would become a medical missionary.

Ten years later he arrived at Stout Memorial Hospital in Wuchow, South China. War was brewing between the warlords of Kwangsi Province and the government of Chiang Kai-shek, and many missionaries had fled. Wallace remained at the hospital, performing surgery, making rounds, and sharing Christ.

He survived the dangers only to face a greater one. It was Japan, intent on a conquest of the Chinese mainland. Still Wallace stayed, treating the wounded and performing surgery amid exploding bombs and flying bullets. Not until 1940 did he return to America on furlough. When time came to return, his friends questioned him, but he said, "When I was trying to decide what I should do with my life, I became convinced God wanted me to be a medical missionary. That decision took me to China. And that, along with the fact that I was extremely happy there, will take me back." He returned on *August 14, 1942*, and began dispensing medical and spiritual help during World War II.

Then an even greater threat emerged—the Communist takeover of China. Still Wallace stayed, performing duties with a hero's valor. Finally during predawn of December 19, 1950, Communist solders came to arrest the "best surgeon in China" on trumped-up espionage charges. He was placed in a small cell, where he preached to passersby from a tiny window. Brutal interrogations followed, and Wallace, wearing down, stuck verses of Scripture on the walls of his cell. When he died from the ordeal, the Communists tried to say he had hanged himself, but his body showed no signs of suicide. He was buried in a cheap wooden coffin in a bamboo-shaded cemetery. The inscription on his grave simply said: For to Me to Live Is Christ.

I honestly expect and hope that I will never do anything to be ashamed of. Whether I live or die, I always want to be as brave as I am now and bring honor to Christ. If I live, it will be for Christ, and if I die, I will gain even more. (Philippians 1:20–21)

My Victory

Rev. William Anderson of Philadelphia's North United Presbyterian Church saw a boy dart into a grocery store. He followed him, asking, "Where do you go to Sabbath school?" Nine-year-old Robert McQuilkin replied, "Nowhere." Anderson invited him. "And I can promise you a wonderful teacher too," he added. "William Parker. He has a fine class of boys."

At age twelve, Robert united with the church, saying, "When I grow up I am going to be a minister; the Lord wants me." But as a teen he grew dissatisfied with his Christian experience. Though active among his church's youth, he wrestled with anxiety and doubt. On Christmas Eve 1904, he wrote, "Have come much closer to Christ, advanced spiritually but not near enough." He entered the University of Pennsylvania and the following summer took time to attend a missionary conference on the New Jersey coast. The speaker, Dr. Charles Trumbull, shared his testimony, admitting that there had been great fluctuations in his own spiritual life. But he had discovered that "the resources of the Christian life, my friends, are just—Jesus Christ. That is all. But that is enough."

McQuilkin sought out Trumbull, the two talked, and on *August 15, 1911*, McQuilkin entered a prayer room. "There came to me this impression: I am going into that room, and I do not want to come out before this matter is settled, and I have taken Christ as my Victory for daily living.

McQuilkin knelt and consciously surrendered every sector of his life to Christ—his sins, his "doubtful things," his loved ones, his fiancée, his past failures, his future. "When I finished, I had no special emotion, and I saw no vision. But it did seem for the first time consciously in my life that there were just two persons in the universe—my Lord and I, and nothing else mattered except the will of that other person."

For the next forty years, the Holy Spirit flowed through McQuilkin like rivers of living water—and out of his ministry came Columbia Bible College/Columbia International University in South Carolina, today one of the great Christian and missionary training centers on earth.

Every child of God can defeat the world, and our faith is what gives us this victory. No one can defeat the world without having faith in Jesus as the Son of God. (1 John 5:4–5)

High Water

Count Nikolaus Ludwig von Zinzendorf was among the most eligible bachelors in eighteenth-century Europe—wealthy, intelligent, charming, handsome. And utterly devoted to Jesus Christ. After finishing studies at the University of Paris, he spent a year touring Europe and in the process became ill in Castell. There he fell in love with eighteen-year-old Theodora von Castell. He proposed to her, and she replied, saying, "If God should incline me to it more than at present, I will not resist."

Zinzendorf wasn't sure what to make of those words, but he gave the impression the two were virtually engaged. He resumed his travels only to be waylaid again, this time by high water. He took the occasion to visit his close friend, Count Henry von Reuss. As the two talked, Reuss admitted that he, too, was looking for a girl to marry. Zinzendorf said (in effect), "Well, what about Theodora? To be honest, she didn't seem all that enthusiastic about marrying me. Why don't you have a go at it?" Henry hesitated, saying, "But she's *your* fiancée!" Zinzendorf nevertheless took his friend to Castell, where Henry and Theodora promptly fell in love and married.

Zinzendorf, though magnanimous, was miserable. He spent hours studying the Old and New Testaments on the subject of marriage, celibacy, and God's will. And his eyes were opened.

They were opened to Henry's sister—Countess Erdmuth Dorothea von Reuss, whom he had met while detained by the high waters. Erdmuth loved Christ, and in her Zinzendorf found a soul mate. They were engaged on *August 16, 1722*. On that day the young count wrote a hymn of praise to God and a letter of intent to Erdmuth's mother, saying: "I foresee many difficulties in this case; as I am but a poor acquisition for any person, and the dear Countess Erdmuth must not only enter upon a life of self-denial with me, but also co-operate with me in my principal design, namely, to assist me in gaining souls for Christ."

And that's exactly what they did—from their marriage on September 7, 1722, until the Countess's death in 1756.

What if I could have
sixty queens, eighty wives,
and thousands of others!
You would be my only choice,
my flawless dove . . .
The young women, the queens,
and all the others
tell how excited you are
as they sing your praises. (Song of Songs 6:8–9)

August 17 The Two Lips of God

When the British monarchy was reinstated in 1660, a series of new laws stifled religious liberty. The Act of Uniformity, for example, required all ministers to use *The Book of Common Prayer* as a format for worship. Many non-Anglicans refused, and in August 1662, over two thousand of England's finest ministers were ejected from their pulpits. Among them was Thomas Watson of Cambridge, who preached his farewell sermon on *August 17, 1662*:

> I have exercised my ministry among you for sixteen years and have received many demonstrations of love from you. I have observed your reverent attentions to the word preached. I have observed your zeal against error; and as much as could be expected in a critical time, your unity. Though I should not be permitted to preach to you, yet shall I not cease to love and pray for you; but why should there be any interruption made? Where is the crime? Some say that we are disloyal and seditious. Beloved, what my actions and sufferings for his majesty have been is known. I desire to be guided by the silver thread of God's word and of God's providence. And if I must die, let me leave some legacy with you before I go from you, some counsel.
>
> First, keep your constant hours every day with God. Begin the day with God, visit God in the morning before you make any other visit; wind up your hearts towards heaven in the morning and they will go the better all the day after! Oh turn your closets into temples; read the scriptures. The two Testaments are the two lips by which God speaks to us; this will make you wise unto salvation. Besiege heaven every day with your prayer, thus perfume your houses.

Watson proceeded to give his listeners nineteen more "directions," then ended, saying: "I have many things yet to say to you, but I know not whether God will give me another opportunity. My strength is almost gone. Consider what hath been said, and the Lord will give you understanding in all things."

Enemies spend the whole day
finding fault with me;
all they think about
is how to do me harm.
They attack from ambush,
watching my every step
and hoping to kill me.
You have kept record
of my days of wandering.
You have stored my tears
in your bottle
and counted each of them. (Psalm 56:5–6, 8)

One Hundred Hymns

Can you imagine singing a hundred hymns in one evening? One church did with history-shattering results.

Count Nikolaus Ludwig von Zinzendorf, born in 1700, grew up in an atmosphere of Bible reading and hymn singing. He married a Christian countess, and the two began allowing Protestant refugees to camp on their German estate. A Moravian community named Herrnhut ("Under the Lord's Watch") soon developed.

One day a potter named Leonard Dober arrived to establish artistic pottery as a profitable product for Herrnhut. Not long thereafter Zinzendorf returned from a trip to Copenhagen with reports of slaves in the West Indies having no one to tell them of Christ. Dober spent a sleepless night. "I could not get free of it," he said. "I vowed to myself that if one other brother would go with me, I would become a slave."

He found his brother in David Nitschmann, a carpenter.

On *August 18, 1732*, in an extraordinary, emotion-packed service, the two were commissioned. One hundred hymns were sung that night as the congregation bade them good-bye and Godspeed.

The two sailed from Copenhagen on October 8, sustained by Numbers 23:19: "God is no mere human! He doesn't tell lies or change his mind. God always keeps his promises."

They arrived on St. Thomas in December, and a planter named Lorenzen took them in. Their first Sunday saw them beginning their search for souls, preaching to a small group of slaves, several of whom soon followed Christ. Dober ministered to those suffering from malaria, at one point nearly dying of the fever himself. On another occasion he almost starved. But reinforcements began arriving from Herrnhut in 1734. Though many died, the Moravian tide of missionaries continued—to Greenland, to Lapland and Georgia, to Surinam, to Guinea, to South Africa, to Algeria, to North American Indians, to Ceylon and Romania and Constantinople. From 1732 to 1742, more than seventy Moravian missionaries were sent from Herrnhut, a community of six hundred.

It has been called the Golden Decade. It was the dawn of Protestant missions.

Tell every nation on earth,
"The LORD is wonderful
and does marvelous things!" (Psalm 96:3)

A Dog's Tale

God both guides and provides. He leads and feeds his people, and sometimes in ways unusual—as John Craig once learned. Craig was born in Scotland in 1512, studied at the University of St. Andrews, and entered the ministry. While living on the Continent, he found a copy of Calvin's *Institutes* and in reading them found himself becoming a Protestant. As a result he was arrested by agents of the Inquisition, taken prisoner to Rome, and condemned to death at the stake. On the evening of *August 19, 1559*, while awaiting execution the next day, dramatic news arrived that Pope Paul IV had died. According to custom, the prisons in Rome were thrown open, the prisoners temporarily released.

Craig took advantage of the opportunity, escaping to an inn on the city's outskirts. A band of soldiers tracked him down, but as the captain of the guard arrested him, the soldier paused, looking at him intently. Finally he asked Craig if he remembered helping a wounded soldier some years before in Bologna. "I am the man you relieved," said the captain, "and providence has now put it into my power to return the kindness—you are at liberty." The soldier gave Craig the money in his pockets and marked out an escape route for him.

As he made his way through Italy, Craig avoided public roads, taking the circuitous route suggested by the captain and using the money for food. But at length Craig's money was exhausted, and so were his spirits. He lay down in the woods and gloomily considered his plight. Suddenly the sound of steps was heard, and Craig tensed. It was a dog and in its mouth, a purse. Craig waved the animal away, fearing a trick. But the dog persisted, fawned on him, and left the purse in his lap.

Using money from the purse, Craig reached Austria, where Emperor Maximilian listened to his sermon and gave him safe conduct. He thus returned to his native Scotland, where he preached Christ and abetted the Reformation until his death many years later at age eighty-eight.

Elijah was a prophet from Tishbe in Gilead . . . The LORD said to Elijah, "Leave and go across the Jordan River so you can hide near Cherith Creek. You can drink water from the creek, and eat the food I've told the ravens to bring you." Elijah obeyed the LORD and went to live near Cherith Creek. Ravens brought him bread and meat twice a day, and he drank water from the creek. (1 Kings 17:1–6)

Study in Contrasts

Jesus, the very thought of Thee, With sweetness fills my breast;
But sweeter far Thy face to see, And in Thy presence rest.

This hymn, sung for almost a thousand years, is attributed to a puzzling man in France named Bernard, a deeply spiritual Christian who advanced a militant Christianity.

Bernard seemed destined for a promising secular career until as a youth he turned toward Christ and persuaded more than two dozen of his friends to give themselves to celibacy and to the monastery of Citeaux. He soon became the most famous figure there and was sent to found a similar institution at Clairvaux.

The monastery of Clairvaux became his headquarters, and he seldom left it, but his influence radiated from its walls like spokes of a wheel. During his lifetime he founded seventy more monasteries and oversaw ninety others. He loved the Scripture and became deeply acquainted with its teachings; but he loved the sword almost as much. He advanced monastic military orders—communities of knights and men-at-arms living under monastic discipline committed to the defense of church and faith. He wrote the rule book for the Knights Templar and inspired German military orders that forcibly Christianized parts of Europe. He envisioned the Second Crusade and persuaded Pope Eugene, his former pupil, to authorize it. And when it ended in disaster, Bernard commented, "It is better that they blame me than God."

Many Christians today do blame Bernard. He was a fighter who battled the devil in his own life by rigid disciplines; heresy, by asserting orthodoxy at every stop; paganism, by preaching with a Bible in one hand and a sword in the other; and Muslims, by sending Europe's finest on an ill-fated crusade. He didn't give up his battles until *August 20, 1153*, when at age sixty-three he departed—"Thy face to see and in Thy presence rest."

We question his judgment, but we still sing his song. And we remember his life every August 20, the feast day of St. Bernard of Clairvaux.

One of Jesus' followers pulled out a sword. He struck the servant of the high priest and cut off his ear. But Jesus told him, "Put your sword away." (Matthew 26:51–52)

August 21 The Warrior Pope

Giuliano della Rovere began climbing the ecclesiastical ladder as a youth, aided by his uncle, Pope Sixtus IV. In 1503, Giuliano himself became Pope Julius II. He secured his office by promising the cardinals to seek their advice on important issues, to call a general council, and to continue the war against the Turks.

He kept his promises just as he had kept his monastic vow of celibacy, which is to say, loosely. He was a powerful, restless man—massive head, deep eyes, lips tight with resolution, face somber, temper violent. He kept Italy at war and Rome in turmoil. He liberated the papal states, leading his own troops and actually scaling the walls of Bologna himself.

He tore down the old St. Peter's Cathedral and, at age sixty-three, climbed down a long, trembling rope ladder to lay the cornerstone for the new one. He also instituted the sale of indulgences to pay for the new basilica, provoking Luther. His love for architecture prompted prelates, nobles, bankers, and merchants to build opulent palaces. Broad avenues were cut through the ancient city, hundreds of new streets opened, and Rome again began looking like the home of a Caesar.

Julius discovered and developed Michelangelo and Raphael, moved the center of the Renaissance from Florence to Rome, financed hundreds of promising artists, and gave the world the Sistine Chapel ceiling.

But his enemies and adversities increased. Julius was stricken with a severe illness and hovered near death three days. On *August 21, 1511*, as he lay unconscious, the cardinals prepared to name his successor. Julius disappointed them by recovering. He wasn't finished yet. He soon formed England's King Henry VIII, Germany, Spain, and Switzerland into a military alliance against France. They launched the war, but during the campaign the warrior-pope's energy finally ran out. Consumed by a fever (thought by some to be caused by venereal disease or by his immoderate eating and drinking), he gave instructions for his funeral, confessed himself a great sinner, and died.

The LORD says:
Don't brag about your wisdom
or strength or wealth.
If you feel you must brag,
then have enough sense
to brag about worshiping me,
the LORD.
What I like best
is showing kindness,
justice, and mercy
to everyone on earth. (Jeremiah 9:23–24)

Twenty-Three Days

He was a has-been, a fossil, a relic, an old fogey . . . but as a child, George Frideric Handel had accompanied his father to the court of Duke Johann Adolf. Idly wandering into the chapel, the boy found the organ and started improvising, causing Duke Adolf to exclaim, "Who is this remarkable child?"

This remarkable child soon began composing operas, first in Italy, then in London. By his twenties he was the talk of England and the best-paid composer on earth. He opened the Royal Academy of Music. Londoners fought for seats at his every performance, and his fame soared around the world.

But the glory passed. Audiences dwindled. His music became outdated. The academy went bankrupt, and newer artists eclipsed the aging composer. One project after another failed, and Handel grew depressed. The stress brought on a case of palsy that crippled some of his fingers. "Handel's great days are over," wrote Frederick the Great, "His inspiration is exhausted."

Yet his troubles also matured him, softening his sharp tongue. His temper mellowed, and his music became more heartfelt. One morning Handel received by post a script from Charles Jennens. It was a word-for-word collection of various biblical texts about Christ. The opening words from Isaiah 40 moved Handel: "Comfort ye my people . . ." (KJV).

On *August 22, 1741*, he shut the door of his London home and started composing music for the words. Twenty-three days later, the world had *Messiah*. "Whether I was in the body or out of the body when I wrote it, I know not," Handel later said, trying to describe the experience. *Messiah* opened in London to enormous crowds on March 23, 1743. Handel led from his harpsichord, and King George II, who was present that night, surprised everyone by leaping to his feet during the "Hallelujah Chorus." No one knows why. Some believe the king, being hard of hearing, thought it the national anthem.

No matter—from that day audiences everywhere have stood in reverence during the stirring word: "Hallelujah! For He shall reign forever and ever."

Then I heard what seemed to be a large crowd . . . They were saying,
"Praise the Lord!
Our Lord God All-Powerful
now rules as king.
So we will be glad and happy
and give him praise." (Revelation 19:6–7)

August 23 Bartholomew's Day

When ten-year-old Charles IX became king of France in 1560, his mother, Catherine de' Medici, seized power as queen regent then tried to stabilize her religiously divided country. She tilted first toward Protestants then toward Catholics. Skirmishes broke out, and between 1561 and 1572, there were eighteen massacres of Protestants, five of Catholics, and thirty assassinations. Civil war loomed.

In a bid for peace Catherine, a Catholic, offered her daughter in marriage to Protestant Henry of Navarre. Henry came to Paris for the wedding, accompanied by thousands of Huguenots (French Protestants). The city trembled, and rumors spread that Huguenots were planning to kidnap the royal family. Clanging anvils across Paris betrayed the making of weapons. On *August 23, 1572*, Catherine and Charles were sequestered in the palace. About 10:00 PM Catherine warned Charles of imminent insurrection, working him into a fever, telling him Huguenots were planning to seize him. Charles suggested the rebels be arrested. It was too late for that, Catherine retorted. She roared and raged and threatened to flee France. Charles, nerves racked, ran from the room about midnight screaming, "By the death of God, since you choose to kill . . . I consent! But then you must kill all the Huguenots in France . . . Kill them all! Kill them all!"

The gates of the city were closed. Word spread among the troops, "Kill! The king commands it." As church bells pealed 3:00 AM, swords were drawn. Protestant leader Gaspard de Coligny was seized, strung by the heels, and his hands and genitals were lobbed off and sold. Huguenots and their children were dragged into the streets and slain. Embryos torn from dead mothers were smashed against the pavement. The sun, rising over Paris on St. Bartholomew's Day, revealed thousands of Protestant corpses.

The cries of butchered Huguenots rang in the king's head, day and night. "Who but you is the cause of all this?" he shouted to his mother. "God's blood, you are the cause of it all!" His constitution failed, and he began seeing visions of his victims. He ranted and raved and died at age twenty-three. "What evil counsel have I followed!" he cried. "O my God, forgive me! I am lost!"

The wicked are a restless sea
tossing up mud.
But I, the LORD, have promised
that none who are evil
will live in peace. (Isaiah 57:20–21)

The Tale of Two Cities

Barbarian invaders stampeded across Europe like herds of elephants, trampling everything in their path. Roman legions, unable to defend their ten-thousand-mile frontier, collapsed; the intruders penetrated Italy to the gates of Rome itself. And on *August 24, 410*, the Eternal City fell to Alaric and his swarms. For three days Rome was plundered. Women were attacked, the wealthy slaughtered, art destroyed, and the city battered beyond recognition.

The world reeled in shock, and Christians suddenly found themselves blamed. The empire had, after all, been an invincible fortress of iron before becoming "Christianized" with Constantine's conversion in 312. Now less than a century later, the greatest city and empire in history were no more. The old gods had been offended and had withdrawn their protection.

Across the Mediterranean the world's greatest theologian listened to the reports, saw the refugees, heard the charges, and spent thirteen years writing a response. Augustine's twenty-two-volume *The City of God* was written as a defense of Christianity, and it became the first great work to shape and define the medieval mind.

The first volumes of *The City of God* declare that Rome was being punished, not for her new faith but for her old sins—immorality and corruption. Augustine admitted that he himself had indulged in depravity before coming to Christ. But, he said, the original sin could be traced back to Adam and Eve, and we have but inherited the sinful nature unleashed by them.

Mary's child, Jesus Christ, offers forgiveness, and Christ alone provides eternal salvation. "Through a woman we were sent to destruction; through a woman salvation was restored to us. Mankind is divided into two sorts: such as live according to man, and such as live according to God. These we call the 'two cities,' the one predestined to reign eternally with God, and the other condemned to perpetual torment with Satan.

"The Heavenly City outshines Rome," Augustine wrote. "There, instead of victory, is truth; instead of high rank, holiness; instead of life, eternity."

Because Abraham had faith, he lived as a stranger in the promised land. . . . Abraham did this, because he was waiting for the eternal city that God had planned and built. (Hebrews 11:9–10)

Curtain Call

The last great Roman persecution against the church occurred during the reign of Diocletian, a son of slaves who became emperor in 284. Diocletian seemed tolerant of Christians at first. His wife and daughter studied Christian writings. But as the new faith grew and large church buildings began appearing in major cities, the emperor put Christianity to the rack. One of the strangest incidents occurred in 303, when Diocletian attended a play in Rome. In the performance actors clothed in white made fun of Christian rituals and habits. One of them, Genesius, ran onto the stage and fell to the floor crying, "I feel so heavy. I want to be made light. I want to die as a Christian that on that day I may fly up to God as a refuge." A mock priest and an exorcist ran to his side, performing rituals including a fake baptism.

The crowd roared with laughter. But Genesius had grown up in a Christian home, and his pagan ways had failed to destroy his Christian roots. He was suddenly haunted with pangs of conviction so strong that he cried out, "I want to receive the grace of Christ, that I may be born again, and be set free from the sins which have been my ruin."

Many in the crowd thought he was still acting. But he rose, interrupting the play. Looking at the audience he said, "Illustrious emperor, and all you people who have laughed loudly at this parody, believe me! Christ is the true Lord!"

Diocletian, enraged, immediately ordered Genesius stretched onto a device of agony called the hobbyhorse. As the tortures increased, his skin was torn with sharp hooks and his sides burned with torches. But the actor kept repeating, "There is no king except Christ, whom I have seen and worship. For him I will die a thousand times. I am sorry for my sin, and for becoming so late a soldier of the true king."

The tortures failed to dissuade him, and the curtain fell on his life when he was beheaded on this day, *August 25, 303.*

The LORD our God was with our ancestors to help them, and I pray that he will be with us and never abandon us. May the LORD help us obey him and follow all the laws and teachings he gave our ancestors. I pray that the LORD our God will remember my prayer day and night. (1 Kings 8:57–59)

The Ravings of a Wife

Blessed is the man whose wife speaks with wisdom even when she's out of her mind.

Ebenezer Erskine was a minister but not a good one. His Scottish congregation wearied of his preaching, but he seemed unable to do better. "I began my ministry without much zeal, callously and mechanically," he later wrote, "being swallowed up in unbelief and in rebellion against God." He had no enthusiasm for the Lord or his Word. No devotional life. No fresh insights from Scripture. His sermons were long, formal, and memorized; he preached them word for word in a monotone, never looking up or glancing into the jaded faces of his audience.

His wife, barely able to endure it, dreaded each approaching Sunday. For years she wept secretly over her husband's unregenerate heart and unspiritual ministry. She prayed earnestly for God, yet she said little to Ebenezer until . . . . until she contracted a raging fever. Ebenezer, then twenty-eight years of age, anxiously hovered over her as she twisted and tossed, body shrouded in sweat. In her delirium, she babbled her opinions of his ministry—it was lifeless and long-winded. And his heart? It was lost and languishing. Her words pierced him.

"At last," Ebenezer wrote in his diary, "the Lord was pleased to calm her spirit and give her a sweet serenity of mind. This, I think, was the first time ever I felt the Lord touching my heart in a sensible manner. Some few weeks after, she and I were sitting together in my study, and while we were conversing about the things of God, the Lord was pleased to rend the veil and to give me a glimmering view of salvation which made my soul acquiesce in Christ."

His acquiescence came on *August 26, 1708*. He wrote, "I offer myself up, soul and body, unto God the Father, Son, and Holy Ghost. I flee for shelter to the blood of Jesus. I will live to him; I will die to him. I take heaven and earth to witness that all I am and all I have are his."

Ebenezer Erskine became a popular preacher in eighteenth-century Scotland and the founder of the Scottish Secession Church.

The right word
at the right time
is like precious gold
set in silver.
Listening to good advice
is worth much more
than jewelry made of gold. (Proverbs 25:11–12)

August 27

The Prayer Chain

In 1722, Count Nikolaus Ludwig von Zinzendorf, troubled by the suffering of Christian exiles from Bohemia and Moravia, allowed them to establish a community on his estate in Germany. The center, known as Herrnhut, grew quickly and so did its appreciation for the power of prayer.

On *August 27, 1727*, twenty-four men and twenty-four women covenanted to spend an hour each day in scheduled prayer, praying in sequence around the clock. Soon others joined the prayer chain. Days passed, then months. Unceasing prayer rose to God twenty-four hours a day as someone—at least one—was engaged in intercessory prayer each hour of every day. The intercessors met weekly for encouragement and to read letters and messages from their brothers in different places. A decade passed, the prayer chain continuing nonstop. Then another decade. It was a prayer meeting that lasted more than a hundred years.

Undoubtedly this prayer chain helped birth Protestant missions. Zinzendorf, twenty-seven, suggested the possibility of attempting to reach others for Christ in the West Indies, Greenland, Turkey, and Lapland. Twenty-six Moravians stepped forward. During the first two years, twenty-two missionaries perished and two more were imprisoned, but others took their places.

By the time William Carey became the Father of Modern Missions, more than three hundred Moravian missionaries had already gone to the ends of the earth. And that's not all. The Moravian fervor sparked the conversions of John and Charles Wesley and indirectly ignited the Great Awakening that swept through Europe and America.

The prayer meeting lasted a hundred years. The results will last for eternity.

Jesus told his disciples a story about how they should keep on praying and never give up. Won't God protect his chosen ones who pray to him day and night? . . . He will surely hurry and help them. (Luke 18:1, 7–8)

A Hymnbook Under His Arm

Levi (Matthew) wasn't the only tax collector to follow Christ into full-time ministry. Ira Sankey did too. Sankey was born on *August 28, 1840*, in a small Pennsylvania town. His family later moved to New Castle, where his father became president of a local bank. Sankey served in the Union Army during the Civil War, then returned home to serve as the local internal revenue collector.

His real love, however, was singing, and he was in demand through Pennsylvania and Ohio as a soloist at meetings. His father, hoping he would enter politics, complained, "I am afraid that boy will never amount to anything. All he does is run about the country with a hymnbook under his arm." His mother replied that she would rather see him with a hymnbook under his arm than a whiskey bottle in his pocket.

In 1870, Sankey attended the national convention of the YMCA, meeting in Indianapolis. One of the convention sessions was dragging along so badly that Sankey offered to lead some hymns. At the end of the session, he was approached by a big, burly man who pelted him with questions. "Where are you from? What is your business? Are you married?"

When Sankey told him he was married, lived in Pennsylvania, and worked for the government, the man abruptly announced, "You will have to give that up."

"What for?" asked Sankey in amazement.

"To come to Chicago and help me in my work."

Sankey replied that he could not possibly leave his business. To this, the man said, "You must; I have been looking for you for the last eight years."

Thus began one of the most famous partnerships in evangelistic history: D. L. Moody and Ira Sankey. For the next quarter century Moody and Sankey traveled around the world. As Moody preached the gospel, Sankey sang solos, conducted the singing, and composed music for the gospel hymns. His *Gospel Hymns and Sacred Songs and Solos* sold more than fifty million copies. He became his generation's most beloved gospel singer.

Once again, Jesus went to the shore of Lake Galilee. A large crowd gathered around him, and he taught them. As he walked along, he saw Levi, the son of Alphaeus. Levi was sitting at the place for paying taxes, and Jesus said to him, "Come with me!" So he got up and went with Jesus. (Mark 2:13–14)

Mass Escape

John Dick, son of an Edinburgh lawyer, was a graduate of Edinburgh University, where he studied theology in hope of becoming a minister of the gospel. He didn't make it, for he was among the Presbyterians deemed outlaws during the reign of Charles II. He lived a fugitive's life until betrayed by a poor woman who later lost her mind over the incident.

John was brought before the Committee of Public Affairs on *August 29, 1683*, found guilty of treason, and sentenced to die by hanging. The Canongate tollbooth contained two large upper cells, and John, tossed into one of them, found there two dozen other religious prisoners. The men joined hearts in prayer, asking God's help as they planned a mass escape. News seeped out, and Presbyterians all over Edinburgh prayed for a successful breakout. On the appointed night the men begin sawing painstakingly through the iron bars of their glassless window.

The first bar was cut about nine o'clock, but to the horror of all, before any of them could catch it, it fell down into the narrow street near the sentry. They held their breath and watched and prayed, but no alarm sounded. They continued their furtive work; then one by one, the men dropped from the window and disappeared into the night.

The next morning confusion erupted through official Edinburgh. Police, city fathers, guards and sentries were questioned; but none of the prisoners was ever recaptured—except John Dick. He enjoyed but six months of freedom, using the time to write his fifty-eight-page "Testimony to the Doctrine, Worship, Discipline, and Government of the Church of Scotland and the Covenanted Work of Reformation in the Three Kingdoms," which, despite its unwieldy title, circulated widely. Then, his book finished, he was captured. On the scaffold he sang Psalm 2, read Ezekiel 9, and preached his last sermon, saying: "Remember when Abraham was about to sacrifice his son? Isaac said, 'Here is the wood, and the fire, but where is the sacrifice?'" John Dick turned and gazed upon the gallows. "Now blessed be the Lord," he said. "Here is the sacrifice."

They arrested the apostles and put them in the city jail. But that night an angel from the Lord opened the doors of the jail and led the apostles out. (Acts 5:18)

Two Martyrs

Christianity became firmly rooted in North Africa in the 200s, but the Roman emperors exerted every effort to pull it up. Among their targets were an urban bishop and a small-town pastor. The urban bishop was Thascius Caecilius Cyprianus, who had turned his back on a promising political career to represent Christ. Though a relatively new convert, Cyprian was appointed bishop of Carthage in 248. "The stain of my earlier life had been washed away by the help of the water of birth [baptism]," he wrote, "and the second birth restored me so as to make me a new man."

He served for ten years, steering the Carthage church through stormy days of persecution. At length Roman Emperor Decius ordered the liquidation of all leading Christian bishops. News came of bishops executed in Rome, Jerusalem, Antioch, Caesarea. Then the soldiers came for Cyprian too. He was beheaded on *August 30, 258.*

Several years later during the reign of Emperor Diocletian, a village pastor outside Carthage faced similar jeopardy. The persecution unleashed by Diocletian was the worst of all. Churches were destroyed, Bibles burned, and all civil rights of Christians were suspended. Diocletian required everyone to sacrifice to the gods. When Roman magistrates came to the village, they summoned leading Christians and ordered them to surrender their Bibles. The believers replied that their pastor, Felix, had them in his possession, and he was away in Carthage. When Felix returned the next day, he was surrounded by troops who demanded he turn over the Bibles.

He refused. "It is better that I should be burnt myself than the Scriptures," he told them. They gave him three days to reconsider his answer, then sent him to the proconsul in Carthage, who suggested he wriggle out of the dilemma by offering some old Bibles and spare books.

Felix refused. "I have Bibles," he said, "but I will not surrender them." He was escorted to the lowest cell in the city's filthiest prison for a month of misery, then shipped to Italy bound in heavy chains. He died en route on *August 30, 303*, in the hold of a ship carrying horses.

I chose you and sent you out to produce fruit, the kind of fruit that will last . . . So I command you to love each other. If the people of this world hate you, just remember that they hated me first. (John 15:16–18)

Solidarity

No one played a larger role in the collapse of Communism in Eastern Europe than Karol Wojtyla of Krakow. During the Nazi occupation of Poland, Wojtyla had attended an underground Catholic seminary by dodging military patrols and taking secret classes in convents, churches, and homes. At length he graduated, donned clerical robes, and traveled to a small Polish village to serve as priest. Communists, meanwhile, were replacing Nazis as the oppressors of Eastern Europe, but with intrepidity, Wojtyla performed baptisms, heard confessions, offered mass, foiled the secret police, and thwarted authorities.

The years passed, and by 1978, the village priest had advanced to become the first non-Italian pope in 456 years—John Paul II. On one of his first outings, the new pope heard someone in the crowd shout, "Don't forget the Church of Silence!" (that is, the church under Communism). John Paul replied, "It's not a Church of Silence anymore because it speaks with my voice."

John Paul soon returned in triumph to Warsaw, where his plane landed over the protests of Soviet leader Leonid Brezhnev. Oceans of faces met him everywhere, weeping, praying, shouting. Communist leaders in Russia and Poland trembled as they listened to his words: "Dearest brothers and sisters! You must be strong with the strength that flows from faith! There is no need to be afraid. The frontiers must be opened."

Within a year spontaneous strikes occurred throughout Poland; and in Gdansk, Lech Walesa stood atop an excavator and announced a strike in the shipyards. Back at the Vatican John Paul watched, prayed, and spoke to a group of Polish pilgrims in St. Peter's Square. "All of us here in Rome are united with our compatriots in Poland," he said, signaling his blessings on the strikers. Within a week the Communists made historic concessions, and on *August 31, 1980*, the Gdansk Accords were signed, permitting the first independent union in Eastern Europe. There was no mistaking the role of the Polish pope, for Lech Walesa signed the papers using a brightly colored Vatican pen featuring a picture of John Paul II.

The Iron Curtain was crumbling.

I'll tell you
what it really means
to worship the LORD.
Remove the chains of prisoners
who are chained unjustly.
Free those who are abused! (Isaiah 58:6)

On This Day in Christian History…

SEPTEMBER

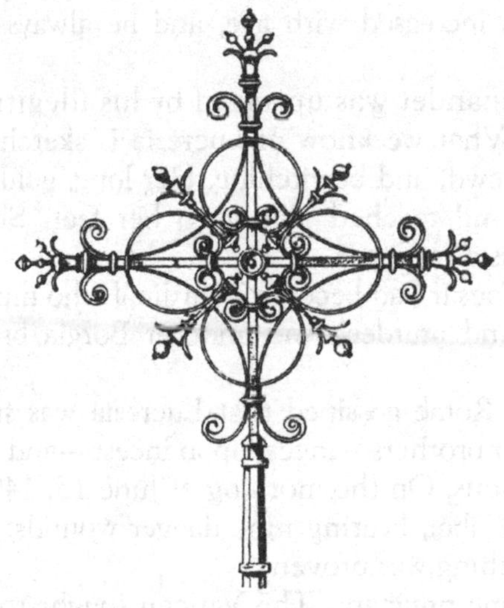

September 1 The Pagan Pontiff

The history of the church tells lessons good and bad. Its heroes include the noblest saints who ever lived, but its rosters also record scoundrels who have blackened its name. For example . . .

In 1460, twenty-nine-year-old Cardinal Rodrigo Borgia of Spain fumed as he opened the letter from the reigning pope. Pius II was upset over news of another wild Borgia party. "None of the allurements of love was lacking," the pope complained. He condemned Borgia's orgies, warning him of "disgrace" and "contempt."

But Borgia, ever more unrestrained, advanced in office until he purchased the papacy itself in 1492. He called himself Pope Alexander VI. His sinful exploits increased with age, and he always kept a stable of women.

But Pope Alexander was upstaged by his illegitimate daughter, Lucrezia Borgia. What we know of Lucrezia is sketchy but vivid. She was charming, shrewd, and bewitching. Her long, golden hair crowned her angelic face and reached almost to her feet. She inherited her father's lustiness as a teenager.

Her brother Caesar had become a cardinal who mixed church work with immorality and murder. And another Borgia brother, Juan, was equally immoral.

In the 1490s, Rome gossiped that Lucrezia was sleeping with her father and both her brothers—incest upon incest—and that the brothers were violently jealous. On the morning of June 15, 1497, Juan's corpse was found in the Tiber, bearing nine dagger wounds. Caesar was suspected though nothing was proven.

Lucrezia became pregnant. The Vatican sought to hide her condition, but word filtered out. The child was named Giovanni. But who was his father? On *September 1, 1501*, Pope Alexander VI issued two extraordinary edicts. The first, which was made public, identified Giovanni as Caesar's child. But the second, hidden in church vaults, identified Giovanni as the pope's own son, making Pope Alexander both the child's father and his grandfather.

A young monk named Martin Luther was watching.

I have heard terrible things about some of you. In fact, you are behaving worse than the Gentiles. A man is even sleeping with his own stepmother. Don't you know how a little yeast can spread through the whole batch of dough? Get rid of the old yeast! (1 Corinthians 5:1, 6–7)

Find a Verse and Put Your Name in It

Educating missionary children is exciting and exacting. On one hand few people are more fortunate than missionary kids. They grow up as internationals with the world their home. They roam across Europe or explore Africa as easily as other children go around the block. On the other hand many missions settings do not offer adequate schooling or needed interaction with other youth.

Ruth Bell Graham vividly remembered *September 2, 1933*. She was thirteen. Her father, a missionary surgeon in China, and her mother were sending her to boarding school in what is now Pyongyang, North Korea. For Ruth it was a brutal parting, and she earnestly prayed she would die before morning. But dawn came, her prayers unanswered; she gripped her bags and trudged toward the riverfront. She was leaving all that was loved and familiar: her parents, her Chinese friends, the missionaries, her home, her memories. The *Nagasaki Maru* carried her down the Whangpoo River into the Yangtze River and on to the East China Sea.

A week later waves of homesickness pounded her like a churning surf. Ruth kept busy by day, but evenings were harder, and she would bury her head in her pillow and cry herself to sleep, night after night, week after week. She fell ill, and in the infirmary she read through the Psalms, finding comfort in Psalm 27:10—"Even if my father and mother should desert me, you will take care of me."

Still, the hurt and fear and doubt persisted. Finally she went to her sister Rosa, also enrolled in Pyongyang. "I don't know what to tell you to do," Rosa replied matter-of-factly, "unless you take some verse and put your own name in it. See if that helps." Ruth picked up her Bible and turned to a favorite chapter, Isaiah 53, and put her name in verse 5: "He was wounded and crushed because of Ruth's sins; by taking Ruth's punishment, he made Ruth completely well."

Her heart leaped, and the healing began.

Has anyone believed us
or seen the mighty power
of the LORD in action?
Like a young plant or a root
that sprouts in dry ground,
the servant grew up
obeying the LORD. (Isaiah 53:1–2)

September 3 Gregory the Great

None of us are all good, and few of us are all bad. We often struggle with decisions, sometimes finding our well-intended efforts producing unfortunate results. Thus with Gregory. Born in Rome about five hundred years after Christ, his family provided wealth and rank, and he became mayor of Rome at the age of thirty-three. After his father's death Gregory gave his inheritance to the church and the poor, turned his mansion into a monastery, and became a monk.

He was consecrated as Pope Gregory I on *September 3, 590*, and did much good. Burdened for the evangelization of England, he sent Augustin to evangelize the British Isles. Gregory also appointed wise and competent men as church leaders, and he fought apostasy. He encouraged the Visigoths to turn from heresy to orthodox doctrine. He wrote evangelistic tracts to barbarian tribes and upheld biblical morality. He prepared a training manual for clergy. He wrote liturgy and popularized the Gregorian chant.

But Gregory also established the dogmas of purgatory and the mass. He encouraged the worship of relics (the remains of deceased Christians) and popularized unlikely legends about the saints. He glorified the past and held tradition equal with Scripture. He drew wild, allegorical lessons from the pages of the Bible. And he claimed universal jurisdiction over Christendom.

With Western Europe in chaos and the Roman Empire shattered, Gregory assumed broad civil control. He ruled most of Italy. He raised an army and defeated the Lombards. He negotiated treaties to avoid Rome's destruction. He ransomed captured individuals. He collected taxes and supplied food and services to the poor. He, in effect, turned the church into the state.

In so doing, Gregory became the father of the medieval papacy—with all the good and bad that entailed.

Jesus answered, "My kingdom doesn't belong to this world . . . I was born into this world to tell about the truth. And everyone who belongs to the truth knows my voice." (John 18:36–37)

The Niger Expedition

In 1840, three strands of purpose—missionary advance, humanitarian resolve, and slavery abolition—merged into the Niger Expedition, brainchild of Foxwell Buxton of the Church Missionary Society and of the Society for the Extinction of the Slave Trade. The British government funded the enterprise, and all England followed the course of the three new state-of-the-art steamships named *Albert, Wilberforce*, and *Soudan*. The iron vessels had a novel system of ventilation using chemical filters to neutralize the swamp gases thought to produce malaria.

The fleet sailed in early 1841, loaded with sailors, scientists, agriculturists, philanthropists, liberated slaves (as interpreters), and missionaries J. F. Schon and Samuel Adjai Crowther. They arrived in African waters in mid-August, but on *September 4, 1841*, the chief medical officer, Dr. McWilliams, logged that "fever of a most malignant character" had broken out, and the whole expedition was paralyzed. The sick were loaded onto the *Soudan* to return to healthier harbors, and the *Wilberforce* followed her.

The *Albert* forged up the Niger River alone, but soon the captain and crew were sick. Men threw themselves overboard in their deliriums. The dead were buried on the riverbanks by the missionaries. With no one left to navigate the ship, Dr. McWilliams did his best to control the reeling ship, using a textbook found in the captain's cabin. But he had to repeatedly leave the bridge to attend the sick and dying. Of the 145 Europeans on board, 130 contracted malaria, and many died.

But the mission wasn't a complete failure. The missionaries returned with valuable recommendations that led to establishing a missionary center in Fourah Bay for training liberated slaves to evangelize West Africa. Within four years its foundation stone was laid on the very spot, where forty years before, a factory had stood that engaged in the slave trade. And the rafters of the new roof were made almost entirely from the masts of old slave ships.

Tell the whole world to sing
a new song to the LORD!
Tell those who sail the ocean
and those who live far away
to join in the praise.
Tell the tribes of the desert
and everyone in the mountains to celebrate and sing.
Let them announce
his praises everywhere. (Isaiah 42:10–12)

September 5 No Stone Unturned

Allen Francis Gardiner grew up in a Christian home, took to the sea, and achieved a successful British naval career with little thought for God. But in 1822, he fell ill and reevaluated his life. He scribbled in his journal: "After years of ingratitude, unbelief, blasphemy and rebellion, have I at last been melted? Alas, how slow, how reluctant I have been to admit the heavenly guest who stood knocking without!"

Traveling around the world had given Captain Gardiner a glimpse of the need for missionaries, and he gave himself for the task. Leaving England for South America, he hoped to minister among the Araucanian or Mapuche Indians of southern Chile. Government interference and intertribal fighting forced him back to England. Three years later he was at it again, visiting the Falklands and investigating the possibility of taking the gospel to the islands of Patagonia and Tierra del Fuego. Sensing opportunity at hand, Gardiner returned to England and on July 4, 1844, established a small organization called the Patagonian Missionary Society. He wrote, "I have made up my mind to go back to South America and leave no stone unturned, no effort untried, to establish a mission among the aboriginal tribes. While God gives me strength, failure will not daunt me."

Gardiner visited South America a third time, but his efforts were again thwarted by intertribal fighting and governmental interference, the land being strongly Catholic, intolerant of Protestant missions. He returned to England, recruited six missionaries, and set sail for Tierra del Fuego. But all seven men died of disease, starvation, and exposure on Picton Island. Gardiner, the last to die, dated his final journal entry *September 5, 1851*: "Good and marvelous are the loving kindnesses of my gracious God unto me. He has preserved me hitherto and for four days, although without bodily food, without any feelings of hunger or thirst."

Captain Allen Gardiner died without seeing a single soul saved among those for whom he was most burdened. But he lit a fire that has never gone out. His South American Missionary Society (as it came to be called) has been sending missionaries and saving souls for more than one hundred fifty years.

My dear friends, stand firm and don't be shaken. Always keep busy working for the Lord. You know that everything you do for him is worthwhile. (1 Corinthians 15:58)

Whipped with Roses September 6

Visitors to Boston Commons with its graceful swan boats might be surprised to learn what once happened there to Obadiah Holmes. In 1651, Holmes was arrested for preaching Baptist doctrine in nearby Lynn. Friends tried to pay his fine, but Holmes refused. On *September 6, 1651*, he was taken to Boston Commons, stripped to the waist, and tied to a whipping post. He later wrote: "As the man began to lay the strokes upon my back, I said to the people, Though my flesh should fail, yet God would not fail. So it pleased the Lord to come in and fill my heart and tongue; and with an audible voice I broke forth praying unto the Lord not to lay this sin to their charge. In truth, as the strokes fell upon me, I had such a manifestation of God's presence as the like thereof I never had nor felt, nor can with fleshy tongue express; and the outward pain was so removed from me, that indeed I am not able to declare it to you. It was so easy to me that I could well bear it, yea and in a manner felt it not although it was grievous, the man striking with all his strength (spitting on his hands three times as many affirmed) with a three corded whip, giving me therewith thirty strokes. When he loosed me from the post, having joyfulness in my heart and cheerfulness in my countenance, I told the magistrates, 'You have struck me with roses.'"

If so, they were covered with thorns. The whipping was so severe that blood ran down Holmes's body until his shoes overflowed. A friend reported: "Holmes was whipt thirty stripes in such an unmerciful manner that in many days, if not some weeks, he could take no rest, but lay on knees and elbows, not being able to suffer any part of his body to touch the bed."

But the suffering wasn't wasted. The trial and whipping of Obadiah Holmes occasioned the conversion of Henry Dunster, president of Harvard, to the Baptists and led to the organization of Boston's first Baptist church.

We gladly suffer, because we know that suffering helps us to endure. And endurance builds character, which gives us a hope that will never disappoint us. All of this happens because God has given us the Holy Spirit, who fills our hearts with his love. (Romans 5:3–5)

September 7 — Turf Wars

In twelfth-century Europe the relationship between pope and emperor was like the dance of the porcupines. The emperor needed the pope to instill reverence; the pope needed the emperor to protect the church. But which of the two was supreme?

On *September 7, 1159*, Cardinal Orlando Roland was proclaimed Pope Alexander III, but he wasn't well received by Holy Roman Emperor Frederick II, for Roland had once quipped, "From whom does the emperor receive his dignity if not from the pope?" Frederick immediately named a rival pope, Octavian, who moved into the Vatican. France, Spain, and England sided with Alexander. Germany, Hungary, Bohemia, Norway, and Sweden supported Octavian. Italy was divided.

War broke out. In November 1166, Frederick crossed the Alps, attacking and routing the armies supporting Alexander. But he soon found himself facing a mightier enemy than the pope's. The Roman Fever broke out among his troops, sweeping away his noblemen, knights, and soldiers. Frederick broke camp in haste and recrossed the Alps with a few straggling survivors.

He eventually took steps to reconcile with Alexander, the spiritual head of his enemies; and after eighteen years of conflict, the two men met to sign peace accords in front of St. Mark's Cathedral in Venice on July 24, 1177. The pope sat in his pontifical dress, surrounded by cardinals, archbishops, and other dignitaries. The emperor arrived in a magnificent gondola with a train of nobles. He emerged from his conveyance and proceeded toward the cathedral. Overcome by feelings of reverence, he cast off his mantle, bowed, and fell at the pope's feet. Alexander wept, raised him up, and kissed him. The multitude burst into song.

Legend persists of a whispered exchange in which Frederick reputedly said in the pope's ear, "I do this homage to Peter, *not* to thee," to which Alexander replied, "To Peter *and* to me."

It wasn't a lasting peace; Alexander III was again driven from Rome to Civata Castellana, where he died in exile in 1181.

Jesus called the disciples together and said: You know that foreign rulers like to order their people around. And their great leaders have full power over everyone they rule. But don't act like them. If you want to be great, you must be the servant of all the others. (Matthew 20:25–26)

Terrible Day at Anagni

Proverbs 16:18—"Too much pride will destroy you"—finds a perfect illustration in Benedetto Gaetani. Gaetani, a clergyman, carried himself with aplomb, serving the Vatican well in various capacities across Europe. When he became Pope Boniface VIII in 1294, he determined to raise the papacy to its highest point. His crown contained 48 rubies, 72 sapphires, 45 emeralds, and 66 large pearls. The Roman pontiff, he said, "is most high over princes, and monarchs receive their light from him as the moon receives its light from the sun." He sometimes appeared before pilgrims crying, "I am Caesar. I am emperor."

France's young King Philip IV would have none of it, and he continually outmaneuvered Boniface in diplomatic skirmishes. Things came to a head when Philip arrested the pope's legate. Boniface roared back with a document known as *Ausculta fili*—"Give ear, my son"—charging Philip with arrogance toward the clergy and with plundering church property. Philip assembled the French Parliament and asserted his independence from the church.

The pope then issued another edict, the most extreme assertion of papal power in church history, called *Unam sanctam.* The pope is the vicar of Christ, it said, and every human must obey him. The pope further announced that on *September 8, 1303*, he would appear at the church of Anagni, Italy, near his summer residence, and with great solemnity pronounce a ban on Philip.

September 8 never came. On September 7, Philip's commandos attacked the papal residence and burst in on the eighty-six-year-old pope. He was roughly treated. His palace was looted, and the cathedral was burned, its relics destroyed. Its most priceless possession, a vase reportedly containing milk from Mary's breasts, was shattered.

Boniface remained prisoner for three days till forces loyal to him retook the palace. But the old man never recovered. He lost his mind and began beating his head against the wall. He refused to eat. A month later he died. The event is known to history as the Terrible Day at Anagni, and it marked the beginning of the decline of the papacy in medieval Europe.

Too much pride
will destroy you.
You are better off
to be humble and poor
than to get rich
from what you take by force. (Proverbs 16:18–19)

Jabez

Mary Redfern lived in the small English village of Haddon in Derbyshire. Her mother was bedfast, and all the care for her eight younger siblings fell onto Mary's shoulders. One day in 1769, she heard a commotion in the street. A little man was preaching before a crowd in the open. His name was John Wesley.

Soon after, Richard Boardman, one of Wesley's evangelists, came preaching. He had recently lost his wife, and his demeanor was tender and poignant. He spoke from 1 Chronicles 4:9 about Jabez, "the most respected son in his family." Mary was deeply moved and never forgot the story of Jabez. She moved to Manchester, married, and named her firstborn Jabez. And when Wesley preached in Manchester's Oldham Street Church, Mary brought little Jabez. The great evangelist touched the child and blessed him.

Little did he know he was blessing his future successor.

Young Jabez often heard Wesley preach, and he developed a great love for the gospel. As a lad he would walk miles to hear preaching, returning to deliver his own little sermons to long-suffering sisters, using his father's shirts as ministerial robes. When nineteen he preached his first official sermon in Sodom, near Manchester, and shortly thereafter he was ordained to the ministry.

Jabez quickly advanced in Methodism, but he often proved hard-headed and strong-willed. When he rose to leadership following Wesley's death, he ruled with a strong hand. His slogan was: "Methodism hates democracy as it hates sin." One of several controversies occurred on *September 9, 1825*, when the Brunswick Chapel opened in Leeds, England. A dispute arose over whether an organ should be installed. Many members opposed it, but the leaders installed it anyway. The organ, it was later said, cost one thousand pounds and a thousand Methodists.

Jabez was called the Pope of Methodism. But he preached a clear gospel and brought Methodist theological training and world missions into their own. His influence lasts to this day.

You must watch over everyone God has placed in your care. Do it willingly in order to please God, and not simply because you think you must . . . Don't be bossy to those people who are in your care, but set an example for them. (1 Peter 5:2–3)

49 City Road

Jabez Bunting was buried near John Wesley, but other early Methodists actually ended up in Wesley's grave. They considered it high honor to have their death dust mingled with that of the great evangelist. The crowded tomb is located behind Wesley's Chapel on London's City Road. In the late 1770s, Wesley built his new chapel there, then built a manse next door. He moved in on *September 10, 1779*, writing in his journal, "This night I lodged in the new house in London. How many more nights have I to spend here?"

The answer—eleven years. He died in ripe old age, his longevity attributable to several secrets contained in his new home. Today's visitors are shown an exact replica of his chamber horse. Wesley valued exercise and considered horseback riding the best, so he designed a towering chair with tall coils and springs that allowed him to bounce up and down, hair flying and falling until his heart was racing and his clothing drenched with sweat.

Wesley's house also contains a primitive tabletop device for generating electricity. He believed that regular shocks of electricity were good for one's health, and he became such a forceful advocate of electrical medicine that his sick friends lined up at his door each day for the treatment.

The real power room of Methodism was Wesley's tiny prayer closet with its small table, tall window, and open Bible. It adjoined his bedroom, and Wesley stayed spiritually fit.

Here at 49 City Road in London, a narrow brick building of five floors, Wesley realized he was dying. He went to his room and asked for a half hour alone. The message flew through London, "Mr. Wesley is very ill! Pray!" Friends gathered, and on February 27, 1791, he recited a hymn to them: "I'll praise my maker while I've breath / And when my voice is lost in death, / Praise shall employ my nobler powers. / My days of praise shall ne'er be past." He spoke his last words, "The best of all is, God is with us. Farewell." And then John Wesley, who often said that his followers "died well," did so himself.

As the saying goes,
"Exercise is good
for your body,
but religion helps you
in every way.
It promises life
now and forever."
These words are worthwhile and should not be forgotten. (1 Timothy 4:8–9)

Spunk

Isaac Watts faced criticism when he began writing hymns, for it was believed only psalms should be sung in worship. But the little songwriter had inherited spunk from his grandfather and father.

Grandfather Thomas Watts, commander of a British warship, was attacked once by a tiger in India. Running into the river, he turned to see the tiger swimming after him. He faced the creature, gripped its head, and forced it under water until it drowned.

Isaac Senior fought a different kind of tiger—persecution. He rejected the state Church of England and joined British Nonconformists. That was considered treasonous, and he was thrown into Southampton Jail, a huge, gloomy place where Dissenters languished in iron shackles. He emerged from prison in time to marry Sarah Tauton on *September 11, 1673*, but the new couple was under constant watch. The stress caused Sarah to prematurely give birth to a weak, stunted baby, Isaac Junior. Within weeks, the senior Watts was jailed again. He found comfort in his pocket Bible, but his wife worried endlessly. Every day she crept to the prison, sat on a stone outside, nursed her baby, and wept.

Watts was released at last, and a few years passed. One morning young Isaac "tittered" during family prayers. His father sternly demanded an explanation. "Because," said the spunky boy, pointing to a bell rope, "I saw a mouse running up that; and the thought came into my mind, 'There was a mouse for want of stairs / Ran up a rope to say his prayers.'" Isaac Senior, unimpressed, reached for the rod. The boy fell to his knees, begging and crying, "Oh father, father, pity take / And I will no more verses make." But he did make more verses.

When sometime later he grumbled about the music in his church, his father told him to write his own songs if he thought he could do better than King David. So he wrote "Joy to the World," "O God Our Help in Ages Past," "I Sing the Mighty Power of God," "When I Survey the Wondrous Cross," and six hundred others.

He became the father of English hymns.

With thankful hearts, sing psalms, hymns, and spiritual songs to God. Whatever you say or do should be done in the name of the Lord Jesus. (Colossians 3:16–17)

No, I Am Not Dead!

Thomas Webb was a portly, homely, ragged fireball who helped establish Methodism in America. Born in England, Webb had initially chosen a soldier's career and had fought with the British army in 1759. He was wounded and returned to England, only to be retired on captain's pay. About 1764, he was converted to Christ in Bristol under the preaching of John Wesley, and he soon began applying his military mind in the Methodist campaign for souls. He became an ardent preacher in England and Ireland; then in 1766, he came to America as a soldier for Christ.

In New York City Captain Webb fired up a discouraged preacher named Philip Embury, assisting him in preaching the gospel. New York's population was only about fifteen thousand. But Webb saw the potential and joined several others in constructing a small chapel, forty-two by sixty feet, with a seating capacity of seven hundred. It was built of stone, covered with blue plaster. The benches had no backs. Candles provided light. It was a plain building, but worshippers claimed it had "the beauty of Holiness." The John Street Church, the first Methodist chapel in New York City, has been called the Mother Church of Methodism in America.

Afterward Captain Webb traveled far and wide—to Long Island, Philadelphia, Baltimore, Delaware, Jamaica, and Europe. And during his periodic stops in England, he continually urged Wesley to send more preachers to the colonies.

Those who met Webb never forgot him, chiefly because of his dangling sword and the large, green oversized patch that covered his left eye, the result of his war wounds of *September 12, 1759*, during the Battle of Louisburg. It was described this way:

> A ball hit him on the bone which guards the right eye, and taking an oblique direction, burst the eyeball, and passing through his palate into his mouth, he swallowed it. A comrade said, "He is dead enough." Webb replied, "No, I am not dead." In three months, he was able to rejoin his comrades. He was never ashamed of his scars.

All that matters is that you are a new person. If you follow this rule, you will belong to God's true people. God will treat you with undeserved kindness and will bless you with peace. (Galatians 6:15–16)

Jesus' Kinsmen

Jesus Christ, the Son of God, had neither wife nor children. But he did have brothers, sisters, nieces, and nephews. Have you ever wondered what happened to his family, the descendants of Joseph and Mary? They are not entirely lost to history. His brothers, James and Judas, after initially rejecting his ministry, were converted, became leaders in the early church, and wrote the New Testament epistles that bear their names—James and Jude.

But there's more.

On *September 13, 81*, the Roman emperor Titus died at age forty after a two-year reign. He was replaced by his brother, Titus Flavius Domitianus, twenty-nine, who reigned until 96 as Domitian. As a youth Domitian was handsome and tall and modest. In later years he developed a protruding belly, spindle legs, and a bald head (though he had written a book, *On the Care of the Hair*).

The historian Pliny described Domitian as the beast from hell who sat in its den, licking blood. He relished sadistic cruelty. He caught flies just so he could stab them with his knife and entertained himself with gladiatorial fights between women and dwarfs.

He was the first Roman emperor to title himself *God the Lord* and insisted others cheer him with the phrases *Lord of the earth! Invincible! Glory! Thou Alone!* The Jews and Christians refused to utter such blasphemy and were targeted for intense persecution.

Eusebius, Bishop of Caesarea, the Father of Church History, cites Hegesippus, a church historian from the second century, as saying that among the oppressed were the great-grandsons of Joseph and Mary: "Domitian brought from Palestine to Rome two kinsmen of Jesus, grandsons of Judas, the brother of the Lord, but seeing their poverty and rustic simplicity, and hearing their explanation of the kingdom of Christ as not earthly, but heavenly, to be established by the Lord at the end of the world, when he should come to judge the quick and the dead, he let them go."

He taught in their meeting place, and the people were so amazed that they asked, "Where does he get all this wisdom and the power to work these miracles? Isn't he the son of the carpenter? Isn't Mary his mother, and aren't James, Joseph, Simon, and Judas his brothers? Don't his sisters still live here in our town?" (Matthew 13:54–56)

Golden Mouthed

For fifteen centuries this day in church history has belonged to John Chrysostom, who died on *September 14, 407*, at age sixty. His powerful sermons gave him the reputation as the greatest orator in Christian history. Indeed, the name Chrysostom means "Golden Mouthed."

John was born in Antioch, Syria. His father, a high-ranking Roman officer, died shortly after John's birth. His mother, Anthusa, devoted herself to raising John in the nurture of the Lord. She placed him in the finest schools, and under the well-known orator Libanius, John mastered the art of rhetoric.

John became a lawyer, well known for powerful speaking. His legal studies led him to reexamine Christianity's beliefs, and he became so impressed with Scripture that he resigned the law, was baptized, and wanted to join a monastery. When his mother persuaded him to remain home and comfort her in her old age, John turned his home into a personal monastery, eating simply, making few purchases, and spending much time in study.

After his mother's death, John studied and worked quietly as a monk for six years, followed by two more Elijah-like years in a hermit's cave. Then he began preaching. His messages were practical, powerful, and sprinkled with humor. He effectively led his listeners through the Bible in exegetical fashion. His oratory was so powerful that his audiences frequently burst into spontaneous applause, a practice he disliked.

In 398, John was elected patriarch of Constantinople, but when his plainspoken messages riled priests and politicians there, he was banished to a remote spot on the Black Sea. "The doctrine of Christ did not begin with me," he told saddened parishioners, "and it shall not die with me." His forced departure caused a riot in Constantinople, and on the night of the riot, a powerful earthquake shook the city. The public officials immediately sent for him, and he returned in triumph. But John's blunt, biblical sermons continued to rankle the authorities, and he was again deposed and entered a period of ministry through letters and epistles before dying on this date in the year 407, his last words being, "Glory be to God for all things. Amen."

Ezekiel, I am sending you to the people of Israel. They are just like their ancestors who rebelled against me and refused to stop. They are stubborn and hardheaded. But I, the LORD God, have chosen you to tell them what I say. Those rebels may not even listen, but at least they will know that a prophet has come to them. (Ezekiel 2:3–5)

My Parish

Antoinette Brown, born in a log cabin in New York, was moved by the ministry of Charles Finney at the age of six and joined the Congregational Church at age nine. She excelled in school. After graduating from Oberlin College in 1847, she created a stir among the faculty when she returned for graduate studies in theology. No woman had yet studied theology at Oberlin. Her family grew alarmed and stopped supporting her. At the end of her studies, she was given no part in the commencement exercises, and her name didn't appear in the alumni catalog.

When she attended the World's Temperance Convention in New York City, she was not allowed to speak. This so incensed Horace Greeley of the *New York Tribune* that he reported: "This convention has completed three of its four business sessions, and the results may be summed up as follows: First Day—Crowding a woman off the platform. Second Day—Gagging her. Third Day—Voting that she shall stay gagged. Having thus disposed of the main question, we presume the incidentals will be finished this morning."

Greeley's words catapulted Antoinette Brown to prominence, and she was offered a preaching ministry at a large New York City church. But she felt too inexperienced for a large metropolitan pulpit, accepting a call instead to a small Congregational church, having "neither steeple or bell," in South Butler, New York.

There on *September 15, 1853*, Antoinette Brown became the first regularly ordained woman minister in America. Rev. Luther Lee preached the ordination message from Galatians 3:28: "Faith in Christ is what makes each of you equal with each other, whether you are a Jew or a Greek, a slave or a free person, a man or a woman."

Brown wrote in her journal: "This is a very poor and small church, ample I believe for my needs in this small community. My parish will be a miniature world in good and evil. To get humanity condensed into so small a compass that I can study each individual, opens a new chapter of experience. It is what I want . . ."

All of you are God's children because of your faith in Christ Jesus. And when you were baptized, it was as though you had put on Christ in the same way you put on new clothes. Faith in Christ Jesus is what makes each of you equal with each other, whether you are a Jew or a Greek, a slave or a free person, a man or a woman. (Galatians 3:26–28)

Friends of Israel

The reestablishment of the State of Israel in 1948 was a crowning achievement for the Zionist movement of the nineteenth and twentieth centuries. Among the Zionists were many Christians, especially in Great Britain, who believed the restoration of the Jews to Palestine was part of God's plan for the final chapters of history. Even before the end of the 1600s, at least twelve publications appeared in England advocating the return of the Jews to Palestine. Many British Christians viewed this as a mandate of biblical prophecy and linked it with the return of Christ. On *September 16, 1840*, Scottish minister Robert Murray McCheyne wrote to his friend in Belfast, George Shaw:

> You cannot tell how much real joy your letter gave me when you tell of the dear brethren who meet with you on Monday mornings, to read and pray concerning Israel. I feel deeply persuaded from prophecy, that it will always be difficult to stir up and maintain a warm and holy interest in outcast Israel. The lovers and pleaders of Zion's cause will be always few. Do you not think this is hinted at in Jeremiah 30:13: "There is none to plead thy cause, that thou mayest be bound up."? And is not this one of the very reasons why God will take up their cause?
>
> It is sweet encouragement to learn, that though the friends of Zion will probably be few, yet there always will be some who will keep watch over the dust of Jerusalem, and plead the cause of Israel with God and with man. See Isaiah 62:6–7: "Ye that make mention of the LORD, keep not silence, and give him no rest, till he establish, and till he make Jerusalem a praise in the earth." Oh, my dear brethren, into whose hearts I trust God is pouring a scriptural love for Israel, what an honor is it for us, worms of the dust, to be made watchmen by God over the ruined walls of Jerusalem, and to be made the Lord's remembrancers, to call His own promises to His mind, that He would fulfill them, and make Jerusalem a blessing to the whole world!

Jerusalem, on your walls
I have stationed guards,
whose duty it is
to speak out day and night,
without resting.
They must remind the LORD
and not let him rest
till he makes Jerusalem strong
and famous everywhere. (Isaiah 62:6–7)

The Rat Pit

Soon after the Civil War, reporter Oliver Dyer wrote that if all the bars, prostitution houses, and gambling dens of New York City ran along one street, it would stretch thirty miles. Each night on that street, he said, there would be a murder every half mile, a robbery every 165 yards, six outcasts at every door, and eight preachers barking the gospel. And Dyer pronounced barkeeper John Allen the "wickedest" of the city's wicked.

A minister, having read the story, entered Allen's bar on Water Street to witness to him. To his surprise, Allen, though not converted, was seized by pious pangs and offered to open his saloon to daily prayer meetings. Hundreds began flocking there. Newspapers puffed the story, and Allen became a media sensation. He soon announced his bar would become a house of worship, adding that since he was now famous he intended to join a church . . . someday.

The success of the meetings led organizers to rent the nearby rat pit at Kit Burns's Saloon, a makeshift amphitheater with seats rising above a pit in which scores of rats were released. Dogs were turned loose, and bets taken on the number of rats they could kill within a certain time. Burns's son-in-law often ended shows by jumping into the pit and killing surviving rats with his teeth. Kit Burns cleaned the blood from the floor each day and rented out his pit for prayer. As soon as services ended each afternoon, rat shows resumed (to "ratify" the prayers, Burns quipped).

On *September 17, 1868*, John Allen, basking in publicity, prepared to leave on a lecture tour of New England. He made it to Connecticut before getting so drunk he was ejected. Public interest plunged, and within a month Allen took his saloon back. But Christians rented another building down the street, and it became the first home of the McAuley Water Street Mission.

That's not all. Kit Burns's place was eventually transformed into a home for reformed prostitutes; the bar became a chapel, and the rat pit became a kitchen.

Turn to the LORD!
He can still be found.
Call out to God! He is near.
Give up your crooked ways
and your evil thoughts.
Return to the LORD our God.
He will be merciful
and forgive your sins. (Isaiah 55:6–7)

Jerry McAuley

McAuley Water Street Mission was named for Jerry McAuley, born in Ireland in 1839. His father, a counterfeiter, fled home to escape the law, and Jerry never knew him. His mother evidently languished in prison, and the boy was raised by his grandmother. When she couldn't control him, he was sent to New York, where he lived under the docks, drinking, fighting, and stealing from boats. In 1857, he was caught and sent to Sing Sing.

Sing Sing inmates were forced to live in unbroken silence in cell blocks five tiers high. Each cell was a little coffin—three feet wide, six feet high, seven feet long. It was wet in the summer; icy in winter; always grim. There was no plumbing, just buckets. Cells, never disinfected, filled with vermin, lice, and fleas. Infractions were punished by flogging, the "iron collar," or the "shower bath," in which prisoners were repeatedly drowned and revived.

One Sunday Jerry was herded into the chapel. He was moody and miserable until he glanced on the platform and recognized a well-known prizefighter, Orville Gardner. The boxer told of finding Jesus, and Jerry listened attentively. He soon began reading the Bible, page after page, day after day. He read it through twice; then in great agony he fell to his knees—but jumped up immediately in embarrassment. He did this several times. Finally one night, resolving to kneel until he found forgiveness, he prayed and prayed. "All at once it seemed something supernatural was in my room. I was afraid to open my eyes; the tears rolled off my face in great drops, and these words came to me, 'My son, thy sins, which are many, are forgiven.' "

He was released in 1864, having been incarcerated seven of his twenty-six years. He thereafter devoted himself to rescuing other incorrigibles. Twenty years later on *September 18, 1884*, the huge Broadway Tabernacle was packed for his funeral, with multitudes flooding surrounding streets. His Water Street Mission, a pioneer among America's rescue missions, has been a haven of hope for more than one hundred years.

"I tell you that all her sins are forgiven, and that is why she has shown great love. But anyone who has been forgiven for only a little will show only a little love." Then Jesus said to the woman, "Your sins are forgiven." (Luke 7:47–48)

Glory, Laud, and Honor

As the 700s rolled into the 800s, the greatest man in the world was Charlemagne, king of the Franks and Holy Roman Emperor. Having gained control of most of Western Europe, he set himself to reform the legal, judicial, and military systems of his empire. He established schools and promoted Christianity, and in his capital scholars and saints gathered from across Europe.

Among them was Theodulf. He was about fifty years old in 800, and he possessed an established reputation as churchman, poet, and scholar. Charlemagne made him bishop of Orleans in Spain, and Theodulf traveled widely, taking part in the great events of the empire. Upon the death of Alcuin, Charlemagne's secretary of education, Theodulf advanced to that position. Unfortunately, Theodulf's fortunes died when Charlemagne did. Accused by the new emperor of treason, he was imprisoned. He maintained his innocence and was pardoned in 818, but he died shortly afterward and was buried on *September 19, 821*.

Theodulf worked vigorously to provide the clergy with a good education. Among his books is *Directions to the Priests of the Diocese*, in which he issued maxims such as these:

- No woman is allowed to live in the house with a priest.
- Priests must not get drunk or frequent taverns.
- Priests must teach everyone the Lord's Prayer and the Apostle's Creed.
- Daily, honest confession of sins to God ensures pardon.
- True charity consists in the union of good deeds with a virtuous life.

Theodulf of Orleans is best remembered, however, for his beautiful hymn *Gloria, Laus et Honor*, which has been sung every Palm Sunday for more than a thousand years in churches around the world: "All glory, laud, and honor / To Thee, Redeemer, King, / To whom the lips of children / Make sweet hosannas ring: / Thou art the King of Israel, / Thou David's royal Son, / Who in the Lord's name comest, / The King and blessed one!"

Many people spread clothes in the road, while others put down branches which they had cut from trees. Some people walked ahead of Jesus and others followed behind. They were all shouting, "Hooray for the Son of David! God bless the one who comes in the name of the Lord. Hooray for God in heaven above!" (Matthew 21:8–9)

Ten More Days

Her name, Pandita Pamabai, though unfamiliar to many today, is etched in glory. Her father was a Brahmin priest who, at age forty-four, married a nine-year-old girl. Wanting to educate her, he took her to a remote forest in southern India, built a house, and, having removed all distractions, taught her all he knew. Here in 1858, Pandita was born. Her father determined to give her, too, an education, and by the time she was twelve, Pandita had memorized eighteen thousand Sanskrit verses and had become fluent in various languages.

But the little family encountered mounting debts, then hunger. Pandita's father "held me tightly in his arms, and stroking my head and cheeks, told me he loved me, how he had taught me to do right, and never to depart from the way of righteousness."

Then he died of starvation, followed by her mother. Pandita set off across India, sleeping in the open, suffering from cold, eating berries. She began doubting her father's idols, and finally in Calcutta, she learned of Jesus Christ.

Educated women were novelties in India, and Pandita began lecturing here and there, seeking to raise the standard of life for women. Traveling to England and America, she embraced Christ and was baptized. She studied mathematics and medicine in Western universities, and she sought financial support for a home for child-widows in India. In the late 1880s, she returned to India and opened the Mukti (Salvation) Mission. It was thronged by hundreds of desperate girls. She and her workers dug wells, planted trees, tilled the land, and preached the gospel. Hundreds were converted. Thousands were rescued from starvation. She established schools to educate her girls. Then a church was built with these lines inscribed on the foundation: *Praise the Lord. Not by might, nor by power, but by my Spirit, saith Jehovah of Hosts. That Rock was Christ. September 20, 1899.*

Her last years were spent translating the Bible into Marathi. She had almost completed the task when she fell ill. She prayed for ten more days in which to complete her work; and ten days later, on April 5, 1922, she died, having just finished the last page.

I am the LORD All-Powerful. So don't depend on your own power or strength, but on my Spirit. (Zechariah 4:6)

Any One of Us

Young, athletic scholars often make the best missionaries, especially when, like John Coleridge Patteson, they abandon all for Christ. Patteson, great-nephew of poet Samuel T. Coleridge, was "finely educated" at Oxford, where he excelled in sports, especially in rowing. Following graduation he became a curate of the Church of England and soon sailed to New Zealand to assist his missionary friend, Bishop George Selwyn.

Patteson conducted schools for Melanesian Christians, preached the gospel, and translated the Scriptures. He spoke twenty-three dialects and translated the New Testament into local languages. In 1861, he was consecrated Bishop of Melanesia, and after twenty years, only forty of the eight hundred natives on the chief island, Mota, remained unbaptized.

But European slave traders sullied the atmosphere by sailing among the islands, kidnapping native boys. In all, an estimated seventy thousand young men were captured into servitude. Patteson fought the practice tooth and nail, but a fear of Europeans emerged among the islanders, and many held Patteson at arm's length. Might he, too, be wanting their boys, not for the purposes of educating them but for enslaving them?

On *September 21, 1871*, Patteson anchored alongside an island. He spoke to local schoolboys about Stephen, the first Christian martyr. He concluded, saying, "We are all Christians here on this ship. Any one of us might be asked to give up his life for God, just as Stephen was in the Bible. This might happen to any one of us, to you or to me. It might happen today."

Patteson closed his Bible and went ashore. He was met by a barrage of arrows. An unmanned canoe was found shortly after, drifting in the water. It contained Patteson's pierced body, covered by a palm with five knotted fronds, showing that Patteson's life had been taken in exchange for five island boys who had been kidnapped. Patteson was in his mid-forties. His death sparked such protest that South Pacific kidnapping was eventually ended, and his martyrdom inspired many young men who gave their lives to South Seas missionary work.

As Stephen was being stoned to death, he called out, "Lord Jesus, please welcome me!" He knelt down and shouted, "Lord, don't blame them for what they have done." Then he died. (Acts 7:59–60)

The Polish Reformer

The outward reform of the church is useless unless accompanied by spiritual reform of the inner life of the Christian. So taught Caspar Schwenckfeld, known today as the forgotten reformer. Caspar grew up on an estate in Poland. He gained a good education and became involved in civil affairs. About 1519, he experienced what he called a "visitation of the divine," and thereafter began earnestly studying Scripture. His Bible, printed in Worms, Germany, by Anton Koberger, became underlined and well marked with extensive scribbles in the margins.

In 1525, he journeyed one hundred miles by horseback to Wittenberg, and on December 1, he asked Martin Luther for an appointment. "(As) Doctor Martin was accompanying us to the door, I drew him aside to a window and called his attention to the fact that I had previously written to him . . . and that I wished to speak with him . . . He thereupon replied: Dear Caspar, I will be glad to confer with you, come tomorrow, as early as you wish, six, seven, or eight o'clock. Nothing shall hinder me . . ."

Caspar arrived early the next morning, about seven, but soon found himself at odds with Doctor Martin. Caspar feared that the tenet of justification by faith, if interpreted wrongly, would create moral danger; he was unable to accept Luther's view of the Lord's Supper; he believed that Christians feed on Christ's celestial flesh by faith; he opposed participation in war and oath-taking; he rejected infant baptism; he opposed denominations.

He thus became part of the Radical Reformation and found himself persecuted by both Catholics and Protestants. After much oppression from both church and state, he died on December 10, 1561. But his disciples multiplied through the years, and in 1734, a group of one hundred eighty of them sailed from Holland to America aboard the *St. Andrews* with brightly painted chests containing their belongings and books. They arrived in Philadelphia on *September 22, 1734*, calling themselves Confessors of the Glory of Christ. The Quakers welcomed them. The Confessors planted themselves in the Mennonite countryside, and five Schwenkfelder churches still exist today as part of the Pennsylvania Dutch heritage.

Can anyone really harm you for being eager to do good deeds? Even if you have to suffer for doing good things, God will bless you. So stop being afraid and don't worry about what people might do. Honor Christ and let him be the Lord of your life. (1 Peter 3:13–15)

Fulton Street Revival

The mood of America was grim during the mid-1850s. The country was teetering on the brink of civil war, torn by angry voices and impassioned opinions. A depression had halted railroad construction and factory output. Banks were failing; unemployment soared. Spiritual lethargy permeated the land.

In New York City, layman Jeremiah C. Lanphier accepted the call of the North Reformed Dutch Church to a full-time program of evangelism. He visited door-to-door, placed posters, and prayed. But the work languished and Lanphier grew discouraged.

As autumn fell over the city, Lanphier decided to try noontime prayer meetings, thinking that businessmen might attend during their lunch hours. He announced the first one for *September 23, 1857*, at the Old Dutch Church on Fulton Street. When the hour came, Lanphier found himself alone. He sat and waited. Finally one man showed up, then a few others.

But the next week, twenty came. The third week, forty. Someone suggested the meetings occur daily, and within months the building was overflowing. The revival spread to other cities. Offices and stores closed for prayer at noon. Newspapers spread the story; even telegraph companies set aside certain hours during which businessmen could wire one another with news of the revival.

In all these cities prayer services began at noon and ended at one. People could come and go as they pleased. The service opened with a hymn, followed by the sharing of testimonies and prayer requests. A time limit of five minutes per speaker was enforced by a small bell when anyone exceeded the limit. Virtually no great preachers or famous Christians were used. It was primarily a lay movement, led by the gentle moving of God's Spirit.

The revival—sometimes called the Third Great Awakening—lasted almost two years, and between five hundred thousand and one million people were said to have been converted. Out of it came the largest outlay of money for philanthropic and Christian causes America had yet experienced.

> You, LORD, are my shepherd.
> I will never be in need.
> You let me rest in fields
> of green grass.
> You lead me to streams
> of peaceful water,
> and you refresh my life. (Psalm 23:1–3)

Off Course

Sometimes our plans don't work out as hoped because God detours us, leading us elsewhere in his overruling providence. Thomas Coke, a sophisticated Oxford-educated Welshman, left his ministry in the Anglican Church in 1777, to become John Wesley's chief assistant in the new and quickly growing Methodist movement.

On *September 24, 1785*, Coke packed his books and bags and sailed out of England for Nova Scotia, where he wanted to establish the three missionaries who accompanied him. But the voyage was ill-fated and grew more perilous by the day, the ship being caught in mountainous waves and mast-splitting winds. The ship's captain, determining that Coke and his missionaries were bringing misfortune on his ship as did Jonah, considered throwing them overboard. He actually gathered some of Coke's papers and tossed them into the ocean.

The voyage took three months rather than the expected one, and instead of landing in Nova Scotia, the damaged ship ended up in the Caribbean, limping into St. John's harbor on the island of Antigua on Christmas Day. Coke knew that at least one Methodist lived somewhere on Antigua, a missionary named John Baxter. After rowing ashore from their shattered ship in the predawn morning, Coke and his missionaries started down the street in St. John's and stopped the first person they found, a fellow swinging a lantern in his hand, to inquire of Baxter.

It was John Baxter himself. He was on his way to special Christmas morning services he had planned for the island, and Coke's sudden appearance seemed too good to be true. It took three services that day to accommodate the crowds. After it was over, Coke and his associates abandoned any idea of going to Nova Scotia. Instead, they planted the missionary team on Antigua and neighboring islands. By the time of Coke's death in 1814, there were more than seventeen thousand believers in the islands' Methodist churches.

I am the LORD, your holy God,
Israel's Creator and King.
I am the one who cut a path
through the mighty ocean.
I invite the whole world
to turn to me and be saved. (Isaiah 43:15–16; 45:22)

Problems?

Pope Clement VII, son of Giuliano de' Medici, was among the most unfortunate occupants of the Vatican. He was tall, slender, and moderately handsome, though wearing a "permanently sour" expression. He was upright and intelligent but unprepared for the hornet's nest of the papacy. When faced with hard decisions, he vacillated. The Venetian ambassador wrote, "The pope is 48 years old and is a sensible man but slow in decision, which explains his irresolution in action."

Clement, finding his treasury bankrupt, was chagrined that no Italian banker trusted him. The citizens of Rome didn't like him either. And Clement agonized over his failure to stem Luther's Reformation and to promote reform within his own church. At the same time he was caught between the conflicting aims of the kings of France and Spain. His attempts to steer a middle course invited the sack of Rome in 1527. As Clement watched helplessly from a tower, his city was plundered, raped, butchered, and burned.

He was caught once again between two kings—Henry VIII of England and Charles V of Spain, the Holy Roman Emperor. King Henry, frustrated he had no male heir, wanted an annulment from Catherine of Aragon to marry Anne Boleyn. Pope Clement had the prerogative to set aside the marriage. But he was under the thumb of Charles—Catherine's nephew. To grant the annulment invited disaster, including the alienation of the Holy Roman Empire from Catholicism. To refuse invited the fury of Henry VIII and the probable loss of England.

Clement tried to steer a middle course, hemming and hawing, at his wit's end, worrying that whatever happened, "the church cannot escape utter ruin." He made catastrophic errors. King Henry seized his nation's monasteries, split with the Vatican, and established the Reformation in England by the Act of Supremacy.

On *September 25, 1534*, having barely survived his previous misfortunes, he met a final one—a miserable death, reportedly from gobbling down a bowl of poisonous mushrooms.

Moaning and groaning are my food and drink,
and my worst fears
have all come true.
I have no peace or rest—
only troubles and worries. (Job 3:24–26)

How One Sermon Killed Another

At age eighteen, while studying in a city near his home, Aeneas Sylvius de' Piccolomini heard a friar preaching. He was impressed and entered church life but without giving up his vices. Aeneas worked his way up the religious ladder and was elected as Pope Pius II at age fifty-three. He understood world politics as few did, and he was brilliant. He was a grammarian, geographer, historian, novelist, and orator. But he wasn't pious. He wrote explicit love stories, fathered children here and there, and instructed young men in ways to indulge themselves.

He also had something to say to princes. On *September 26, 1460*, Pius called European leaders together in Mantua to discuss his life's dream—a new crusade against the Turks. He preached three hours at the opening session, telling the princes they must emulate Stephen, Peter, and Andrew, who were willing to lay down their lives in holy warfare. The Turks had robbed Christianity of its greatest treasures, he said—Jerusalem, where Christ lived; Bethlehem, where he was born; the Jordan River, where he was baptized; Calvary, where he was crucified; and Antioch, where the disciples were first called Christians. Joshua had fought for this land. So had Gideon, Jephthah, and Samson. Earlier crusaders had demolished Muslim strongholds and liberated Christian sites. "O! That Godfrey were once more present, and Baldwin and the other mighty men who broke through the ranks of the Turks and regained Jerusalem!"

His message greatly stirred the assembly, and for a moment the princes appeared ready to rush from the room to undertake a new crusade. But the pope was followed by another preacher, Cardinal Bessarion, who spoke for another three hours. By the end of the day, the princes were so worn-out by the preaching that they had no passion for the cause.

The congress became mired in political rivalry, and the promises made there were never kept; the days of the crusades were over. Yet Pope Pius continued dreaming of one, and his dying words were "Pray for me, for I am a sinner. Bid my brethren continue this holy expedition."

It takes strong winds to move a large sailing ship, but the captain uses only a small rudder to make it go in any direction. Our tongues are small too, and yet they brag about big things. (James 3:4–5)

Staring in the Mirror

When King Louis XIV waltzed into his ornate chapel to worship and be worshipped, he often heard Jacques Benigne Bossuet, one of the most eloquent French Catholics. Bossuet, born in Dijon on *September 27, 1627*, had discovered the Bible, opened it to Isaiah, and was gripped. Running to his father, he read him chapter after chapter. In time Bossuet learned the Bible almost by heart.

Bossuet also gained a reputation as an orator, keeping fellow students in rapt attention during addresses. Eventually he was appointed court preacher at Versailles. His sermons were "unexcelled upon earth." It was said, "Bossuet is the most powerful, the most truly eloquent speaker that our language has ever known."

He was also blunt. In some sermons he addressed the king by name; and on one occasion he earnestly implored Louis to abandon his adulteries and return to his wife. Unfortunately Bossuet's eloquence did little good. The nobility sat listening to him, dressed in powdered wigs, high-heeled shoes, and gaudy costumes. They wept during Bossuet's messages but left unchanged. Here, for example, is an excerpt from one of his sermons that should have made an impact. As it was, the nobility listened and cried and nodded and went their way as before:

> The honour of the world makes us attribute to ourselves all that we do, and ends by setting us upon pedestals like little gods. Well, proud and self-complacent soul, thus deified by the honour of the world, see how the eternal, the living God abases Himself in order to confound you! Man makes himself God through pride, God makes Himself man through humility! Man falsely attributes to himself what belongs to God; and God, in order to teach him to humble himself, takes what belongs to man. This is the remedy for insolence! This alone can confound the honour of the world—that Hill of Calvary, that Cross of Shame, Jesus Christ the Incarnate God, our Pattern, our Master, our King.

Obey God's message! Don't fool yourselves by just listening to it. If you hear the message and don't obey it, you are like people who stare at themselves in a mirror and forget what they look like as soon as they leave. (James 1:22–24)

King Wenceslas

We know of good King Wenceslas primarily because he happened to look out his window "on the feast of Stephen, while the snow lay round about, deep and crisp and even."

Actually, we aren't even certain of that.

Wenceslas was born in Bohemia, modern Czechoslovakia, in the early 900s. His father, the Czech ruler, Duke Ratislav, gave him a good education supervised by his grandmother, Ludmilla. Ludmilla, a devout woman, did a good job.

He became a king. When his father died, Wenceslas, seeing his mother mishandle affairs of state, stepped in and seized the reins of government. But he took control on his terms. From the beginning King Wenceslas was a different sort of king. He sought good relations with surrounding nations, particularly with Germany. He took steps to reform the judicial system, reducing the number of death sentences and the arbitrary power of judges. He reportedly encouraged the building of churches. Most of all he showed heartfelt concern for the poor of the realm. He cut firewood for orphans and widows, it is said, often carrying the provisions on his own shoulders through the snow—thus inspiring J. M. Neale's Christmas carol.

Wenceslas's brief reign ended suddenly. His brother Boleslav, pagan and rebellious, invited him to a banquet then murdered him the next morning, *September* 28, 929, as he left for church. There is no direct evidence, apart from his virtuous reputation, that Wenceslas was a genuine Christian, for he left behind no written testimony. Much of our information about him comes from legend. But his people venerated him as a martyr, and today he is the patron saint of Czechoslovakia.

Therefore, Christian men be sure,
Wealth or rank possessing,
Ye who now will bless the poor,
Shall yourselves find blessing.

Religion that pleases God the Father must be pure and spotless. You must help needy orphans and widows and not let this world make you evil. (James 1:27)

September ~ **29**

The Candle Burns Out

Evangelist George Whitefield longed to die preaching, and he almost did. In 1770, on a final tour through the American colonies, he ignored the pleas of doctors and friends to rest. When too tired to preach, he lifted his voice all the more. When asthmatic colds caused breathing crimps, he ignored them. He claimed that a good "pulpit sweat" was beneficial. But the vomiting, diarrhea, and shivering increased as autumn arrived.

On Saturday, *September 29, 1770*, Whitefield rode to Exeter, New Hampshire, where someone, seeing his appearance, told him he was more fit to go to bed than to preach. "It's true," Whitefield replied; then he burst into prayer: "Lord, I am weary *in* thy work, but not *of* it. If I have not yet finished my course, let me speak for Thee once more and come home and die."

A crowd assembled and Whitefield stood precariously atop a barrel. He quoted 2 Corinthians 13:5—"Test yourselves and find out if you really are true to your faith"—then began to preach. "He rose up sluggishly and wearily," reported an eyewitness, "as if exhausted by his labors. His face seemed bloated, his voice hoarse, his enunciation heavy. But then his mind kindled, and his lionlike voice roared to the extremities of his audience." He told the crowd he would rather climb to the moon by a rope of sand than try to achieve heaven by works. Whitefield kept his audience spellbound for two hours. Then he suddenly cried, "I go! I have outlived many on earth, but they cannot outlive me in heaven. My body fails, my spirit expands."

Finishing his sermon, he was helped from the barrel to his horse, and he continued to Newburyport. That evening a group of friends gathered and asked Whitefield to speak to them. He begged off, citing asthma. But then he rose and took a lighted candle, starting up the steps. Turning, he delivered a brief but moving message. When the candle died out, he continued up the stairs and went on to his bed, where he died during the night.

Test yourselves and find out if you really are true to your faith. If you pass the test, you will discover that Christ is living in you. But if Christ isn't living in you, you have failed. I hope you will discover that we have not failed. (2 Corinthians 13:5–6)

The Contrarian

The Lord has often used people in church history whom we may not have liked had we lived during their days. Jerome, for example, possessed a brilliant mind, a sharp tongue, hot blood, and thin skin. He was a contrarian, remembered as one of the church's most irritable scholars and among the first of the great Bible translators who have spread the gospel abroad.

Jerome was an Italian, born about 330, who early fell in love with women and books. After indulging in the former, he joined an ascetic group to enjoy the latter, but his sandpaper personality caused the group to disintegrate. As Jerome struggled to control his sexual energy, he began advancing the doctrine of the perpetual virginity of Mary. He believed that after Jesus' birth, Mary continued to live a virgin's life, and his own Herculean efforts to remain celibate led to his so exalting virginity that he considered marriage beneficial only because it brought virgins into the world.

Perhaps the answer for him was a hermit's life in the desert, practicing severe self-disciplines. It didn't work. He still dreamed of Roman dancing girls. Returning to Rome, he faced the temptations head-on and avoided the dancing girls. But he didn't avoid Paula, a young widow who became not a sexual partner but a lifelong soul mate. In Rome in the early 380s, he discovered his life's work. Pope Damasus suggested he prepare a new Latin version of the Gospels and Psalms. Jerome set to work on it, and for the next twenty-two years he labored tirelessly as a Bible translator.

His sharp tongue made trouble in Rome, so he and Paula moved to Bethlehem in 386. Near the birthplace of Jesus, they established separate monasteries for men and women, where Jerome balanced his need for companionship with a corresponding need for solitude, study, and asceticism. He poured himself into the Latin translation of the Bible, his life's crowning achievement. He died, white haired and wrinkled, on *September 30, 420.*

With my whole heart I agree with the Law of God. But in every part of me I discover something fighting against my mind, and it makes me a prisoner of sin that controls everything I do. What a miserable person I am. Who will rescue me . . . ? Thank God! Jesus Christ will rescue me. (Romans 7:22–25)

On This Day in Christian History…

OCTOBER

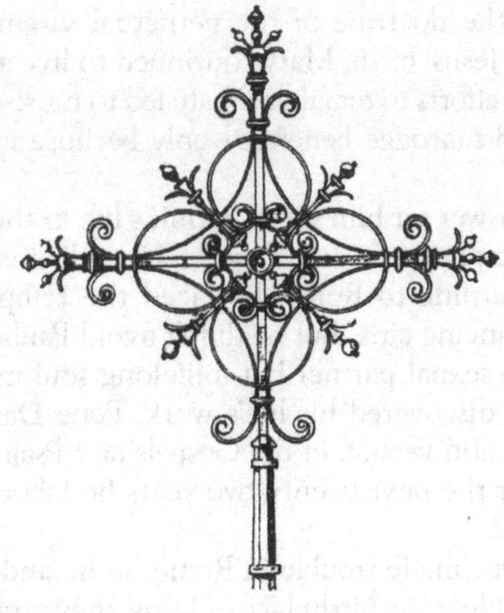

The Fifteenth Point

Unity is essential among Christians, but unity does not mean uniformity, and one of the most remarkable patterns in church history is that God uses his church and blesses his children even when they disagree. History's first missionary team, Paul and Barnabas, argued over John Mark. Wesley and Whitefield were at odds over various points of theology. And the reformers, themselves strong-willed men, crossed swords over, among other things, the nature of the Lord's Supper.

The Swiss reformers, led by Ulrich Zwingli, insisted that the Lord's Supper was a memorial service while the German reformers, led by Martin Luther, insisted that Christ is actually present in the consecrated bread and wine.

The conflict was so sharp that a local political leader invited the men to his castle in Marburg on *October 1, 1529*. In the banquet hall a long table covered with a velvet runner sat in the middle of the room. Before the proceedings began, Luther reportedly took a piece of chalk and on the cloth in front of him wrote the words "This is my body."

The debate raged for three days. Zwingli insisted that the verb *is* in the phrase "This is my body" should be interpreted as "represents." Luther said, "Where in the Bible does the verb 'is' ever mean 'represent'?" Zwingli showed him several places. But Luther wouldn't budge. At the end of the three-day conference, the delegates had agreed on fourteen of fifteen areas of former confusion. But on the fifteenth—the Lord's Supper—they failed to reach agreement, and the reformers were unable to join the German and Swiss factions. As a result Zwingli lost the support of the German princes. The five Catholic Cantons of Switzerland sent an army against him, and he died in the Battle of Kappel.

But nothing could stop the reformers' fire, and despite the failure of the Marburg meetings, the doctrine of justification by grace through faith spread across the continent.

During the meal Jesus took some bread in his hands. He blessed the bread and broke it. Then he gave it to his disciples and said, "Take this. It is my body." Jesus picked up the cup of wine and gave thanks to God. He gave it to his disciples, and they all drank some. Then he said, "This is my blood, which is poured out for many people . . ." (Mark 14:22–24)

October 2

Four Centuries

Protestants were slow to embrace the missionary cause. In the sixteenth century, they struggled to liberate themselves from moribund Catholicism. The seventeenth century was consumed with bloody efforts for liberty within the state. Not until the eighteenth century could their attention be drawn overseas. The Moravians were the first, sending missionaries to such fields as the West Indies and Labrador. But still there was no organized missionary enterprise supported by a strong home base.

Then came a failure-prone shoemaker named William Carey. His sermons, conversations, and his book, *Enquiry*, finally nudged his fellow Baptists to adopt this resolution at an associational meeting: *Resolved that a plan be prepared against the next Ministers' meeting at Kettering, for forming a Baptist Society for propagating the Gospel among the Heathen.*

Five months later on Tuesday, *October 2, 1792*, fourteen men huddled in the back parlor of widow Wallis's house in Kettering, in a room twelve feet by ten. There were twelve ministers, a student, and a deacon. Carey, then thirty-one years old, reviewed the achievements of the Moravians and recounted the Bible's missionary mandate. By and by a resolution was worded: *Humbly desirous of making an effort for the propagation of the Gospel amongst the Heathen, according to the recommendations of Carey's Enquiry, we unanimously resolve to act in Society together for this purpose; and as, in the divided state of Christendom, each denomination, by exerting itself separately, seems likeliest to accomplish the great end, we name this the Particular Baptist Society for the Propagation of the Gospel among the Heathen.*

Andrew Fuller passed around his snuff box with its picture of Paul's conversion on the lid, taking up history's first collection of pledges for organized, home-supported Protestant missions.

Suddenly missionary societies popped up everywhere, especially in London: in 1792, the British Missionary Society; in 1795, the London Missionary Society; in 1799, the Religious Tract Society and the Church Missionary Society. In 1804, the British and Foreign Bible Society came into being. The era of missions had begun, making the nineteenth century the Great Century in the advancement of the gospel around the globe.

Afterwards, Jesus appeared to his eleven disciples as they were eating. He scolded them because they were too stubborn to believe the ones who had seen him after he had been raised to life. Then he told them: Go and preach the good news to everyone in the world. (Mark 16:14–15)

One Woman's Crusade

Was the first Thanksgiving really held by the pilgrims shortly after the Mayflower anchored at Plymouth? Texans claim the first Thanksgiving in America was proclaimed in Palo Duro Canyon by Padre Juan De Cadilla for Coronado's troops in 1541, seventy-nine years before the Pilgrims.

At any rate Thanksgiving as an annual national holiday was slow in coming. Throughout early American history, some leaders issued Thanksgiving proclamations; some did not. Many were against it for various reasons, and Thanksgiving was an on-again, off-again affair . . . until Sarah Hale got hold of it. Sarah was a young widow with five children and a millinery shop. She used spare moments for writing, and in 1823, her first book appeared. She was soon hired as editor of a small magazine; then in 1837, she was named editor of *Godey's Lady's Book*, the nation's foremost women's magazine. Circulation mushroomed.

Godey's wasn't a Christian magazine, but Sarah, an Episcopalian, was a devout Christian who injected religious issues into her editorials. In 1846, she launched a crusade to establish Thanksgiving as a holiday. She wrote stirring editorials about it, and November issues featured Thanksgiving poetry, stories, and turkey recipes. She pelted politicians with personal letters on the subject, and by 1859, thirty governors had agreed to a common day of Thanksgiving.

Still, no national holiday emerged. As America lurched toward civil war, Sarah tried a new tactic. Disunion, she wrote in 1859, could be averted by Thanksgiving: "If every State would join in union Thanksgiving on the 24th of this month, would it not be a renewed pledge of love and loyalty to the Constitution!"

But war erupted in 1861. In 1863, she wrote President Lincoln, "laying before you a subject of deep interest . . . the day of our annual Thanksgiving made a national and fixed union festival. The beleaguered president finally agreed, and on *October 3, 1863*, he established Thanksgiving as a national holiday for the last Thursday of November. Even in war, Lincoln said, we can count our blessings: "They are gracious gifts of the most high God, who, while dealing with us in anger for our sins, hath nevertheless remembered mercy."

Tell the LORD
how thankful you are,
because he is kind
and always merciful. (Psalm 118:1)

October 4 Pre-answers to Prayer

Occasionally God answers our prayers before we offer them. William Tyndale put his life at risk when he decided to translate the Bible into the English language during the days of King Henry VIII. Both the church and government opposed him. On October 6, 1536, he was burned at the stake for his efforts. His last words were, "Lord, open the King of England's eyes."

He perished without knowing the Lord had already answered his prayer—one year earlier, almost to the very day. The answer? Miles Coverdale. Born in 1488, Coverdale came under the influence of Robert Barnes at Cambridge, who discussed ideas "out of Germany" with him. When Coverdale picked up the Bible and began reading it for himself, he fell in love with it. "Now I begyne to taste of Holy Schryptures; now (honour be to God) I am sett to the most swete smell with the godly savour of holy and awncyent Doctoures."

Soon he began preaching an evangelical message, but it proved impossible for him in England, so he fled to the Continent, where he spent seven years translating the Bible from Latin into English for his own people. It was published in 1535, the first complete edition of the Bible in English. He wisely dedicated it to King Henry VIII, who, being flattered, allowed it to become the first English rendering of Scripture to circulate without official hindrance—thus answering Tyndale's prayer one year in advance.

In his preface Coverdale said he had not coveted the task of translating Scripture, but "it greued [grieved] me yt other nacyons shulde be more plentously prouyded [provided] with ye scripture in theyr mother tongue than we . . ."

Coverdale became rector of St. Magnus Church near London Bridge, and visitors today can read a memorial plaque on the east wall of the church: ". . . he spent many years of his life preparing a translation of the Scriptures. On the *4th of October, 1535*, the first complete printed English version of the Bible was published under his direction."

I will answer their prayers
before they finish praying. (Isaiah 65:24)

Toothpicks and Oranges

The Tower of London, sitting forbiddingly on the Thames, is a small village within impregnable walls. It has served as a palace, a fortress, and, more ominously, a prison. Here a young Catholic named John Gerard suffered for his faith during the reign of Protestant Queen Elizabeth I.

He was a Jesuit priest, educated on the Continent, who began covertly performing priestly work in England at age eighteen, moving from place to place one step ahead of the law. He was eventually captured and taken to the Clink, a prison so infamous that its name lives to this day. For three years he was kept there, sometimes chained, often attempting to escape. Then he was moved to the Tower.

One of the buildings there, the White Tower, contains a deep vault without windows or outer doors. There in the eerie glow of flickering torches, Gerard was hung by his hands for hours, day after day. When he fainted, he was revived, and the torture reapplied. His arms swelled monstrously, his whole body throbbed, his bones screamed, and his hands became so damaged he couldn't even feed himself.

The torture was finally suspended for a while. The young priest did finger exercises, and within three weeks he could again feed himself. Soon he asked for oranges and toothpicks. The toothpicks became pens. Orange juice became ink, visible only when heated. Messages flew back and forth. A rope, a boat, and outside helpers were recruited. On *October 5, 1597*, Gerard climbed through a hole to the roof of Cradle Tower, threw a rope over the side, and slid down it, wincing as it mutilated his hands. Friends whisked him to a hiding place outside London.

He was soon back at his clandestine priestly work, always a mere step from recapture. Finally it became untenable for him to stay in England, and he sadly slipped out of the country in the retinue of the Spanish and Dutch ambassadors. He labored in Rome until July 27, 1637, when he passed away at age seventy-three. He is known today as one of an elite handful of people who outwitted the Tower of London.

Surrender your heart to God,
turn to him in prayer,
and give up your sins—
even those you do in secret.
Then you won't be ashamed;
you will be confident
and fearless.
Your troubles will go away
like water beneath a bridge. (Job 11:13–16)

Tyndale

The "father of the English Bible" was apparently born in a hamlet near the Welsh border about 1490. He arrived at Oxford with a gift for languages and began studying the writings of the greatest linguist in the world, Erasmus. He pored over Erasmus's Greek New Testament and other writings, and he soon began lecturing from them. The Bible was still virtually unavailable in English, and an idea formed in William Tyndale's mind.

He began proclaiming the value of pure Scripture and of the need to translate it. He was threatened and opposed. "We are better to be without God's laws than the pope's," one man said, voice rising. Tyndale's reply is among the most famous in church history: "If God spares me, I will cause a boy that drives the plow to know more of the Scriptures than you do."

He approached the Bishop of London for help in rendering the Bible into English but was rebuffed. Tyndale nevertheless began working on his project. Finding his life in danger, he fled to the Continent. There he continued translating, smuggling copies of Matthew and Mark back into London. Spies combed Europe for him, and Tyndale played a cloak-and-dagger game, hiding and running, translating and smuggling. By 1525, complete copies of the New Testament were being secretly read in England.

On May 21, 1535, Tyndale was betrayed and seized. He languished in a miserable prison cell. His witness there converted the jailer and the jailer's family. On *October 6, 1536*, he was tied to the stake outside of Brussels, strangled, and burned. He was forty-two.

A year earlier King Henry VIII had given approval for a new English Bible by Miles Coverdale, Tyndale's friend. Henry never realized that Coverdale's Bible was nearly 70 percent Tyndale's work. In 1604, James I approved a new translation of the Bible into English, and Tyndale's work became the basis of 90 percent of the King James Version.

The Scriptures say, "Humans wither like grass,
and their glory fades
like wild flowers.
Grass dries up,
and flowers fall
to the ground.
But what the Lord has said
will stand forever."
Our good news to you is what the Lord has said. (1 Peter 1:24–25)

From *The Narratives of George Mueller*

When at the end of the year 1829, I left London to labour in the Gospel, a brother in the Lord gave to me a card containing the address of a well-known Christian lady, Miss Paget, who then resided in Exeter, in order that I should call on her. Three weeks I carried this card in my pocket without making an effort to see this lady; but at last I was led to do so.

"Miss Paget gave me the address of a Christian brother, Mr. Hake, who had a Boarding School for young ladies and gentlemen at Northernhay House. To this place I went. Miss Groves, afterwards my beloved wife, was there. I went week after week. At this time my purpose had been not to marry at all, but to remain free for traveling about in the service of the Gospel; but after some months I saw, for many reasons, that it was better for me as a young pastor under 25 to be married. The question now was, to whom shall I be united?

"Miss Groves came before my mind; but the prayerful conflict was long before I came to a decision. At last this decided me, I had reason to believe I had gotten an affection in the heart of Miss Groves for me, and therefore I ought to make a proposal of marriage to her. On Aug. 15th, I wrote to her proposing to her to become my wife, and on Aug. 19th, she accepted me. The first thing we did after I was accepted was to fall on our knees and to ask the blessing of the Lord on our intended union. On *October 7, 1830*, we were united in marriage.

"Our marriage was of the most simple character. We walked to church, had no wedding breakfast, but in the afternoon had a meeting of Christian friends in Mr. Hake's house and commemorated the Lord's death; and then I drove off in the stagecoach with my beloved wife to Teignmough, and the next day we went to work for the Lord.

"This was God's way of giving me an excellent wife."

With all your heart
you must trust the LORD
and not your own judgment.
Always let him lead you,
and he will clear the road
for you to follow. (Proverbs 3:5–6)

October 8 What a Day!

Dwight L. Moody came to the Lord in a Boston shoe store while a teenager. Though poorly educated, he possessed boundless energy that quickly funneled itself into soul-winning. He moved to Chicago, took up children's work, and grew his Sunday school to over a thousand pupils. But though outwardly flourishing, Moody was inwardly frustrated, sensing a lack of spiritual power, struggling with the notion that God wanted him to leave Chicago to become an itinerant evangelist, something he wasn't willing to do.

On *October 8, 1871*, Moody spoke to his Sunday school listeners, asking them to consider responding to Christ on the following Sunday, but they never got that chance. As services ended, fire alarms sounded in the streets. The meeting closed in panic, and the young people left the building to find the city in terror. Flames leapt into the sky, swallowing whole buildings. Gas mains were exploding, and the streets became clogged with fleeing humanity. The Great Chicago Fire burned from Sunday to Wednesday, and Moody lost both his church building and his home.

Deeply shaken, Moody quickly left Chicago for New York, seeking funds for rebuilding his work, but "my heart was not in the work of begging." While walking down Wall Street, he had a spiritual experience so powerful that he seldom referred to it afterward. "I was crying all the time that God would fill me with His Spirit. Well, one day, in the city of New York—ah, what a day!—I cannot describe it. I seldom refer to it, it is almost too sacred an experience to name—Paul had an experience of which he never spoke for fourteen years—I can only say that God revealed Himself to me, and I had such an experience of His love that I had to ask Him to stay His hand."

From that day, whenever, wherever Moody preached, hundreds of people were saved, and he spent the rest his life traveling the globe as the most famous and effective evangelist for Christ in the nineteenth century.

God told us to announce clearly to the people that Jesus is the one he has chosen to judge the living and the dead. Every one of the prophets has said that all who have faith in Jesus will have their sins forgiven in his name. (Acts 10:42–43)

Scandalous Pursuits

The modern Baptist movement began in the early 1600s, and though its leaders suffered imprisonment and death at the hands of British officials, they persevered. Among them was Benjamin Keach, born in 1640. He was converted to Christ at eighteen and began pastoring ten years later. He served the Horsley Down Baptist Church in Southwark near London, where he was described by associates as "earnest, self-educated, intensely evangelical, his outlook narrowed to the denomination and almost to the congregation, but wielding great influence within those limits."

Keach loved both children and singing, and that's what got him into trouble. Wanting to explain Baptist beliefs to the young, he wrote a primer for them. The children loved it. The king didn't. British constables arrested him, and on *October 9, 1664* he stood a prisoner in the court of Aylesbury while the chief justice roared: "Benjamin Keach, you are convicted of writing and publishing a seditious and scandalous book; you shall go to prison for a fortnight and the next Saturday stand in a pillory for two hours from eleven o'clock until one with a paper upon your head with this inscription: 'For writing and printing and publishing a schismatical book entitled, *The Child Instructor* or *A New and Easy Primer*,' and the next Thursday to stand in the same manner and for that same time in the market at Winslow, and there your book shall openly be burnt before your face by the common hangman in disgrace of you and your doctrine, and you shall forfeit to the king's majesty the sum of twenty pounds."

Keach actually spent two months in prison and paid one hundred pounds, but he didn't learn his lesson. Some time afterward he got into trouble again, this time for publishing a hymnal. English-speaking churches had previously sung only the psalms of David, usually to ponderous tunes. In 1691, Keach published *Spiritual Melody*, a book of three hundred lively hymns. Such a radical innovation upset his congregation, and he watched with alarm as many members left. But Keach nevertheless spent the rest of his life in the seditious and scandalous pursuits of teaching children and singing hymns.

Memorize his laws and tell them to your children over and over again. Talk about them all the time, whether you're at home or walking along the road or going to bed at night, or getting up in the morning. Write down copies . . . (Deuteronomy 6:6–8)

October 10

Sixty Ounces of Blood

Little is known of the early life of Sir Archibald Johnston, otherwise known as Lord Warriston. He grew up in seventeenth-century Scotland and became active in the Scottish government and in Presbyterian church life, rising to a position of great respect. His mind was as sharp as any on the British islands, and he witnessed freely to world leaders of his faith. During the Puritan revolt, he sided with Cromwell as King Charles I was deposed and executed. When Charles II restored the British monarchy in 1660, Johnston found himself in danger, and on *October 10, 1660*, he was pronounced a condemned fugitive.

Johnston fled to the Continent but while there became sick. As it happened, one of King Charles's physicians, Dr. Bates, attended him. Intending to kill him, Dr. Bates injected him with poison and drew from him sixty ounces of blood. While Johnston didn't die, he was permanently impaired in his mind and could never again remember what he had said or done a quarter hour before.

Aided by friends Johnston fled to France, but Charles's agents were looking for him there, too, and he was seized while at prayer. In January 1663, he was returned to England and imprisoned in the Tower of London. At length he was transported to Edinburgh for execution though, according to his nephew, "he was so disordered in body and mind that it was a reproach to any government to proceed against him."

He slept well on the night before his execution, and he took his last lunch cheerfully, "hoping to sup in heaven, and to drink the next cup fresh in his Father's kingdom." At two o'clock he was taken from the prison to the scaffold. There he pulled a paper from his pocket, being unable to remember what he wanted to say. He read from it front and back; then as if in a rapture, he looked up and prayed: "Abba, Father! Accept this thy poor sinful servant, coming unto thee, through the merits of Jesus Christ."

He was hanged, and his head was nailed beside that of James Guthrie on Netherbow Port.

Christ died for us at a time when we were helpless and sinful. No one is really willing to die for an honest person, though someone might be willing to die for a truly good person. But God showed how much he loved us by having Christ die for us, even though we were sinful. (Romans 5:6–8)

The Battle of Tours

In 570, the woman Amina bore a son who, according to Eastern storytellers, cried out immediately at birth, "There is no god but Allah, and I am his prophet!" He was Mohammed, the "Promised One," and it was he who gave the Arabs their religion. The ensuing years saw Mohammed's followers leap from conquest to conquest until the Middle East and North Africa were under their feet. Then they moved like a swarm of locusts across Spain before climbing the southern slopes of the Pyrenees and gazing lustfully into France.

Europe had fallen into its Dark Ages just as the Arabs were coming into their Golden Age, and in the early 700s, the Muslims were threatening to pounce on the remnants of the old Roman Empire. Across Europe echoed the cry: "The Arabs are coming!" They *were* coming, and they seemed unstoppable. In the streets of Paris, men and women trembled, and from their midst came a strong, young, long-haired Frank: Charles, son of Pepin. Charles Martel—Charles the Hammer.

Charles gathered his Franks and a few allies on the plain between Tours and Poitiers. It wasn't much of an army, just a motley crew of miscellaneous, frightened barbarians. Charles told them just to stand firm, to hold their ground, to die if necessary, to do anything but break lines.

On *October 11, 732*, the two forces met—two cultures, two languages, two creeds, two civilizations battling for the fate of Western civilization. The Muslims charged toward the amassed Franks, the thundering roar of their hoofbeats and shouts heard miles away. The defenders held firm. A second charge came, but Charles's soldiers stood spread-eagled over their dead. A third charge failed, then a fourth. Charles galloped among his men, shouting orders, closing gaps. For five days the attacks came in waves. On the sixth day the Arabs cut through the lines only to find themselves surrounded and trapped. Their morale was spent, and the surviving invaders fled.

The battlefield was carpeted with the dead, but Europe was saved for Christianity.

Be smart, all you rulers,
and pay close attention.
Serve and honor the LORD;
be glad and tremble.
Show respect to his son
because if you don't,
the LORD might become furious
and suddenly destroy you. (Psalm 2:10–12)

October 12 A Pinch of Poison

Luke, who bolted New Testament events into world history, refers to Roman emperor Claudius in Acts 11 and 18.

Tiberius Claudius Caesar Augustus Germanicus, born shortly before Christ, became Roman emperor in 41 at age fifty. As a young man he had suffered infantile paralysis, and his long, spindly legs barely supported his stout frame. His head wobbled when he walked, he stuttered, and he laughed in outbursts. When angered, he foamed at the mouth and trickled at the nose.

But when he became emperor, he surprised everyone by showing promise. He lowered taxes, extended the empire into Britain and Mauritania, and refused to be worshipped as a god. Many were granted Roman citizenship under his rule. Civil service was expanded, the legal system was reformed, and public works grew.

It didn't last. The latter years of Claudius were marred by intrigue, much of it centered around his wife, Agrippina. The emperor's first wife had died on their wedding day. Others had been divorced or slain. Then he met and married the wily Agrippina.

The empress, at age thirty-two, had but one aim: to secure the throne for her own son. To do that, she had to dispatch both Claudius and his son Britannicus. As she assumed more and more power, she plotted the deaths of her enemies and unleashed a reign of terror. It took Claudius five years to realize what was happening, and by then it was too late. On *October 12, 54*, she fed him mushrooms well seasoned with a potent pinch of poison. He suffered twelve agonizing hours, unable to speak a word, before dying. Britannicus eventually tasted poison as well.

Agrippina's son became emperor. He thanked her by plotting her murder. First he tried poisoning her, but she knew all the tricks. He next tried drowning her, but she swam to safety from the prearranged shipwreck. Finally paid assassins plunged swords into her womb. Viewing her uncovered corpse, the young emperor remarked, "I did not know I had so beautiful a mother."

His name? Nero.

During this time some prophets from Jerusalem came to Antioch. One of them was Agabus. Then with the help of the Spirit, he told that there would be a terrible famine everywhere in the world. And it happened when Claudius was Emperor. (Acts 11:27–28)

Relics

Medieval crusaders returning from Palestine and Constantinople brought with them a treasure trove of relics—sacred objects from the Holy Land. All Europe was astir, bishop vying with bishop, church competing with church, to acquire and display various holy items. Cathedrals became virtual museums, and these relics were soon objects of veneration and pilgrimage.

In various churches worshippers could view barbs from the crown of thorns, splinters from the cross of Christ, or the finger that Thomas thrust into Jesus' side. The church of Halberstadt acquired the sponge and reed of Golgotha. A church in St. Omer claimed the lance that pierced the Savior's side. The cathedral of Amiens enshrined the head of John the Baptist in a silver cup. Three different churches in France boasted a complete corpse of Mary Magdalene. In various other European churches, one could view Noah's beard, Jacob's rock, Moses's rod, or the stone of Christ's sepulcher. Elsewhere, his robe, his chalice (the Holy Grail), or shavings from his beard thrilled wide-eyed pilgrims.

Even the Lord's foreskin, his naval cord, and milk from Mary's breasts were reportedly discovered and displayed. The basilica of St. Peter in Rome enshrined the bodies of Peter and Paul, making it the ultimate goal of Christian pilgrimage.

It isn't surprising then that England was beside itself on *October 13, 1247*, when some of Christ's blood arrived in London. The crusaders vouched for its authenticity, and it bore the seals of the patriarch of Jerusalem and the archbishops of the Holy Land. King Henry III fasted and prayed through the night of October 12; then as morning broke, he marched through London's streets, accompanying the priests in full regalia. He held aloft the vase containing the holy liquid. The procession moved from St. Paul's to Westminster; then the Bishop of Norwich preached a great sermon regarding the relic in the vase.

But he would have done better to have ignored the relic and preached the reality, proclaiming nothing more nor less than the truth of Ephesians 1:7: "Christ sacrificed his life's blood to set us free, which means that our sins are now forgiven."

Christ sacrificed his life's blood to set us free, which means that our sins are now forgiven. Christ did this because God was so kind to us. God has great wisdom and understanding, and by what Christ has done, God has shown us his own mysterious ways. (Ephesians 1:7–9)

October 14 Backus's Crusade

George Whitefield had just finished preaching in Norwich, Connecticut, when a young man stepped up to shake his hand. Isaac Backus, heir of a family fortune, had been deeply moved, and he soon gave his life to Christ, was baptized, and became a pastor, church planter, and Baptist evangelist. As a home missionary Backus made more than nine hundred trips in colonial America, covering more than sixty-eight thousand miles on horseback.

He is best known, however, as a champion of religious liberty. From the beginning of his ministry, Backus fought doggedly for separation of church and state in the American colonies. When he entered his ministry, a tax in Massachusetts supported the state church—the Congregational Church in New England. Backus refused to pay the tax, was imprisoned, and when released, mounted a tireless campaign to abolish the state-supported church system.

In 1774, when the First Continental Congress met in Philadelphia, Backus was there, lobbying the representatives. On *October 14, 1774*, he and his fellow ministers arranged a meeting with the Massachusetts representatives to the Congress and presented a petition requesting full religious liberty. The politicians were irritated. John Adams insisted that taxes collected to support the Congregational Church did not impinge on the freedom of other religious groups, and he ended the four-hour meeting saying, "Gentlemen, if you mean to try to effect a change in Massachusetts laws respecting religion, you may as well attempt to change the course of the sun in the heavens!"

Backus determined to take his petition to John Hancock, then before the entire Continental Congress, but John Adams was always working to frustrate his efforts. Yet his ideas took root, and twenty-seven years after Backus's death, the last state church in Massachusetts was finally disestablished. More than any other man, Isaac Backus is credited with formulating and publicizing the evangelical position of church and state that ultimately prevailed in America.

We don't obey people. We obey God. You killed Jesus by nailing him to a cross. But the God our ancestors worshipped raised him to life and made him our Leader and Savior. (Acts 5:29–31)

God Looked Down . . .

"Think of what you were when you were called," said Paul. "Not many of you were wise . . . influential . . . of noble birth. But God chose the foolish things . . ." (1 Cor. 1:26–27 NIV).

It had started on a bus in England. Gladys Aylward, a poorly educated twenty-eight-year-old parlor maid, was reading about China and the need for missionaries there, and from that moment, China became her life and passion. She applied to a missionary agency only to be turned down. Crushed with disappointment, she returned to her small servant's room and turned her pocketbook upside down. Two pennies fell on top of her Bible. "O God," she prayed, "here's my Bible! Here's my money! Here's me!" Gladys began hoarding every cent to purchase passage to China. She knew she couldn't afford to travel by ship, so she decided to go overland by train, right across Europe and Asia, though it meant slicing through a dangerous war zone on the Manchurian border. On *October 15, 1932*, a little bewildered party gathered at London's Liverpool Street Station to see Gladys Aylward off for China. The journey was hair-raising and nearly cost her life. But eventually Gladys reached China, showing up at the home of an older missionary who took her in—but didn't quite know what to do with her.

Yet Gladys Aylward became one of the most amazing single-woman missionaries of modern history. Her missions career was so extraordinary that the world finally took notice. Her biography was made into a movie starring Ingrid Bergman. She dined with such dignitaries as Queen Elizabeth and spoke in great churches. She even became a subject of the television program *This Is Your Life.*

But Gladys never grew accustomed to the limelight, for her heart was always in Asia. "I wasn't God's first choice for what I've done for China," she once said. "There was somebody else . . . I don't know who it was—God's first choice. I don't know what happened. Perhaps he died. Perhaps he wasn't willing. And God looked down . . . and saw Gladys Aylward."

My dear friends, remember what you were when God chose you. The people of this world didn't think that many of you were wise. Only a few of you were in places of power, and not many of you came from important families. But God chose the foolish things of this world to put the wise to shame. He chose the weak things of this world to put the powerful to shame. (1 Corinthians 1:26–27)

Latimer's Light

It is a mistake to nail the English Reformation just to the door of King Henry VIII. While Henry broke relations with Rome, he still believed Catholic doctrine. He just wanted Catholicism without the pope.

The real English Reformation is better credited to a scholar at Cambridge University named Thomas Bilney, who embraced Reformation truth after reading Erasmus's Greek New Testament. Bilney gathered a group at White Horse Inn for secret Bible study and prayer. He was eventually found out, and he perished in the flames at Norwich on August 19, 1531—but not before influencing Hugh Latimer, a spiritual giant who is known as the Apostle to the English.

Latimer had bitterly opposed the Reformation, but Bilney, hearing him preach a scathing sermon at Cambridge against Lutheranism, sought him out and succeeded in persuading him otherwise. Soon Latimer was preaching the faith he had once labored to destroy. As a result he fell from favor during Henry's reign and spent time in the Tower of London.

When Edward VI came to the throne, Latimer was released for ministry, but when Edward died, Latimer was among those caught and condemned by officials of Queen Mary. On *October 16, 1555*, he and Nicholas Ridley were tied back-to-back to the stake in Oxford and set aflame. "Be of good comfort, Mr. Ridley," Latimer cried. "Play the man! We shall this day light such a candle, by God's grace, in England, as I trust shall never be put out."

And the flames leaped up, but the blinding smoke
Could not the soul of Hugh Latimer choke;
For, said he, "Brother Ridley, be of good cheer,
A candle in England is lighted here,
Which by the grace of God shall never go out!"—
And that speech in whispers was echoed about—
Latimer's Light shall never go out,
However the winds may blow it about.
Latimer's Light can come to stay
*Till the trump of a coming judging day.**

So keep your mind on Jesus, who put up with many insults from sinners. Then you won't get discouraged and give up. (Hebrews 12:3)

---

*From A *Frank Boreham Treasury*, complied by Peter F. Gunther (Chicago: Moody Press, 1984), p. 11.

The Bishop's Sepulcher

When the apostle John addressed his readers as "my children," he perhaps had in mind his pupil Ignatius, a young man whose name doesn't appear in the New Testament but who figures prominently in early church history. Ignatius became the third bishop of the church in Antioch (where the Lord's followers were first called Christians—Acts 11:26) around AD 69, and he became the first to use the terms *Christianity* and *Catholic*.

We know little of his ministry, but he faithfully served the church at Antioch for forty years. When persecution arose, Ignatius was arrested, chained, and entrusted to ten soldiers. The story of his prison-voyage to Rome reads as though it leaped from the pages of the New Testament.

The party made its way overland and by the shipping routes, following the footsteps of Paul. As they passed Smyrna, Ephesus, Philippi, and Thessalonica, Christians gathered to ask his blessings. Along the way Ignatius wrote seven letters that rank among the most famous documents in church history. In his letter to Rome, intended to precede his arrival, Ignatius begged the brothers there to avoid using their political connections to hinder his expected martyrdom. "You cannot do me a greater favor," he wrote, "than allow me to be poured out as an offering to God while the altar is ready." Not wanting to bother them with the burial of his remains, he desired to be entirely consumed by the beasts in the arena. "Entice the beasts to become my sepulcher," he wrote, "that they may leave nothing of my body."

And so were his prayers answered. He reportedly died on *October 17, 108*, under the claws and teeth of lions or tigers as entertainment for Emperor Trajan. But his influence did not die. Fourteen hundred years later a young Spanish soldier was so moved by reading Ignatius's story that he dedicated his life to God and changed his name to Ignatius—of Loyola.

My children, I am writing this so that you won't sin. But if you do sin, Jesus Christ always does the right thing, and he will speak to the Father for us. Christ is the sacrifice that takes away our sins and the sins of all the world's people. (1 John 2:1–2)

October 18 Come Before Winter

Scottish Presbyterians cast long shadows. Catherine Robertson grew up in Scotland, where her father owned the largest cotton factory in the world. She was refined, wealthy, passionately Christian, and strongly Presbyterian. She married a preacher-professor, and the two began ministry in rural Ohio. They had seven children, and the last one—Clarence Edward Noble Macartney—became one of the greatest Presbyterian leaders of the twentieth century.

Clarence excelled in both studies and debating, but he wrestled with doubt and suffered serious bouts of shyness. He enrolled in Princeton Seminary and studied under Archibald Hodge and B. B. Warfield. During his long and distinguished career, Clarence pastored three churches in Pennsylvania. He averaged six hours a day in study and as a pastime wrote books and delivered lectures on the Civil War. He was a lifelong bachelor.

In 1924, he was named Moderator of the General Assembly of the Presbyterian Church in the United States of America. He was described as dignified, eloquent, Napoleon-like, aloof. He wrote fifty-seven books and was a staunch conservative in a liberal time. To those who denied the authority of Scripture, he thundered, "A deleted Bible results in a diluted gospel. Protestantism, as it loses faith in the Bible, is losing its religion." We can decaffeinate coffee, he said, and de-nicotine tobacco, but we can't de-Christianize Christianity.

The pulpit was his throne, and he preached well-crafted sermons without notes. His best-known message, repeated many times around the country, was an evangelistic sermon entitled "Come Before Winter," taken from 2 Timothy 4:21 and first preached in Philadelphia, *October 18, 1915*. It emphasized the need to receive Christ now, not later: "The Holy Spirit, when he invites men to come to Christ, never says, 'Tomorrow' but always 'Today.' If you can find me one place in the Bible where the Holy Spirit says, 'Believe in Christ tomorrow' or 'Repent and be saved tomorrow' I will come out of the pulpit and stay out of it—for I would have no gospel to preach.

Make good use of God's kindness to you. In the Scriptures God says,
"When the time came,
I listened to you,
and when you needed help,
I came to save you."
That time has come. This is the day for you to be saved. (2 Corinthians 6:1–2)

Case of Knives

"Fits of depression come over most of us," Charles Spurgeon once told his students. "The strong are not always vigorous; the joyous are not always happy." Spurgeon himself was living proof, for he often suffered agonizing periods of depression. One of the worst occurred when he was only twenty-two years old. His congregation had outgrown its building, so Spurgeon arranged to rent Royal Surrey Garden's Music Hall, London's most commodious and beautiful building, for Sunday night services. Surrey Hall usually accommodated secular concerts, carnivals, and circuses. Using it as a place of worship was unheard-of in its day, and the news spread through London like lightning.

On Sunday morning, *October 19, 1856*, Spurgeon preached at New Park Street Chapel, saying: "I may be called to stand where the thunder-clouds brew, where the lightnings play, and tempestuous winds are howling on the mountain top. Well, then, amidst dangers he will inspire me with courage; amidst toils he will make me strong; we shall be gathered together tonight where an unprecedented mass of people will assemble, perhaps from idle curiosity, to hear God's Word; see what God can do, just when a cloud is falling on the head of him whom God has raised up to preach to you."

That evening twelve thousand people streamed into Surrey Hall and an additional ten thousand overflowed into the surrounding gardens. The services started, but as Spurgeon rose to pray, someone shouted "Fire! Fire! The galleries are giving way!" There was no fire, but the crowd bolted in panic, and in the resulting stampede seven people were trampled to death. Twenty-eight more were hospitalized.

The young preacher, reeling in shock, was literally carried from the pulpit to a friend's house, where he remained in seclusion for weeks. He wept by day and suffered terrifying dreams at night. He later said, "My thoughts were all a case of knives, cutting my heart to pieces." At last, while meditating on Philippians 2:10, the Lord's Word began to restore his soul.

It was this disaster, horrible as it was, that vaulted Charles Spurgeon to overnight fame as a preacher all the world wanted to hear.

So at the name of Jesus
everyone will bow down,
those in heaven, on earth,
and under the earth.
And to the glory
of God the Father
everyone will openly agree,
"Jesus Christ is Lord!" (Philippians 2:10–11)

October 20

By *His* Stripes

Peter Damian died on February 23, 1072, but not before beginning one of the strangest fads in Christian history. Damian, a Benedictine monk, advocated a life of extreme austerity. In denying worldly pleasures, he found it useful to whip himself, and he taught the practice to others. Monks began lashing themselves while reciting the Psalms. Each psalm was accompanied by a hundred strokes with a leather strap to the bare back. The whole Psalter was good for an additional fifteen hundred strokes. It reenacted the suffering of Christ and of the martyrs, they thought, and served as an act of penance. Some monks flogged themselves to death for their own benefit and to release souls from purgatory.

Self-flagellation remained localized and limited to monasteries for two hundred years, but in the thirteenth century, it enflamed the masses. The Black Death was causing many people to believe the end of the world was near, and bands of flagellants appeared across Europe calling people to repentance. In the outbreak of 1259, great parades of thousands from all classes and of all ages marched through the streets stripped to their waists, carrying crosses and banners, singing hymns and scourging themselves.

The flagellant movement reignited repeatedly during the next two centuries, and the frenzy of 1349 exceeded all previous demonstrations. Bands of enthusiasts suddenly appeared in all areas of Europe. They marched from town to town, dressed in white, with red crosses on caps and mantles, singing hymns and carrying banners. They camped in public squares, and twice daily they bared themselves to the waist, fell to their knees and scourged themselves. Their whips with needle-pointed iron tips drew blood as they struck to the rhythmic music of hymns.

On *October 20, 1349*, self-flagellation was condemned by a papal bull and rightly so. We can never pay for our sins by our own blood, however painfully shed. By *his* stripes we are healed. Our bodies are his temples to be guarded, not abused.

Flagellants were nevertheless seen in Rome as late as 1870, and even today there are isolated outbreaks.

He was wounded and crushed
because of our sins;
by taking our punishment,
he made us completely well.
All of us were like sheep
that had wandered off.
We had each gone our own way,
but the LORD gave him
the punishment we deserved. (Isaiah 53:5–6)

My God, I Am Thine

James Hannington grew up peacefully enough near Brighton, England, working in his father's countinghouse. But then he entered the ministry and offered himself to the Church Missionary Society. His first trip to Africa was interrupted by sickness. After recovering, he made a second attempt and arrived off the African coast July 23, 1884. He started inland toward Uganda, but he unwittingly chose the most dangerous path imaginable. Compatriots sent runners after him, but they arrived too late. Hannington was seized by warriors of the lawless Mwanga tribe. His small diary, crammed with tiny handwriting, is among the most moving missionary documents on record.

> *October 21, 1885.* About 20 ruffians set upon us. They violently threw me to the ground. Twice I nearly broke away from them, then grew faint from struggling and was dragged by the legs over the ground, my clothes torn to pieces, wet through, strained in every limb, expecting death.
>
> October 22. In a fair-sized hut, but with no ventilation, floor covered with rotting banana peel and leaves and lice, fearfully shaken, scarce power to hold a small Bible. Shall I live through it? My God, I am Thine.
>
> October 23. I woke full of pain and weak. I don't see how I can stand all this, yet I don't want to give in.
>
> October 27. I am very low; it looks so dark. I don't know what to think, and would say from the heart, "Let the Lord do what seemeth Him good."
>
> October 28. A terrible night, first with my drunken guard and secondly with insects, which have found my tent and swarm. I don't think I got one hour's sleep, and woke with fever fast developing. O Lord, do have mercy upon me and release me. I am quite broken down and brought low. Comforted by reading Psalm 27.
>
> October 29. I was held up by Psalm 30, which came with great power. A hyena howled near me last night, smelling a sick man, but I hope it is not to have me.

That was his last entry. That day they killed him.

You, LORD, are the light
that keeps me safe.
I am not afraid of anyone.
You protect me,
and I have no fears.
Brutal people may attack
and try to kill me,
but they will stumble . . .
Armies may surround me,
but I won't be afraid;
war may break out,
but I will trust you. (Psalm 27:1–3)

Disappointment

The churches of northeastern America grew rapidly in the early 1800s, fueled by one revival after another. The new Christians had little theological education, yet many of them began to discuss details of biblical prophecy with great vigor. Speculation boiled over as to the exact day and year when Christ would return, and among the speculators was William Miller of New York.

Miller, when newly converted, had torn into the prophecies of Daniel, concluding in 1818 that Christ would return in 1843 or 1844. When he later began preaching, this became a keynote of his messages, and his listeners, finding him earnest, eloquent, and sincere, multiplied. He finally announced that Christ would return to earth on October 22, 1844.

The financial panic of 1839 contributed to the belief that the end of the world was approaching. Enthusiasm for Christ's return became so great that prophetic charts were added alongside stock-market listings and current events in the newspapers. Miller's teachings swept through New England, and large numbers espoused Millerism.

As the morning of *October 22, 1844*, dawned, a sense of fear and foreboding fell over New England. People gathered on mountaintops and in churches. Normal activities ceased as everyone awaited the sudden rending of the skies and the end of the world. When the day passed uneventfully, many Christians grew disillusioned. The unsaved became cynical. The following years saw a decline in conversions, and the period of revivals came to an abrupt end. The event became known as the Great Disappointment.

Some of Miller's followers, however, pressed on, and their efforts evolved into the Seventh-day Adventist movement.

No one knows the day or hour. The angels in heaven don't know, and the Son himself doesn't know. Only the Father knows. When the Son of Man appears, things will be just as they were when Noah lived. People were eating, drinking, and getting married right up to the day that the flood came and Noah went into the big boat. They didn't know anything was happening until the flood came and swept them all away. That is how it will be when the Son of Man appears. (Matthew 24:36–39)

A Priceless Bible

Among Christianity's greatest treasures is the *Codex Alexandrinus* (Alexandrian Manuscript), a manuscript of the Greek Bible written in the early 400s. It contains virtually the entire Bible, along with the Apocrypha, some hymns, and letters written by Clement of Rome.

It was housed in Alexandria until 1627, when Cyril Lucar, the patriarch of Alexandria, presented it to England's King Charles I, who placed it in his Royal Library at St. James Place. But when the Puritan Revolution occurred, Charles was beheaded, and troops were quartered at St. James's. The books in his library lay on the floor in heaps, subject to rain and dust and rats.

The monarchy was restored in 1660, under Charles II, but conditions at the Royal Library didn't improve. In 1693, Richard Bentley, a brilliant classical scholar, temporarily took the Alexandrian Manuscript to his own lodgings for safekeeping.

In the early 1700s, the Royal Library was moved to Cotton House, and the priceless Bible was kept in a narrow, damp room with only a small window at each end. Christopher Wren considered the building so ruinous that most of it "should be demolished," and the library "purged of much useless trash." In 1730, the Royal Library was moved into Ashburnham House which, on Saturday morning, *October 23, 1731*, caught fire. The alarm was given, and Arthur Onslow, Speaker of the House of Commons, came across from his nearby residence to direct the rescue. Many precious volumes were thrown from the windows in an effort to save them, but the invaluable Codex Alexandrinus was treated with better care. An eyewitness told of the learned Dr. Bentley "in nightgown and great wig" fleeing the building with the *Codex Alexandrinus* under his arm.

The disastrous fire drew public attention to the plight of the Royal Library, and a generation later it found a home in the newly founded British Museum, where today the *Codex Alexandrinus* is securely displayed.

Many people have tried to tell the story of what God has done among us. They wrote what we had been told by the ones who were there in the beginning and saw what happened. So I made a careful study of everything and then decided to write and tell you exactly what took place . . . . (Luke 1:1–3)

Living Water

John Paton's life was molded by his childhood in a little cottage in Kirkmahoe, Scotland. The cottage had ribs of oak, stone walls, a thatched roof, and three rooms filled with eleven children. The front room served as bedroom, kitchen, and parlor. The rear room was his father's stocking-making shop. The middle room was a closet where John's father retired each day for prayer and Bible study. The sound of his father's prayers through the wall made a powerful impression on young John.

Years later when Scotland's Reformed Church issued a plea for missionaries for the South Pacific, John went to his parents for advice. They told him something they had never before disclosed—he had been dedicated to foreign missions before birth.

John sailed from Scotland April 16, 1858, landing on the islands in November. He found himself among cannibals and endangered again and again. "They encircled us in a deadly ring," he wrote of one incident, "and one kept urging another to strike the first blow. My heart rose up to the Lord Jesus; I saw him watching all the scene. My peace came back to me like a wave from God. I realized that my life was immortal till my Master's work with me was done."

The turning point came when Paton decided to dig a well to provide fresh water for the people. The islanders, terrified at bringing "rain from below," watched with deepest foreboding. Paton dug deeper and deeper until finally at thirty feet he tapped into a stream of water. Opposition to his mission work ceased, and the wide-eyed islanders gave him their full respect. Chief Mamokei accepted Christ as Savior; then a few others made the daring step. On *October 24, 1869*, nearly eleven years after his arrival, Paton led his first communion service. Twelve converted cannibals partook of the Lord's Supper. "As I put the bread and wine into those hands once stained with the blood of cannibalism, now stretched out to receive and partake the emblems of the Redeemer's love," he wrote, "I had a foretaste of the joy of Glory that well nigh broke my heart to pieces."

The Lord meant that when you eat this bread and drink from this cup, you tell about his death until he comes. (1 Corinthians 11:26)

Council of Ephesus

Orthodox Christianity teaches that Jesus Christ is one person, having both a human and a divine nature. Nestorius, powerful fifth-century preacher, disagreed. Two separate persons indwelled the incarnate Christ, he taught, one divine and the other human. "I separate the natures, but I unite the worship. Consider what this must mean," he said. "He who was formed in the womb of Mary was not himself God, but God assumed him."

A violent controversy ensued. Nestorius, a popular orator, had been named patriarch of Constantinople by Emperor Theodosius II. Preachers, monks, and bishops exploded in their pulpits against him. The pope condemned him in a set of twelve anathemas (the word *anathema* means "cursed") and demanded he recant within twelve days.

Emperor Theodosius, stunned by the theological war fragmenting his empire, called a general church council in Ephesus in 431. From the beginning it proved to be animated and stomach-wrenching. Nestorius arrived with sixteen bishops, an armed escort, and the backing of the emperor. But he was badly outnumbered, and the verdict went against him: "Whosoever does not anathematize Nestorius, let him be anathema; the true faith anathematizes him; the holy council anathematizes him. Whoever holds fellowship with Nestorius, let him be anathema. We all anathematize the letter and doctrines of Nestorius. We all anathematize Nestorius and his followers and his ungodly doctrine."

But Emperor Theodosius declared the decree invalid because not all the bishops had yet arrived in Ephesus. More politics, intrigue, and anxiety followed, but in the end the result was the same. Nestorius was deposed as patriarch of Constantinople, and on *October 25, 431*, his successor was nominated. Nestorius was banished to Egypt, where he died after writing his autobiography and titling it *Tragedy*.

The Council of Ephesus was one of the bitterest councils in church history, but it preserved the orthodox doctrine of Christ. A small group of Eastern bishops, however, refusing to accept its decisions, constituted themselves into a separate church, centered in Persia. Remnants of the Nestorian Church survive to this day in western and central Asia.

This good news is about his Son, our Lord Jesus Christ! As a human, he was from the family of David. But the Holy Spirit proved that Jesus is the powerful Son of God, because he was raised from death. (Romans 1:3–4)

October 26 A Charming Man

Thomas More was hard to dislike. "I am entirely devoted to this man," wrote Italian scholar Niccolo Sagundino. "I often relax in his delightful company as one might lodge in some beautiful place. I never see him without his sending me away better informed and more attached to him. You could not imagine, I assure you, a more agreeable, charming, and amusing man. His wonderful elegance as a writer, his choice of words and well-rounded sentences are universally admired, but no more so than his keen mind, set off by fairness, humor, wit, and courtesy."

Dean Swift thought More the greatest man of virtue "this kingdom ever produced." Erasmus agreed. He described More as cheerful, having quick humor and ready smile, being a faithful husband, a persuasive orator, a man alert. "In short," said Erasmus, "what did Nature ever create milder, sweeter, and happier than the genius of Thomas More."

These merits propelled More to the highest office in England on *October 26, 1529*, when he was named Lord Chancellor under King Henry VIII. But it proved his undoing, for More was a deeply religious man. He gave liberally to the needy, sang in the choir of his parish church in Chelsea, led in family prayer each night, and built a small chapel by his house for personal prayer and Bible study. Here he occasionally engaged in self-flagellation with a whip of knotted cords in the medieval manner. He was devoted to his church. He forcibly opposed Protestants. He was a man of principle.

Henry VIII didn't like men of principle, and he was incensed when his Lord Chancellor refused to obtain from the pope the desired divorce from Catherine of Aragon. He was further enraged when More refused to recognize him as head of the Church of England. Henry imprisoned him in the Tower of London and tried him for treason. On July 7, 1535, Thomas More mounted the scaffold and told the hushed crowd that he died being the "king's good servant, but God's first." Then he read Psalm 51 and laid his head carefully on the block.

I have sinned and done wrong
since the day I was born.
But you want complete honesty,
so teach me true wisdom.
Wash me with hyssop until I am clean
and whiter than snow. (Psalm 51:5–7)

My Very Heart Melted

At the 1771 Methodist Conference in England, John Wesley said, "Our brethren in America call for help. Who is willing to go over?" Francis Asbury, five foot six, 150 pounds, sat listening. For months the young man had longed to visit America. "So I spoke my mind, and made an offer of myself. It was accepted by Mr. Wesley, who judged I had a call."

Asbury returned home to break the news to his parents. "Though it was grievous, they consented to let me go. My mother is one of the tenderest parents in the world; I believe she was blessed in the present instance with Divine assistance to part with me."

He sailed on September 4. "For three days I was very ill with the seasickness; and no sickness I ever knew was equal to it." But he soon recovered enough to gather his thoughts: "I will set down a few things that lie on my mind. Whither am I going? To the New World. What to do? To gain honor? No, if I know my own heart. To get money? No: I am going to live to God, and to bring others so to do."

Asbury arrived in America on *October 27, 1771*. "This day we landed in Philadelphia where we were directed to the house of Mr. Francis Harris who kindly entertained us and brought us to a large church where we met with a considerable congregation. The people looked on us with pleasure, receiving us as angels of God. When I came near the American shore, my very heart melted within me, to think from whence I came, where I was going, and what I was going about. I feel that God is here . . ."

Asbury never returned to England. He plunged into the American wilderness, traveling day and night for years in all kinds of weather and through all kinds of hardship. He traveled 270,000 miles and wore out one horse after another. All he owned was carried in two saddlebags. When Asbury arrived in America, there were fewer than 80 Methodist preachers and 14,000 members. When he died there were 2,000 preachers and 200,000 members.

We are not preaching about ourselves. Our message is that Jesus Christ is Lord. He also sent us to be your servants. The Scriptures say, "God commanded light to shine in the dark." Now God is shining in our hearts to let you know that his glory is seen in Jesus Christ. (2 Corinthians 4:5–6)

In this Sign Conquer

By the early fourth century Christianity was straddling the Roman Empire, boasting of churches from Britain to Carthage and Persia. The gospel had spread mouth to mouth, person to person until, despite relentless persecution, it had taken root. "Every time a drop of blood was shed," said pastor Charles Spurgeon, "that drop became a man."

The final storm occurred when Emperor Diocletian suddenly unleashed the Great Persecution, fiercest of all purges. But Romans eventually sickened of the blood, and the Christian holocaust created far-reaching sympathy for believers. When Diocletian abdicated, a power struggle erupted between two titans: Constantine and Maxentius. Their armies met at the Milvian Bridge outside Rome; Constantine, as he later told the historian Eusebius, turned to the Christian God for help. In a dream on *October 28, 312*, he saw a cross in the sky with the words *in this sign conquer* written in Greek. Thus encouraged he advanced and prevailed. After the battle he openly espoused Christianity, and the outcast church suddenly found itself on top of the world.

Constantine extended great liberties to bishops. He abolished crucifixions and ended gladiatorial contests as punishments. He issued the Edict of Milan, which said in part: "Every one who has a common wish to follow the religion of the Christians may from this moment freely proceed without any annoyance or disquiet." He made Sunday a holiday, built church buildings, financed Christian projects, and gathered bishops to discuss theology.

But whether Constantine was genuinely born again is doubted. He treated church leaders as political aides. He banished churchmen he didn't like and retained paganism he did like. Under his rule the church, while enjoying freedom, deteriorated from an army of noble martyrs to a mixed multitude of semiconverted pagans. An alignment between church and state developed that set the stage for the Middle Ages and continues to this day in the state churches of Europe.

The conversion of Constantine was at once both the best thing that could have happened to the church and the worst.

Let the name of the LORD
be praised now and forever.
From dawn until sunset
the name of the LORD
deserves to be praised. (Psalm 113:2–3)

The Archbishop's Arrow

Maurice Abbot was a clothier in a village twenty miles from London. One night his pregnant wife, Alice, dreamed that if she could catch a pike, her child would be a boy. She rushed to the nearby river and trapped a young pike in her pitcher. She cooked it, ate it, and on *October 29, 1562*, bore a son.

The story spread through the superstitious town, and many people offered to finance the boy's education. Consequently George entered Oxford at age sixteen. The Abbots were staunch Protestants, and the young man entered the ministry. His powerful, Puritan-leaning sermons, though often dull, were always scholarly. When King James approved a new version of the Bible, George became a translator of the Gospels, Acts, and Revelation.

In 1611, the year the King James Bible was published, George became head of the Church of England, the archbishop of Canterbury—the only KJV translator to reach that office. When James died, it was George Abbot who crowned the new king, Charles I. He thus became the only KJV translator to crown a monarch.

But he was also the only archbishop of Canterbury and translator ever to kill a man. It happened when he joined friends in a hunting party, midsummer of 1621. Abbot was stout, stodgy, and unfamiliar with bows. When a buck came into sight, he drew back his arrow and let it fly—right into poor Peter Harkins, who quickly bled to death. All England was stunned, and many were critical of the archbishop, who was himself doubled over in grief. A special council absolved him of guilt, more or less, and the king issued a pardon. But many churchgoers whispered doubts about the holiness of a man who had killed another. Abbot soon became ill with "the stone and gravel," and with gout. He began fasting every Tuesday in sorrow for his poor marksmanship. But he was never again well—or well accepted by the people. Yet he still speaks to us every time we read the Gospels, Acts, or Revelation in the King James Version of the Bible.

I am about to collapse
from constant pain.
I told you my sins,
and I am sorry for them.
Many deadly and powerful
enemies hate me,
and they repay evil for good
because I try to do right. (Psalm 38:17–20)

October 30 Demoralized Leaders

October 31, 1517, is the best-known date in Protestant history—the day Martin Luther nailed his convictions to the Wittenberg door. But an incident that happened sixteen years before helps us understand Luther's boldness. Rodrigo Borgia was named a cardinal in 1456, and "no sooner had he donned his red hat than he removed it, together with the rest of his raiment, for a marathon romp with a succession of women whose identity is unknown to us and may well have been unknown to him."* His immorality only increased when in 1492, he became Pope Alexander VI.

On *October 30, 1501*, Pope Alexander presided over the infamous Ballet of the Chestnuts. Guests approaching the papal palace saw living statutes of naked, gilded young people in erotic poses. Inside, after the dishes were cleared from the banquet hall, the city's most beautiful prostitutes danced with the guests, shedding their clothes a bit at a time. Eventually the pope and his sons became judges of a contest in which guests stripped and performed with one another. Alexander awarded prizes to the men.

The corruption of the papacy continued under Alexander's successor, Julius II, and when Luther visited Rome in 1510, he was shocked to find the papal court served by "twelve naked girls." Down to his old age Luther remembered seeing and hearing of sexual abominations taking place in the name of Christ by those who were thought to be spiritual leaders. He later wrote, "I would not have missed seeing Rome for a hundred thousand florins. If I did I should ever had been uneasy lest I might have done injustice to the pope."

It was the demoralized nature of the papacy as much as its doctrinal failure that convinced Luther to risk prosecution and excommunication with fortitude. Holy living—personal purity—Luther knew, is married to pure doctrine, and the union is inseparable . . . for "the *just* shall live by *faith*."

You are God's people, so don't let it be said that any of you are immoral or indecent or greedy. Don't use dirty or foolish or filthy words. Instead, say how thankful you are. Being greedy, indecent, or immoral is just another way of worshipping idols. (Ephesians 5:3–5)

---

*William Manchester, *A World Lit Only by Fire* (Boston: Little, Brown, & Co., 1992), p. 76.

High Noon

In 1517, Pope Leo X, empty pocketed and needing funds to rebuild St. Peter's basilica, issued a special sale of indulgences. The very word *indulgence* tends to convey dubious moral connotations, but these indulgences were particularly questionable. What was an indulgence? It was a special sort of forgiveness for sins, issued by the pope in consideration of various acts of merit, in this case donations to Leo's treasury. Indulgences could even be purchased on behalf of loved ones in purgatory.

Dominican friar Johann Tetzel became the pontiff's peddler, a P. T. Barnum traveling around with a brass-bound chest, a bag of printed receipts, and an enormous cross draped with a papal banner. Whenever Tetzel came to a town, church bells pealed, crowds gathered, and street performers kicked up their heels. Tetzel would set up shop in the nave of the local church, open his bags, and shout, "I have here the passports to lead the human soul to the celestial joys of Paradise. As soon as the coin rings in the bowl, the soul for whom it is paid will fly from purgatory and straight to heaven."

He usually exceeded his quota.

But many were troubled, and when the hard eyes of Martin Luther fell on the indulgences purchased by fellow villagers in Wittenberg, he studied them carefully and pronounced them frauds. At high noon on *October 31, 1517*, Luther, a thirty-three-year-old university professor, walked to the door of Castle Church in Wittenberg, Germany, and tacked to it a document. The door served as the town bulletin board, and Martin Luther had an announcement to post. He called for a "disputation on the power and efficacy of indulgences."

A few curious passersby drew near and scanned the words: "Out of love for the faith and the desire to bring it to light, the following propositions will be discussed at Wittenberg under the chairmanship of the Reverend Father Martin Luther, Master of Arts and Sacred Theology . . ." There followed a list of ninety-five items.

Luther did not yet know what mighty blows he had struck.

God is our mighty fortress,
always ready to help
in times of trouble.
Nations rage! Kingdoms fall!
But at the voice of God
the earth itself melts.
The LORD All-Powerful
is with us.
The God of Jacob
is our fortress. (Psalm 46:1, 6–7)

On This Day in Christian History...

NOVEMBER

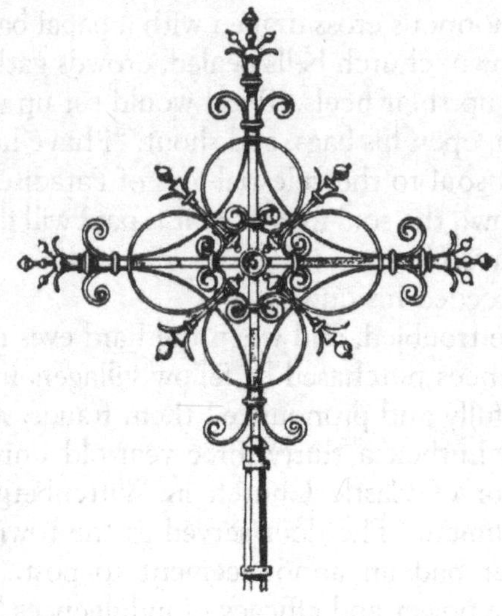

Council of Chalcedon

The old church of St. Euphemia, sitting atop a hill in Chalcedon across the Bosphorus from Constantinople, hosted the fourth great council of the church in the fall of 451. The emperor called the bishops together to combat a series of heresies about the person of Christ and to formulate a creed that would unite Christianity.

The nature of Christ was the chief theological question of the first four hundred years of church history. Christendom as a whole remained unified in an orthodox faith, but periodic assaults by heretics forced the church in its councils to state its definition of Christ. The Council of Nicaea in 325 had affirmed Christ as fully God. But how, then, could he also be truly human?

The Council of Chalcedon tackled that problem, and it wasn't pretty. Bishops and delegates shouted at each other in rough-and-tumble debates, interrupting each other, losing their tempers, shouting down speakers, and wreaking havoc. In the end, however, it managed to affirm that Jesus: (1) is fully God, (2) is fully human, (3) is one person, and (4) possesses two distinct natures. The Chalcedon document, one of the most important in church history, says in part:

> Following the holy fathers, we confess with one voice that the one and only Son, our Lord Jesus Christ, is perfect in Godhead and perfect in manhood, truly God and truly man, that he is of one substance with the Father as God, he is also of one substance with us as man. He is like us in all things without sin. This one and the same Christ, Son, Lord, Only-begotten is made known in two natures (which exist) without confusion, without change, without division, without separation. The distinction of the natures is in no way taken away by their union, but rather the distinctive properties of each nature are preserved.

The Council of Chalcedon thus affirmed that Jesus Christ is one person having both a divine and a human nature. He is one Lord. He is both God and man.

And with that, the council dissolved on *November 1, 451.*

Here is the great mystery of our religion: Christ came as a human. The Spirit proved that he pleased God, and he was seen by angels. Christ was preached to the nations. People in this world put their faith in him, and he was taken up to glory. (1 Timothy 3:16)

City Aflame

Citywide conflagrations seldom happen today, having gone the way of the plague. But Christians of earlier eras often ministered and suffered amid such holocausts. Believers in Nero's day were unjustly blamed for Rome's fiery destruction. Eighty-nine churches perished in London's 1666 fire. D. L. Moody lost virtually all his property in the great Chicago fire of 1871. But none of them exceeded the fire and fear that engulfed Canton during the days of Protestants' first missionary to China.

Robert Morrison ministered in Canton despite the misgivings of the East India Company and the antagonism of the Chinese themselves. Yet he plodded on, finally baptizing his first convert after seven years of labor.

On Friday night, November 1, 1822, Morrison became aware of panic in the city. A fire, starting in a baker's shop and driven by strong winds, was roaring like a furnace through acres of crowded wooden houses. Multitudes fled in hysteria. The East India Company's fire equipment was of little use, for the streets were clogged with fleeing humanity, and the water supply was poor.

Morrison, transfixed by the sea of flames, hurriedly penned a letter in Chinese before dawn on *November 2, 1822*, begging officials to pull down buildings in front of the fire to stop the inferno's advance. But the Chinese refused to even read his letter though he took it to the governor in person. By 8:00 AM, the flames consumed the city's manufacturing sectors. Shifting winds drove the fire along the riverfront, westward for a mile and a half. Multitudes were killed, burned, or left homeless. Thousands of shops and houses were destroyed. It was the end of the world in miniature.

Looters tried to beat the flames to abandoned valuables, and Morrison recorded that twenty-eight people were trampled while scrambling for money after a robber cut open a man's cash-stuffed backpack. The missionary himself was relatively fortunate. He lost nothing of great value beyond a hundred pounds of paper intended for a new edition of his translation of the New Testament.

The earth came out of water and was made from water. Later it was destroyed by the waters of a mighty flood. But God has commanded the present heavens and earth to remain until the day of judgment. Then they will be set on fire, and ungodly people will be destroyed. (2 Peter 3:5–7)

Bobby Wild Goose

Robert Raikes was born in 1735, in Gloucester, England, where his father published the *Gloucester Journal.* When the elder Raikes died in 1757, Robert, then twenty-two years old, inherited the newspaper and immediately used it to crusade for moral reform. English prisons, for example, were inhumane places of misery where prisoners, crowded into tiny compartments with no ventilation or sanitary facilities, died of "gaol fever." Raikes visited them, raised money for them, and taught them to read. His penetrating newspaper columns repeatedly called attention to their plight.

One Saturday afternoon in 1780, Robert discovered another cause to champion. He entered a slummy suburb of Gloucester to interview a prospective gardener. Swarms of children surrounded him, and Raikes recoiled in horror at their fighting, profanity, stench, gambling, and filth. He returned home shaken and almost immediately conceived a plan for Sunday schools. Such schools had already been tried but without widespread backing. Raikes hired four Christian women to open schools on Sunday. Why Sunday? Children worked in the factories the other six days of the week, but on Sunday they ran wild.

The portly Raikes, primly dressed and carrying an elegant snuffbox and tasseled cane, ambled through the ghettoes day after day recruiting pupils. The children began calling him Bobby Wild Goose. But in his Sunday schools, they were taught to read; then they learned the Bible, the catechism, and other subjects.

Three years later after the schools were clearly working, Raikes used his newspaper to promote them. On *November 3, 1783*, the *Gloucester Journal* published an article on the success of Sunday schools. To Raikes's surprise, London papers picked up the story and inquiries poured in from across England. The movement spread rapidly. And the rest, as they say, is history.

The form of Sunday school changed, yet millions of all ages find their way each week to Sunday school to learn of Christ.

Some people brought their children to Jesus, so that he could place his hands on them and pray for them. His disciples told the people to stop bothering him. But Jesus said, "Let the children come to me, and don't try to stop them! People who are like these children belong to God's kingdom." (Matthew 19:13–14)

Rock of Ages

On *November 4, 1740*, a baby in Farnham, England, was given the formidable name of Augustus Montague Toplady. His father died in a war, his mother spoiled him, his friends thought him "sick and neurotic," and his relatives disliked him.

But Augustus was interested in the Lord. "I am now arrived at the age of eleven years," he wrote on his birthday. "I praise God I can remember no dreadful crime; to the Lord be the glory." By age twelve he was preaching sermons to whoever would listen. At fourteen he began writing hymns. At sixteen he was soundly converted to Christ while attending a service in a barn. And at twenty-two he was ordained an Anglican priest.

As a staunch Calvinist he despised John Wesley's Arminian theology. He accused Wesley of "lying and forgery." "I believe him to be the most rancorous hater of the gospel-system that ever appeared on this island," Augustus wrote. "Wesley is guilty of satanic shamelessness," he said on another occasion, "of acting the ignoble part of a lurking, shy assassin." He described the evangelist as a prizefighter and a chimney sweep.

In 1776, Augustus wrote an article about God's forgiveness, intending it as a slap at Wesley. He ended his article with an original poem:

Rock of Ages, cleft for me,
Let me hide myself in Thee;
Let the water and the blood,
From Thy wounded side which flowed,
Be of sin the double cure,
Save from wrath and make me pure.

Augustus Toplady died at age thirty-eight, but his poem outlived him and has been called "the best known, best loved, and most widely useful" hymn in the English language. Oddly, it is remarkably similar to something Wesley had written thirty years before in the preface of a book of hymns for the Lord's Supper: "O Rock of Salvation, Rock struck and cleft for me, let those two Streams of Blood and Water which gushed from thy side, bring down Pardon and Holiness into my soul."

Perhaps the two men were not as incompatible as they thought.

I love you, LORD God,
and you make me strong.
You are my mighty rock, my fortress, my protector,
the rock where I am safe . . . (Psalm 18:1–2)

The Council of Constance

Two heads aren't always better than one—and three heads can get downright ridiculous. For example . . .

During medieval days, the pope reigned as the most powerful figure on earth, a superleader combining religious and political authority in one gilded role. But between thirteen hundred and fifteen hundred political leaders in England and France began defying the papal father.

The harshest conflict arose when troops of France's King Philip burst into the bedroom of eighty-six-year-old Pope Boniface, more or less frightening him to death. A Frenchman, Pope Clement V, replaced him and moved the papal residence to France. Thus began a seventy-two-year period of six successive French popes, all of whom chose to live in the small town of Avignon, France, rather than in Rome. This "exile" has been called the Babylonian Captivity of the papacy. Tensions between France and Italy eventually led to the election of two popes, one chosen by the Italian faction and the other by the French. This Great Papal Schism lasted for thirty-nine years, each pope having his own College of Cardinals, each claiming to be the true vicar of Christ.

In 1409, a majority of cardinals from both camps agreed to end the schism by deposing both popes and electing a new one from scratch. The result? When neither of the old popes resigned, the number increased to three. The ridiculous spectacle of three popes led to the Council of Constance, convening on *November 5, 1414*—the largest church council in history and the most important since the Council of Nicaea in 325. Constance, a village of six thousand, swelled with five thousand delegates along with an army of servants, secretaries, peddlers, physicians, quacks, minstrels, and fifteen hundred prostitutes. The council met for three years and at length persuaded one of the popes to resign and deposed the other two. In 1417, it chose a new leader, Pope Martin V, thus effectively ending the Great Schism and the Babylonian Captivity.

But the damage to the Vatican's prestige had been wrought, helping pave the way for the Reformation exactly a hundred years later.

It is truly wonderful
when relatives live together
in peace. (Psalm 133:1)

November 6 Let a Thousand Fall

Along the edge of western Africa sits Liberia, Sub-Saharan Africa's first independent state. It was established in the early 1800s, through the efforts of the American Colonization Society, an organization devoted to repatriating American ex-slaves in colonies along the African coast.

The first missionary of the Methodist Episcopal Church, Melville Beveridge Cox, was directed there in 1833. He was a young widower, pale and prostrate with grief who had been planning for missions service in South America. "Why not go to Liberia?" asked his bishop, seeking someone to send to that land of fatal fevers.

"If the Lord wills," replied Cox. "I have no lingering fear. A grave in Africa shall be sweet if he sustain me." To a friend Cox wrote, "I know I cannot live long in Africa, but I hope to live long enough to get there; and if it please God that my bones shall lie in an African grave, I shall have established such a bond between Africa and the church at home as shall not be broken until Africa be redeemed."

To students of Connecticut's Wesleyan University, he said, "If I die in Africa, you must come over and write my epitaph." When a student asked what they should write, Cox replied, "Write, Let a thousand fall before Africa be given up."

He made a final visit to the graves of his wife and small child; then on *November 6, 1832*, Cox boarded the *Jupiter* and set sail. The seas were rough, and at first he doubled over in seasickness. But by mid-ocean he was at work, planning a mission house, school, and farm. Glimpsing the coast, he wrote, "I have seen Liberia and live! It rises up like a cloud of heaven!" He disembarked at Monrovia on March 7, 1833, and threw himself into the work. But on July 21, he awoke from a fitful sleep, bathed in sweat and shouting, "Come, come, Lord Jesus, come quickly!" He died in a fever, having served less than four months.

There were 999 left to go, and because of Cox's example, five other youths were already on their way.

I know what it is to be poor or to have plenty, and I have lived under all kinds of conditions. I know what it means to be full or to be hungry, to have too much or too little. Christ gives me strength to face anything. (Philippians 4:12–13)

Passages of Trouble

The Scottish Reformation came painfully, costing the lives of many staunch Protestants, including John Nisbet, whose sixteen-year-old son later penned this account in a "neat old-fashioned hand":

On the *7th of November, 1685*, my father, with other three, desired to go and end a controversy in one of their Christian societies; upon which he left me to the kind care of Providence, and went on his intended journey. But early on Sabbath morning, he and the other three were seized by forty of the enemy. The night before, I had gone to the Earl of Loudon's house; and in my sleep I dreamed of all the passages of trouble my father was in. I awoke with much sorrow of spirit, and immediately rose and essayed prayer. But alas, alas, I was dead, lifeless and overwhelmed with such a flood of sorrow that I could do nothing all that day but sigh to the breaking of my heart. At night, two young ladies came and sat down by me, and seeing me in such sorrow, asked me if I had got any meat. It was told them I would eat none all that day. Upon which they opened their skirts wherein they had some meat, and both very kindly urged me to eat. But I would eat none. At which the young ladies burst into tears; and one of them says, "This morning, forty of the enemy came upon your father near to Fenwick Kirk; they have killed the other three and your father has received seven wounds and is prisoner." At the hearing of which sad news I was struck to the heart. I arose immediately and went out to the fields. But kind Providence ordered the matter so, that though very dark, I met an eminent Christian, William Woodburn, my father's friend, who counseled me to acquiesce in and submit to the sovereign will of God who is a father to the fatherless. Upon this blessed advice and seasonable counsel, the weight of my burden was much taken off, my sorrow alleviated, and all fretting at the dispensation prevented. I spent this night looking to the Lord, that my father might be strengthened to be faithful unto the death.

Our LORD, you will always rule,
but nations will vanish
from the earth.
You listen to the longings
of those who suffer.
You offer them hope,
and you pay attention
to their cries for help.
You defend orphans
and everyone else in need. (Psalm 10:16–18)

November 8 The Subtle Doctor

John Duns Scotus was born in Scotland, studied theology at Oxford, England, and was ordained. About 1304, he migrated to Paris and obtained his doctorate degree. Pressing on to Cologne, Germany, he taught theology for about a year before dying on *November 8, 1308*, at a relatively young age, probably under forty. A monument was erected to John Scotus in 1513, in the Franciscan church in Cologne, reading, "Scotia [Scotland] gave me birth, England nursed me, Gaul educated me, Cologne holds my ashes."

Scotus possessed a brilliant mind that shook up medieval theology. He had few qualms about criticizing earlier Catholic theologians—Thomas Aquinas and Anselm and the others—and he delighted in rattling students by challenging established beliefs. But, like many theologians, he was better at questioning than answering. His own theology is difficult to follow, and for that reason he is known to church history as the Subtle Doctor. He has perplexed and frustrated so many students that the word *dunce* was coined from the Duns in the middle of his name.

Scotus became the first major theologian to advocate the doctrine of Mary's immaculate conception: that Mary herself was conceived without any sin, that she was pure and sinless from the moment of her conception. At a public debate in Paris, it is said, Scotus pummeled the followers of Thomas Aquinas with two hundred arguments on this subject, and the two camps waged one of the most bitter controversies in the pre-Reformation church.

Yet Scotus did not teach his position as dogma but as probability, writing: "Upon this question I say that God was able to effect it that Mary was never in original sin. He was able also to effect it that she remained in sin for a moment or for a certain time and was cleansed of it in the last instant of that time. Which of the solutions really took place . . . God knows."

His position on the subject, nonetheless, became established church teaching when Pope Pius IX proclaimed it a dogma in 1854.

Keep your minds on whatever is true, pure, right, holy, friendly, and proper. Don't ever stop thinking about what is truly worthwhile and worthy of praise. You know the teachings I gave you, . . . So follow my example. And God, who gives peace, will be with you. (Philippians 4:8–9)

Cost of Discipleship

Berlin's leading psychiatrist and neurologist, Karl Bonhoeffer expected his son to take up a respectable profession such as science or the law. Instead, young Dietrich declared he wanted to be a theologian. When his family pointed out flaws in the German church, he replied, "In that case, I'll reform it."

He tried, but he came of age during the days of Adolf Hitler, who duped most German churchmen. "It is because of Hitler that Christ has become effective among us," said one minister. "National Socialism is positive Christianity in action." Bonhoeffer, opposing the Nazis with all his might, called the church to repentance. His outspokenness put him at risk; every day, every year, the crisis grew, and the tension deepened.

On Kristallnacht (Crystal Night), *November 9, 1938*, the Nazis unleashed their full fury against Jewish communities in Germany. Windows were shattered, houses stormed, synagogues burned, families brutalized, Jews imprisoned. Bonhoeffer, away from Berlin, raced back to the capital and stood like an intrepid prophet against the violence. He was furious with Christians who justified the violence by saying the Jews were reaping only what they deserved as the crucifiers of Christ. He marked the calamitous date alongside Psalm 74:7–8, which he underlined in his Bible.

He was eventually incarcerated at Telgel Prison outside Berlin. His six-by-nine-foot cell contained cot, shelf, stool, and bucket. Here he lived eighteen months, writing letters and poems. Some of them were addressed to Maria von Wedemeyer, his fiancée. They never married, and the letters he wrote to her were at Harvard University, sealed at her request until the year 2002.

Eventually Bonhoeffer was taken to Flossenburg Concentration Camp. As he led a small worship service on April 8, 1945, the Gestapo burst in and dragged him away. He cried, "This is the end—for me, the beginning of life." Shortly after five o'clock the next morning, he was taken to an execution site in a grove of trees and forced to strip. He knelt naked and prayed, then ascended the gallows to God.

They burned down your temple
and badly disgraced it.
They said to themselves,
"We'll crush them!"
Then they burned every one
of your meeting places
all over the country. (Psalm 74:7–8)

The Warrior

In 1942, a missionary to Malaysia named Paul Fleming contracted cerebral malaria and returned home. While recovering, he spent hours talking with pastor Cecil Dye about the need for reaching remote tribes for Christ. They formed an interdenominational agency named New Tribes Mission, and soon Dye, his brother, and three other men arrived with their families in Bolivia to establish a ministry among the Ayores, a wild tribe of Indians. Bolivians warned them of danger, but the men nonetheless moved their families into the heart of the jungle and established a base. From there the five plunged into the thicket in search of Ayores.

A month passed, and a search party set out along a rocky path over the hills. They found nothing but a cracked camera lens, a sock, a machete, and some other personal items. A second search found more effects at an abandoned Ayore site. Army troops prepared to invade the area in retribution for the apparent murders, but a mission representative stopped them, saying, "Don't go! We want to reach them for Christ."

Years passed, and the women moved deeper into Ayore territory, still hoping their husbands were alive. Then in 1948, a band of naked Indians appeared at the camp, took proffered gifts, and disappeared. Later they returned for more gifts and told the women their husbands were dead.

Gradually more details emerged: On *November 10, 1944*, the five missionaries had approached an Ayore village, creating great excitement. An impatient warrior had released an arrow, wounding one of them. Another missionary pulled out the arrow, and the five walked rapidly away. Upoide, an enraged warrior, led a band after the men, and one by one the missionaries were clubbed, speared, and killed.

The wives soon learned that it was Upoide himself who had approached their camp, telling the story. When he sensed the women would forgive him, he confessed his involvement, repented, and came to Christ. A permanent Christian settlement was soon established among the Ayores as a base for other missionary activity, and a fruitful ministry to South American aboriginals continues to this day.

The LORD is my strength,
the reason for my song,
because he has saved me.
I praise and honor the LORD—
he is my God
and the God
of my ancestors.
The LORD is his name,
and he is a warrior! (Exodus 15:2–3)

Imitating Christ

Thomas Hemerken, better known as Thomas of Kempen (Kempen being a German village forty miles from Cologne) or Thomas à Kempis, wrote the most famous devotional book in Christian history.

He was born about 1380, and his parents, though poor, managed to send him to Holland to be educated by the Brethren of the Common Life. The Brethren emphasized spiritual conversion, practical holiness, and meditation on Christ. These teachings hit a chord with the young student, and he became a deeply pondering disciple of the Lord Jesus. In 1399, Thomas, then about twenty years old, entered the Augustinian convent of Mount St. Agues, near Zwolle, Holland, and this became his home the rest of his life. There he preached, copied manuscripts, dispensed spiritual counsel, and wrote books until his death at age ninety. A monument was dedicated to his memory at St. Michael's Church in Zwolle on *November 11, 1897*.

Though Thomas's life was a quiet one, its echoes reverberate through history. His best-known work is *The Imitation of Christ*, originally a series of four books published anonymously (causing years of speculation about its author). *The Imitation* was widely popular, embraced by both Protestants and Catholics, and it reached its ninety-ninth printing by the end of the fifteenth century. Today it is known as one of the greatest devotional classics of all time. In terms of circulation it has reportedly been more widely distributed than any book in church history besides the Bible. Readers are challenged to deny themselves, embrace humility, and love God. Here is a sample:

> Strive to turn your heart from loving things that are seen, and to set it upon things that are not seen . . . How much better is a lowly peasant who serves God than a proud philosopher who watches the stars and neglects knowing himself . . . We must not trust every word of others or feeling within ourselves, but cautiously and patiently try the matter, whether it be of God. The more humble a man is in himself, and the more obedient toward God, the wiser will he be in all things, and the more shall his soul be at peace.

You have been raised to life with Christ. Now set your heart on what is in heaven, where Christ rules at God's right side. Think about what is up there, not about what is here on earth. You died, which means that your life is hidden with Christ, who sits beside God. (Colossians 3:1–3)

November 12 Pilgrim in the World

If *The Imitation of Christ* has a rival in sales, it is *The Pilgrim's Progress*, written by John Bunyan. On *November 12, 1660*, Bunyan left home to conduct a small worship service in a friend's house. Earlier that year King Charles II of England, Bible clutched to breast, had returned from exile to restore the monarchy and to return the Church of England to its position of authority. All non-Anglican houses of worship were closed, making Bunyan's preaching of the gospel now treasonous.

Arriving at the farmhouse, Bunyan learned that a warrant had been issued for his arrest. His friends urged flight. "No!" he replied. "I will not stir neither have the meeting dismissed. Let us not be daunted. To preach God's Word is so good a work that we shall be well rewarded if we suffer for that." The service was soon disrupted by the local constable, and Bunyan managed only a few parting words before being arrested. He spent the next twelve years imprisoned in Bedford, England, during which time his family suffered, and his beloved blind daughter, Mary, passed away.

Bunyan supported his family by making laces in prison; but shortly he discovered a hidden gift—the ability to write. His fame as an imprisoned writer fueled sales of his books, and he eventually wrote sixty volumes, one for every year he lived. His most famous work, written during the final phase of incarceration, is *The Pilgrim's Progress.* It sold one hundred thousand copies during Bunyan's lifetime and millions since. It joins *The Imitation of Christ* in being publishing history's top best seller, apart from Scripture.

Bunyan spent his final years in his little cottage in Bedford, where visitors often found him studying, his library consisting only of a Bible and some of his own works. On his deathbed, battling high fever, Bunyan rambled in tortured, fractured words, but even these were collected and published as *Mr. Bunyan's Dying Sayings.* They include this one: "The spirit of prayer is more precious than treasure of gold and silver. Pray often, for prayer is a shield to the soul, a sacrifice to God, and a scourge for Satan."

When people talk this way, it is clear that they are looking for a place to call their own. If they had been talking about the land where they had once lived, they could have gone back at any time. But they were looking forward to a better home in heaven. (Hebrews 11:14–16)

The Synod of Dort *November* 13

One of the things Christians disagree about is the importance of their disagreements, observed C. S. Lewis. Today many Calvinists and Arminians work hand in hand, but for hundreds of years they battled one another as bitterest foes.

The Arminians derive their name from Jacobus Arminius, who was born in the Dutch village of Oudewater in 1559 or 1560. He received a good education, but his studies at the University of Marburg were interrupted by tragedy. Spanish troops attacked his hometown of Oudewater, and Arminius, hearing the news, immediately returned home to find his family massacred.

He spent the next several years wandering through Europe, going from university to university, soaking up knowledge like a sponge. In 1587, he finally settled in Amsterdam, having been appointed a pastor there by city fathers. Arminius, who understood suffering better than most, made a good pastor. He visited the sick even during outbreaks of the plague, admonished the wayward, and counseled tolerance in theological matters. His sermons were powerful and popular.

After several years Arminius moved to Leiden to teach at the university, and there his six remaining years became embroiled in conflict with the prevailing interpretation given to Calvinism by Theodore Beza, Calvin's successor at Geneva. Beza hardened Calvin's belief that God decrees to save and damn certain individuals by his own sovereign pleasure. Arminius, worrying that Beza's position made God the author of sin, insisted that election to salvation is conditioned by faith. The controversy became so acute that the Dutch national assembly asked both sides to submit their positions in writing.

Arminius died before responding, but the controversy was just beginning. A war of pamphlets, books, and sermons so divided Holland that the national assembly convened the Synod of Dort, which began *November 13, 1618*. From the beginning the synod regarded the followers of Arminius as heretics, and on January 14, 1619, the Arminians were condemned. All two hundred Arminian pastors in Holland were thrown from office, and any who would not be silent were banished from the country. But the issue wasn't settled. Christians have been arguing these doctrines—and about their importance—ever since.

Peter said, "Turn back to God! Be baptized in the name of Jesus Christ, so that your sins will be forgiven. Then you will be given the Holy Spirit. This promise is for you and your children. It is for everyone our Lord God will choose, no matter where they live." (Acts 2:38–39)

Smiling Bill

Civil war erupted in the Congo (Zaire) in the 1960s, and among the missionaries caught in the crossfire was William McChesney with Worldwide Evangelization Crusade. Though only five foot two, 110 pounds, Bill had an outsized personality that radiated cheer wherever he went. His coworkers dubbed him Smiling Bill.

On *November 14, 1964*, suffering from malaria, Bill, twenty-eight years old, was seized by Congolese rebels. Ten days later he was beaten mercilessly, his clothing ripped off, and he was thrown into a filthy, crowded cell. Catholic priests gave him their garments, for he was shaking violently from malarial fever. The next day he was dragged from the cell and killed.

Before leaving for Africa, Bill had written a poem explaining his desire for overseas missions. It said, in part:

I want my breakfast served at eight,
With ham and eggs upon the plate;
A well-broiled steak I'll eat at one,
And dine again when day is done.

I want an ultramodern home
And in each room a telephone;
Soft carpets, too, upon the floors,
And pretty drapes to grace the doors.

I want my wardrobe, too, to be
Of neatest, finest quality,
With latest style in suit and vest:
Why should not Christians have the best?

But then the Master I can hear
In no uncertain voice, so clear:
"I bid you come and follow Me,
The lowly Man of Galilee."

If he be God, and died for me,
No sacrifice too great can be
For me, a mortal man, to make;
I'll do it all for Jesus' sake.

Yes, I will tread the path He trod,
No other way to please my God;
So, henceforth, this my choice shall be,
My choice for all eternity.

You cannot be my disciple unless you carry your own cross and come with me. (Luke 14:27)

His Utmost

Oswald Chambers wrote one of Christianity's greatest books, but he never knew it.

He had early displayed the gifts of an artist, and with his scholarship his future seemed assured to any of the leading art centers of Europe. But being won to Christ by Charles Spurgeon, he instead enrolled in Dunoon Bible Training College, telling his family, "Do not be sorry that I cannot go for a university curriculum, maybe I shall be best without it. I will to the limit of my power educate myself for His sake." He further explained in his diary: "From my childhood the persuasion has been that of a work strange and great, an experience deep and peculiar."

While at Dunoon Chambers heard Dr. F. B. Meyer speak about the Holy Spirit. He returned to his room feeling he knew nothing of spiritual power, and he was miserable. "Nothing but the grace of God and the kindness of friends kept me out of an asylum," he said. "I knew that if what I had was all the Christianity there was, the thing was a fraud."

Then he found a verse of scripture, Luke 11:13: "As bad as you are, you still know how to give good gifts to your children. But your heavenly Father is even more ready to give the Holy Spirit to anyone who asks."

"I claimed the gift of the Spirit in dogged committal on Luke 11:13," he said. "I had no vision of heaven or angels. I was dry and empty as ever, no power or realization of God. Then I was asked to speak at a meeting, and forty souls came to the front." Chambers had found a power and peace in ministry that impacted the world both during and after his life.

He died suddenly in Egypt on *November 15, 1917*, while serving British troops during World War I, and was buried in Cairo under a headstone bearing the words of Luke 11:13. Only later did his widow, Gertrude Hobbs, compile his manuscripts, notes, lectures, and sermons into the classic *My Utmost for His Highest*, a book that challenges Christians to this day.

Which one of you would give your child a scorpion if the child asked for an egg? As bad as you are, you still know how to give good gifts to your children. But your heavenly Father is even more ready to give the Holy Spirit to anyone who asks. (Luke 11:12–13)

The Legacy

On Sunday, *November 16, 1572*, Robert Fairley of Edinburgh didn't go home after church. The reformer John Knox lay dying nearby, and he went to see him. Fairley sat at a table near Knox's bed, both men sharing food and fellowship.

Fairley, longing to be the last to see the great reformer alive, followed Knox's illness. Sensing the end, he visited again on Thursday. Waiting until everyone else had left the room, he crept beside the dying man. Knox looked over and whispered, "I have been greatly indebted to you. I shall never be able to recompense you, but I commit you to One who is able to do it—to the Eternal God."

Fairley never forgot those words. He told his children. They told theirs. The story passed from generation to generation until young Marion Fairley was told, "Your great grandfather was committed in prayer to the Eternal God by his servant, John Knox." Moved by that legacy and by her father's preaching, Marion gave herself to Christ.

Marion grew up to marry godly William Veitch. One night soldiers burst in, carrying William to prison for his gospel preaching. "All the time the officers were in the house," Marion later wrote, "[The Lord] supported me so that I was not in the least discouraged before them."

Presently, news arrived that William was to be hanged. Marion rode horseback through a blinding January snowstorm to Morpeth jail, arriving at midnight. At daybreak she was given a few moments with her husband; "then I went to a friend's house and wept my fill." That day prosecutor Thomas Bell announced, "Veitch will hang tomorrow as he deserves."

But that evening prosecutor Bell tarried at a friend's house, drinking and talking until past ten. The night was dark and cold when he left for home. He never arrived. Two days later his body was found in the river, frozen up to his arms in solid ice.

William Veitch was released, and he and Marion lived to a ripe old age, passing their godly heritage on to their children and grandchildren.

These are things we learned
from our ancestors,
and we will tell them
to the next generation.
We won't keep secret
the glorious deeds
and the mighty miracles
of the LORD. (Psalm 78:3–4)

C. H. Mason

Charles H. Mason was born outside Memphis near the end of the Civil War to Jerry and Eliza Mason, freed slaves. Eliza prayed earnestly that her son would be dedicated to God. The child soaked up those prayers and was soon joining his mother at the throne of grace, asking for faith like that of the old slaves and of his parents.

When Charles was twelve years old, yellow fever broke out in the area. The Masons packed their scant belongings and quickly moved to Plumersville, Arkansas, where they became tenant farmers on a swampy plantation. The plague followed them, took Jerry's life, and wrapping its deadly tentacles around young Charles, laid him low with chills and fever. His death seemed certain. But early one Sunday morning "the glory of God appeared to Charles as never before," as his wife later put it. "Being instantly healed by the divine presence, [he] got out of bed and walked outside all by himself. There under the morning skies, he prayed and praised God for his healing. During these moments, [he] renewed his commitment to God." Meanwhile his mother, who had risen to check on him, was astonished to find his bed empty. She discovered him outdoors, trotting and skipping and shouting, "Glory to God! Hallelujah! Praise his holy name!"

Not surprisingly, C. H. Mason grew up to become a preacher, but his holiness message rankled fellow Baptists. One day while walking down a street in Little Rock pondering 1 Thessalonians 2:14, a name came to mind: the Church of God in Christ. Mason and the Baptists parted company, and he began organizing his like-minded brethren into a new group. Between 1897 and 1906, the fledgling organization grew in fits and starts. Then in 1907, at the Azusa Street Revival in Los Angeles, Mason received the baptism of the Holy Spirit. He returned home with dramatic zeal, and the young denomination was reorganized and enflamed.

The Church of God in Christ was the first major denomination to emerge from the ardor of Azusa Street, and by the time of Mason's death on *November 17, 1961*, it was among the largest Pentecostal denominations in America.

We always thank God that you believed the message we preached. It came from him, and it isn't something made up by humans. You accepted it as God's message, and now he is working in you. My friends, you did just like God's churches in Judea and like the other followers of Christ Jesus there. (1 Thessalonians 2:13–14)

The Lord Will Provide

Hudson Taylor established his China Inland Mission in 1865, on the premise that it would never solicit funds but simply trust God to supply its needs. While this policy may not be appropriate for every ministry, it provided Taylor with thousands of examples of God's faithfulness, like this one described in a letter on *November 18, 1857*:

> Many seem to think I am very poor. This is true enough in one sense, but I thank God it is "as poor, yet making many rich." My God shall supply all my needs; to him be the glory. I would not, if I could, be otherwise than I am—entirely dependent myself upon the Lord, and used as a channel of help to others.
>
> On Saturday we supplied, as usual, breakfast to the destitute poor, who came to the number of 70. Sometimes they do not reach 40, at other times exceeding 80. They come to us every day, Lord's Day excepted, for then we cannot manage to attend to them and get through all our other duties, too. Well, on that Saturday morning we paid all expenses, and provided ourselves for the morrow, after which we had not a single dollar left between us. How the Lord was going to provide for Monday we knew not; but over our mantelpiece hung two scrolls in the Chinese character—Ebenezer, "Hitherto hath the Lord helped us"; and Jehovah-Jireh, "The Lord will provide"—and he kept us from doubting for a moment. That very day the mail came in, a week sooner than was expected, and Mr. Jones received $214. We thanked God and took courage. On Monday the poor had their breakfast as usual, for we had not told them not to come, being assured that it was the Lord's work, and that the Lord would provide. We could not help our eyes filling with tears of gratitude when we saw not only our own needs supplied, but the widow and the orphan, the blind and the lame, the friendless and the destitute, together provided for by the bounty of him who feeds the ravens.

Don't worry and ask yourselves, "Will we have anything to eat? Will we have anything to drink? Will we have any clothes to wear?" Only people who don't know God are always worrying about such things. Your Father in heaven knows that you need all these. But more than anything else, put God's work first and do what he wants. Then the other things will be yours as well. (Matthew 6:31–33)

Silenced

Who was the greatest English preacher of them all? Some claim that distinction for seventeenth-century British Puritan Richard Baxter. And yet for ten of his best years, Baxter's voice was stilled, his sermons silenced, and his pulpit empty.

Baxter's life spanned the seventeenth century. He was born in 1615 and lived during the churning days of England's Civil War, the beheading of King Charles I, and the Commonwealth under Cromwell. The Puritans, at the heart of these events, found the political tide turning against them in 1660. Charles II restored the monarchy and shortly afterward Baxter (forty-five years old at the time) and two thousand other Puritan preachers were ejected from their pulpits. Baxter was arrested, spent several spells in prison, lost most of his possessions, and suffered repeatedly from various illnesses, including a constant cough, frequent nosebleeds, migraine headaches, digestive ailments, kidney stones, gallstones, and an ongoing battle with tuberculosis.

For ten years Baxter was away from his pulpit, unable to legally proclaim the Word of God. But he was a man of prayer, and from his sufferings came some of the most powerful books ever written, including the *Saints' Everlasting Rest, The Reformed Pastor*—and 138 others!

Finally his exile ended. We read in his diary about *November 19, 1672*: "The 19th of November was the first day, after ten years' silence, that I preached in a tolerated public assembly, though not yet tolerated in any consecrated church, but only, against law, in my own house."

If only tape recorders had been invented—to have heard Baxter's powerful voice after ten years of pent-up prayer, meditation, study, and passion! "Study hard," Baxter once wrote, "for the well of spiritual knowledge is deep, and our brains are shallow."

Baxter studied hard and labored tirelessly until he passed to the saints' everlasting rest in 1691 at age seventy-six.

Everything in the Scriptures is God's Word. All of it is useful for teaching and helping people and for correcting them and showing them how to live. The Scriptures train God's servants to do all kinds of good deeds . . . I command you to preach God's message. (2 Timothy 3:16—4:2)

November 20

A Doctor's Vow

On *November 20, 1759*, the *Arundel* approached an unknown ship in the waters off the West Indies. The tense, tanned sailors stood by their guns as Captain Charles Middleton sent a boarding party to investigate. The *Swift* proved to be a slaver bound for Guinea. It carried the plague.

Middleton summoned his surgeon, James Ramsay, a young man he had led to Christ. The doctor clambered aboard the *Swift* and reeled in horror. The holds were jammed with naked slaves, chained row upon row, writhing and groaning and sweating and dying of the plague. The stench was unbearable, the filth unbelievable. Ramsay left the *Swift*, vowing to do his utmost for slaves.

Shortly afterward he retired from naval service and became pastor on the West Indies island of St. Kitts. He purchased ten slaves from tyrants, and Ramsay became their servant, teaching them Scripture and treating them medically. His hatred of slavery grew as he visited nearby plantations, treating wounds inflicted by whips and branding irons. Owners threatened him when he advocated humane treatment of slaves, and when Ramsay called for the abolition of slavery, he was attacked in the local papers, censured by the citizens, and driven from the island.

Ramsay took a pastorate in the English countryside of Kent. Though only forty-eight years old, he looked old and drawn. Day and night the cries of slaves haunted him, and the memories of November 20, 1759, never left him. He put his feelings into print and braced himself for another storm. It came, but this time he had an ally—his old captain, Charles Middleton, now a member of Parliament. Middleton joined Ramsay's crusade but looked around for a younger more eloquent member of Parliament to be leader. He chose William Wilberforce.

Wilberforce's lifelong crusade to abolish slavery in Britain is well known. But few remember that it can be traced back to a quiet Christian doctor who made a vow on a November's day in 1759.

Jesus went back to Nazareth, . . . and went to the meeting place on the Sabbath. When he stood up to read from the Scriptures, he was given the book of Isaiah the prophet. He opened it and read,

"The Lord's Spirit
has come to me,
because he has chosen me
to tell the good news
to the poor.
The Lord has sent me
to announce freedom
for prisoners." (Luke 4:16–18)

Vatican II

Torrential rains trailed off by nine o'clock, and the morning sun blazed down on twenty-five hundred white-clad Roman Catholic bishops as they wound through St. Peter's Square for the historic opening of the Second Vatican Council. It was October 11, 1962. Pope John XXIII, who convened the council, had been elected pope at age seventy-seven, and few had expected a dramatic tenure. Instead, he had surprised everyone by calling this council, attributing the idea to a sudden inspiration of the Holy Spirit.

As the bishops found their places in the basilica, the old man slowly rose to speak. He reminded his audience that the church now lives in a modern age. Though the "deposit of faith" is unchanging, how it is presented is another matter. Forms, methods, and attitudes must be updated.

For the next three years the bishops thought and debated and agonized and prayed. Lines were drawn between Conservatives and Progressives. Pope John died on June 3, 1963; but Paul VI, his successor, carried on. In the end, sixteen documents were overwhelmingly adopted. Catholic liturgy was simplified, with permission given to celebrate the rites of the church in the languages of the peoples rather than in Latin. More scripture was to be used, with greater participation by worshippers. Biblical exposition and congregational singing were encouraged. A new emphasis on freedom became an overarching theme of the council.

Equally important the attitude of Catholics toward other Christian bodies shifted. In calling Vatican II, Pope John had dreamed of dialogue and fellowship with the "separated brethren" of East and West, of a new unity in Christendom. *November 21, 1964*, was the solemn close of the third session, and three documents were approved on that day, including the Decree of Ecumenism, adopted by the council by a vote of 2,137 to 11. It declared that both Catholics and Protestants share blame for divisions in the church, and it extolled the growth of the ecumenical movement. Dialogue with other Christian groups should replace suspicion and competition, said the decree.

While no basic doctrines were revised at Vatican II, the changes made in attitudes and approaches changed the Catholic Church forever.

But a time is coming, and it is already here! Even now the true worshippers are being led by the Spirit to worship the Father according to the truth. These are the ones the Father is seeking to worship him. God is Spirit, and those who worship God must be led by the Spirit to worship him according to the truth. (John 4:23–24)

Sea Billows

In November 1873, Chicago lawyer Horatio G. Spafford took his wife and four daughters, Maggie, Tanetta, Annie, and Bessie, to New York and boarded them on the luxurious French liner, SS *Ville du Havre.* The Great Chicago Fire had destroyed everything they owned, and Spafford was sending his girls to an English academy until the Chicago schools—and his own life—could be rebuilt. As he saw his family settled into their cabin, an unease filled his mind, and he moved them to a room closer to the bow of the ship. Then he said good-bye, promising to join them later in France.

During the small hours of *November 22, 1873*, as the *Ville du Havre* glided over smooth seas, the passengers were suddenly thrown from their bunks in a jolt. The ship had collided with an iron sailing vessel, the *Lochearn.* Water poured in like Niagara, and the *Ville du Havre* tilted dangerously. Screams and prayers and oaths merged into a nightmare of unmeasured terror. Passengers, losing their footing, clung to posts, tumbled through darkness, and were drenched by powerful currents of icy, inrushing sea. Loved ones fell from each other's grasps and vanished into foaming blackness. Within two hours the mighty ship disappeared beneath the nocturnal waters. The 226 fatalities included Maggie, Tanetta, Annie, and Bessie. Mrs. Spafford was found nearly unconscious, clinging to a piece of the wreckage. Nine days later when the survivors landed in Cardiff, Wales, she cabled her husband: "Saved alone."

He immediately booked passage to join his wife. On the way over on a cold December night, the captain called him aside and said, "I believe we are now passing over the place where the *Ville du Havre* went down." Spafford went to his cabin but found it hard to sleep. He said to himself, "It is well; the will of God be done," and later wrote his famous hymn based on those words:

When sorrows like sea billows roll,
Whatever my lot, Thou hast taught me to say,
It is well, it is well with my soul.

Your vicious waves
have swept over me
like an angry ocean
or a roaring waterfall.
Every day, you are kind,
and at night
you give me a song
as my prayer to you,
the living LORD God. (Psalm 42:7–8)

Short, Sick, and Spectacular

His was a short, sick, spectacular life. He died before reaching forty, yet not before leaving an enduring mark. Blaise Pascal, born in France in 1623, was educated in Paris and started making contributions to geometry, physics, and mathematics at age sixteen. His fame and wealth accumulated quickly as did his religious inclinations. In January 1646, his father fell and broke his leg. His nurses were devout Catholics, and Pascal, after extended conversations with them, began taking his Catholic faith seriously. His reputation in the Paris scientific community grew by leaps, and the more he studied nature, the more evidence he saw of the Creator. On *November 23, 1654*, while reading John 17, he personally encountered Jesus Christ and jotted his impressions on a parchment: "From about half-past ten in the evening until about half-past twelve, *fire*! God of Abraham, God of Isaac, God of Jacob, not of the philosophers and scholars. Certitude. Feelings. Joy. Peace. This is eternal life, that they might know thee, the only true God, and the one whom Thou hast sent, Jesus Christ."

Pascal sewed the paper inside his coat lining and often in moments of temptation slipped his hand over it to press its message into his heart. His life changed, and he began giving much of his money to the poor. His scientific studies, world famous to this day, became second to his spiritual pursuits.

His books display great craftsmanship of words, and even the infidel Voltaire remarked that Pascal's writings were the first work of genius to appear in France. He became France's Shakespeare, its Dante, its Plato, its Euclid. He designed the world's first calculator and the first bus service and paved the way for the invention of the barometer and the theories of probability.

As his health failed, Pascal wanted to leave behind a final work, a defense of the Christian faith, challenging atheists and agnostics with the evidences for Christianity. He began making notes, but his headaches worsened. He died, leaving some one thousand fragments that were soon assembled into one of the classics of Christian literature, the *Pensées*.

God has also said that he gave us eternal life and that this life comes to us from his Son. And so, if we have God's Son, we have this life. But if we don't have the Son, we don't have this life. (1 John 5:11–12)

The Bifocals of Faith

Perhaps it was his Scottish accent. Perhaps his playful smile. Perhaps the simplicity of his preaching, or maybe it was his prayers with their pungent twists of boldness. For whatever reason Peter Marshall is remembered as one of the most beloved Senate chaplains in American history.

Marshall immigrated to the United States, arriving at Ellis Island in 1927, only nineteen years before being named Senate chaplain. He pastored in Georgia, then at Washington's New York Avenue Presbyterian Church. On January 5, 1947, he was named Senate chaplain, and his prayers immediately touched the nation.

Here is his Bifocals of Faith prayer, offered before the United States Senate on *November 24, 1947:*

> God of our fathers and our God, give us the faith to believe in the ultimate triumph of righteousness, no matter how dark and uncertain are the skies of today.
>
> We pray for the bifocals of faith—that see the despair and the need of the hour but also see, further on, the patience of our God working out his plan in the world he has made.
>
> So help thy servants to interpret for our time the meaning of the motto inscribed on our coins. Make our faith honest by helping us this day to do one thing because thou hast said, "Do it," or to abstain because thou hast said, "Thou shalt not."
>
> How can we say we believe in thee, or even want to believe in thee, when we do not anything thou dost tell us? May our faith be seen in our works. Through Jesus Christ our Lord. Amen.*

Just over a year later Peter Marshall, forty-six years old, was rushed to the hospital with severe pain in his chest and arms. A massive heart attack took his life, and the entire nation mourned his death. But his prayers, sermons, and life have been immortalized in Christian literature through the efforts of his wife and biographer, Catherine Marshall.

When you pray, don't talk on and on as people who don't know God. They think God likes to hear long prayers. Don't be like them. Your Father knows what you need before you ask. You should pray like this:

> Our Father in heaven,
> help us to honor
> your name. (Matthew 6:7–9)

---

*Catherine Marshall, *The Prayers of Peter Marshall* (New York: McGraw-Hill Book Company, 1949), p. 188.

White Blood?

The truth of the Bible is hard and clear as diamonds, providing a solid basis for both life and death. "You can't argue with the Scriptures," Jesus said in John 10:35. But you *can* argue with some of the legends and half-truths of church history. Take, for example, the remarkable story of Saint Catherine of Alexandria.

Born in the third century to a noble Christian family in Alexandria, the beautiful Catherine gave herself to Christ and refused to sacrifice to pagan gods. Emperor Maxentius, lusting after her, offered her pardon if she would sleep with him. She refused, saying she was the bride of Christ. Hoping to dissuade her, Maxentius summoned fifty brilliant scholars to debate her. She conquered all of them, winning all fifty to the Christian faith. They paid for their conversions by being burned alive, compliments of the emperor.

Catherine, meanwhile, converted the emperor's wife, his top general, and two hundred of his best troops. These, too, were immediately executed. Maxentius, enraged, ordered Catherine attached to a spiked wheel to be tortured and broken. When the wheel fell apart, Maxentius demanded the executioner behead her. Milk rather than blood flowed from her severed neck.

The virgin martyr became one of the most venerated women of antiquity, and *November 25* was appointed Catherine's feast day on the church calendar. She was admired and adored without measure by medieval worshippers, becoming the patron saint of young women, wheelwrights, attorneys, and scholars.

But how much of her story is true? Perhaps not much. Behind the legends there may have been a beautiful martyr whose full story is known only in heaven. But the earliest mention of Catherine dates from the ninth century, when her bones were reportedly transferred to the monastery of Mount Sinai, and the earliest biographies of her date from the tenth century. Though she was among the greatest heroes to the masses of the Middle Ages, there is scant evidence that Catherine of Alexandria ever existed.

Warn them to stop wasting their time on senseless stories and endless lists of ancestors . . . You must teach people to have genuine love, as well as a good conscience and true faith. There are some who have given up these for nothing but empty talk. (1 Timothy 1:4–6)

A Tiny Spark

The power of simple words is immense, as James 3:5 (NIV) indicates: "Consider what a great forest is set on fire by a small spark." Never was this truer than on *November 26, 1095*, the date of the most effective sermon ever preached by pope, preacher, or prince. It was Pope Urban II's sermon in Clermont, France, launching the Crusades.

For many years the Christian world had fretted over the capture of Palestine by the Muslim Turks. Finally Pope Urban addressed the subject at the church council in Clermont. He spoke in an open field to both clerics and the general public, passionately describing how the Turks, an "accursed race," had devastated the kingdom of God by fire, pillage, and sword. Jerusalem, the "navel of the world," was laid waste. Antioch was ruined. The Holy Land was in the hands of barbarians. It must be liberated.

The crowd, whipped into a frenzy, began chanting, "God wills it! God wills it!" Urban II replied, "It *is* the will of God. Let these words be your war cry when you unsheathe the sword. You are soldiers of the cross. Wear on your breasts or shoulders the blood-red sign of the cross."

Thousands immedately sewed the cross on their clothing or had it branded with flaming irons to bare skin. The fervor swept across the Continent. A new era in European history began as the crusading passion, inspired by its pope, took hold of its people. The era of the Crusades stretched from 1096 to 1291, and in the light of history is seen as a horrible mistake. The kingdom of God cannot be furthered militarily. The Crusades, only partially and temporarily successful in "liberating" Palestine, produced two hundred years of abuses, excesses, deaths, diseases, violence, cruelty, and reproach.

It takes only a spark to start a forest fire! The tongue is like a spark. It is an evil power that dirties the rest of the body and sets a person's entire life on fire with flames that come from hell itself. All kinds of animals, birds, reptiles, and sea creatures can be tamed and have been tamed. But our tongues get out of control. (James 3:5–8)

Tuan Change

Earnest Presswood was born on the Canadian prairie in 1908, and came to Christ in a Sunday school class at age eleven. Later, under the preaching of Gipsy Smith, he surrendered to Christian service. He enrolled in the Christian and Missionary Alliance Institute at Nyack, New York, and by 1930, he was in Borneo.

Rumors of the young white man whose message could turn evil men into good ones, drunken men into sober ones, and violent men into men of God soon flew across the island. Islanders called him Tuan Change because his message changed lives. "When I heard," said one man, "I could not sleep for desire. We all went to meet him. He preached the Resurrection. Right from the beginning it hit me. I was drinking it in. When I first heard I believed."

Ernie, twenty-five years old, crisscrossed mountain trails to remote villages. His feet became ulcerated by leech bites, but his passion was relentless. "What a time I have had," he wrote after one tour. "Physically it has been hard, but the results have been glorious. Around 600 were reached with the message." Another time he wrote, "From early morning till late at night I have kept busy with scarcely a break. Pray for me for the strain is very great. I have baptized 130, and I expect at least twice as many more."

Returning to America on furlough, Ernie fell in love with Laura Harmon, married her, and took her back to Borneo. She died suffering a miscarriage, and Ernie buried her in a coffin made with timbers from the house they were building. Then he pressed on, alone again.

His service was disrupted between 1940 and 1945 by war in the South Pacific. For five years Ernie wondered and worried about his suffering flock. On *November 27, 1945*, when he returned, he found the graves of many Christians, but the church in Borneo was triumphant. By now Ernie was old beyond his thirty-eight years, and he died three months later of pneumonia after a rafting accident—having planted a church and reaped a harvest that thrives to this day.

The LORD forgives our sins,
heals us when we are sick,
and protects us from death.
His kindness and love
are a crown on our heads.
Each day that we live, he provides for our needs
and gives us the strength
of a young eagle. (Psalm 103:3–5)

A One-Year Ministry

Hugh MacKail was a bright young man who preached the outlawed Reformation truth in Scotland—but not for long. He was licensed to preach at age twenty and preached his last message at twenty-one, saying, "The people of God have been persecuted sometimes by an Ahab on the throne, sometimes by a Haman in the state, and sometimes by a Judas in the church."

That very day Scottish authorities—"Ahab, Haman, and Judas"—came after him, forcing him to flee for safety. His capture was inevitable, and his trial occurred on *November 28, 1666.* When he refused to recant, he was affixed in a chair, with a tight iron boot enclosed around his leg and knee. An iron wedge was inserted, and a jailer stood by with a sledgehammer, awaiting his orders. A surgeon sat near, his thumb on the young man's pulse. The judge nodded. The jailer gripped the mallet, took aim, and slammed it down on the wedge. Bone and muscle were crushed. A second blow. A third. Blood ran down Hugh's leg and dripped from his toes. More blasts of pain. The eleven blows crushed Hugh's leg to pulp. Radiating waves of agony surged through every inch of his body. Rough hands then jerked him from his chair and threw him into the dungeon.

Some days later, asked how his leg felt, Hugh smiled dismally and said he had stopped worrying about his leg and started worrying about his neck. He had reason. He was shortly taken to the gallows and forced to climb a ladder to the platform. A large crowd gathered, and MacKail, raising his voice, said, "I care no more to go up this ladder than if I were going home to my father's house." He awkwardly dragged his useless leg up the rungs, turning and saying, "Every step is a degree nearer heaven." At the top he took out his pocket Bible, read from its last chapter, and spoke of Christ. The rope tightened around his thin neck, his boyish smile faded from earth, and his feet danced in the air until his soul ascended to God.

I am coming soon! And when I come, I will reward everyone for what they have done. I am Alpha and Omega, the first and the last, the beginning and the end. God will bless all who have washed their robes. They will each have the right to eat fruit from the tree that gives life, and they can enter the gates of the city. (Revelation 22:12–14)

A Good One, Too

When James Gilmore sailed for China in 1870, he was young, strong, and in need of a wife. He plunged into reopening the London Missionary Society's work in Mongolia, but with no one to lean on. "Companions I can scarcely hope to meet," he wrote, "and the feeling of being alone comes over me." As labors increased, so did loneliness. "Today I felt a good deal like Elijah in the wilderness," he told his journal. "He prayed that he might die . . . I felt drawn towards suicide. Two missionaries should always go together. Oh! the intense loneliness."

The pain deepened when his proposal to a Scottish girl was rejected. "I then put myself and the direction of this affair—I mean the finding of a wife—into God's hands, asking him to look me out one, a good one, too."

In 1873, Gilmore visited friends in Peking, a Mr. and Mrs. Meech. Seeing a picture of Mrs. Meech's sister, Emily Prankard, James asked about her. As his hostess described Emily, James found himself falling in love. He gazed at her picture, saw some of her letters, and asked more and more questions.

Early the next year James wrote to Emily, proposing marriage in his first letter. By the same mail he informed his parents in Scotland: "I have written and proposed to a girl in England. It is true I have never seen her, and I know very little about her; but I have put the whole matter into the hands of God, asking him, if it be best, to bring her, if it be not best, to keep her away, and he can manage the whole thing well."

Receiving Gilmore's letter, Emily took it at once to the throne of grace. Later Gilmore recalled, "The first letter I wrote her was to propose, and the first letter she wrote me was to accept." By autumn Emily was in China, arriving on this day, *November 29, 1874*. A week later they were married. Gilmore acquired both wife and colleague, and they labored faithfully side by side for years, reaching northern China for Christ.

"A man's greatest treasure is his wife," says Proverbs 18:22. "She is a gift from the LORD."

A truly good wife is the most precious treasure
a man can find!
Her husband depends on her,
and she never lets him down.
She is good to him
every day of her life. (Proverbs 31:10–12)

November 30

Forlorn Hope

John Clough was called to the harvest field while working in one. He had grown up without religious inclinations, and in college seemed resistant to evangelistic efforts by friends. His roommate tried to read the Bible and pray with him each evening, but John, growing exasperated, drew a chalk line down the middle of the room, forbidding prayer or Scripture on his side of the line.

But the Holy Spirit worked on his heart, and one evening, unable to study and overwhelmed with his need, he crossed the line and knelt by his roommate. Shortly after, hearing a missionary sermon, John wondered if God would have him overseas, and he applied. He was atop a four-horse reaper breaking off grain when a farmhand approached him with a letter from Boston. Clough wiped away his sweat and tore open the news from the Baptist Foreign Mission Board. "What do you know!" he shouted. "They want me to go to India as a missionary!"

Missions officials wanted to send him to "Forlorn Hope"—Telugu, India—where seventeen years of painful, plodding effort had produced no apparent results. On *November 30, 1864*, Clough and his wife sailed from Boston on a tiny ship, hardly seaworthy, called the *James Guthrie.* It rolled and pitched its way across the ocean, finally limping into India the following April. John, leaping into service, was immediately confronted with a dilemma. The higher caste of Indians refused to attend church with the lower caste and outcasts. Praying for wisdom, Clough randomly opened his Bible and read in 1 Corinthians 1:26–29 of God choosing the lowly. Across the room at the same moment, his wife randomly opened her Bible to the same place. Clough, amazed, took it as divine guidance. He announced that all were welcome in his church, that he would not accept a segregated congregation.

He started preaching, and conversions multiplied. Fifteen months later two Indian preachers stood in a river and began baptizing the converts. When they grew weary, other preachers relieved them. By five o'clock 2,222 had been baptized, and the baptisms continued for two more days.

My friends, if you have faith in our glorious Lord Jesus Christ, you won't treat some people better than others . . . God has given a lot of faith to the poor people in this world. He has also promised them a share in his kingdom that he will give to everyone who loves him. (James 2:1, 5)

On This Day in Christian History...

DECEMBER

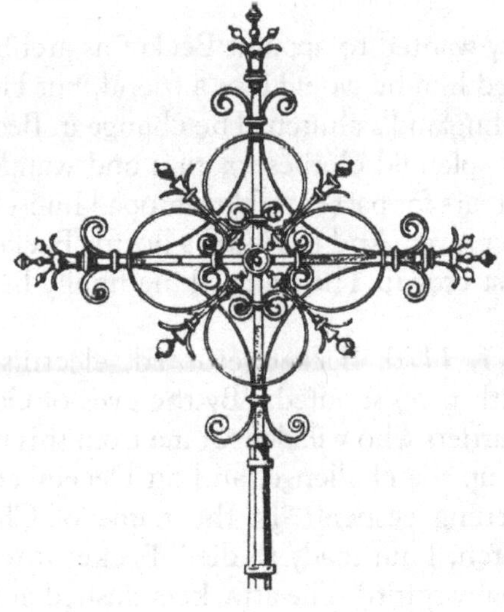

Thunderstorm over Canterbury

Henry II was among England's most remarkable kings, forceful and brilliant. But he is best known for his quarrel with close friend Thomas Becket. Becket was born in London in 1118. His father was a crusader, his mother a princess. He was Henry's equal in appearance—handsome, tall, commanding, affable, athletic, and alert. Henry appointed Becket, age thirty-seven, chancellor of England, the highest civil post in the land, and for seven years Becket lived in splendor, traveled in style, and ruled in power. He became *de facto* king, Henry's closest ally.

In 1162, Henry wanted to appoint Becket as archbishop of Canterbury. Becket warned him he would lose a friend, but Henry nonetheless made him head of England's church. The change in Becket was immediate. He traded his splendid clothes for rags and wandered through his cloisters shedding tears for past sins. He whipped himself, read the Bible, and spent hours in prayer. And to Henry's horror Becket endlessly sided with church against crown. The frantic king finally banished him from the country.

On *December 1, 1170*, Becket returned, electrifying all England. Henry, foaming with rage, shouted, "By the eyes of God, is there none of my cowardly courtiers who will deliver me from this turbulent priest?" Four knights took up the challenge, and on December 29, they fell on Becket during evening vespers. "In the name of Christ and for the defense of his church, I am ready to die," Becket uttered as the blows fell. "Lord, receive my spirit." The attackers slashed at his head, spilling his blood and brains on the floor. A violent thunderstorm broke over the cathedral.

The Christian world reeled with horror, and Henry saw the tide turn against him. Walking through Canterbury's streets with bleeding feet, he entered the cathedral, kissed the spot where Becket had died, and placed his head and shoulders on Becket's tomb. There he was flogged by the priests. But the rest of his days were calamitous, and he died broken in spirit, cursing his life.

Controlling your temper
is better than being a hero
who captures a city.
We make our own decisions,
but the LORD alone
determines what happens. (Proverbs 16:32–33)

Consecrated, Lord, to Thee

Frances Ridley Havergal received Christ at a young age but struggled for years with Christian victory. "I had hoped that a kind of tableland had been reached in my journey, where I might walk awhile in the light, without the weary succession of rock and hollow, crag and morass, stumbling and striving; but I seem borne back into all the old difficulties of the way, with many sin-made aggravations. I think the great root of my trouble and alienation is that I do not make an unreserved surrender of myself to God; until this is done I shall know no peace. I am sure of it."

She struggled throughout her twenties and thirties, pulled in one direction by the acclaim of great London crowds who loved her singing and in another direction by the Holy Spirit. Then one day, at age thirty-six, she read a booklet entitled *All For Jesus*, which stressed the importance of making Christ King of every corner and cubicle of one's life. Frances made a fresh, complete consecration to God. Years later her sister asked her about it, and she replied: "Yes, it was on Advent Sunday, *December 2, 1873*, I first saw clearly the blessedness of true consecration. I saw it as a flash of electric light. There must be full surrender before there can be full blessedness. God admits you by the one into the other. He showed me this most clearly."

Shortly after, Frances found herself spending several days with ten people, some of them unconverted and others of them Christians not fully surrendered. "Lord," she prayed, "give me all in this house." Before she left, all ten were yielded Christians. On the last night of her visit, Frances, too excited to sleep, wrote her "Consecration Hymn," the song that became her life's theme. She took its words seriously and prayed earnestly over them every December 2 making changes to her life and lifestyle as needed. The first verse says:

Take my life and let it be,
Consecrated, Lord, to Thee,
Take my hands and let them move
At the impulse of Thy love.

I have been nailed to the cross with Christ. I have died, but Christ lives in me. And I now live by faith in the Son of God, who loved me and gave his life for me. (Galatians 2:19–20)

December 3 The Power of a Hero

Never underestimate the influence of your child's heroes. Sixteen-year-old Francis Xavier moved to France from northern Spain, enrolled in the University of Paris, and gained a reputation for being "charming, witty, urbane, athletic, musical, good-looking, successful with women, and somewhat vain . . . a complete worldling until one day he met . . . Ignatius Loyola."* Loyola sought reformation within the Roman church. Loyola's convictions so affected Francis that for the rest of his life he knelt when writing to Loyola or reading a reply. Together the two men established the Society of Jesus—the Jesuits—in 1534.

In the late 1530s, Loyola and Xavier set off as ministers to Venice, where they preached and worked in hospitals. Then with the blessing of Pope John III, Xavier left Europe as a missionary to the Orient. Arriving in India in 1542, he walked throughout the countryside, wearing poor clothing, incessantly ringing a little bell, and calling the inhabitants to turn from paganism to Christ. He focused on the children, advising a coworker, "I earnestly recommend to you the teaching of the children . . . since the grown-ups have no hankering for Paradise."

Xavier journeyed on to Japan, where he laid aside his rags, put on expensive clothing, and publicly debated Buddhist monks. Numbers of Japanese entered the Christian faith, but Xavier felt that the key to winning Japan was to first win the Chinese, so he set off for China. Waiting for an audience with the Chinese emperor and permission to preach, Xavier developed a fever, weakened, and died on *December 3, 1552*.

Francis Xavier is the father of modern Catholic missions. He started life spoiled but became one of the most courageous figures in missionary history. He laid the groundwork for the Catholic evangelism of the Orient and did it all in just a ten-year period.

Such is the power of a hero.

Wise friends make you wise,
but you hurt yourself
by going around with fools.
You are in for trouble if you sin,
but you will be rewarded
if you live right. (Proverbs 13:20–21)

*Robert D. Linder, "Francis Xavier," in *Great Leaders of the Christian Church*, ed. John D. Woodbridge (Chicago: Moody Press, 1988), p. 234.

Last of the Greek Fathers

About six hundred years after the apostle Paul was converted in Damascus, a boy was born there named John Mansour. Damascus was by then ruled by the Muslims, but John's father, the treasurer of Caliph Abdulmeled, was a Christian who represented church interests before the court. John became a Christian himself and was educated by an Italian monk whom his father had ransomed from slavery. He excelled in academics, and upon the death of his father, he was appointed by the caliph to high position.

In time, however, John felt the Lord calling him to the ministry. He left Damascus and settled in the Convent of St. Sabas between Jerusalem and the Dead Sea. There he became a priest and spent out his days in study, writing, and humble tasks. His feast day is *December 4*.

John vigorously defended the Eastern church's practice of worshipping icons and images. But he is most famous for his encyclopedic summary of theology. He systematized Greek theology much as Thomas Aquinas summarized and systematized Latin doctrine five hundred years later. "Like a bee," he wrote, "I gather all that conforms to the truth . . . I am not offering my own conclusions, but those which were laboriously arrived at by the most eminent theologians. I have merely collected them and summarized them, as far as was possible in one treatise."

John also wrote hymns, and those who take time to thumb through old hymnals find his great resurrection hymn, *Come, Ye Faithful*, now fourteen hundred years old. Its words still paint beautiful pictures in our minds:

'Tis the spring of souls today, Christ hath burst his prison,
And from three days' sleep in death as a sun hath risen.
All the winter of our sins, long and dark is flying
From his light, to whom we give laud and praise undying.

Alleluia! now we cry to our King Immortal
Who, triumphant, burst the bars of the tomb's dark portal;
Alleluia! with the Son, God the Father praising,
Alleluia! yet again to the Spirit raising.

Christ has been raised to life! And he makes us certain that others will also be raised to life. Just as we will die because of Adam, we will be raised to life because of Christ. (1 Corinthians 15:20–21)

December 5 — Peace and Quiet

St. Sabas was born in 439, to parents who didn't want him. His father, an army officer, traveled widely, taking the boy's mother with him. Sabas was entrusted to an uncle who mistreated him. He ran away twice and at age ten sought peace and quiet in a monastery. There he learned of the Lord.

Ten years later the young man traveled to Jerusalem, intrigued by reports of religious hermits and monks who lived in the Palestinian deserts. The ascetic St. Euthymius became his mentor but refused his requests for total solitude. When Sabas reached age thirty, he again begged Euthymius for a life of silence. This time he was allowed to spend five days a week in a remote cave in prayer and manual labor. Every Sunday night Sabas would leave the monastery carrying bundles of palm twigs, and every Saturday morning he would return with fifty baskets he had made.

When Euthymius died, Sabas retired into a cave near the brook Cedron. He lived there, totally separated from human interaction, for years. But at length pilgrims began disturbing him, coming for counsel, wanting to become his disciples. Sabas consented at last and formed a community of ascetics. Soon one hundred hermits were cloistered together. Sabas, by then fifty-three years old, was ordained a priest. Hospitals and inns were built, and benevolent ministries were established. In 493, the patriarch of Jerusalem appointed Sabas head of all the hermits of Palestine.

Sabas found himself in demand from his own monks and by the church at large. Several heresies were threatening, and Sabas became a powerful advocate for orthodoxy. He journeyed to Constantinople to instruct the emperor on doctrinal matters, and he traveled widely preaching the faith and defending orthodoxy.

He was ninety-one when he made his last journey to Constantinople to intervene with the emperor about political repression in Palestine. His mission was successful, and he returned to his community of monks, where he fell sick and asked for peace and quiet. He lingered four days, then died on *December 5, 532*, at age ninety-four.

"In the desert someone is shouting, 'Get the road ready for the Lord! Make a straight path for him. Fill up every valley and level every mountain and hill. Straighten the crooked paths and smooth out the rough roads. Then everyone will see the saving power of God.'" (Luke 3:4–6)

The Dumb Ox

Potential is hard to spot. Who would have thought, for example, that a quiet, overweight, lumbering boy nicknamed "the Dumb Ox" would become the greatest theologian of the Middle Ages and establish the theology of Catholicism for centuries to come?

Thomas Aquinas, born a noble about 1225, enrolled in the University of Naples at age fourteen. His family encouraged him to pursue church office, but they were horrified when he renounced the prestige of ecclesiastical rank for a Dominican vow of poverty. His siblings kidnapped him, and he was imprisoned fifteen months by his family. His brothers tempted him with money and even hired a prostitute to corrupt him. Thomas escaped through a window and fled to Paris, where he sat under the great teacher Albertus Magnus.

Two intellectual forces were colliding in the classrooms of the day. The first was traditional theology; the other was Aristotle and other non-Christian writers, such as Averroes and Avicenna, the Muslims. The philosophers' emphasis on reason seemed to undercut the theologians' emphasis on faith. Thomas determined to bridge the two. All truth is coherent, he believed. The author of creation is the author of Scripture; thus, true fact and true faith never conflict. Yet reason alone would be insufficient. Revelation, theology, and the doctrines of faith show us the Triune God in greater detail.

Thomas's towering intellect was accompanied by pulpit prowess. He would sometimes have to pause in mid-sermon, giving congregations time to recover from their weeping. Even more intense was his prayer life. "Every time he wanted to study, discuss, teach, write, or dictate," said a friend, "he first had recourse to the privacy of prayer, weeping before God to discover the divine secrets."

On *December 6, 1273*, while conducting mass in the Chapel of St. Nicholas, a tremendous mystical experience broke over him. Thomas never again wrote theology. "I can do no more," he told his servant. "Such things have been revealed to me that all that I have written seems to me as so much straw. Now I await the end of my life."

But God has given us his Spirit. That's why we don't think the same way that the people of this world think. That's also why we can recognize the blessings that God has given us. (1 Corinthians 2:12)

December 7 "... And My House"

James Taylor, eighteenth-century English villager, hated Wesley's circuit riders, viewing them as nothing but targets for his rotten eggs. But one day as he readied his missiles one of the preachers quoted Joshua 24:15: "As for me and my house, we will serve the LORD!" (KJV). James, about to be married, was smitten. On his wedding day he prayed so long that he arrived late for the ceremony. He announced he had become a Christian. Burdened for his new wife, he picked her up, carried her to the bedroom, and forced her to her knees, where she, too, became a Christian.

Their faith passed from generation to generation until it reached their great-grandson, James Hudson Taylor, who founded the China Inland Mission and opened the interior of China to the gospel.

His grandson, James Hudson Taylor II, continued the legacy by taking his family to China as missionaries during the days before World War II. The children's boarding school was located in a Chinese city, a thousand miles from their parents, and they were there on *December 7, 1941*, when Japanese planes attacked Pearl Harbor. When news reached Mrs. Taylor, she writhed in fear and fell on her knees, unable to pray. Worried, a paraphrase of Matthew 6:33 came to mind: if you will take care of the things that are dear to God, God will take care of the things that are dear to you.

Meanwhile, far away, the four Taylor children were herded into a concentration camp in Japanese-occupied territory while singing, "God is our refuge and our strength, a very present help in trouble." The children were detained for five years until liberated by the Americans and allowed to rejoin their parents.

One of the boys, James Hudson Taylor III, grew up to become the general director of China Inland Mission (now Overseas Missionary Fellowship)—the great-grandson of the great-grandson of the man who resolved on his wedding day: "As for me and my house, we will serve the LORD!"

If you don't want to worship the LORD, then choose right now! Will you worship the same idols your ancestors did? Or since you're living on land that once belonged to the Amorites, maybe you'll worship their gods. I won't. My family and I are going to worship and obey the LORD! (Joshua 24:15)

Providence

He was an Anglican, then a Puritan, then a Separatist, then a Baptist, then a Seeker. He quarreled with civil leaders, frustrated church leaders, and loved the Indians. He founded an American colony and established the first Baptist church on American soil. Most of all, he trusted the overruling providence of God so much that he named a city in honor of it.

Who was he? He was Roger Williams, born about 1603, in England. He grew up in London near a square in front of Newgate Prison, famous as the site of execution for condemned heretics. Young Williams witnessed many such executions, and he developed an abhorrence for the persecution of those with differing religious beliefs. As an eighteen-year-old, he worked as recording secretary in a British courtroom, transcribing the cases of heretical prosecution. By the time Williams graduated from Cambridge, he was a powerful preacher and a relentless advocate of religious liberty.

In 1630, under King Charles I, Williams was infuriated by the treatment given his friend, Dr. Alexander Leighton, a Puritan—life imprisonment, heavy fine, defrocking, public whipping, ears cut off, nose split on both sides, and branding of a double *S* (for "sower of sedition") on his face.

With righteous wrath Williams began preaching and writing against the church/state unions and their resulting policies of coercion and persecution. Finding himself at risk, he accepted an invitation from Puritans in Boston and embarked secretly on a ship for America on *December 8, 1630*. But Puritan leaders in America were intolerant too. They sought to impose their beliefs through legal constraint. One night news reached him that authorities were plotting to seize him and return him in chains to England. Bundling himself against the cold, he fled through the snow into Indian country. On the shores of Narragansett Bay, he purchased land from the Indians, and there he founded a settlement, naming it Providence, where all could worship in freedom. There he established the first Baptist church in America. And there he established the colony of Rhode Island.

John said, "Master, we saw a man using your name to force demons out of people. But we told him to stop, because he isn't one of us." "Don't stop him!" Jesus said. "Anyone who isn't against you is for you." (Luke 9:49–50)

December 9 The Dream Team

They have been called the Dream Team of missions, seven young aristocratic athletes from Cambridge who stunned England by renouncing fame and fortune to serve Christ in the back country of Asia as missionaries with the China Inland Mission. The greatest speaker among them was Stanley Smith, who was captain of Cambridge's rowing team. Charles T. Studd, captain of the Cambridge cricket team, was a poor speaker but imposing in appearance. Smith, Studd, and their five compatriots toured the British Isles, preaching Christ and promoting missions prior to their departure for the field. They were a media sensation.

On Tuesday, *December 9, 1884*, Smith and Studd arrived in Edinburgh to speak to students at the university there. They had been staying up all night at various colleges, praying and talking to students, and were in a "mortal funk," as Studd later described it. Organizers had rented the Free Assembly Hall, distributed bundles of flyers, and put men in placards on sidewalks. There were two fears. Some worried that few of the skeptical Scottish students would show up; others were afraid the meetings would be disrupted by heckling. Stanley and Smith spent the afternoon in prayer, "till they got the victory."

The building was crammed well before the appointed hour, and when the two athletes entered the hall, they were loudly cheered. Studd spoke first. His remarks were halting, but his devotion to Christ melted the crowd. Then Smith spoke about the hypocrisy of Christians lacking full commitment. The atmosphere was tense with spiritual power, and when Smith finished, the students surged around him, wanting to hear more of Christ and the Great Commission. Later that evening the two young men arrived at the train station and found it thronged with young people shouting, "Speech! Speech!" As the train pulled from the platform, the students ran after it singing, "God be with you till we meet again."

The Cambridge Seven catapulted the China Inland Mission to the attention of the world. When they arrived in China in 1885, CIM had 163 missionaries there. By 1900, there were 800.

When the good news about the kingdom has been preached all over the world and told to all nations, the end will come. (Matthew 24:14)

Perseverance

Moses persevered, says Hebrews 11, because he saw him who is invisible. The word *persevere* comes from the prefix *per* meaning "through" and *severe*—to press by faith through severe circumstances. Consider, for example, Marcus and Narcissa Whitman, missionaries to Native Americans in the American Northwest.

Marcus, born in New York in 1802, was converted and eventually joined a Presbyterian church. He studied medicine and felt God calling him as a missionary physician to the Indians of the West. His girlfriend, Narcissa, shared his burden, and on the day after their wedding, they set out for Oregon. Narcissa became the first white woman to cross America, and she was awed by the splendor of God's creation. Her heart was in a vast adventure, and there, somewhere between Elkhorn and the Loup, she became pregnant.

After two thousand rugged miles, the Whitmans reached Oregon, settling down among the fierce Cayuse. Marcus built a hut for himself and his pregnant wife, and on *December 10, 1835*, they moved in. Daughter Alice was born three months later.

Marcus and Narcissa worked themselves to exhaustion, building a mission compound, developing agriculture, treating the sick, and sharing their faith. Unbelievable hardship and sorrow overwhelmed them. They became overworked, tired, and sometimes discouraged. Relationships with other missionaries deteriorated. Worst of all, little Alice, one day during her second year, wandered away while her dad was reading, fell into a nearby stream, and drowned. But the Whitmans pressed on, ministering selflessly to orphans, to the diseased, to the disinterested, and to whoever would listen.

Their passion cost them their lives. In 1847, several Indians died during an outbreak of measles, and Marcus was blamed. Late on a dark fall day, the mission was attacked by a band of Cayuse. Marcus and Narcissa died by tomahawk, along with a dozen coworkers. But the gospel had been planted on the American frontier by a couple willing to remain faithful through severe circumstances. They had persevered, seeing him who is invisible.

Because of his faith, Moses left Egypt. Moses had seen the invisible God and wasn't afraid of the king's anger. His faith also made him celebrate Passover. He sprinkled the blood of animals on the doorposts, so that the first-born sons of the people of Israel would not be killed by the destroying angel. Because of their faith, the people walked through the Red Sea on dry land. (Hebrews 11:27–29)

December 11 Nine Rabid Teeth

Susan Talbott Wengatz, Methodist missionary in Malange, Angola, began Wednesday, *December 11, 1929*, by strolling through her garden, soaking up the fragrances of the roses and the brilliance of the sunshine. She gathered as many blossoms as she could carry, then turned toward the house to prepare her morning Bible class. Suddenly she saw a large dog tramping toward her. "Shoo!" Susan cried. "Shoo! Go back!"

But the dog snarled, bared its teeth, and lunged. Susan dropped her roses and threw her arms over her face. The dog tore into her, sinking nine rabid teeth into the flesh. Mr. Wengatz rushed his wife to a nearby hospital, but there was no rabies serum. They sped to another hospital. No serum. They rushed to the port to find a boat leaving the country, but the ships had left. They considered driving to the Belgian Congo, but heavy rains had washed out the roads.

Cables flashed to Lisbon, Capetown, Johannesburg, and the Congo, where pharmacists quickly wrapped and sent packages of rabies serum. Days of unbearable suspense passed as local Christians in Angola wept, fasted, and prayed. For various reasons the serums were delayed in transit. Meanwhile Susan felt no pain or sickness. Her wounds healed, and she returned to business as usual. When one of the packages finally arrived, she began taking the shots.

One month after the attack Susan found her husband in the workshop and told him, "It's aching today, my arm." The ache grew worse, and she was put to bed. She declined rapidly. "I hear the music of heaven," she whispered. "I see Jesus. My anchor holds. Does yours? I'll see you in the morning. Now I'm going to sleep in Jesus' name."

No one understands why God permitted a rabid dog to enter Susan Wengatz's garden that morning in 1929. He allows us unanswered questions—the stuff of faith. Southern preacher Vance Havner, mulling over similar imponderables, spoke of being "shipwrecked on God and stranded on Omnipotence." Charles Spurgeon put it like this: "When we can't trace God's hand we can trust his heart."

Martha said to Jesus, "Lord, if you had been here, my brother would not have died." Jesus then said, "I am the one who raises the dead to life! Everyone who has faith in me will live, even if they die. And everyone who lives because of faith in me will never really die." (John 11:21, 25–26)

Rivers of Blood

History is littered with the names of infamous rogues who drank rolling rivers of blood with devilish delight. Among them was the Spanish General Fernando Alvarez de Toledo, the Duke of Alva, whose cruelty can only be described as demonic.

He was born into a noble Spanish family in 1508, at the onset of the Reformation. His grandfather, Frederick of Toledo, dominated his youth and trained him to be a warrior and a soldier, tough as iron. He fought his first battle at age sixteen and climbed the military beanstalk with cunning and prowess. As a general he was brilliant, but like his commander-in-chief, Philip II of Spain, Fernando was also deceitful, fanatical, cruel, and merciless.

The Reformation, especially Calvinism, had found fertile ground in Holland, for the Bible had been translated there into Flemish several years earlier. But the Netherlands were under the control of Spain and its hated King Philip. Philip established the Inquisition in Holland, provoked a rebellion, and in 1567, sent the Duke of Alva with ten thousand troops into the Netherlands to quell the Reformation, to extinguish the evangelical heresy, and to regain control of the citizens.

Over the next six years, six thousand lowlanders were sentenced to death in the duke's "Council of Blood." Some estimates put the total number of martyrs at one hundred thousand, including women and children. One historian claims that more Christians lost their lives during this bloodletting than during all the Roman persecutions of the first three hundred years of church history. Alva imposed oppressive taxes, destroyed the economy of Holland, violated civil liberties, tortured citizens, and provoked a war of independence that lasted eighty years.

One reaps, however, what one sows. In 1580, Alva was sent against Portugal. He was victorious, but on the way back, a fever developed. A dark foreboding drew itself around him like a curtain. His life drained out of him like sand through the glass, and the man who had gulped the blood of Christians lay in helpless suffering, able to sip only milk drawn from a woman's breast.

On *December 12, 1582*, his soul was required of him.

Those who plant seeds of evil
harvest trouble,
and then they are swept away
by the angry breath of God.
They may roar and growl
like powerful lions.
But when God breaks their teeth,
they starve. (Job 4:8–11)

December 13 The Hermit-Pope

Peter of Morone craved a hermit's life. His asceticism appealed to certain others, and in 1254, he founded an order known as the Hermits of St. Damian. He lived as a recluse in a mountain cave until his eighties.

Meanwhile in Rome, Pope Nicholas IV died, and church officials spent twenty-seven months trying to choose a replacement. Unable to agree, they finally pulled Peter's name from the hat. Three bishops traveled one hundred fifty miles and clawed their way up the rocky side of the hermit's mountain to tell him of his election. Panting and sweating, they inched around the narrow ledge and spied Peter peeking curiously through the bars of his makeshift door. He was unkempt, pale, disheveled, sick, aged, and hardly able to understand them.

Peter gathered a knapsack, wrapped himself in a tunic, mounted a donkey, and accompanied the bishops to Aquila, Italy, where he was crowned before two thousand people. He took up residence in Naples, calling himself Pope Celestine V. He built a tiny wooden cell to hide in and wandered through his palace, nibbling crusts of bread.

Celestine knew nothing of church government, world affairs, or political intrigue. His misjudgments multiplied like rabbits, and he soon found himself hopelessly entangled. The church descended into crisis. "O God!" he cried, "While I rule over other men's souls, I am losing my own!" Churchmen trembled at his ineptitude, and according to one story, Cardinal Gaetani finally inserted a reed through the wall of Celestine's private room and spoke as a voice from heaven, telling him it was God's will for him to resign.

In the last act of his pontificate, Celestine issued a constitution giving popes the right to quit, then shocked the world by resigning on *December 13, 1294*, just fifteen weeks after his coronation. It was explained that he was abdicating in the quest of a better life and an easy conscience and on account of the frailty of his body and the badness of men.

The "voice from heaven," Gaetani, was elected Pope Boniface VIII. He imprisoned Celestine in the castle of Fumone until the old man died in 1296.

> I wish I had wings
> like a dove,
> so I could fly far away
> and be at peace.
> I would go and live
> in some distant desert.
> I would quickly find shelter
> from howling winds
> and raging storms. (Psalm 55:6–8)

A Good Monument

The area around Wheaton, Illinois, was first settled by Erastus Gray from Connecticut in 1831. Six years later Warren Wheaton, another Connecticut native, arrived and built a home at the corner of what is now Roosevelt Road at Naperville Street. The railroad came through; a grocery store was built, then an inn and a liquor store. Soon the population reached eight hundred.

A number of slavery-hating Wesleyan Methodists settled in Wheaton. Horrified that their children might be trained by professors sympathetic to slavery, they decided to establish a school of their own. On a sizzling summer's day in 1852, a group of them knelt in the grass on the crest of a small hill overlooking the rolling prairie about a mile from the train station. They prayed that "the hill and all that should be built upon it" would be dedicated to God. A plain, three-story limestone building went up for ten thousand dollars, and on *December 14, 1853*, Illinois Institute opened under the direction of Rev. John Cross. It soon filled with students—and with smoke, for the stoves vented improperly.

But the Wesleyan founders were "mostly men who had little of this world's goods," wrote one of their sons a generation later. "They were reformers, especially interested in the antislavery struggle. The purpose was not so much to start a denominational school as to provide a place where their principles should not be smothered out."

Because they possessed so little of this world's goods, the Institute failed financially, and in 1860, the trustees requested help from the wealthier Congregationalists. Jonathan Blanchard, Presbyterian pastor and academic, was appointed president. He approached Warren Wheaton for a large donation of property and offered to name the school Wheaton College. "That will at least save your heirs the expense of a good monument," Blanchard said.

The school reopened under the Congregationalists with the support of the Wesleyans and with a Presbyterian president. And for more than a century since, Wheaton College has been training young people "for Christ and His Kingdom."

> If you are already wise,
> you will become even wiser.
> And if you are smart,
> you will learn to understand
> proverbs and sayings,
> as well as words of wisdom
> and all kinds of riddles.
> Respect and obey the LORD!
> This is the beginning
> of knowledge. Only a fool rejects wisdom
> and good advice. (Proverbs 1:5–7)

Neither Suit nor Service

The surprising thing about John Oldcastle was the number of roles he played. During his approximately thirty-nine years, he was a knight, a politician, a soldier, a preacher, a baron, a fugitive, a martyr, and the inspiration for Shakespeare's character, Falstaff.

"Over a century before Luther, John Wycliffe proclaimed Reformation views in England, and a group of preachers, the Lollards, spread his message through the country. After Wycliffe's death, John Oldcastle sought to protect and advance the Lollard ministry. Against him arose the archbishop of Canterbury, imploring the king to silence Oldcastle and the Lollards. Henry met with his baron and beseeched him to "submit to his mother the holy Church." Oldcastle replied, "I am always prompt and willing to obey you, forasmuch as I know you are a king and the anointed minister of God . . . But as touching the pope and his spirituality, I owe him neither suit nor service."

Henry withdrew his support. Oldcastle, finding himself "compassed on every side with deadly dangers," was seized, imprisoned in the Tower of London, and condemned. But before his execution could occur, "in the night season [it is not known by what means], he escaped out and fled to Wales."

Henry offered a great reward for his recapture, but Oldcastle remained at large four years. Then "the Lord Powis, whether for greediness of the money or for hatred of the true doctrine of Christ, seeking all manner of ways how to play the part of Judas, and outwardly pretending great favor, at length obtained his bloody purpose and most cowardly and wretchedly took him and brought him bound up to London" (wrote John Foxe).

On *December 15, 1418*, Oldcastle was taken to Smithfield in London, where martyrs were killed, and "hanged up by the middle in chains of iron, and so consumed alive in the fire, praising the name of God so long as his life lasted."

By faith we have been made acceptable to God. And now, because of our Lord Jesus Christ, we live at peace with God . . . So we are happy, as we look forward to sharing in the glory of God. But that's not all! We gladly suffer. (Romans 5:1–3)

The Earthquake

On *December 16, 1811*, a massive earthquake rocked the southern United States, its tremors and aftershocks spreading so far as to make church bells ring in Philadelphia. Tennessee's Reelfoot Lake was formed by the upheaval. Methodist preacher Peter Cartwright, one of America's most colorful itinerant evangelists, recorded several earthquake experiences in his autobiography. Cartwright, who had been converted through the Cane Ridge revival and subsequently traveled throughout the South and Midwest for almost seventy years preaching, spreading revival, and starting churches, wrote:

> It seemed to stop the current of the Mississippi, broke flat-boats loose from their moorings, and opened large cracks or fissures in the earth. This earthquake struck terror to thousands of people, and under the mighty panic hundreds and thousands crowded to and joined the different churches. There were many interesting incidents connected with the shaking of the earth at this time. I had preached in Nashville the night before the second dreadful shock came, to a large congregation. Early the next morning I arose and walked out on a hill near the house where I had preached, when I saw a Negro woman coming down the hill to the spring, with an empty pail on her head. When she got within a few rods of where I stood the earth began to tremble and jar; chimneys were thrown down, scaffolding around many new buildings fell with a loud crash, hundreds of citizens suddenly awoke, sprang into the streets; loud screaming followed, for many thought the day of judgment was come. The young mistresses of the above-named Negro woman came running after her, and begging her to pray for them. She raised the shout and said to them, "My Jesus is coming in the clouds of heaven, and I can't wait to pray for you now; I must go and meet him. I told you so, that he would come, and you would not believe me. Farewell. Hallelujah! Jesus is coming, and I am ready. Hallelujah! Amen." And on she went, shouting and clapping her hands, with the empty pail on her head.

When you hear about wars and threats of wars, don't be afraid. These things will have to happen first, but that isn't the end. Nations and kingdoms will go to war against each other. There will be earthquakes in many places, and people will starve to death . . . No one knows the day or the time . . . So watch out and be ready! (Mark 13:7–8, 32–33)

No Regrets

On *December 17, 1912*, Bill Borden boarded ship for China via Egypt. His missionary career would be among history's briefest—and most effective.

Borden was born into an upper-class family on Chicago's Gold Coast, heir to a fortune in real estate and milk production. His mother became a Christian, and young Bill began attending Chicago's Moody Church with her, soon becoming a Christian himself. Shortly afterward when Pastor R. A. Torrey challenged worshippers to dedicate their lives to God's service, William quietly rose—a little fellow in a blue sailor suit. He stood a long, long time while the service went on, but there was no wavering, and it was a consecration from which he never retreated.

Later at Yale University Bill became well known as a star athlete, good-looking, worth fifty million dollars, and committed to Christ. At a student missions conference in Nashville, he was deeply moved by Samuel Zwemer to reach the Muslims, and following graduation, he announced he was giving his immense inheritance to the cause of world missions. He joined the China Inland Mission, planning to evangelize the Muslims in China. But first came language study in Egypt. On the eve of his departure, his widowed mother wondered if Bill had done the right thing, giving up fortune and homeland. "In the quiet of my room that night, worn and weary and sad, I fell asleep asking myself again and again, 'Is it, after all, worthwhile?' In the morning as I awoke, a still small voice was speaking in my heart, answering: '*God* so loved the world that *he* gave *his* only beloved son . . .'"

A month after arriving in Egypt, Borden contracted spinal meningitis. He was dead in two weeks, but he left a final message on paper stuffed under his pillow: "No reserve! No retreat! No regrets!"

The story of his sacrifice was retold in newspapers across America, and the publication of his biography resulted in a dramatic leap in numbers of young people offering themselves as living sacrifices for the Lord of the harvest.

The LORD said to Abram: Leave your country, your family, and your relatives and go to the land that I will show you. I will bless you and make your descendants into a great nation. You will become famous and be a blessing to others. I will bless anyone who blesses you, but I will put a curse on anyone who puts a curse on you. Everyone on earth will be blessed because of you. (Genesis 12:1–3)

"The Whole Pack of You Heretics"

John Foxe researched and recorded the sufferings of many obscure evangelicals who died during the reign of England's Queen Mary. Here is his story, condensed, of John Philpot who was burned on *December 18, 1555:*

The bishop, seeing his unmovable steadfastness in the truth, did pronounce sentence of condemnation against him. "I thank God," said Philpot, "that I am a heretic out of your cursed church; I am no heretic before God. But God bless you, and give you grace to repent your wicked doings, and let all men beware of your bloody church." So the officers delivered him to Newgate [Prison]. "Well," said Philpot, "I must be content, for it is God's appointment. I pray you show me what you would have me do."

He said, "If you would recant, I will show you any pleasure I can."

"Nay," said Master Philpot, "I shall never recant whilst I have my life, that which I have spoken is certain truth; in witness hereof I will seal it with my blood."

Then Alexander said, "This is the saying of the whole pack of you heretics." Whereupon he commanded him to be set upon the block, and as many irons as he could bear.

Upon Tuesday at supper, being the 17th day of December, 1555, there came a messenger from the sheriffs and bade Philpot make ready, for the next day he should suffer. Master Philpot answered, "I am ready; God grant me strength and a joyful resurrection." He went into his chamber and poured out his spirit unto the Lord God, giving him most hearty thanks, that he of his mercy had made him worthy to suffer for his truth.

In the morning the sheriffs came, about eight of the clock, and he most joyfully came down unto them. When he was come to the place of suffering, he said, "Shall I disdain to suffer at this stake, seeing my Redeemer did not refuse to suffer a most vile death upon the cross for me?" Then in the midst of the fiery flames he yielded his soul into the hands of Almighty God.*

When Christ died, he died for sin once and for all. But now he is alive, and he lives only for God. In the same way, you must think of yourselves as dead to the power of sin. But Christ Jesus has given life to you, and you live for God. (Romans 6:10–11)

*John Foxe: *Foxe's Book of Martyrs* (Springdale, PA: Whitaker House, 1981), pp. 340–343.

Cards and Dice

Hugh Latimer, English reformer, was asked to preach on *December 19, 1529*, at St. Edward's in Cambridge. The students loved playing cards, so Latimer decided to preach about the cards God deals us, using the example of John the Baptist. He suggested that we must all answer the question the Jews asked John—"Who are you?" Without Christ the answer is: "I am under condemnation because of sin." But through repentance and forgiveness we can answer, "I am a Christian." Then as we study the New Testament, it is like turning over cards, one at a time, to learn how God wants us to live.

Latimer ascended the little hexagonal pulpit; his clear voice pealed out the Scripture in Latin, translated it into English, then plunged into his sermon.

A friar named Buckenham preached a countersermon using the idea of a pair of dice. He called it *cinque-quatre*—five, four—saying that God's dice have landed with *five* on one and *four* on the other. He attacked the Reformation using five Scripture passages and four church doctors: Ambrose, Augustine, Jerome, and Gregory. Buckenham ridiculed Latimer's call for an English translation of Scripture. "The common man will not understand the figurative language of Scripture," Buckenham asserted. For example, when the Bible speaks of plucking out one's eye, some may do it literally.

Latimer assured Buckenham that the English were smart enough to understand metaphors. To laughter, he said, "For example, when a painter pictures a fox in a friar's cowl, no one supposes an actual fox preaching. What he means is the hypocrisy, craft, and subtle dissimulation that often lie hidden in a friar's cowl."

John Foxe later said, "Friar Buckenham with this sermon was so dashed that never after he durst peep out of the pulpit against Master Latimer."

Now that God has accepted us because Christ sacrificed his life's blood, we will also be kept safe from God's anger. Even when we were God's enemies, he made peace with us, because his Son died for us. Yet something even greater than friendship is ours. Now that we are at peace with God, we will be saved by his Son's life. (Romans 5:9–10)

Bear with Me, Madam!

Edmund Grindal's love for books saved his life. One day while romping through the fields with a book stuffed into his coat, a hunter's stray arrow flew into him, lodging in the book. Later another book saved him: The Bible brought him to Christ. Grindal grew in faith and entered the ministry, but when "Bloody" Mary rose to the throne, he fled to Germany until Mary was replaced by Protestant-leaning Elizabeth I. Grindal returned to England and was appointed archbishop of Canterbury in 1575.

Elizabeth soon complained to the new archbishop that too much preaching was causing seedbeds of sedition. "Three or four sermons a year" are quite enough, the queen said, and she ordered Grindal to curtail preaching throughout the kingdom.

On *December 20, 1576*, Grindal responded in a long letter, saying in part: "The speeches it hath pleased you to deliver me concerning abridging the number of preachers and the utter suppression of conferences among ministers have exceedingly dismayed and discomforted me. Alas, Madam, is the Scripture more plain in any one thing than that the Gospel of Christ should be plentifully preached? To the building of Solomon's material temple there were appointed 150,000 labourers and 300 overseers, and shall we think a few preachers may suffice to edify the spiritual temple of Christ? St. Paul said, 'Preach the Word.' Public and continual preaching of God's word is the ordinary instrument of salvation. I cannot with safe conscience and without the offense of the Majesty of God consent to their suppressing. Bear with me, I beseech you, Madam, if I choose rather to offend your earthly Majesty than to offend the heavenly Majesty of God. I beseech you, Madam, let the Majesty of God be before your eyes and say, 'Not mine but Thy will be done.' "

Elizabeth, furious, placed Grindal under house arrest. But the gospel was not shut up, and despite the queen's misgivings, gospel preaching spread to every corner of the British Isles.

Keep your mind on Jesus Christ! He . . . was raised from death, just as my good news says . . . I am locked up in jail and treated like a criminal. But God's good news isn't locked in jail. (2 Timothy 2:8–9)

Have They No Souls?

When Hernando Cortes and the other Spanish explorers led conquistadors against the Aztec and Inca empires, their goal was to claim land, seize gold, and share the faith. In the name of Christ, thousands were slaughtered and enslaved. Entire civilizations perished. Some of the conquistadors sincerely believed they were expanding the faith. "Gunpowder against Indians is incense to the Lord," said one of them. But it is important to know that many voices in the church rose in righteous, angry opposition.

On *December 21, 1511*, Antonio des Montesinos stood before his church in Hispaniola with fire on his lips:

> I have climbed to this pulpit to let you know of your sins, for I am the voice of Christ crying in the desert of this island, and you must not listen to me indifferently. You are in mortal sin; you not only are in it, but live in it and die in it because of the cruelty and tyranny you bring to bear on these innocent people. By what right do you wage your odious wars on people who dwelt in quiet and peace on their own islands? Why do you oppress and exploit them, without even giving them enough to eat? They die, or rather, you kill them, so that you may extract more and more gold every day.
>
> Are they not human? Have they no souls? Are you not required to love them as you love yourselves? How can you remain in such profound lethargy? I assure you, in your present state you can no more be saved than Moors or Turks who reject the faith of Jesus Christ.

His audience was stunned, and his words leaped the oceans. In Spain a furious King Ferdinand told Christopher Columbus, "I have seen the sermon . . . and although he was always a scandalous preacher, I am much surprised by what he said, which has no basis in theology or law."

Montesinos refused orders to retract his statements, and increasing numbers joined him in reminding the world that not everything done in the name of Christianity is of Christ.

I command you to preach God's message. Do it willingly, even if it isn't the popular thing to do. You must correct people and point out their sins. (2 Timothy 4:1–2)

Lord, Save Fiji!

As a child John Hunt often sat by the fire, engrossed in his father's tales of military adventure. At sixteen he nearly died of "brain fever." Recovering, he found the Lord in a Methodist chapel. He later married Hanna Summers, and on *December 22, 1838*, they arrived on the Fiji islands as missionaries.

They shuddered at the sight. Two-thirds of all children were boiled and eaten. Every village had its human butcher. Aged parents were butchered and eaten by their children. A man would often cook his best wife or most tender child as a feast for his closest friends.

Some time after their arrival the chief's youngest son was lost at sea. Seventeen women were killed and roasted as a result, and Hanna was forced to watch. The islanders then insisted the missionaries leave. But the Hunts refused. They found increasing numbers willing to listen. The queen of Viwa came under such conviction that she fainted twice, then, coming to, pleaded for mercy. A revival swept her village, then others.

Hunt translated the New Testament into Fijian and kept preaching fearlessly. Converts increased, and chapels were built. At length Hunt's health broke, and when the islanders realized their missionary was ill, they flocked to the chapels to pray for him. "O Lord," cried one of them, Elijah Verani, "we know we are very bad, but spare thy servant. If one must die, take me! Take ten of us! But spare thy servant to preach Christ."

But Hunt realized he was dying. He committed his wife to the Lord and began crying, "Lord, bless Fiji! Save Fiji!" Later, turning to Hanna, he said, "If this be dying, praise the Lord!" and "I want strength to praise him abundantly . . . Hallelujah!"

With that he breathed his last. The island was moved by his death, and even the wicked King Thakombau confessed Christ openly. Much of Fiji was transformed, causing one missionary historian to call Fiji a "jewel in the missionary diadem."

God's people must learn to endure . . . Then I heard a voice from heaven say, "Put this in writing. From now on, the Lord will bless everyone who has faith in him when they die." The Spirit answered, "Yes, they will rest from their hard work, and they will be rewarded for what they have done." (Revelation 14:12–13)

A Father's Advice

Heinrich Bullinger was a good pastor and a better father. He was born in 1504, to a priest who embraced Reformation views. Though it cost him his church, it gained him his son. Young Heinrich loved Luther's writings, Melanchthon's books, and the study of the Bible. At the age of twenty-seven, he took the place of slain Swiss reformer Ulrich Zwingli as pastor of the Grossmunster of Zurich, on *December 23, 1531.*

Heinrich continued Zwingli's practice of preaching through books of the Bible, verse by verse. His home was open from morning till night, and he freely distributed food, clothing, and money to the needy. His wisdom and influence spread across Europe.

No one was more affected than his own son, Henry. When the young man packed his bags and set out for college in Strasburg, Heinrich gave him ten rules for living:

1. Fear God at all times, and remember that the fear of God is the beginning of wisdom.
2. Humble yourself before God, and pray to him alone through Christ, our only Mediator and Advocate.
3. Believe firmly that God has done all for our salvation through his Son.
4. Pray above all things for a strong faith active in love.
5. Pray that God may protect your good name and keep you from sin, sickness, and bad company.
6. Pray for the fatherland, for your dear parents . . . for the spread of the Word of God.
7. Be reticent, be always more willing to hear than to speak, and do not meddle with things you do not understand.
8. Study diligently . . . Read daily three chapters of the Bible.
9. Keep your body clean and unspotted, be neat in your dress, and avoid above all things intemperance in eating and drinking.
10. Let your conversation be decent, cheerful, moderate.

The advice was taken; and Henry Bullinger became, like his father and grandfather, a minister of the gospel of Jesus Christ.

Parents, don't be hard on your children. Raise them properly. Teach them and instruct them about the Lord. (Ephesians 6:4)

Behold Your God!

Many people celebrate Christmas without Christ, the glory of a holy day being supplanted by the glitz of a holiday—a problem that reaches back to the days of St. Francis of Assisi. Francis was born in 1182, in central Italy, the son of a rich merchant. After a scanty education, he joined the army and was captured in war. He came to Christ shortly after his release, and soon he began traveling around the countryside, preaching the gospel. During a mass in February 1209, Francis was gripped by words being read from Matthew 10: "As you go, preach this message: 'The kingdom of heaven is near.' Heal the sick, raise the dead, cleanse those who have leprosy, drive out demons. Freely you have received, freely give. Do not take along any gold or silver or copper in your belts; take no bag for the journey, or extra tunic, or sandals or a staff" (vv. 7–8 NIV).

Francis felt that Christ himself was speaking directly to him. He decided to obey those words as literally as possible, preaching the kingdom and possessing nothing. It is as though a tweve-hundred-year bridge were crossed, putting Francis in the shoes of the original wayfaring apostles themselves.

He spent his remaining days making Christ real to everyone he met—a passion leading to history's first living nativity scene. On *December 24, 1223*, Francis found a cave near Greccio, Italy, and brought in animals traditionally associated with the birth of Christ. (Francis loved animals and sometimes even preached to them.) He built the crib, arranged the hay, and finished the scene. Crowds gathered full of curiosity and wonder, and there on Christmas Eve, Francis preached the wonder of God made man, born a naked infant and laid in the manger. "Behold your God," he said, "a poor and helpless child, the ox and donkey beside him. Your God is of your flesh."

Glitz gave way to glory that evening as the people of Greccio learned afresh the meaning of Christmas.

She gave birth to her first-born son. She dressed him in baby clothes and laid him on a bed of hay, because there was no room for them in the inn. That night in the fields near Bethlehem some shepherds were guarding their sheep. All at once an angel came down to them from the Lord, and the brightness of the Lord's glory flashed around them. The shepherds were frightened. But the angel said, "Don't be afraid! I have good news for you . . . a Savior was born." (Luke 2:7–11)

Mass Conversion

Not all who sing Christmas carols are Christians. Superficial sentiment is sometimes substituted for genuine faith.

Take Clovis, for example. After the breakup of the Roman Empire, disorder reigned. Anarchy prevailed. Fifteen-year-old Clovis inherited a small kingdom in the corner of Gaul. King Clovis seized adjoining lands, united Gaul, moved his capital to Paris, and founded the nation of France.

In 493, Clovis married a Christian. When Queen Clothilde wanted to baptize their newborn son, Clovis agreed, but when the child died in his baptismal robe, Clovis blamed the Christian God. When a second child grew ill following baptism, Clothilde prayed earnestly, the child recovered, and the king was impressed.

When Clovis was thirty, he was routed in battle. "Jesus Christ," he cried, "Clothilde says you are the Son of God and can give victory to those who hope in you. Give me victory, and I will be baptized!" The tide turned, and Clovis, true to his word, entered the Cathedral of Rheims on *December 25, 496*. "Worship what you once burned," the priest told him, "and burn what you worshipped."

On that day three thousand troops followed Clovis in baptism. The army marched alongside a river where priests, chanting the baptismal formula, dipped branches into the stream and flung the water, supposedly making them Christians.

This was a momentous day in church history, for it was the first of the great mass conversions that turned Europe into a Christian continent. Little change was detected in Clovis or his troops who were as pagan as ever, apparently viewing Christ merely as a war god who ensured them victory. But the stage was set for many genuine believers who spread the message of the Babe of Bethlehem throughout emerging Europe.

The angel told Mary, "Don't be afraid! God is pleased with you, and you will have a son. His name will be Jesus. He will be great and will be called the Son of God Most High. The Lord God will make him king, as his ancestor David was. He will rule the people of Israel forever, and his kingdom will never end." (Luke 1:30–33)

This Is No Dream

Dwight L. Moody, badly overweight, grew ill in Kansas City, canceled his engagements, and returned home to Northfield, Massachusetts. He lugged himself up to his bedroom to dress for dinner, but felt so exhausted that he took to bed. He declined quickly, and it became clear he was dying of "fatty degeneration of the heart." On December 22, he suddenly opened his eyes and spoke clearly: "Earth recedes! Heaven opens before me." His son, sitting near him, suggested he was dreaming. "This is no dream, Will," Moody replied. "It is beautiful! It is like a trance! If this is death, it is sweet! God is calling me, and I must go!"

The family gathered around. "This is my triumph!" said Moody. "This is my coronation day! I have been looking forward to it for years." His face suddenly lit up. "Dwight! Irene! I see the children's faces!" (Dwight and Irene were his recently deceased grandchildren.) Moody closed his eyes and appeared unconscious. Then he spoke again. "No pain! No valley! If this is death, it's not bad at all! It's sweet!"

A little later he raised himself on an elbow and exclaimed, "What does all this mean? What are you all doing here?" His wife explained he had not been well. Moody fell back on the bed and said, "This is very strange! I've been beyond the gates of death to the very portals of heaven, and here I am back again. It is very strange."

Then he said, "I'm not at all sure but that God may perform a miracle and raise me up. I'm going to get up and sit in that chair. If God wants to heal me by a miracle, all right; if not, I can meet death in my chair as well as here." To everyone's shock, Moody rose, walked across the room, and sat in an easy chair. But he soon returned to bed exhausted, spoke tenderly to them some more, and finally slipped on to heaven. His funeral was conducted at 10:00 AM on *December 26, 1899*, by C. I. Scofield, and he was laid to rest atop Northfield's Mount Hermon.

But we are citizens of heaven and are eagerly waiting for our Savior to come from there. Our Lord Jesus Christ has power over everything, and he will make these poor bodies of ours like his own glorious body. (Philippians 3:20–21)

Robert and Mary

Robert Moffat was a strong, healthy young man who loved working outdoors. He was hired by James Smith, owner of Dukinfield Nurseries, but Smith had misgivings, for he knew two things: first, that Robert's good looks would appeal to his only daughter, Mary; second, that Robert wanted to be a missionary.

It happened just as Smith feared. As Robert worked in the gardens, he met Mary and discovered that she, too, was a Christian with an interest in missions (having been educated in a Moravian school). Unknown to her parents, she had secretly prayed two years before that God would send her to Africa.

An intense attachment formed quickly, but when the young couple announced to family members their plans to marry and leave England as missionaries to South Africa, the reaction was violent. Robert's parents seemed resigned, but the Smiths refused to give their consent. All pleading and imploring failed. At last with his heart breaking, Robert decided to abandon hope of marriage and leave for the field alone. "From the clearest indications of his providence," he wrote his parents, "he bids me go out alone. It is the Lord, let him do what seemeth him good." So on October 18, 1816, Robert Moffat sailed for South Africa, leaving his heart behind.

He arrived in the field suffering deep loneliness. "I have many difficulties to encounter, being alone," he wrote his parents. Meanwhile in England Mary, too, was miserable. Three long years passed, and she finally told Robert in a letter that she had given up all prospect of joining him.

But her next letter a month later contained different news: "They both yesterday calmly resigned me into the hands of the Lord," she wrote, "declaring they durst no longer withhold me." Mary quickly packed her trunks, told her anguished parents good-bye with no expectation of ever seeing them again, and left for South Africa. There she and Robert were married before a handful of friends on *December 27, 1819*. And there they labored side by side for fifty-three years, becoming one of the greatest husband-wife teams in missionary history.

Do what the LORD wants,
and he will give you
your heart's desire.
Let the LORD lead you
and trust him to help.
Then it will be as clear
as the noonday sun
that you were right.
Be patient and trust the LORD. (Psalm 37:4–7)

Seeing the Stars

Vance Havner once lamented that many churchgoers sit and yawn over the truths for which their forefathers shed blood; thus, "the living faith of the dead has become the dead faith of the living." It wasn't so for Charles Hodge, one of America's greatest theologians, who was born on *December 28, 1797*. He studied the old and familiar Scriptures with fresh excitement. Three thousand pastors prepared for ministry in his theology classes at Princeton, and multitudes have benefited from his three-volume *Systematic Theology*. In a sermon once, Hodge warned his listeners against becoming bored with the Bible. Referring to Romans 3:29 "Does God belong only to the Jews? Isn't he also the God of the Gentiles? Yes, he is!" Hodge said:

> We are so familiar with the truth contained in these words that we do not appreciate its importance. Accustomed to the varied beauties of the earth, we behold its manifold wonders without emotion; we seldom even raise our eyes to look at the beauteous canopy of heaven, which every night is spread over our heads. The blind, however, when suddenly restored to sight, behold with ecstasy what we regard with indifference. Thus the truth that God is not a national God, not the God of any one tribe or people, but the God and Father of all men, and that the Gospel is designed and adapted to all mankind, however little it may affect us, filled the apostles with astonishment and delight. They were slow in arriving at the knowledge of this truth; they had no clear perception of it until after the day of Pentecost; the effusion of the Spirit which they then received produced a most remarkable change in their views and feelings. Before that event, they were Jews; afterwards, they were Christians.

Ralph Waldo Emerson observed that if the constellations appeared only once in a thousand years, what an exciting event it would be. Because they are there every night, we barely look.

"Don't lose the wonder," Gipsy Smith said. God's mercies are new every morning, and his Word is fresh every day.

> You, LORD, are all I want . . .
> I praise you, LORD,
> for being my guide.
> Even in the darkest night,
> your teachings fill my mind.
> With all my heart,
> I will celebrate,
> and I can safely rest.
> You have shown me
> the path to life,
> and you make me glad
> by being near to me.
> Sitting at your right side, I will always be joyful. (Psalm 16:5, 7, 9, 11)

Pure Bliss

Philip Paul Bliss was born to singing parents in a log cabin in the northern Pennsylvania woods. He left home to work at age eleven and made a public confession of Christ at age twelve. He spent his teen years in lumber camps and sawmills. But he loved to sing, and he did his best to get an education in music. His voice was remarkably full, resonant, and elastic with a range from low D-flat to high A.

With an old horse named Fanny and a twenty-dollar melodeon, Philip started traveling around as a professional music teacher. In 1858, he married Lucy Young, a musician and poet who encouraged him to develop his gifts. As a result he wrote and sold his first composition in 1864. It was well received, and he moved to Chicago the next year as an associate of music publishers Root & Cady. Presently he found himself in demand, conducting musical institutes, giving concerts, and composing Sunday school melodies. Moody championed his work, and Bliss wrote many of the gospel songs we love today: "Let the Lower Lights Be Burning," "Man of Sorrows—What a Name!", "Jesus Loves Even Me," "The Light of the World Is Jesus!", "Almost Persuaded," "Wonderful Words of Life." He also wrote the music to such hymns as "It Is Well with My Soul."

During the Christmas holidays of 1876, the Bliss family visited his mother in Pennsylvania. On *December 29, 1876*, they boarded the *Pacific Express* in Buffalo to return to Chicago. About eight o'clock that evening in a blinding snowstorm as the train crossed a ravine, the wooden trestle collapsed. The cars, packed with holiday passengers, plunged seventy-five feet into the icy river and caught fire. More than one hundred people perished in the wreck, among them were Philip Bliss and his family. He was thirty-eight.

By coincidence Philip's trunk had been placed on another train, and it arrived safely in Chicago. Inside, his friends found a last hymn:

I will sing of my Redeemer
And his wondrous love to me.
On the cruel cross he suffered
From the curse to set me free.

Tell everyone on this earth
to sing happy songs
in praise of the LORD.
Make music for him on harps.
Play beautiful melodies!
Sound the trumpets and horns
and celebrate with joyful songs
for our LORD and King! (Psalm 98:4–6)

Lemonade Lucy

Among those mourning the deaths of Philip Bliss and the other victims of the *Pacific Express* was the president-elect of the United States, Rutherford B. Hayes, who would soon be officially proclaimed winner of the 1876 election by only one electoral vote. The nation was reeling at the time from Reconstruction, economic depression, and the political scandals of Ulysses S. Grant. Hayes brought to the presidency a keen mind, a love for literature, and courage (in the Civil War, he was wounded four times and had four horses shot from under him). He also had a secret weapon—his wife, Lucy, whom he had married on *December 30, 1852.* Lucy brought to Washington a college degree (she was the first president's wife to have one), a gift for hospitality, and an open commitment to Jesus Christ.

But she didn't bring any alcohol.

Official Washington was shocked by her banning of alcoholic beverages from the executive mansion, and the First Lady was dubbed Lemonade Lucy. She was unapologetic. "It is true I violate a precedent," she said, "but I shall not violate the Constitution, which is all that, through my husband, I have taken an oath to obey." She later told a friend, "I had three sons coming to manhood and did not feel I could be the first to put the wine cup to their lips."

Among those displeased was Hayes's secretary of state, who grumbled after one state dinner, "It was a brilliant affair. The water flowed like champagne."

President and Mrs. Hayes began each day with morning prayers, making no secret of their lifelong custom of family devotions. They ended most days with music and singing. They were devout Methodists. During their years in Washington they attended the Foundry Methodist Episcopal Church, and when the Woman's Home Missionary Society of the Methodist Episcopal Church was organized, Lucy became its first president. Sunday evenings at the White House were times of worship. Hymnbooks were distributed, and Lucy sang vigorously the hymns of Philip Bliss and others.

Kings and leaders
should not get drunk
or even want to drink.
Drinking makes you forget
your responsibilities,
and you mistreat the poor.
Beer and wine are only
for the dying
or for those
who have lost all hope. (Proverbs 31:4–6)

December 31 Ashes of Wycliffe

The darkest times are ripest for revival. John Foxe observed: "What time there seemed to be no spark of pure doctrine remaining, Wycliffe, by God's providence, sprang up, through whom the Lord would waken the world." John Wycliffe was a brilliant professor at Oxford whose logic and popularity made him England's leading theologian. But to the horror of the church—and long before Luther—Wycliffe denounced the arrogance, power, and wealth of the Catholic clergy, rejecting the infallibility of pope and council. Taking the Bible as the only source of truth, he proclaimed the gospel of justification by grace through faith. Wycliffe wasn't the first to criticize the papacy, but he was among the first to attack the doctrines that undergirded papal theology. For that reason, he's called the Morning Star of the Reformation.

Church authorities counterattacked: "It hath been intimated that one John Wycliffe, professor of divinity, hath gone to such a pitch of detestable folly, that he feareth not to teach and preach, or rather to vomit out of the filthy dungeon of his breast, certain erroneous and false propositions and conclusions." But Wycliffe enjoyed support from the people. When the archbishop of London prohibited his preaching, Wycliffe spent his time preparing the first English translation of the Bible.

The strain of his public battles aged Wycliffe, and in his sixtieth year, on the last Sunday of 1384, presiding over the Lord's Supper, he was struck with paralysis and fell to the ground. His friends carried him to bed, where he died on *December 31, 1384*. Forty-one years later, still hated by his enemies, his bones were exhumed, burned, and thrown into the river. As an ancient biographer wrote, "They burnt his bones to ashes and cast them into the Swift, a neighboring brook running hard by. Thus the brook conveyed his ashes into the Avon, the Avon into the Severn, the Severn into the narrow seas and they into the main ocean. And so the ashes of Wycliffe are symbolic of his doctrine, which is now spread throughout the world."

God blesses those people
who refuse evil advice
and won't follow sinners
or join in sneering at God.
. . . Those people succeed
in everything they do. (Psalm 1:1, 3)

Index of Selected Topics